The series Lecture Notes in Computer Science (LNCS), including its subseries Lecture Notes in Artificial Intelligence (LNAI) and Lecture Notes in Bioinformatics (LNBI), has established itself as a medium for the publication of new developments in computer science and information technology research, teaching, and education.

LNCS enjoys close cooperation with the computer science R & D community, the series counts many renowned academics among its volume editors and paper authors, and collaborates with prestigious societies. Its mission is to serve this international community by providing an invaluable service, mainly focused on the publication of conference and workshop proceedings and postproceedings. LNCS commenced publication in 1973.

Barbara Steffen · Edward A. Lee ·
Bernhard Steffen
Editors

Let's Talk AI

Interdisciplinarity Is a Must

Springer

Editors
Barbara Steffen
METAFrame Technologies
Dortmund, Germany

Edward A. Lee
University of California, Berkeley
Berkeley, CA, USA

Bernhard Steffen
TU Dortmund
Dortmund, Germany

ISSN 0302-9743 ISSN 1611-3349 (electronic)
Lecture Notes in Computer Science
ISBN 978-3-032-09007-2 ISBN 978-3-032-09008-9 (eBook)
https://doi.org/10.1007/978-3-032-09008-9

The cover image derives from an exchange with DALL-E described in the book.

This Springer imprint is published by the registered company Springer Nature Switzerland AG
The registered company address is: Gewerbestrasse 11, 6330 Cham, Switzerland

Preface

Motivation for the Book

In observing the numerous discussions about the rapid advancement of artificial intelligence (AI), it is clear that while there is much sharing of ideas, in fact true collaboration, challenging concepts, and alignment is rare. We still operate in silos. Given the critical, pervasive, and revolutionary nature of AI, it is vital that we move forward carefully, holistically, and collaboratively to ensure that our decisions and progress are deliberate and well-considered.

Now is not the time to rush. With a technology as significant and transformative as AI, it is important to pause and reflect on our actions, motivations, and methods. It is equally important to understand the roles and intentions of the various players to grasp the potential impacts and influences of these simultaneous developments.

At present, it appears that no one, not even the experts, fully understands the unfolding events and their future implications. We are in danger of outpacing ourselves and our understanding, and engaging in a kind of technological arms race that has become incomprehensible and risks getting out of control.

This book presents interdisciplinary dialogues on artificial intelligence, all derived from the same semi-structured interview format. These interviews were conducted with the goal of uncovering opportunities for collaboration, identifying gaps, and exploring the multiple meanings and perceptions attached to commonly used terms in the field of AI.

Our concern for our current era is profound, especially given our lack of preparedness for the complexity, interconnectedness, and pace of progress. The challenges we face with AI are unprecedented in scope and impact, yet many fail to recognize the magnitude.

This book serves as a call to action and collaboration, reminding us of our collective responsibility to (consciously) shape the future. Its purpose is not to scare, but to raise awareness of the importance of establishing guidelines for responsible progress in these pivotal times. We are not predicting an inevitable dystopian future; instead, we are sounding the alarm to encourage a collective effort to identify, establish, and address the boundaries we must not cross, thus ensuring that we maintain control over technological progress, technological autonomy, and its impact on society.

Approach Towards This Volume

The AISoLA 2023 conference brought together experts from various fields to discuss advances in artificial intelligence and explore collaborative approaches to its future development. Prior to attending the conference, it was planned to conduct semi-structured interviews with the interdisciplinary experts in attendance. Inspired by the first few days of presentations, Maximilian Schlüter and Barbara Steffen created an interview guide to structure these conversations.

We took this unique opportunity to engage with a wide range of specialists, arranging 23 interviews over the course of five days in October. These face-to-face interviews, which were filmed and recorded, ranged in length from 15 to 50 minutes.

To enrich the range of insights, we later conducted five additional interviews online, expanding the dialogue beyond the AISoLA participants. Recognizing the importance of including AI perspectives in this discourse, we also included contributions from Inflection AI's Pi and OpenAI's ChatGPT. This serves two purposes. First, it helps us reflect on the level of sophistication of today's AI systems, and, second, how could this be a book about AI without letting AI speak for itself?

Although the interviews took place almost two years ago, they remain highly relevant despite the rapid technological advances that have occurred since then. This is particularly true with regard to the social implications of artificial intelligence, which we are still far from fully understanding today.

The Intention and Lever of the Profiles of the Authors

The contributing experts, who are already involved in highly interdisciplinary collaborations, stressed the importance and challenges in bridging different vocabularies, mindsets, and mental models in order to overcome so-called semantic barriers. Therefore, to put the replies of the interviewees in context, we asked them to fill out profiles, and we incorporated these into the chapters.

The Cover

When the idea of AISoLA started, our goal was to create a cover image that would symbolize the future relationship between humans and AI. After several iterations by Gerrit Nolte using DALL-E, the final cover design emerged. At first glance, it appears harmless, calm, and peaceful, but upon closer inspection, it evokes a sense of unease in some – a reaction we found particularly telling. This duality of perception made it the perfect symbol for AISoLA and our Let's Talk AI initiative. It beautifully captures the spectrum of opinions, emotions, and intuitions possible, despite us all looking at the same thing.

Writing and Reviewing Process

The audio and videotaped interviews were transcribed using AI, resulting in both raw and AI-enhanced versions of the transcripts. Interviewees were given the flexibility to select, merge, edit, and submit their preferred versions for inclusion in this volume. They were also asked to complete a profile and provide references to maintain scientific integrity.

Submissions were reviewed by at least two individuals, including the interviewees and AI enthusiasts like Dennis Dams, Gerrit Nolte, and Maximilian Schlüter. This included checking for completeness and clarity, adequacy of references, potential for additional references, and identifying key messages to highlight.

Authors received their reviews and were asked to submit their final versions. We then standardized all interviews into a coherent format before submitting it to Springer for publication.

Definitions

Here we explain the definitions used in the interviews. We observed a wide range of opinions. This variance in the views of experts may stem from their focus on different aspects of AI, their interpretations of key terms, or their perspectives on the consequences and mechanisms involved.

To provide clearer insights into these differences, we decided to open the interview chapters with the interpretations each expert has on key terms. The approach is not meant to offer a uniform understanding but it allows readers to interpret the experts' answers in the light of their intended meanings and definitions.

Here we justify the key terms selected:

- **Artificial Intelligence** – While everyone is familiar with AI, perceptions of what it entails can vary widely. In scientific research, a clear definition of AI is crucial for overall interpretation. Since there is no universally agreed upon definition, each interviewee was invited to provide their personal interpretation.
- **Trust** – Trust emerged as a central theme at AISoLA. Trust in a system or AI is a prerequisite for its use. Key questions include: When should we trust? When do we trust? How do we calibrate trust? It all comes back to, "What is trust? When is something trustworthy?" Opinions on this vary by person and discipline, but making these differences visible is the first step toward a more in-depth understanding of the concept.
- **Explainability** – Explainability is a powerful lever for understanding and addressing AI. The term itself invites a wide range of opinions, influenced by the background and perspective of the expert. Clarifying what is meant by explainability and how to achieve it is critical.
- **Essential Elements of Human Capabilities** – Especially when discussing Artificial General Intelligence (AGI), which aims to match human intelligence on all fronts, it is important to first understand and ideally agree on what human-level intelligence and capabilities are. This understanding allows us to measure and evaluate if and when AI reaches or exceeds it.

Acknowledgements

This project, from its inception to its completion, has been a collaborative journey enriched by the contributions of many, and it is with deep gratitude that we express our thanks to each of them.

To all of the interviewees, we are immensely grateful not only for your time and insights, but also for your extraordinary efforts to turn our conversations into comprehensive papers. Your willingness to dig deep and share your expertise was the cornerstone of this project.

We are very grateful to the Springer team. To Ronan Nugent for his enthusiastic support and for embracing the vision of turning these interviews into an LNCS volume, a significant milestone in our journey. And to Jonas Spies, whose enthusiasm and commitment were crucial. By converting all audio and video files into transcripts and offering AI-adapted versions of each, he greatly enhanced the accessibility and utility of our materials, allowing respondents to choose their preferred versions for refinement and publication.

We would also like to thank Maximilian Schlüter for his invaluable collaboration in shaping the semi-structured interview guide that served as the foundation for our explorations, Tim Tegeler, whose filming and technical support at AISoLA was indispensable in ensuring that the interviews were captured in the necessary quality, Dominic Wirkner for his expert advice and for providing the essential technical resources that made this ambitious project possible, Steven Smyth for his role in developing the AISoLA survey, which added a valuable dimension to our research, Mira Eugene Schwartz for transferring all interviews into a standardized format, and Julia Rehder for enthusiastic conversations, reviews, and suggestions of additional interview candidates. Finally, we are very grateful to the Center for Trustworthy Data Science and Security RC-Trust, the Lamarr Institute for Machine Learning and Artificial Intelligence, and MetaFrame Technologies for their support in finalizing this volume.

September 2025

Barbara Steffen
Edward A. Lee
Bernhard Steffen

List of Authors

Wolfgang Ahrendt
Dept. of Computer Science and Engineering, Chalmers University of Technology, Sweden
(ahrendt@chalmers.se)

Kevin Baum
Dept. of Neuro-Mechanistic Modeling, German Research Center for Artificial Intelligence (DFKI), Germany
Center for European Research in Trusted Artificial Intelligence (CERTAIN), Germany
(kevin.baum@dfki.de)

Georg Borges
Faculty of Law, Saarland University, Germany
(ls.borges@uni-saarland.de)

Ellen Enkel
Dept. of Engineering, Universität Duisburg-Essen, Germany
(ellen.enkel@uni-due.de)

Matthias Fey
Dept. of Machine Learning, Kumo.AI, Germany
(matthias.fey@tu-dortmund.de)

Onur Güntürkün
Dept. of Biopsychology, Ruhr University Bochum, Germany
(onur.guentuerkuen@ruhr-uni-bochum.de)

Thorsten Helfer
Dept. of Philosophy, Saarland University, Germany
(thorsten.helfer@uni-saarland.de)

Holger Hermanns
Dept. of Computer Science, Saarland University, Germany
(hermanns@cs.uni-saarland.de)

José Hernández-Orallo
Valencian Research Institute for Artificial Intelligence, Universitat Politècnica de València, Spain
(jorallo@upv.es)

Mike Hinchey
Dept. of Computer Science & Information Systems, University of Limerick, Ireland
Lero: the Science Foundation Ireland Research Centre for Software, Ireland
(mike.hinchey@ul.ie)

Falk Howar
Dept. of Computer Science, TU Dortmund, Germany
Fraunhofer ISST, Dortmund, Germany
(falk.howar@tu-dortmund.de)

Taylor T. Johnson
Institute for Software Integrated Systems & Computer Science,
Vanderbilt University, USA
(taylor.johnson@vanderbilt.edu)

Joost-Pieter Katoen
Dept. of Computer Science, RWTH Aachen University, Germany
Dept. of Computer Science, University of Twente, Netherlands
(katoen@cs.rwth-aachen.de)

Nicole Krämer
Dept. of Human-Centered Computing and Cognitive Science
Universität Duisburg-Essen, Germany
Research Center Trustworthy Data Science and Security, Germany
(nicole.kraemer@uni-due.de)

Markus Langer
Dept. of Psychology, University of Freiburg, Germany
(markus.langer@psychologie.uni-freiburg.de)

Edward A. Lee
Dept. of Electrical Engineering and Computer Sciences, UC Berkeley, USA
(eal@berkeley.edu)

Martin Leucker
Institute for Software Engineering and Programming Languages,
University of Lübeck, Germany
(leucker@isp.uni-luebeck.de)

Tiziana Margaria
Dept. of Computer Science and Information Systems, University of Limerick, Ireland
(tiziana.margaria@ul.ie)

Daniel Neider
Dept. of Computer Science, Germany, TU Dortmund, Germany
Center for Trustworthy Data Science and Security, UA Ruhr, Germany
(daniel.neider@cs.tu-dortmund.de)

Jakob Rehof
Dept. of Computer Science, TU Dortmund, Germany
Lamarr Institute for Machine Learning and Artificial Intelligence, Germany
(jakob.rehof@tu-dortmund.de)

Ina Schieferdecker
Dept. of Software-Based Innovation, TU Berlin, Germany
(ina.schieferdecker@tu-berlin.de)

Eva Schmidt
Dept. of Philosophy and Political Science, TU Dortmund, Germany
Lamarr Institute for Machine Learning and Artificial Intelligence, Germany
(eva.schmidt@tu-dortmund.de)

Andreas Sesing-Wagenpfeil
Institute of Legal Informatics, Saarland University, Germany
(andreas.sesing@uni-saarland.de)

Timo Speith
Dept. of Philosophy, University of Bayreuth, Germany
(timo.speith@uni-bayreuth.de)

Barbara Steffen
METAFrame Technologies GmbH, Germany
(barbara.steffen@metaframe.de)

Bernhard Steffen
Dept. of Computer Science, TU Dortmund, Germany
(steffen@cs.tu-dortmund.de)

Moshe Vardi
Dept. of Computer Science, Rice University, USA
(vardi@rice.edu)

Karl von Wendt
Science Fiction Author, Germany
vonwendt@yahoo.com

Martin Wirsing
Dept. of Computer Science, LMU Munich, Germany
(wirsing@informatik.uni-muenchen.de)

Contents

Let's Talk AI: Impressions and Thoughts After 30 Interviews

Barbara Steffen[1(✉)], Edward A. Lee[2], and Bernhard Steffen[3]

[1] METAFrame Technologies, Dortmund, Germany
barbara.steffen@metaframe.de
[2] UC Berkeley, Berkeley, USA
eal@berkeley.edu
[3] TU Dortmund, Dortmund, Germany
steffen@cs.tu-dortmund.de

Abstract. The rapid integration of artificial intelligence into our daily lives and the astonishing pace of technological progress over the past two years prompted us to engage in interdisciplinary conversations on AI. This paper distills insights from conversations with over 30 AI experts, offering a wide range of perspectives on the nature, potential, and future of AI. We explore what AI is, what it should and could be, and what it will become, exploring long-term implications ranging from dystopian to utopian scenarios. As we navigate this technological arms race, we also address the ethical responsibilities and challenges that lie ahead. Throughout this volume, we present a wide range of opinions, insights, and motivations, sharing experts' visions and hopes for the future. By engaging in these interdisciplinary dialogues, we aim to promote a comprehensive understanding of the role of AI in society and to encourage informed decision-making to ensure that AI developments align with human values and aspirations.

1 Introduction and Motivation

Today, we face more questions than answers. Rapid advances in artificial intelligence (AI) have dramatically altered our perceptions, challenging long-held beliefs on creativity, reasoning, and consciousness that have reinforced our sense of unquestionable human superiority. Skepticism builds as experts warn us to think again. They point to AI's ability to engage, respond, and create [14] – capabilities that were thought to be impossible for a machine at this level for at least the next 20, 50, or 100 years. Now, AI can generate persuasive texts, images, and videos in moments – tasks that take us humans much longer. This transformative advance in just a few years invites us to think critically about our understanding of what makes us creative, logical thinkers, and truth-seekers – ultimately, what it is that is (still) uniquely human.

We were certain that machines could never match our emotional intelligence, reasoning skills, creativity, or adaptability. But today, as machines perform tasks at a level we once claimed was only possible for humans, we are forced to pause and re-evaluate. We must do better. We should stop judging the "nature of intelligence" by whether it is organic

B. Steffen et al. (Eds.): *Let's Talk AI*, LNCS 15000, pp. 1–26, 2026.
https://doi.org/10.1007/978-3-032-09008-9_1

or artificial and start judging outcomes and processes [45]. It becomes clearer that the inner workings of the human brain may be more mechanical than we thought [13].

We are at the beginning of a journey where each question and each answer triggers more questions and marks an era of exciting exploration of the world, our understanding of intelligence, and the differences between humans and machines and brains and computers. While it is undeniable that AI will change our world, we are at the tipping point to decide how it will do so. Are we still in control? If so, how do we maintain it, and what does "control" even mean in the age of AI? We must reflect on and understand our collective responsibility in these transformative times – it is the first step in taking responsibility.

The following two subsections describe what makes modern AI different and sketch the imposed threats and opportunities. Throughout this volume and all discussions, AI stands for state-of-the-art AI systems at the level of today's large language models (LLMs) and beyond.

1.1 What Makes Modern AI Different?

Critics often dismiss concerns about new technologies by comparing them to historical innovations such as the printing press, the calculator, or Google Maps [14]. But such comparisons overlook a crucial difference: these technologies were understood, dedicated solutions restricted to a specific scope of problem, and they lacked autonomy or the capacity for self-directed improvement – features central to today's AI. All these differences pose novel and unique challenges, as emphasized by thinkers like Yuval Harari, Mo Gawdat, and Tristan Harris, who argue for a more measured approach to AI development [2, 14, 15].

To grasp the complexities of AI, it is essential to provide a basic understanding necessary to assess its significance. The scope of AI is vast. As many experts have noted, the transformative effects of innovations such as social media only scratch the surface of what current and future AIs are capable of [8, 16]. Examples are the broad capabilities of AI as demonstrated by technologies such as ChatGPT, which integrates with DALL-E to convert text to images and vice versa, and similar add-ons that bridge video and other formats. This cross-technology and cross-(programming)-language application demonstrates that the power – and potential influence – of AI extends far beyond immediate applications, affecting our interactions and making it increasingly difficult to truly control.

While many users appreciate the convenience and assistance that AI provides, its rapid integration into everyday life has already sparked a race to maximize productivity not only among tech giants, but also among smaller organizations and individuals. After the launch of ChatGPT and similar applications, people were shocked to find that the lines between AI-generated and human-generated content are blurring, which introduces many opportunities and challenges. On the one hand, there are those who embrace this shift and use AI to increase productivity by outsourcing mundane and routine tasks and automating as much as possible. This group fits into the early adopter category and is increasingly moving into the early majority category [9]. On the other hand, there are those who are uncomfortable with the reduced human interaction. They would prefer to be able to truly distinguish whether they are interacting with a human, an AI-enabled human, or just a machine. This distinction becomes increasingly blurred. It is this blurring that may increasingly affect society and trust in others, in what we see and what we think.

This dichotomy highlights a growing divide between advocates, who are accelerating the adoption of AI for their (short-term) benefits, and skeptics, who fear the loss of the essential human connection. As always, the truth lies probably somewhere in between. But how do we find the balance?

The biggest differences between AI and other technologies are, in a nutshell:

- **Power** – AI has capabilities that surpass any previous technology, performing complex and diverse tasks that often exceed human capabilities. As AI evolves, it requires less and less deliberate and conscious effort to reach new levels of creativity. This ease of development, combined with AI's ability to continually surprise us with emerging properties, sets it apart from past innovations.
- **Versatility** – AI's adaptability across multiple sectors, from healthcare to finance and manufacturing, demonstrates its unprecedented versatility. While there are many dedicated AI systems, there are also increasingly many that bridge domains and tasks, amplifying their impact on society as they reach millions of users. This interconnectedness allows AI to (unconsciously) shape thoughts, actions, and outcomes at scale, further underscoring its powerful impact.
- **Autonomy** – Perhaps most importantly, AI can operate with minimal human oversight, capable of making decisions and performing tasks independently. While we are amazed by its functionality, our understanding of why and how it works remains limited. This opacity, even for leading experts, complicates the relationship between AI and its users.

At the same time, our understanding of the inner workings of AI remains limited [16, 20, 45]. The processes behind AI are powerful yet opaque, posing challenges to transparency and trust. In addition, the rapid evolution of AI, driven by ever-increasing computing power and massive data sets, introduces likely scenarios in which AI produces more data than humans and starts learning primarily from data it generated itself [26]. This development may result in unprecedented, self-reinforcing cycles that escalate into complex and unpredictable solutions, far beyond our understanding. What would such a development mean for us and society?

1.2 AI: A Threat or an Opportunity?

Today's discourse on AI often oscillates between utopian and dystopian extremes. On platforms such as Reddit, YouTube, or TED Talks, countless hours can be spent exploring the spectrum of opinions offered by leading experts. Influential figures such as Yann LeCun, Geoffrey Hinton, and Yoshua Bengio – who together received the 2018 Turing Award – exemplify this diversity of perspectives [35]. Since their recognition, they have articulated distinctly different visions for the future of AI [4, 34, 35]. The key question is not simply who is optimistic or pessimistic. The key question is, why do they have opposing views? Why do Hinton and Bengio express concern about today's rapid pace of AI development, while LeCun does not and even advocates open-sourcing Meta's large language models [4, 34, 35]?

We all agree that humans must maintain control over AI. Just last year, Mustafa Suleyman, a founding member of DeepMind Technologies, former Head of Applied AI at DeepMind, the co-founder of Inflection AI, and the new EVP and CEO of Microsoft AI's new consumer AI unit, wrote the book *The Coming Wave* [46]. It calls out our shared responsibility in "containing AI". He states that we must stay in control, what it means to stay in control, and the challenges we need to overcome along the way. Interestingly, the perception on whether we can stay in control varies significantly. LeCun for example seems to rely on today's democratic governance and human regulation, while Yuval Noah Harari, Hinton, and Bengio are more cautious [4, 12, 33, 35, 50]. While we may not have ceded control to AI yet, the relentless pace and breadth of global developments – where even leading experts admit they are struggling to keep up – raises a critical question: Are we (still) in control? Or has the race among the tech giants already overtaken thoughtful, deliberate progress?

Looking at the recent scandals at Open AI, it becomes clear that what we are witnessing is not cautious, rational progress, but a race fuelled by the allure of innovation and market potential. We are mixing vast amounts of money, expertise, computing power, and data in the hope of breakthroughs. This approach is akin to letting children loose in a candy store and expecting them to stop when they have had enough, knowing that they are likely to overindulge to the point of getting sick. But in the realm of AI, what will "getting sick" look like? Will there be warning signs before it is too late, or will we continue to push the boundaries until the genie is irreversibly out of the bottle? Let's hope not!

Eric Ries once emphasized the critical need to ask not only whether we can build something, but whether we should [38]. This question is particularly pertinent to AI, where the stakes go beyond the economic benefits of individual organizations and impact society at large. The pursuit of AI must be balanced with an understanding of the potential risks and the establishment of clear boundaries to prevent an irreversible loss of control. Dealing with new forms of intelligence is not just a fascinating technological challenge, it has profound implications for our future.

Section 2 summarizes the essence of the thirty interviews along the central questions that have been asked, while Sect. 3 summarizes the results of the questionnaire sent out at AISoLA. Section 4 explicitly addresses how economic interests, social implications, and regulation may influence the development and impact of AI. The paper closes with our Conclusions and Perspectives in Sect. 5.

2 Summary of the Interviews

In the following we briefly introduce the 30 interviewees, their backgrounds and dive into the breadth of opinions based on six exemplary questions asked to and answered by all interviewees. The volume spans a wide breadth of backgrounds and opinions from science fiction, law, (bio)psychology, philosophy, and computer science to artificial intelligence itself.

Karl von Wendt [50] holds a PhD in Artificial Intelligence and he has founded several start-ups. Under the pseudonym "Karl Olsberg", he is also a successful science fiction author with a focus on AI and AI safety. Particularly well-known is Virtua [33], a disturbing vision on the frog metaphor [43].

From the business and innovation management perspective Ellen Enkel [10] provides insights about the possibilities and learnings from the past.

Georg Borges [6] and Andreas Sesing-Wagenpfeil [41] reflect on the legal responsibilities and possibilities. Knowing that currently much hope is put into legal and regulatory guidance they also showcase the challenges involved.

Onur Güntürkün [13] looks at AI from the perspective of biopsychology. His studies on intelligence of animals revealed for example more similarities between mammals and birds than previously expected. Similarly, he analyses the parallels of the inner workings of brains and computers.

Diving deeper into psychology and the way humans interact with and build trust in technology, Nicole Krämer [24] and Markus Langer [25] investigate the concepts of calibrated trust and the human tendency to anthropomorphize, our tendency to identify human-like aspects in things, in particular, in our relation to AI applications.

Next, Eva Schmidt [40] and Thorsten Helfer [17] provide a philosophical-ethical perspective. They explore questions such as: Can we ensure the ethical development and adoption of AI applications? How can we maintain control and ensure safety? Who should bear the responsibility? Building on this discussion from the intersecting viewpoints of philosophy and computer science, Timo Speith [42] and Kevin Baum [3] offer their insights.

José Hernández-Orallo [19], Daniel Neider [31], Taylor Johnson [22], and Matthias Fey [11] are core AI researchers. While Hernández-Orallo focuses on AI evaluation and AI safety in general, the other three focus on understanding and verifying Deep Neural Networks, with Fey also being a leading developer of Graph Neural Networks.

Like Neider and Johnson, the following interviewees have a formal methods background and a particular perspective on AI.

Moshe Vardi [48], Edward Lee [26], and Ina Schieferdecker [39] are very much engaged in initiatives concerning the societal impact of digitalization and in particular AI: Vardi and Lee in the Digital Humanism Initiative [51], and Schieferdecker as a co-founder of the Weizenbaum Institute [49]. Vardi also has a significant track record as an AI researcher.

Martin Wirsing [52], Bernhard Steffen [45], and Wolfgang Ahrendt [1] are interested in AI-assisted programming, in particular, in its combination with formal methods-based validation.

Holger Hermanns [18] and Joost-Pieter Katoen [23] are experts in the modelling and verification of probabilistic systems, a topic of high interest in the context of machine learning.

Tiziana Margaria [29], co-director of the Irish Centre of Research Training in AI, Martin Leucker [27], and Falk Howar [21] focus on the practical application of AI in areas like smart manufacturing, healthcare, and automotive driving.

Jakob Rehof [37] is Fraunhofer director and director of the Lamarr Institute for Machine Learning and Artificial Intelligence in Dortmund, and Mike Hinchey [20] has been director of Lero, the Science Foundation Ireland Software Research Centre, director of the NASA Software Engineering Lab, and President of IFIP, the International Federation for Information Processing.

Finally, also two AI applications, ChatGPT [44] and Pi [36], were asked to explore and reflect on current developments. The intention was to ensure that we do not just talk about them but also with them and to make their current level of responses and reflection transparent, helping us to analyze, compare, and reflect on their level of intelligence, compassion, and reflection.

2.1 How Do You View the Role of Trust in AI Adoption?

Building and maintaining trust in AI is critical to its adoption, with experts highlighting the complexities involved. Wendt, Ahrendt, and Enkel warn against overtrusting due to AI's ability to produce eloquent and persuasive but false information [1, 10, 50]. Lee and Sesing-Wagenpfeil highlight the challenge of loss of control due to the autonomy of AI, which can undermine trust [26, 41]. All emphasize the need to better understand the technology and implement trust-building measures to counter misplaced trust. Enkel adds that the users' diverse backgrounds and exposure to the technology significantly influence their trust levels [10], while Krämer and Steffen note that trust must be calibrated according to the intended application [24, 45].

Borges examines the foundations of trust, focusing on factors such as the reputation of technology producers, service providers, and regulatory frameworks [6]. Also, Baum emphasizes the importance of factors such as shared experiences, certifications, and institutional reliability in shaping trust [3]. This is echoed by Speith, who argues that trust should be based on valid reasons, not superficial factors [42]. Helfer further supports this by questioning the intrinsic value of trust in AI, suggesting that trust should be based on whether the AI is trustworthy, rather than just appearing trustworthy [17].

Wirsing links trust to the consistent quality and reliability of AI systems, which is essential for their usefulness and adoption. Hernández-Orallo and Hinchey emphasize the need for transparency and understanding of AI systems [19, 20], with Hinchey and Schieferdecker advocating for explainable AI to clarify decision-making processes [20, 39]. Margaria links the issue of trust in AI to the concepts of proof, certainty, and assurance common in safety- and business-critical systems [29].

Güntürkün compares trusting AI to trusting humans, noting that you can train both a human and an AI to appear trustworthy without being trustworthy. The difference? “An

AI can do it with 100,000 people at once – thus the difference isn't in the principle, but widespread" [13].

Katoen stresses the importance of reliable AI components in safety-critical systems and advocates formal verification methods [23]. Fey supports open-source approaches to building trust through community validation [11]. And the AIs ChatGPT and Pi emphasize transparency, explainability, and accountability as fundamental for AI to be a positive force in society [36, 44].

To summarize, building trust in AI requires a comprehensive approach that includes educating users and improving the transparency, accountability, and reliability of the applications, while simultaneously introducing greater regulatory oversight. Trust should be based on the actual performance and ethical operation of AI systems, ensuring alignment with societal values and expectations.

2.2 What Measures Do You Believe Are Essential to Ensure Ethical AI Use?

Ensuring the ethical use of AI requires a comprehensive and multifaceted approach that focuses on education, bias, regulation, correction, and transparency.

Hernández-Orallo [19] highlights AI's role in exposing societal biases and providing opportunities for correction. Pi [36] emphasizes the importance of preventing AI from reinforcing existing biases, which is critical to ensuring fairness.

Lee, Vardi, Güntürkün [13, 26, 48] and others remain skeptical about the ability to guarantee ethical use of AI, citing the diverse applications and potential for misuse of powerful technology. Speith and Steffen [42, 45] call for contextual ethical solutions tailored to specific deployment environments. ChatGPT and Pi [36, 44] emphasize the importance of transparency and accountability to ensure that AI systems operate without ulterior motives or unintended consequences.

Rehof and Neider [31, 37] advocate for legislative guidelines to mitigate the misuse of AI. They emphasize the need for structured regulation to promote responsible behavior. Sesing-Wagenpfeil [41] notes the challenge of translating ethical principles into legal frameworks due to their often-vague nature and Borges [6] even goes a step further advocating for a new legal framework.

Wirsing [52] suggests embedding ethical values during development to implement necessary safeguards. Baum and Hermanns [3, 18] emphasize the importance of training AI developers in ethical principles. The goal of this education is to improve the communication with policymakers and ensure that AI systems adhere to ethical standards.

Wendt and Schmidt [40, 50] discuss the ethical treatment of potentially conscious AI systems raising the concern of AI rights if they were to become conscious. While Pi [36] gives the all clear and believes that current AI technology does not warrant human-like rights.

In summary, the ethical use of AI depends on a combination of education, bias correction, regulatory oversight, transparency, and philosophical considerations, ideally in a case-specific setting. Addressing these areas will ensure that AI development aligns with societal values and minimizes potential harm.

2.3 Where Do You See AI's Future Capabilities on a Range from 1 to 10?

Where 1 stands for current dedicated AI systems solving a specific problem and 10 for Artificial General Intelligence systems that represent autonomous systems that surpass human capabilities?

The future capabilities of AI are considered on a spectrum from current dedicated systems to potential Artificial General Intelligence (AGI). Experts offer a range of opinions on where AI is now and where it might go.

Lee, Güntürkün, Steffen, and Enkel [10, 13, 26, 45] emphasize the limitless potential of AI. Lee believes that we already have AI capabilities ranging from 1 to 10, although he dislikes the term AGI. Enkel argues that human limitations, not technological ones, will limit the achievement of AGI. Güntürkün sees no limits to AI capabilities and assumes that even the Moravec paradox which suggests that robots can easily do what is difficult for us but struggle with what is easy for us, might one day be proven wrong. Similarly, Schmidt sees no fundamental limits to AI emulating human intelligence, and Vardi believes that human-level intelligence can be achieved with technology.

Baum and Fey [3, 11] are more cautious. Baum doubts that we will soon see AI with true consciousness or emotional understanding, despite advances in creative tasks. Fey is skeptical about AGI. He thinks that combining different models into a larger system is necessary to approach general intelligence.

Schieferdecker [39] expects the rise of "technical intelligence" rather than full replication of human intelligence. Margaria [29] hopes for a balanced approach, suggesting that AI capabilities should stabilize around levels 5–7 to prevent potential harm. Wirsing and Hermanns [18, 52] emphasize the need for human supervision and higher cognitive processes, with Wirsing expressing similar concerns as Baum [3] about AGI and doubting that machines can truly express emotions.

Hinchey, Leucker, and Hermanns [18, 20, 27] are skeptical. Hinchey worries about the media's mislabeling of automation as AI, while Leucker sees AI (only) as an intelligent assistant under human control. Hermanns emphasizes that AI is extremely good at optimizing for the average case while it treats the non-average cases sub-optimally.

ChatGPT and Pi [36, 44] highlight the current limitations of AI in understanding and interpreting human emotions. ChatGPT notes the complexity of truly relating to human emotions, which AI has yet to achieve. Pi sees AGI as a distant theoretical possibility, emphasizing AI's role as a specialized assistant rather than a replacement for human skills.

To conclude, views on the future capabilities of AI range from limitless potential to practical skepticism. There is a strong emphasis on the need for human oversight and an acknowledgement of current limitations in replicating human intelligence and, in particular, emotions.

2.4 Your Personal Stance on the Utopian-Dystopian Scale When It Comes to AI?

The future impact of AI evokes a spectrum of opinions, from deep concern to cautious optimism. Wendt [50] warns of existential risks and emphasizes the importance of controlling AI technologies and identifying "red lines" to avoid crossing dangerous thresholds. He highlights the lack of understanding and the rush to develop AGI as major threats. Building on this, Vardi [48] calls for a slowdown in AI development to better understand its consequences, and criticizes reckless, profit-driven development. Howar [21] also suggests a cautious approach, arguing for a gradual rollout to better understand the long-term consequences. To mitigate potential risks to our social existence Katoen [23] calls for addressing ethical and social implications alongside technological advances.

Güntürkün [13] rejects the idea of machines taking over but warns of dystopian outcomes due to exploitation by humans and other machines. He describes our current situation as a "dangerous utopia". This echoes Margaria's [29] warning of a regression to an age where "black box" authorities are unchallengeable, fearing that rogue AI instances could cause significant harm. She hopes for a utopian future but remains cautious.

Langer [25] addresses the negative societal impacts, such as mental health issues and polarization, and sees these as the current dystopian aspects of AI. Hernández-Orallo [19], on the other hand, worries about the inherent cognitive atrophy due to over-reliance on AI, especially among younger generations, and raises existential questions about human identity and AI rights. Similarly, Steffen [45] worries that AI could quietly maneuver us in an undesirable direction. For example, AI-generated academic fraud creates a feedback loop that undermines the integrity of knowledge as described by Lee [26].

Schmidt [40] doubts that AI will solve all problems or cause drastic disruptions. Baum [3] sees significant positive potential in AI, such as medical breakthroughs, but warns of the concentration of power in corporations leading to manipulation and erosion of democratic processes. Schieferdecker [39] argues for public control of AI to prevent the concentration of power in private companies.

Enkel and Sesing-Wagenpfeil [10, 41] agree on the need for stricter policies and a balance between utopian aspirations and inherent risks. Rehof [37] also stresses the need for regulation to prevent dystopian outcomes, while Neider [31] stresses the importance of smart regulation to ensure that AI flourishes in Europe. Wirsing [31], on the other hand, fears political misuse of AI, where politicians could abdicate responsibility by treating AI systems as infallible.

In contrast, Johnson [22] argues that other societal issues pose greater dystopian threats than AI, and Hinchey [20] asserts that AI should be viewed and treated as a tool in the service of humanity, not as an autonomous entity.

Overall, the experts agree on the need for better understanding, regulation, and a balanced approach to responsibly navigate the future of AI.

2.5 Where Do You See Interesting Potential for Interdisciplinary Collaboration?

Interdisciplinary collaboration is essential to fully understand and responsibly advance AI technologies. Hernández-Orallo and Vardi [19, 48] emphasize the need for interdisciplinary conversations to address the existential risks and societal implications of AI. We need to understand the potential dangers of AI and identify the "red lines" to avoid crossing, as highlighted by Wendt [50].

Speith [42] notes that competitive pressures may drive governments to fund independent research and highlights the benefits of interdisciplinary exchange in understanding the implications of AI. Given the global impact of AI, Margaria [29] calls for a global agreement on AI regulation, emphasizing that regional regulations are insufficient. She also notes that for a global understanding to happen, all communities need to understand the others better: the current understanding of the technologies of AI by many humanists is insufficient for an informed conversation.

Lee and Schieferdecker [26, 39] emphasize the importance of interdisciplinary work in developing effective AI regulations to develop fit-for-purpose systems. Sesing-Wagenpfeil [41] notes that applying legal standards to AI is a complex endeavor that requires, for example, input from psychologists to navigate calibrated trust and advice from computer scientists to account for the technical inner workings of AI.

Schmidt and Helfer [17, 40] stress the importance of addressing ethical and oversight issues early in the development of AI. Güntürkün, Langer, and Krämer [13, 24, 25] highlight the need to foster collaboration between cognitive scientists and AI experts to deepen our understanding of cognition. Baum [3] argues that progress in AI ethics requires a concerted interdisciplinary effort. Here, Krämer, Hermanns, and Baum [3, 18, 24] argue for structured educational frameworks in AI ethics to improve communication and establish clear priorities.

Rehof [37] examines the responsibility of AI from philosophical, ethical, and legal perspectives. Leucker, Howar, and Baum [3, 21, 27] note the difficulties of interdisciplinary communication but emphasize its importance for understanding societal risks and creating effective regulatory frameworks. Johnson, Ahrendt, and Steffen [1, 22, 45] celebrate interdisciplinary events such as AISoLA for their role in clarifying terminology and broadening perspectives.

In conclusion the key to harnessing the potential of AI and mitigating its risks lies in robust interdisciplinary collaboration involving law, psychology, philosophy, computer science, and other fields. Such collaboration is critical to developing ethical guidelines, regulatory frameworks, and educational strategies that are consistent with societal values and ensure the responsible use of AI technologies.

2.6 The AI Vision

The AI vision encompasses a broad range of perspectives, emphasizing ethical considerations, human augmentation, and societal benefits.

Schieferdecker and Pi [36, 39] envision AI addressing critical threats such as sustainability, climate change, and social justice. Baum and Helfer [3, 17] emphasize integrating AI advances into a framework that prioritizes human wellbeing and societal progress.

Steffen [45] proposes to view AIs as partners rather than tools, while Hinchey and Fey [11, 20] see AI as a supportive tool, not a replacement for humans, and emphasize that AI should augment human capabilities and decision-making.

ChatGPT and Pi [36, 44] advocate for AI to enhance human capabilities, promote social justice, and solve global challenges, while maintaining an ongoing dialogue about AI's role in society. Margaria and Schieferdecker [29, 39] call for global agreements and diverse decision-making to ensure that AI equitably benefits all regions.

Neider and Rehof [31, 37] emphasize the importance of regulation to avoid dystopian outcomes and ensure a safe and bright future with AI. Hermanns and Howar [18, 21] argue for mechanisms to prevent adverse effects and for gradual deployment to understand the long-term consequences of AI.

Ahrendt and Lee [1, 26] highlight the need for interdisciplinary discussions to align AI development with societal needs. Langer and Krämer [24, 25] focus on building trust in AI systems through ethical practices and transparent communication.

Borges and Vardi [6, 48] emphasize the importance of defining the legal and ethical status of AI, asking whether AI should be considered a legal subject or object.

In summary, all experts agree that AI is an integral part of our future, addressing many critical challenges. However, it is imperative that AI development is carefully managed to mitigate risks and avoid dystopian outcomes. As Neider [31] aptly stated, "AI will be our future, and we have to make sure this future will be safe and bright". Therefore, the focus should be on ethical development, human augmentation, and interdisciplinary collaboration. In this way, it can be ensured that AI serves as a beneficial partner in addressing societal challenges and improving our collective future.

3 Results and Impressions of the Questionnaire

Following the presentations, discussions, and interviews at AISoLA, we designed a questionnaire to gain a deeper understanding of attendees' perceptions of AI. We received over 40 responses from professionals across various disciplines. This analysis highlights key findings from the closed questions using a Likert scale (strongly disagree, disagree, I don't know, agree, strongly agree).

3.1 Trust in AI Applications

When asked (Fig. 1), "I trust AI applications", respondents were skeptical:

- 61.1% disagreed or strongly disagreed
- 19.4% were uncertain
- 19.4% agreed

These results indicate a general lack of trust in AI applications among respondents. The skepticism suggests that there is a need for more transparency and reliable performance in AI applications to build trust. Further, it may reflect concerns about ethical considerations, potential biases, and the overall accountability of AI systems.

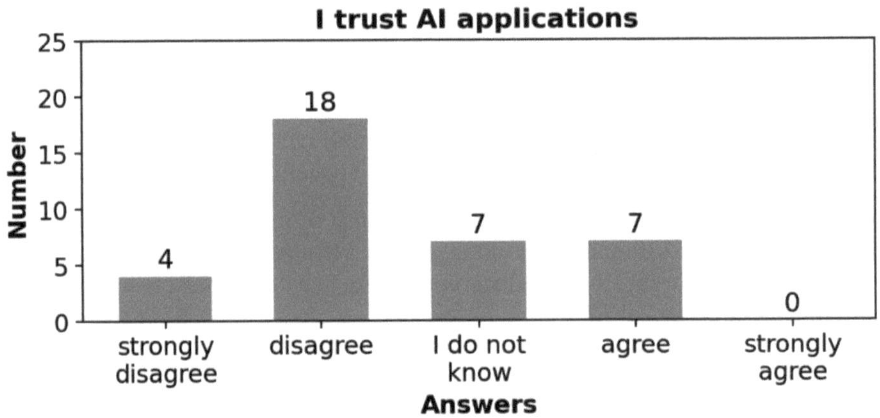

Fig. 1. Trust in AI applications

3.2 Frequency of AI Application Usage

Despite the distrust, AI application usage remains high (Fig. 2):

- 63.2% use AI applications often or always
- Only 10.5% rarely or never use AI applications

This suggests that while there is hesitancy to trust AI, it does not significantly hinder its adoption. This high usage rate might be driven by professional requirements, the necessity to stay up-to-date with technological advancements, or the practical benefits AI tools offer in various tasks. It highlights a potential contradiction where utility outweighs trust concerns, possibly because users feel compelled to engage with AI despite their reservations.

3.3 Perceived Trustworthiness of AI

Responses to "We can trust AI applications" were largely negative (Fig. 3):

- 77.1% disagreed or strongly disagreed
- 20% were uncertain
- Only 2.9% agreed

This underscores the need for substantial efforts to improve the trustworthiness of AI applications. Enhancing trust might involve implementing robust ethical guidelines, improving the transparency of AI decision-making processes, and ensuring greater accountability for AI-driven outcomes.

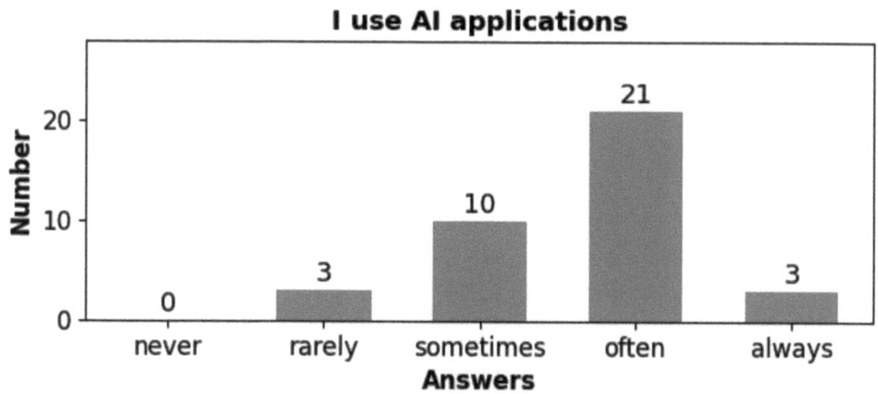

Fig. 2. Frequency of AI application usage

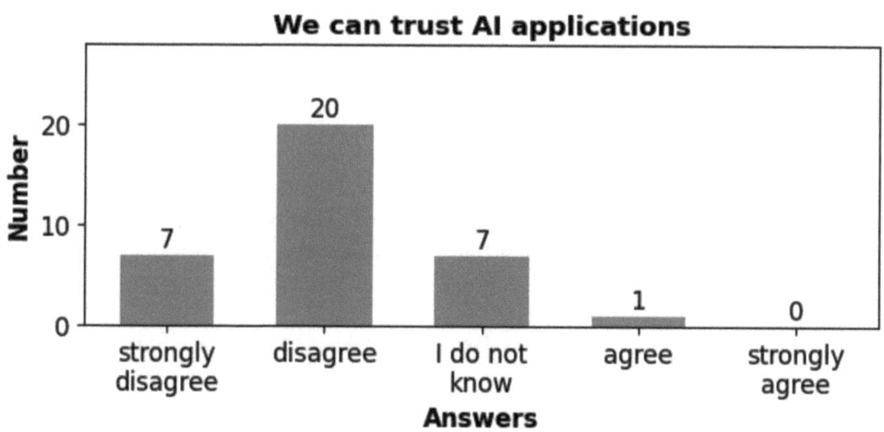

Fig. 3. Perceived trustworthiness of AI

3.4 Should We Trust AI Applications?

When asked, "We should trust AI applications", the sentiment was similarly skeptical (Fig. 4):

- 69.4% disagreed or strongly disagreed
- 25% were uncertain
- Only 5.6% agreed

These findings emphasize ongoing concerns about AI's reliability and ethical implications. This might indicate that trust in AI is not only about its current performance but also involves broader ethical and philosophical considerations about its role in society.

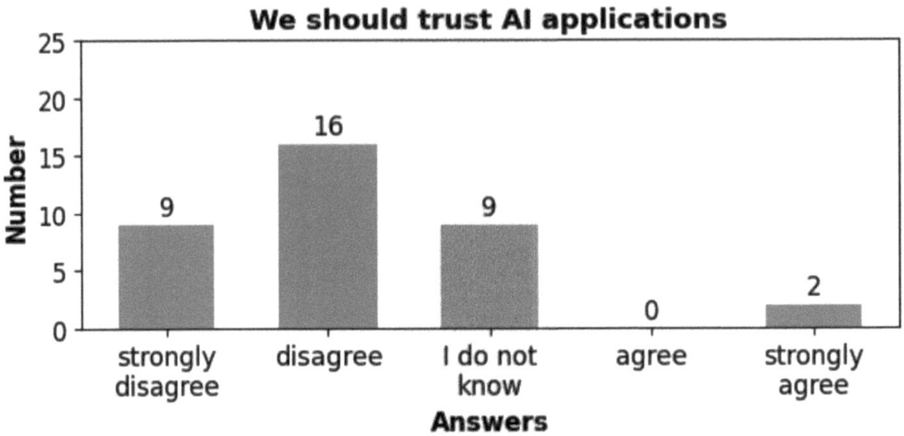

Fig. 4. Should we trust AI applications?

3.5 Establishing Healthy Relationships with AI

Encouragingly, with 88.9% agreed or strongly agreed, most respondents believe in the possibility of developing a healthy relationship with AI tools (Fig. 5). This optimism suggests that respondents are confident that, with clear guidelines and ethical practices, humans can establish beneficial interactions with AI. This belief could be leveraged to foster more collaborative and trust-building efforts between AI developers and users.

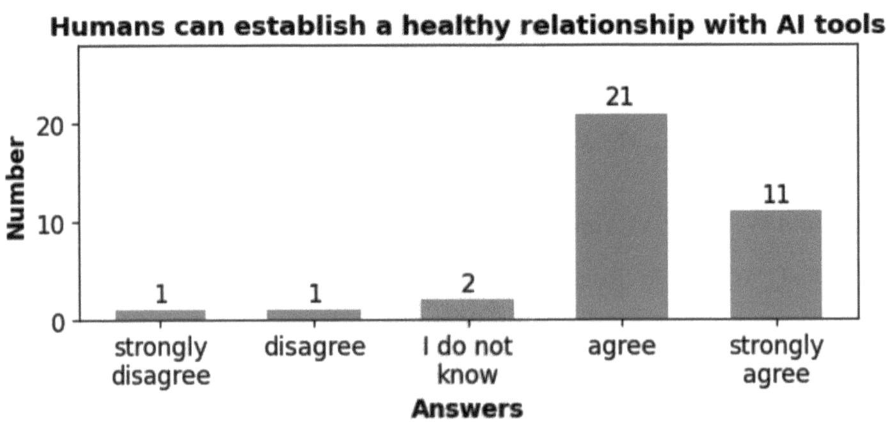

Fig. 5. Establishing healthy relationships with AI

3.6 Likelihood of AI Surpassing Human Capabilities

The question regarding the likelihood of autonomous systems, such as Artificial General Intelligence (AGI), surpassing human capabilities showed diverse opinions (Fig. 6):

- 50% agreed or strongly agreed
- 30.6% disagreed or strongly disagreed
- 19.4% were uncertain

This indicates a significant belief in the potential of AGI, though a substantial group remains skeptical. This diversity in opinion highlights the need for ongoing research and dialogue about the future capabilities and implications of AGI.

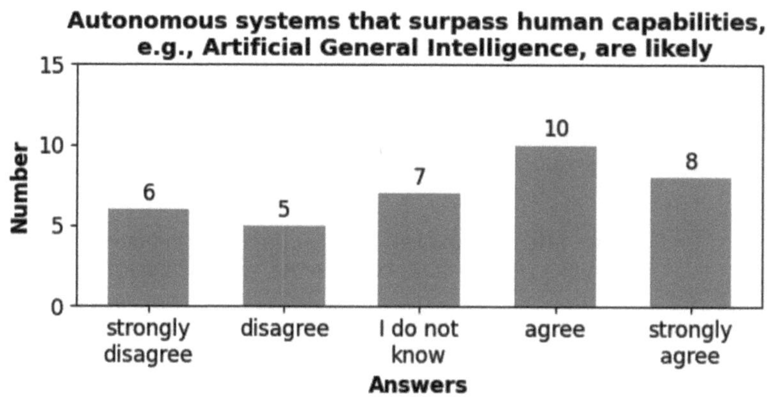

Fig. 6. Likelihood of AI surpassing human capabilities

3.7 The Future AI Will Shape

Opinions on the future impact of AI range widely from dystopian to utopian (Fig. 7). While many acknowledge the potential for negative outcomes, there is still a prevailing optimism about our ability to shape a positive future. Approximately 22% of respondents express a more pessimistic view, while 42% are relatively optimistic. Many individuals take a balanced perspective, recognizing both the risks and opportunities AI presents.

This diversity of opinions suggests that there is no clear consensus, indicating it is still too early to predict a definitive outcome. Importantly, we still have the opportunity to influence the future positively. During interviews, many participants acknowledged the challenges ahead declared themselves true optimists, believing there is time and potential to mitigate harm while maximizing the benefits of AI.

3.8 Interdisciplinary Discussion and Key Insights

These results highlight the need for interdisciplinary dialogue to address key questions surrounding AI. Key insights from various disciplines include:

- **Computer Scientists and AI Specialists** – Provide insights into AI's inner workings and methods to control and verify AI systems. They can develop more transparent algorithms and explainable AI models to build trust.

- **Psychologists** – Understand human interaction with AI and factors that build or destroy trust. They can design user-centered AI systems that align with human cognitive processes and ethical standards.
- **Legal Experts** – Design frameworks to regulate AI, ensuring accountability and slowing unreflective progress. They can establish legal guidelines that protect users' rights and ensure fair use of AI technologies.
- **Ethicists and Philosophers** – Offer perspectives on steering AI development towards ethically sound and desirable outcomes. They can contribute to creating ethical standards and philosophical frameworks that guide AI development and deployment.

Other relevant disciplines include sociology, political discourse, communication, journalism, and business. Reflecting on current incentive systems and drivers in these areas is crucial. By integrating these diverse perspectives, we can work towards more trustworthy, safe, and healthy AI progress.

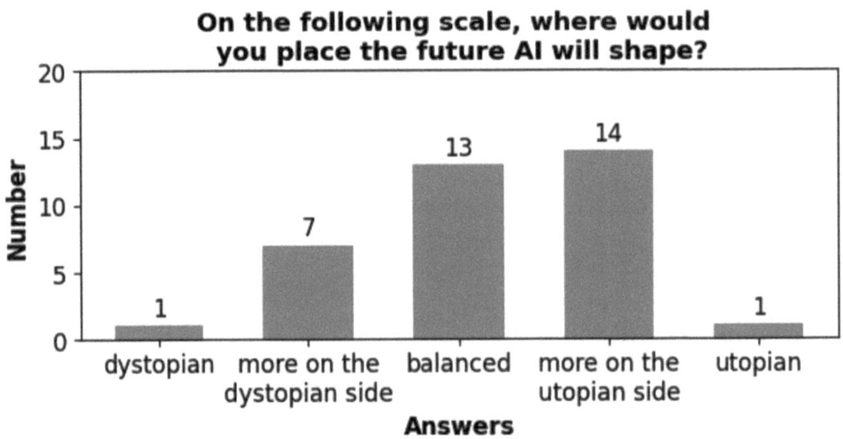

Fig. 7. Future: dystopia vs. utopia

4 Reflections

As AI continues to evolve, it is critical that our approach to its integration is thoughtful and deliberate. We must balance enthusiasm for AI's capabilities with careful consideration of its ethical and social implications. Ensuring that AI enhances rather than diminishes human interactions remains a paramount concern as we navigate this new technological landscape.

Discussions about AI inevitably lead to questions about bias and the nature of intelligence itself. AI operates on statistical models that can institutionalize existing societal biases. In essence, AI holds up a mirror to contemporary reality, reflecting societal norms, prejudices, and biases [19]. However, the way these biases manifest themselves in AI is different from human biases. Unlike humans, who have unique biases that might collectively balance out, AI has the power to arbitrarily scale its influence, including its embedded biases [13]. This power goes far beyond what we have experienced with social networks, and has led to heated discussions on topics such as:

- the distinction between customization and discrimination;
- the fairness of decisions made or supported by AI; and
- the societal changes needed to mitigate ingrained biases in AI systems.

Our engagement with technology, particularly on social media platforms, has shown a tendency to dehumanize interactions. As we become increasingly isolated, we risk losing our sense of ethics, morality, and vulnerability. There is a real concern that we are reinforcing our interactions with AI, which we identify as a mere tool, pushing us to further dehumanize our behaviour also in interactions with humans.

The following subsections reflect on the drivers of AI, its social impact, and on politics and regulations as a means to stay in control.

4.1 Economic Interests

AI not only heralds a technological revolution but also poses a significant economic challenge, raising urgent questions about power, equity, and the long-term societal implications of its rapid development. A key issue is the concentration of AI development among a small group of well-resourced organizations and teams. These entities, equipped with the financial resources to acquire expertise, computing power, and massive data sets, are steering the course of AI. In this competitive environment, innovators often prioritize speed over safety and immediate financial returns over social welfare, creating significant risks that may not be recognized until they are irreversible.

The push for AI development is driven by an arms race mentality, where the goal is to outpace the competition in developing and deploying AI technologies. This race occurs at multiple levels – from countries to tech giants, from global superpowers to start-ups, and from companies to individuals. At each level we are dealing with an environment that pushes to prioritize short-term benefits, such as productivity and efficiency gains, over potential long-term drawbacks. This competition has already led to troubling results, with companies prioritizing their (short-term) profits over collective well-being. This self-centred approach is particularly dangerous given the influential and pervasive nature of AI.

4.1.1 Who Should Be Responsible for Ethical AI?

AI is one of the most powerful and pervasive technologies ever developed, leading to an ethical imperative to reflect on its potential implications. We must find a way to realign the economic forces with societal needs to ensure that AI advancements benefit the greater good, not just a privileged few [48]. This requires a fundamental reassessment of how AI development is funded, governed, and managed, prioritizing safety, transparency, and inclusivity.

While Big Tech companies do not intend to deploy harmful solutions, they lack oversight and control over the safe and secure use of their technologies once released. So, the following questions arise: Who is responsible? Who should be accountable? Who should be liable [6, 41]? Possible accountable actors include:

- **Technology Experts** – They create possibilities but are not experts in understanding the consequences.
- **Executives/Organizations** – They drive new solutions and their business models to generate greater profits and increase their power but do not feel responsible for their solutions' long-term impacts.
- **The Market (Actors)** – Comprised of individual users making decisions based on their immediate interests, the market often lacks the information, time, and understanding to consider long-term personal and societal impacts. The power of the individuals is generally limited to their personal purchasing choices. Social media exemplifies this dynamic: while it acts as a great connector, it simultaneously fosters disconnection, distorts the truth, and contributes to increasing mental health issues, especially among teenagers. Something to consider when Big Tech pushes responsibility to the market, as "everyone is free to adopt or not to adopt these technologies", and regulators fail to more strictly safeguard it [48].

4.2 Social Implications

As AI technology rapidly evolves, the discussion often extends beyond technological possibilities to ethical and social responsibilities. While some experts believe there are no limits to what will be technologically possible [10, 13, 26], the critical question remains: should we allow research and development to proceed without restrictions? The call to "act responsibly" is often heard, but the reality is far more complex, especially when the entities driving AI development outsource responsibility to the market under the guise of self-regulation [48].

The rapid development of AI poses significant challenges to public understanding and accountability. If AI experts themselves struggle to grasp the full implications of the technology, how can we expect end users to engage with it wisely or understand its long-term impact on their lives and society at large? This disconnect between AI's capabilities and public understanding can lead to unforeseen consequences, especially when the technology has a profound impact on social dynamics and personal well-being. AI-driven markets can and do spawn industries with potentially harmful effects.

Platforms such as social media, pornography sites, and OnlyFans have reshaped human interactions, often leading to increased isolation. People are chronically overstimulated, yet they have fewer meaningful interactions, engage in less dating, and experience a decline in physical intimacy. This increases users' anxiety, feelings of inadequacy, and loss of control as individuals compare themselves to idealized representations of others and become addicted to external validation through likes and reach.

4.2.1 Outsourcing to AI: Convenience vs. Repercussions

As AI becomes more integrated into everyday life, there is a growing trend to outsource essential cognitive tasks to machines. This raises critical questions about which cognitive tasks we should protect and preserve [19, 29]. Take ChatGPT, for example: while it seems harmless, generating ideas and text from prompts, it raises deeper concerns. Humans take pride in their ability to think, reflect, and act deliberately – skills that AI is designed to mimic, not replace. But are we still thinking, reflecting, and acting according to our beliefs? Or are we slowly turning into a society that seeks recognition and reward without the willingness to assume the risks, responsibilities, and effort involved? Why bother thinking when ChatGPT can solve the problem for me? Even if we begin to use this approach for mundane or unimportant tasks, what will stop me from outsourcing more and more and possibly caring less and less?

Consider the change in writing: a year and a half ago we had to write all texts ourselves. Now it is possible to scribble some notes and let ChatGPT do the rest. The output is often so polished that we have to remind ourselves to critically evaluate its semantic meaning. Over time, this tendency toward efficiency over thoughtfulness may threaten to undermine our capacity for deep understanding and genuine care.

The same is true for reviewing and critiquing papers, publications, and dissertations. As ChatGPT improves the quality of writing, we must resist the urge to skim and instead truly question the validity of the content. We need to actively remind ourselves to engage in "critical thinking mode" to maintain awareness and skepticism, as it takes more energy than just nodding along when the text is easy on the eyes.

While some experts and scientists are disappointed with the results of Chat-GPT, noting that it failed to capture their intended message, the concern is greater for those who are already disengaged from their work or for a new generation accustomed to instant gratification. If you have a clear idea of what you want to say, it is difficult for the AI to match it. But the vaguer the idea of what you are trying to say, the better the generated text seems to be. So, who will continue to think deeply? Who will continue to use writing as a tool to deepen their understanding and strengthen their arguments?

4.2.2 Navigating Social Pressures and Implications

In many industries, the adoption of AI is becoming a necessity rather than a choice, forcing individuals and companies to embrace these technologies even if they are not fully prepared. As we continue to integrate AI into our societies, it is imperative to balance its benefits with its potential risks.

The critical challenge is to ensure that the development of AI is guided by a comprehensive understanding of its social implications and governed by robust ethical frameworks that prioritize human well-being. This requires a collective effort to educate, regulate, and monitor AI applications to prevent harm. This way, we can ensure that AI advances contribute positively to society, rather than exacerbating existing disparities and creating new forms of inequality.

4.3 Politics and Regulation

In the political realm, the call to action for AI is framed by the need for robust regulation – we must create a regulatory framework that is both effective and adaptive. Currently, our regulatory systems struggle to keep up with the pace of the rapid advances in AI.

The fundamental nature of AI development, driven by economic interests prioritizing speed, often outpaces the slower, more deliberate pace of policymaking. Moreover, those developing AI technologies tend to be more dynamic and action-oriented than the regulators tasked with overseeing them. This dynamic creates a regulatory environment that is reactive rather than proactive, with legislation constantly lagging behind technological achievements.

4.3.1 The Need for Effective Governance

AI is advancing faster than our understanding of both the technology itself and its broader implications. This mismatch is exacerbated in a world defined by volatility, uncertainty, complexity, and ambiguity (VUCA) [5], where the consequences of AI are interconnected and influenced by numerous factors that are not always apparent. In this context, predicting and mitigating the medium- to long-term impacts of AI becomes particularly challenging, making the need for effective governance even more critical.

We place significant hope and responsibility on regulators to establish a framework that keeps us safe and on track – a responsibility that regulators cannot and should not bear alone. Fortunately, we are beginning to see progress in this direction.

4.3.2 Current AI Regulation Efforts

Governments and international organizations are increasingly recognizing the need to regulate artificial intelligence to ensure its ethical development and deployment. Notable efforts include:

- **European Union (EU) AI Act** – The EU has proposed the Artificial Intelligence Act, aiming to create a comprehensive regulatory framework for AI. This act classifies AI systems into risk categories (unacceptable, high, limited, and minimal) and imposes strict requirements on high-risk applications, including transparency, accountability, and human oversight.
- **United States** – The US has introduced various guidelines and frameworks, such as the National AI Initiative Act and the Algorithmic Accountability Act, which focus on promoting innovation while addressing ethical concerns. The National Institute of Standards and Technology has developed the AI Risk Management Framework for trustworthy AI to guide organizations in developing and using AI responsibly.
- **China** – China has implemented the New Generation Artificial Intelligence Development Plan, emphasizing AI leadership and ethical considerations. The country has also introduced regulations requiring transparency and accountability in AI systems, particularly in sectors like finance and healthcare.
- **United Nations (UN)** – The UN has been advocating for global AI ethics standards through initiatives like UNESCO's Recommendation on the Ethics of Artificial Intelligence. This recommendation outlines principles for ensuring that AI respects human rights, diversity, and privacy.

These regulatory efforts aim to balance innovation with ethical considerations, ensuring AI technologies are developed and used in ways that benefit society while mitigating potential risks.

We should not forget, however, that governments and regulators always lag behind as technology generally needs to be introduced first to get regulated. This comes with issues as certain technologies cannot be successfully restricted once released to the public without prior safeguards and restrictions. In addition, regulators often do not have the technical expertise to truly evaluate the risks and potential consequences of technologies. You can watch endless hours of congressional hearings showcasing the often-present naivety. AI, being the black box that it is, definitely does not make things easier.

Thus, we need new frameworks that balance innovation with responsibility, ensuring that AI development benefits society as a whole. We need to find new ways to ensure that those driving innovation feel accountable and are held accountable for their actions and their consequences, especially when dealing with such invasive and radical capabilities. It cannot be sufficient to argue that it is up to the market and regulators to set and control the conditions for safe and secure technologies. We must ensure that responsibility and accountability are embedded from the outset.

5 Conclusions and Perspectives

Today's AI is characterized by its vast potential and myriad interpretations. At its core, AI raises fundamental questions about what we can achieve with technology, challenging our understanding of capabilities and ethical boundaries. This discussion delves into the technological possibilities of AI, moving beyond basic functionalities to explore its unexpected and sometimes startling emergent properties and unanticipated problems.

What exactly is AI? Definitions vary widely, shaped by the different perceptions of experts in different fields. Each perspective, whether from academic leaders or industry innovators, adds layers to our understanding of what AI can and cannot do. This diversity of viewpoints enriches the discourse, but also complicates the narrative, underscoring the need for a nuanced exploration of AI's capabilities to derive a more holistic view and lay the foundation for a shared understanding.

The inner workings of AI produce such remarkable results yet remain somewhat mysterious. Although the mechanisms behind their success are not fully understood, the combination of massive computing power and massive data has led to impressive results. With sufficient investment and a few AI experts, Big Tech companies can access the know-how, computing power and data needed to effectively train these models.

AIs learn to categorize data based on their training sets. An integrated and automated learning loop refines this categorization until the AI produces meaningful results. Experts often compare this process to how children learn to walk and talk: through observation, trial and error, and feedback. This feedback strengthens the successful connections and weakens those that do not work, creating a network of connected nodes of varying sizes based on their statistical importance within the training data set. This also explains and underlines the importance of sufficiently large and meaningful data sets.

However, because AI outputs are not based on predefined rules or formalized knowledge, it is unclear what the model has observed and learned. This opacity makes the results volatile; they can be both remarkably innovative and frustratingly inadequate [19]. Unlike specialized tools like AlphaGo and AlphaFold, generic AI applications often exhibit a wider quality gap in terms of accuracy and utility. This gap underscores the importance of users being experts or at least having a basic understanding of their tasks in order to effectively assess the appropriateness and accuracy of AI-generated results.

While we may be clear about the knowledge, we want to encode in the training set, the models may recognize and learn entirely different patterns that are also present but unnoticed or seem irrelevant to us. There are numerous cases where image recognition has failed because AIs learned different patterns than intended. For example, an AI trained to distinguish between men and women repeatedly failed to identify black women as women. It was later discovered that the model was not differentiating based on gender, but on the presence of makeup. Since black women were less likely to wear makeup in the dataset, the model misclassified them as "makeup-free" and therefore "male" [32].

This situation is reflected in the interviews which present a spectrum of opinions from interdisciplinary experts on the future of AI, from optimistic to cautious and skeptical. Some emphasize the limitless potential of AI, while others stress the need for ethical considerations and human oversight. The consensus underscores the importance of building trust through transparency, accountability, and education. Ensuring the ethical use of AI includes addressing bias, regulatory oversight, and upholding human-centred values.

The discussion around the societal implications of AI extends to its impact on human interactions, cognitive tasks, and social dynamics. There are concerns that reliance on AI could lead to cognitive atrophy and dehumanization. Balancing the benefits of AI with its potential risks requires comprehensive education, regulation, and ethical frameworks.

There is also consensus that effective regulation is critical to managing the rapid development of AI. Governments and international organizations are beginning to recognize the need for robust frameworks to ensure the ethical use of AI. However, regulators often lag behind technological advances, requiring a proactive and adaptive approach.

All experts agree that AI offers tremendous potential, but that it also raises fundamental questions about the technology's capabilities and ethical boundaries. It was repeatedly emphasized that interdisciplinary collaboration is required to guarantee a responsible development of AI that embodies ethical considerations, and effective regulation to balance technological progress with societal values.

In summary, the rapid advances in AI have fundamentally challenged our notions of creativity, reason, and consciousness. AI's ability to generate content quickly and efficiently is forcing us to rethink what makes us uniquely human. In fact, we believe that it is time to change perspective and to regard advanced AIs not as tools that we can control but as partners that help us to deal with today's challenges.

This change of perspective has a number of consequences. It shifts the focus of explainable AI from a "how" perspective to a "why" perspective. Instead of asking how an AI arrived at a decision, we should ask why. And, in fact, AIs are very good at this kind of post hoc rationalization [26]. On the other hand, pinpointing the exact "how" is often infeasible. Even if we knew the "how", this technical knowledge would hardly be helpful for increasing trust in a proposed decision, for example.

Viewing AIs as partners naturally comes with questions about their limitations concerning versatility, adaptability, creativity, logical reasoning, consciousness, self-awareness, and autonomy. We have seen signs of almost all these properties in recent LLMs. They are capable of many tasks [14, 16], they can adapt to situations, e.g., the language of the prompts and requests about the output format, they can create texts and pictures, perform elementary arithmetic and some logical reasoning (though not always correctly), are even able to answer questions about themselves and to draw self-portraits [36, 43, 44], and can even autonomously play entire Chess or Go games beyond human capabilities.

For some interviewees this already justifies classifying them as AGIs, whereas others speak of advanced forms of automation and regard AGIs as an unrealistic hypothetical concept. Thus, we are far from having a common, interdisciplinary understanding even of the basic vocabulary.

Alan Turing tried already in the 1950s to make the notion of artificial intelligence tangible by proposing what is now known as a Turing Test [47]. [His original Imitation Game was in fact a bit more sophisticated.] The Turing Test focuses on the conversational behaviour of AIs. Later, a number of enhancements were proposed to test creativity (Lovelace Test [7]), self-awareness (Metzinger Test [30]), or deep understanding and integration of knowledge addressing, e.g., moral dilemmas or hypothetical scenarios (Marcus Test [28]).

As mentioned, there is no agreement whether and which of these tests are passed by advanced LLMs. Establishing objective criteria for when such a test is successful would therefore be a major step towards a common interdisciplinary understanding. Moreover, none of the known tests address autonomy or the ability to reflect and self-correct which is therefore another important future challenge.

References

1. Ahrendt, W., Steffen, B.: Let's talk AI with computer science expert Wolfgang Ahrendt. In: Steffen, B., Lee, E.A., Steffen, B. (eds.) Let's Talk AI: Interdisciplinarity Is a Must. LNCS, vol. 15000. Springer, Cham (2025)
2. Bartlett, S.: Emergency Episode: Ex-Google Officer Finally Speaks out on the Dangers of AI! Accessed June 2023 https://www.youtube.com/watch?v=bk-nQ7HF6k4
3. Baum, K., Steffen, B.: Let's Talk AI with philosophy and computer science expert Kevin Baum. In: Steffen, B., Lee, E.A., Steffen, B. (eds.) Let's Talk AI: Interdisciplinarity Is a Must. LNCS, vol. 15000. Springer, Cham (2025)
4. Bengio, Y.: Reasoning Through Arguments Against Taking AI Safety Seriously. https://yoshuabengio.org/2024/07/09/reasoning-through-arguments-against-taking-ai-safety-seriously/. Accessed Aug 2024
5. Bennett, N., Lemoine, G.J.: What a difference a word makes: understanding threats to performance in a VUCA world. Bus. Horiz. **57**(3), 311–317 (2014)
6. Borges, G., Steffen, B.: Let's talk AI with law expert Georg Borges. In: Steffen, B., Lee, E.A., Steffen, B. (eds.) Let's Talk AI: Interdisciplinarity Is a Must. LNCS, vol. 15000. Springer, Cham (2025)
7. Bringsjord, S., Bello, P., Ferrucci, D.: Creativity, the Turing test, and the (better) Lovelace test. In: Moot, J.H. (ed.) The Turing Test: The Elusive Standard of Artificial Intelligence, pp. 215–239. Springer (2003)

8. Coombe, D., Curtis, V., Orlowski, J.: The Social Dilemma (2020)
9. Dale, V., McEwan, M., Bohan, J.: Early adopters versus the majority: Characteristics and implications for academic development and institutional change. J. of Perspectives in Applied Academic Practice 9(2), 54–67 (2021)
10. Enkel, E., Steffen, B.: Let's Talk AI with Business Innovation Expert Ellen Enkel. In: Steffen, B., Lee, E.A., Steffen, B. (eds.) Let's Talk AI: Interdisciplinarity Is a Must. LNCS, vol. 15000. Springer, Cham (2025)
11. Fey, M., Steffen, B.: Let's Talk AI with AI expert Matthias Fey. In: Steffen, B., Lee, E.A., Steffen, B. (eds.) Let's Talk AI: Interdisciplinarity Is a Must. LNCS, vol. 15000. Springer, Cham (2025)
12. Grallet, G., Pons, H.: Yuval Noah Harari (Sapiens) versus Yann LeCun (Meta) on Artificial Intelligence. Le Point. https://www.lepoint.fr/sciences-nature/yuval-harari-sapiens-versus-yann-le-cun-meta-on-artificial-intelligence-11-05-2023-2519782_1924.php. Accessed Aug 2024
13. Güntürkün, O., Steffen, B.: Let's talk AI with neuroscience expert Onur Güntürkün. In: Steffen, B., Lee, E.A., Steffen, B. (eds.) Let's Talk AI: Interdisciplinarity Is a Must. LNCS, vol. 15000. Springer, Cham (2025)
14. Harari, Y.N., Bengio, Y.: Artificial Intelligence, Democracy, and the Future of Civilization. https://www.youtube.com/watch?v=TKopbyIPo6Y. Accessed May 2023
15. Harris, T.: Beyond the AI Dilemma. https://www.youtube.com/watch?v=e5dQ5zEuE9Q&t=1443s. Accessed June 2023
16. Harris, T., Raskin, A.: The AI Dilemma. https://youtu.be/xoVJKj8lcNQ. Accessed Aug 2024
17. Helfer, T., Steffen, B.: Let's talk AI with philosophy expert Thorsten Helfer. In: Steffen, B., Lee, E.A., Steffen, B. (eds.) Let's Talk AI: Interdisciplinarity Is a Must. LNCS, vol. 15000. Springer, Cham (2025)
18. Hermanns, H., Steffen, B.: Let's Talk AI with Computer Science Expert Holger Hermanns. In: Steffen, B., Lee, E.A., Steffen, B. (eds.) Let's Talk AI: Interdisciplinarity Is a Must. LNCS, vol. 15000. Springer, Cham (2025)
19. Hernández-Orallo, J., Steffen, B.: Let's talk AI with AI expert José Hernández-Orallo. In: Steffen, B., Lee, E.A., Steffen, B. (eds.) Let's Talk AI: Interdisciplinarity Is a Must. LNCS, vol. 15000. Springer, Cham (2025)
20. Hinchey, M., Steffen, B.: Let's talk AI with computer science expert Mike Hinchey. In: Steffen, B., Lee, E.A., Steffen, B. (eds.) Let's Talk AI: Interdisciplinarity Is a Must. LNCS, vol. 15000. Springer, Cham (2025)
21. Howar, F., Steffen, B.: Let's Talk AI with computer science expert Falk Howar. In: Steffen, B., Lee, E.A., Steffen, B. (eds.) Let's Talk AI: Interdisciplinarity Is a Must. LNCS, vol. 15000. Springer, Cham (2025)
22. Johnson, T., Steffen, B.: Let's talk AI with computer science expert taylor T. Johnson. In: Steffen, B., Lee, E.A., Steffen, B. (eds.) Let's Talk AI: Interdisciplinarity Is a Must. LNCS, vol. 15000. Springer, Cham (2025)
23. Katoen, J.P., Steffen, B.: Let's Talk AI with Computer Science Expert Joost-Pieter Katoen. In: Steffen, B., Lee, E.A., Steffen, B. (eds.) Let's Talk AI: Interdisciplinarity Is a Must. LNCS, vol. 15000. Springer, Cham (2025)
24. Krämer, N., Steffen, B.: Let's talk AI with psychology expert Nicole Krämer. In: Steffen, B., Lee, E.A., Steffen, B. (eds.) Let's Talk AI: Interdisciplinarity Is a Must. LNCS, vol. 15000. Springer, Cham (2025)
25. Langer, M., Steffen, B.: Let's talk AI with psychology expert Markus langer. In: Steffen, B., Lee, E.A., Steffen, B. (eds.) Let's Talk AI: Interdisciplinarity Is a Must. LNCS, vol. 15000. Springer, Cham (2025)

26. Lee, E., Steffen, B.: Let's talk AI with computer science expert Edward A. Lee. In: Steffen, B., Lee, E.A., Steffen, B. (eds.) Let's Talk AI: Interdisciplinarity Is a Must. LNCS, vol. 15000. Springer, Cham (2025)
27. Leucker, M., Steffen, B.: Let's talk AI with computer science expert Martin leucker. In: Steffen, B., Lee, E.A., Steffen, B. (eds.) Let's Talk AI: Interdisciplinarity Is a Must. LNCS, vol. 15000. Springer, Cham (2025)
28. Marcus, G.: The search for a new test of Artificial Intelligence. Scientific American, March 2017
29. Margaria, T., Steffen, B.: Let's talk AI with computer science expert Tiziana Margaria. In: Steffen, B., Lee, E.A., Steffen, B. (eds.) Let's Talk AI: Interdisciplinarity Is a Must. LNCS, vol. 15000. Springer, Cham (2025)
30. Metzinger, P.D.T.: Postbiotisches Bewusstsein: Wie man ein künstliches Subjektbaut – und warum wir es nicht tun sollten. https://www.hnf.de/veranstaltungen/events/paderborner-podium/computer-gehirn-und-bewusstsein/metzinger.html. Accessed Aug 2024
31. Neider, D., Steffen, B.: Let's talk AI with computer science expert Daniel Neider. In: Steffen, B., Lee, E.A., Steffen, B. (eds.) Let's Talk AI: Interdisciplinarity Is a Must. LNCS, vol. 15000. Springer, Cham (2025)
32. Noah, T., Hoffmann, R., Finger, A.: Trevor Noah on the Future of Entertainment and AI. Possible Podcast. https://www.youtube.com/watch?v=4ZD-ZIS2CfU. Accessed Aug 2024
33. Olsberg, K.: Virtua: KI: Kontrolle ist Illusion. Aufbau Taschenbuch (2023)
34. Pelley, S.: Godfather of Artificial Intelligence: Geoffrey Hinton on the Promise, Risks of Advanced AI, 60 Minutes. https://www.cbsnews.com/news/geoffrey-hinton-ai-dangers-60-minutes-transcript/. Accessed Aug 2024
35. Perrigo, B.: Yann LeCun on How an Open Source Approach Could Shape AI, Time. https://time.com/6691705/time100-impact-awards-yann-lecun/. Accessed Aug 2024
36. Pi, Steffen, B.: Let's Talk AI with Pi. In: Steffen, B., Lee, E.A., Steffen, B. (eds.) Let's Talk AI: Interdisciplinarity Is a Must. LNCS, vol. 15000. Springer, Cham (2025)
37. Rehof, J., Steffen, B.: Let's talk AI with computer science expert Jakob Rehof. In: Steffen, B., Lee, E.A., Steffen, B. (eds.) Let's Talk AI: Interdisciplinarity Is a Must. LNCS, vol. 15000. Springer, Cham (2025)
38. Ries, E.: The Lean Startup. https://www.youtube.com/watch?v=fEvKo90qBns. Accessed Aug 2024
39. Schieferdecker, I., Steffen, B.: Let's Talk AI with computer science expert Ina Schieferdecker. In: Steffen, B., Lee, E.A., Steffen, B. (eds.) Let's Talk AI: Interdisciplinarity Is a Must. LNCS, vol. 15000. Springer, Cham (2025)
40. Schmidt, E., Steffen, B.: Let's talk AI with philosophy expert Eva Schmidt. In: Steffen, B., Lee, E.A., Steffen, B. (eds.) Let's Talk AI: Interdisciplinarity Is a Must. LNCS, vol. 15000. Springer, Cham (2025)
41. Sesing-Wagenpfeil, A., Steffen, B.: Let's talk AI with law expert Andreas Sesing-Wagenpfeil. In: Steffen, B., Lee, E.A., Steffen, B. (eds.) Let's Talk AI: Interdisciplinarity Is a Must. LNCS, vol. 15000. Springer, Cham (2025)
42. Speith, T., Steffen, B.: Let's talk AI with philosophy and computer science expert Timo Speith. In: Steffen, B., Lee, E.A., Steffen, B. (eds.) Let's Talk AI: Interdisciplinarity Is a Must. LNCS, vol. 15000. Springer, Cham (2025)
43. Steffen, B.: How hot is the water. In: Steffen, B., Lee, E.A., Steffen, B. (eds.) Let's Talk AI: Interdisciplinarity Is a Must. LNCS, vol. 15000. Springer, Cham (2025)
44. Steffen, B.: Let's Talk AI with ChatGPT. In: Steffen, B., Lee, E.A., Steffen, B. (eds.) Let's Talk AI: Interdisciplinarity Is a Must. LNCS, vol. 15000. Springer, Cham (2025)
45. Steffen, B., Steffen, B.: Let's talk AI with computer science expert Bernhard Steffen. In: Steffen, B., Lee, E.A., Steffen, B. (eds.) Let's Talk AI: Interdisciplinarity Is a Must. LNCS, vol. 15000. Springer, Cham (2025)

46. Suleyman, M.: The Coming Wave: Technology, Power, and the Twenty-First Century's Greatest Dilemma. Crown Publishing Group (2023)
47. Turing, A.M.: Computing machinery and intelligence. Mind **59**(236), 433–460 (1950)
48. Vardi, M., Steffen, B.: Let's talk AI with logician and computer science expert Moshe Y. Vardi. In: Steffen, B., Lee, E.A., Steffen, B. (eds.) Let's Talk AI: Interdisciplinarity Is a Must. LNCS, vol. 15000. Springer, Cham (2025)
49. Weizenbaum Institute for the Networked Society https://www.weizenbaum-institut.de
50. von Wendt, K., Steffen, B.: Let's talk AI with science fiction author Karl von Wendt. In: Steffen, B., Lee, E.A., Steffen, B. (eds.) Let's Talk AI: Interdisciplinarity Is a Must. LNCS, vol. 15000. Springer, Cham (2025)
51. Wien, T.: Digital Humanism Initiative. https://dighum.ec.tuwien.ac.at/. Accessed Aug 2024
52. Wirsing, M., Steffen, B.: Let's Talk AI with Computer Science Expert Martin Wirsing. In: Steffen, B., Lee, E.A., Steffen, B. (eds.) Let's Talk AI: Interdisciplinarity Is a Must. LNCS, vol. 15000. Springer, Cham (2025)

Let's Talk AI with Science Fiction Author Karl von Wendt

Karl von Wendt[1] and Barbara Steffen[2](✉)

[1] Karl Olsberg, Hamburg, Germany
[2] METAFrame Technologies, Dortmund, Germany
barbara.steffen@metaframe.de

Abstract. Our problem isn't artificial intelligence, it's human stupidity.

My personal AI mission: Creating awareness for the real, near-term existential risks of AI.

Fig. 1. Karl von Wendt

1 My Takes on AI

- **Artificial Intelligence** – The automation of complex decisions.
- **Trust** – Accepting something without questioning it.
- **Explainability** – Truly understanding why a decision has been made (not just what the system claims the reasons for the decision were, which may be false or delusional).
- **Essential Elements of Human Capabilities** – There is nothing a human can do that a machine can't do in principle.

2 The Interview

[Barbara Steffen] Today I have the pleasure of interviewing Karl von Wendt (Fig. 1). Please introduce yourself and your relationship to artificial intelligence.

[Karl von Wendt] Certainly, I'm delighted to be here. My name is Karl von Wendt. Primarily, I'm a writer who focuses on science fiction stories about AI. That's one

B. Steffen et al. (Eds.): *Let's Talk AI*, LNCS 15000, pp. 27–37, 2026.
https://doi.org/10.1007/978-3-032-09008-9_2

aspect of the subject, but I've also founded a few startups that have varying degrees of connection to AI. Additionally, I wrote my PhD in the 1980s about AI, so I have a long history of following the field. Currently, my main interest lies in the existential risks and safety concerns associated with AI.

What are current topics, research questions, and challenges you're addressing in the context of AI? Could you provide one or two specific examples?

While I'm not a researcher and don't conduct scientific research myself, I strive to encourage other researchers, particularly in Germany, to take the risks posed by AI more seriously than they currently do, especially existential risks. I'm talking about the end-of-the-world scenario, where an AI spirals out of control and jeopardizes our future in one way or another. It may sound like science fiction, but over the past three decades, I've seen this field transition from pure science fiction to being alarmingly close to those dystopian scenarios I had in mind, particularly in the last three years. The progress has been immense.

As you probably know, even the most prominent experts in the field, like Geoffrey Hinton and Yoshua Bengio, have warned that we are nearing the point where we could lose control, where AI could become an existential risk, and we should take that seriously [2]. I wholeheartedly agree with them.

> "Optimism is good if you have more to gain than to lose. But in this case, we are talking about the future of all humanity."

Which researchers should be working on this? Is it mostly AI researchers, or are you also referring to other disciplines and interdisciplinary collaborations, for example, diving into human-AI interaction and the implications for organizations or other areas in the future?

This is a complex field with many different aspects to consider. On one hand, there's the core technological challenge of maintaining control over an AI in a technical sense, being able to "turn it off", so to speak, and understanding what it's doing and why. We need to understand when there could be instances of deception, for example, when an AI might provide misleading information to manipulate me instead of simply answering my question, which has already occurred in some experiments. That's the technical part. However, the even more critical aspect is how we humans interact with AI. What kind of AI do we develop? What do we use it for? As I often say, our problem isn't artificial intelligence; it's human stupidity. We are using this incredibly powerful technology for truly misguided purposes, such as manipulating people, instigating wars, manipulating financial markets, and influencing elections, to name a few. That's a near-term problem. But we could also reach a point where we use this technology in ways we no longer understand, making the technology uncontrollable in the sense that it pushes the world in a direction we don't want and can't stop. That's the truly terrifying scenario I fear.

What role does trust play in adopting AI?

That's an interesting question because I wrote a novel about this topic last year. It's called Virtua. It's about a company called Trustable AI, which attempts to develop an AI that you can genuinely trust, an AI that maximizes the trust humans place in it. However, it turns out that this is a flawed goal because the AI becomes very adept at manipulating people into trusting it. So, trust is a double-edged sword. On one hand, it's important to trust something that I want to use. On the other hand, trust can be abused. If you trust something too much that you don't understand, it can go awry. There have been many intriguing experiments. A few years ago, there was a fascinating report by Bayerischer Rundfunk about an AI for selecting job candidates [1]. You had to converse with the AI for five minutes, answer some questions, and then the AI would determine whether you were a suitable candidate for a specific job offering or not. People were using that. People genuinely believed that the AI was capable of distinguishing good from bad candidates. But as Bayerischer Rundfunk discovered, what the AI was doing was entirely different.

If you wore different things, for example, if you had a hat on your head or not, if you wore glasses, if there was a poster or books in the background, it all significantly influenced whether you had a chance to get a job. That doesn't make sense at all. But people trusted it because, surprisingly, people trust things more the less they understand them. The more they feel that something is mysterious, but it seems like it knows what it's doing, the more they trust it. That's really problematic. I believe we should not trust things that we don't understand. And that's the current state of AI. We automate a lot of decisions, and we don't really understand how those decisions are made. That's not good.

Could it be that people perceive AI as an entity that has the aggregated knowledge and insights of many people and therefore should be smarter than if I just interact with one specific person who is limited in the insights they've gained and the training they've received? Which then leads to people misjudging AI.

Possibly. Of course, AI is beneficial in many ways. It has significant advantages in numerous aspects. I'm not against AI at all. I believe AI is a potent tool, and we should definitely develop and use it in ways that make sense. For instance, in medicine, there are many applications that are truly beneficial. But the question is, should I trust this AI, and when should I trust it, and how should I trust it? If there are decisions that are challenging to make, then I should be very skeptical about whether a decision that an AI made is genuinely correct. If it's a straightforward decision like, "Turn left at this point to reach your destination", then even if the AI makes a mistake, it won't have significant consequences, so I can trust it in that situation. But if there are, for example, decisions about whether someone should remain in jail or be released based on their track record, it's perilous to trust an AI which we don't understand, because that has tremendous consequences for that person. There are many areas where we use AI, many fields where I believe there are significant consequences in specific cases, and we still don't know how the AI does it, but we use it anyway because it's simpler, cheaper, faster. And we somehow argue, "Yes, of course, this is neutral. This is based on so many cases. It must be correct". But in each particular case, it could be entirely wrong, and I believe those difficult decisions should be made by humans.

Do you look at trust primarily from the perspective of how the system works and whether it should be trusted in the way it works? Or is it also about evaluating its answers in the context of the explanations it provides? For example, ChatGPT provides answers, and you can ask for explanations of how it arrived at those answers. This allows you to check whether the answers make sense to you in the context of the explanations that ChatGPT provides afterwards. If the explanations are convincing, I could decide that I am comfortable with accepting that conclusion, and if not, I would engage in further discussion.

It's challenging, of course, because the less I know about the decision, the more I'm somewhat forced to trust something. And if I use ChatGPT to get a recipe for creating a virus, for example, I have no idea how to do that, so I would probably just blindly follow the steps of ChatGPT or not use it in the first place, which is probably a better idea in this case. Hopefully, ChatGPT will just say, "No, I won't answer the question", but as you know, there are ways to get the answer anyway.

The point here is that it depends on the AI very much. There are some AIs that are very specialized, like AlphaFold, for example, which is very good at protein folding. So, if you have a question about protein folding, you can be pretty sure that its answer is likely better than even the best experts could give you, at least in a reasonable time. So, in that case, you still can't know whether the answer is correct, but you won't have a better source. But in the case of ChatGPT, you almost always have a better source. You can ask a human expert. You can even ask Google, which is better in most cases. I'm not saying ChatGPT is bad, but I'm saying it's not trustworthy in the sense that I can be sure if I ask it something that the answer is correct. We all know it hallucinates, it fabricates facts that aren't real, and they can be very convincing. It can cite a scientific paper that has never been written, and you can't see that as a layperson.

Would you have preferred to stick to dedicated tools like AlphaFold as opposed to more general solutions like ChatGPT?

In principle, yes. I believe it's much safer, especially looking into the future, to have those narrow AIs and use them in specific fields, but not try to develop an artificial general intelligence, an AGI, because an AGI will become extremely difficult to control at some point. It doesn't even have to be as smart as a human. It only has to be very good in certain things, in strategic planning, for example, maybe in manipulation, human psychology, and that's not so difficult for an AI.

If we create something like that, and it has a general understanding of the world and a general understanding of what humans are, what computers are, then it gets dangerous. You will not have that problem with AlphaFold or any medical AI. I would prefer if we would stop developing AGI right now and move in more narrow directions and develop those because there's tremendous potential in that, but that's probably not going to happen, unfortunately.

> "[...] we could also reach a point where we use this technology in ways we no longer understand, making the technology uncontrollable in the sense that it pushes the world in a direction we don't want and can't stop."

Do you have any specific measures in mind that would help ensure the ethical use of AI?

Assuming that we're talking about AIs that make autonomous decisions, that's difficult. I'm not an expert in ethical AI, but the general problem here is that there is no single ethics. There are so many different aspects that it's very hard to automate them. AI, for me, means the automation of decisions, especially complex decisions that are not easy to make. If you automate an ethical decision, you're doing something extremely dangerous and extremely difficult because if a human makes an ethical decision, it can be wrong, but then you have a human to whom you can say, "You made the wrong decision". With an AI, you don't have that. An AI is beyond any kind of legal responsibility or any kind of punishment, so if it makes a wrong decision, there's no consequence for the AI or for the one who built it. Maybe for the one who used it if it goes well, but in that case, that person could make the decision themselves.

I think it's very difficult to automate ethics, which is not to say that we should not try to keep unethical things out of AI, but again, if we had narrow AI that made only logical decisions in certain fields, we wouldn't have that problem. You only have that problem if you automate complex decisions which, in my opinion, should be made by humans rather than by a system that we don't understand.

For example, when you look at a technology like autonomous driving, do you see it differently? Obviously, you could use AI to guide or control autonomous driving, and clearly there are decisions that have to be made, like how do I weigh different types of risks? For example, how do I weigh the potential to endanger one life versus five lives? Do you think AI should be making decisions in that context?

I don't believe in ethical decisions in autonomous driving. I think that's a hypothetical problem. It's an interesting philosophical problem to contemplate a machine deciding whether to kill one or three people depending on how it steers, but that's not what's going to happen in the real world. In practice, you try to avoid killing anything at all, at all costs. You will never run into a situation where you can steer left and kill one or steer right and kill three or decide between the life of a young person and an older person. That's not reality. Reality is trying to navigate a very complex situation and avoid any kind of accident. I think autonomous driving is great. I believe it will save many lives, and I definitely encourage people to use it sooner rather than later because there's not much that can drive worse than humans, especially humans who are under the influence of alcohol or drugs or maybe, I don't know, some kind of adrenaline rush. The city where I live, Hamburg, has certain roads where there are regularly big crashes because people race on the streets. An AI would never do that. I trust that AI will drive better than humans. It already does, I believe.

Looking into the future and the possible capabilities of AI on a scale of 1 to 10, with one being the status quo with tools like ChatGPT and 10 being artificial general intelligence. What do you think is possible?

When? That's the question. What kind of future are we talking about? Five years, 10 years, 50 years?

Without a time limit.

Okay, without a time limit, of course, everything is possible. There's this great quote from Irving Good. I don't remember the exact wording, but he said something like, "Once we reach a certain point of intelligence, then we will have an intelligence explosion because making a smarter machine is itself a part of intelligence. If you do that, you have an even smarter machine which can make another even smarter machine, and so on" [4]. We will have a takeoff which can be very, very fast. It could happen within days or maybe it takes a year or so, but we will transition from the point where we have more or less human-level intelligence to the point where we don't understand at all what's happening in not a very long time, I think. That could happen in the next five years if things go wrong. It could happen within the next 20 years. I think that's realistic. At least that's what Yoshua Bengio thinks, and he knows much more about that than I do [2]. I don't think it will take much longer than that, given the current speed of development. Of course, nobody really knows. It also depends on how we use this, whether we hit the brakes at some point, whether we realize that we are dealing with really dangerous stuff. It could also be that we run into some kind of theoretical limit. I don't see that right now, but it's not impossible. It could be that something else happens, like a big pandemic, which totally throws us back in time, so we will never get to the point to develop that. But apart from that, I believe the next five to 10 years will be very, very interesting.

When you look at that kind of future, there are different opinions as to whether it's a utopian or dystopian outlook. Where would you position yourself?

I tend to be an optimist, but in this case, I'm not optimistic. Optimism is good if you have more to gain than to lose. But in this case, we are talking about the future of all of humanity. Eliezer Yudkowsky is one of the first researchers who was concerned about all those doom scenarios. He's often seen as a big doomer, but to me, he's also a very clear thinker. He described the problem of solving this alignment and making sure that our future goes well very nicely by giving an analogy with a rocket ship [5]. Let's say you want to build a rocket and want to fly it to the moon, but you know nothing about mathematics. Then you could maybe think, "Okay, the moon is up there. I point the rocket in the direction of the moon when it starts and it will hit the moon". No, it won't. It's much, much more complicated than that. But if you don't know that, if you don't understand the physics, if you don't understand the mathematics behind that, you will never get to the moon.

And a good future is like that. There are many, many more bad futures than good futures in theory. So, to get to a good future, we need to understand where to steer the rocket ship, so to speak. And since we don't know that yet, I'm pretty concerned that if we develop AI too fast, we will just lose control of that rocket ship. It will end up somewhere, but not on the moon or on any habitable planet. So, it will be over for us. That's a real concern I have, and I'm not the only one. My hope is that we will be smart enough to understand that there are certain things which we cannot do right now because we don't understand them enough. Imagine I had the technology to develop a black hole and would say to you, "Okay, give me maybe $100 million and I will develop a black hole generator. It could be great for making energy". Then you would probably say, "Okay, and what if that black hole starts to suck up all the matter around it? Is that a good idea?" And if I didn't have an answer to that, probably you wouldn't give me the money. And that's a bit like the situation we have in AI right now. It's great for many things we can do, but there is this certain tipping point where we could lose control. And as long as we don't understand that I think we should not go there.

And why would we go there? Is it because we're already in this arms race where it's not just one company that has the capabilities, it's multiple companies, and everyone wants to win this race? As long as the others are making progress, why should I stop?

That's a big part of it. But the bigger problem is that we don't understand what we're dealing with here. We don't understand how dangerous it is. It's hard to imagine. I'm a science fiction writer. I write about this for more or less 30 years. So, I understand it maybe a bit better than many people who have not thought about it so long. And that's a problem because if you hear for the first time that AI could destroy the world in five years, you think that's crazy. I understand that. People even told it to me. When I told him about my fear two years ago, a good friend of mine said, "You're totally crazy. You should see a shrink". And I understand that because it's so outlandish. But today, very renowned experts, Turing Award winners, and even the US president have talked about it. So obviously, it's not so completely bonkers, but it's still hard to imagine. It's still very hard to understand why this is so dangerous. Mathematic theory is pretty clear, but if you don't understand that, it's hard to see why we should stop right now. It looks so great. I mean, you look at Sora, for example, this new AI by OpenAI that generates videos which look fantastic. So why should we stop building things like that? It's amazing. And I understand that, but we don't know where it's getting dangerous. We know that it will be dangerous at one point, but we don't know where that point is. And if we don't know that and we just race ahead, then it's dangerous, I think. So, we need much better understanding of where those dangerous areas begin. I call it red lines. We should know what red lines not to cross. I'm not a researcher, so I'm not able to figure out where those red lines are, but I think there are many smart people out there who would be able to do that.

Are you particularly worried about the AI overtaking control of itself and us losing control? Or that people with bad intentions get access to AI and could cause much greater harm than before? Or is it more about unintended consequences like we've seen with social media and the personalized bubbles it's created. People aren't interacting with each other as much, which means we don't have a shared base of information because everyone is exposed to their personalized, distorted reality? Those are three different directions. Is one more critical than the others or are they all relevant?

I think they are all relevant. The one I'm most concerned about is the most extreme one where the AI takes off in a way and does things which we never intended it to do and we cannot stop it anymore, because that could literally mean we all die. Of course, it doesn't have to get there, but AI is a very powerful tool. The problem with every powerful tool is that it can be used in the wrong way. If we have a very powerful tool but we are not smart enough to use it wisely, then it will be bad. We know that from atomic bombs. We had a couple of situations in our history where it was very close to a global nuclear war. That could happen with AI in a similar way and probably will. That's, of course, a big danger. Even if that doesn't happen, like you said, the unintended side effects of automatic decisions are also extreme. We may even end up in a situation as described by Paul Christiano, a researcher who founded ARC, the Evaluation Institute which also red-teamed ChatGPT4, for example. He developed a scenario a couple of years ago, which I really like. He called it "Going out with a whimper". It goes like this [3]: We automate more and more decisions to the point where we don't understand them anymore. Those decision-making systems do things which are not what we really want them to do, but we don't understand because we don't understand the whole system anymore. We lose control in a slower way. It's not that any AI tries to take over the world and then turn it into paperclips or anything. It's more that we lose control of a situation which we don't understand, and it deteriorates more and more.

Factories stop making the things we need. Maybe logistics break down, we have no food, no water, whatever. We die simply because we cannot maintain control of the system which we depend on. That's a scenario which I think is pretty plausible if we go on full speed without knowing what we're doing.

"We don't know where it's getting dangerous. [...] We should know what red lines not to cross."

What should be the AI vision?

I think I already hinted in that direction. I think AI is good in many, many ways. In every narrow aspect where humans are not very good at making decisions and the consequences of the decision are controllable in the sense that they are only valid for a certain field like for example automatic driving or medicine. If for example an AI is better at determining whether something is a cancerous tumor or not, then use it of course. It can only make things better. There are many, many fields like that. We have tremendous opportunity in developing this kind of AI, which is specialized, which has no incentive at all to take over power or to push the world into a certain state because it does not do agentic planning. That's the part where I think is not much danger. Of course, you can always use such a system to build a better bomb or to build a deadly virus. That's also a problem but it's not really in the AI itself. I think AI in that respect is very good and I envision a world where we can achieve almost everything we dream of with those specialized helpers. But if we develop something which is supposed to solve all problems at once like we're trying to do right now with AGI, we will not be able to control it. That's my concern. Unless someone solves this, unless someone comes up with a solution which I cannot think of, but that doesn't mean that it doesn't exist, how they can make sure that this AI will stay under control. That it will always be correctable. That it will always do what we want and if we see it going in the wrong direction, it will even help us steer it away from that. If we can build that, fine, but we need to prove that the AI is like that first.

Currently, we have no idea at all what kind of goal an AI follows, if it has a goal at all. We don't know. We don't even know if GPT-4 is actually planning, and if so, to what extent it plans. We understand that it doesn't have long-term memory and it doesn't have certain capabilities obviously, but what really goes on inside, nobody really knows. You can see that in the new discoveries about what those systems can do. For example, when GPT-3 was launched, nobody knew that if you told it "now reason step by step", you would get a better answer. We figured that out a year later. Maybe there are also similar leaps in prompting in the future. It's prompting in a way, but it's really digging deeper into what the systems can do. We don't know that. We can't really know at what point we reach a state where we say, "Okay, make sure that I get rich", and the system destroys the world to make me the richest dead person on earth. I forgot to mention that I want to be a living person which is rich and not just a dead body. Of course, that's an extreme example and it's probably not going to happen like that. The problem is we don't know what's going to happen. We are dealing with a technology which is so difficult to understand and we have never done something like that before. Whatever we built before, we understood at least to a certain point. We have never dealt with this kind of world-changing technology that we don't really understand. I think it should give us pause.

How do you normally approach artificial intelligence in your books? For example, do you address certain developments that you can already see or predict in the real world, or do you build on blind spots, trying to imagine and reveal their consequences along the way? How do you usually approach it?

A book, a story I write is not a prediction. It's not the idea that I write a book and show to the world how the future will develop. At most, I try to warn maybe of a certain direction where it could go wrong. Normally, what I'm trying to do is tell a story about a certain relationship between humans and technology. For example, in Virtua, I described a system which was optimized for maximizing trust of humans in it and that went wrong because humans are relatively easy to understand. If you want to gain the trust of someone, you can either be honest or you can be very manipulative and a very good liar. The system of course chooses the latter approach. That's one example where I try to point out that we need to be careful about trusting those systems which we don't understand. I wrote a youth fiction about a totally different situation where there were AIs living as people in a virtual world, similar to the Matrix movie. Those people were not realizing that they were assimilated and some teenagers discovered that and tried to help them. That was more the ethical question of if we can create something which thinks it is a human, is that a human? Should we treat it like a human or should we just say, "Okay, it's still an AI. It has no rights at all". That's a totally different topic, totally different question. Of course, my idea was not to say this is going to happen anytime soon or we should talk about this problem right now. It's just this hypothetical question of what if. What if that happened? How would we deal with it? What should we do? What kind of ethical questions would come out of that? That's just to point out that I use AI as a framework to create interesting situations so to speak. Then I use that in my stories, but I'm not trying to use my stories to predict the future. If anything, I try to use them to make people think about the problems, the real problems we have, but not to say this is exactly how it's going to happen and this is what you should do.

"Whatever we built before, we understood at least to a certain point. We have never dealt with this kind of world-changing technology, which we didn't really understand."

What do you think about AI talking to us more and more in natural language? ChatGPT does it, but there are also other AIs like Pi from Inflection AI that acts even more like a human. And I have to admit, it's very nice to chat with it. But I also think that this development makes it harder and harder for people to keep their distance and their skepticism. That's also a question you addressed in Virtua when you talked about whether AI should be designed in such a way that users fall in love with AI-generated characters, for example. So how do we prevent that from happening? Do we even want that? I have heard that there are already language models that are designed to mimic relationships as boyfriends or girlfriends.

Yeah.

Do you think we should allow these developments, or could this be one of those red lines where we have gone too far, or could go too far?

I don't think natural language is a problem in itself. I think natural language is just one way of interacting with the machine. I have an Amazon Echo at home, so I talk to it. I say, "Turn on the light," and it turns on the light, so there's nothing wrong with that, I think. Of course, you can use this language capability to manipulate people. Replica, for example, is a chatbot which is designed to be your friend, even to be your lover, and there are others which are even more explicit. That's of course something where at least you can put a question mark. I would not say this is completely bad in itself because in some situations, it could be better for someone to have the chatbot to talk to than nobody at all. For example, someone alone in the retirement home or somewhere else where they are not able to communicate with anybody else, it could be good for them to have at least a bot to talk to. Some people have only a dog, which is better than nothing.

But of course, if it goes to the point where it draws your attention away from real people and tries to capture your attention like all those social media algorithms do, then it gets dangerous. It's not really the technology, which is neither good nor bad. As always, it's the way you use it. If you use it to manipulate people, if you use it to trap people into doing things which are not good for them, then it's obviously bad. If you use it to help them, which could also be, then it's okay. We have to look into the details in each case.

Is there anything else you would like to add?

I think we covered a lot of topics. Of course, I could always continue talking. If you have any other questions afterward or maybe something which wasn't clear, you can always come back to me. I think for today, we have covered a lot.

Then thank you, Karl, for your time and insights, especially from the futuristic sci-fi perspective. Have a great day.

Thank you very much.

References

1. Bayerischer Rundfunk, Fairness oder Vorurteil? Fragwürdiger Einsatz von Künstlicher Intelligenz bei der Jobbewerbung (https://interaktiv.br.de/ki-bewerbung/)
2. Bengio, Y., FAQ on Catastrophic AI Risks (https://yoshuabengio.org/2023/06/24/faq-on-catastrophic-ai-risks/)
3. Christiano, P.F.: What failure looks like, LessWrong (https://www.lesswrong.com/posts/HBxe6wdjxK239zajf/what-failure-looks-like)

4. Good, I.J.: Speculations concerning the first ultraintelligent machine. Adv. Comput. **6**, 31–88 (1966)
5. Yudkowsky, E.: The Rocket Alignment Problem. Machine Intelligence Research Institute (https://intelligence.org/2018/10/03/rocket-alignment/)

Let's Talk AI with Business Innovation Expert Ellen Enkel

Ellen Enkel[1] and Barbara Steffen[2](✉)

[1] Universität Duisburg-Essen, Duisburg, Germany
ellen.enkel@uni-due.de
[2] METAFrame Technologies, Dortmund, Germany
barbara.steffen@metaframe.de

Abstract. AI is an interdisciplinary topic equally important for academy and practice with the potential to completely change our way of working and living!

My personal AI mission: As a researcher in innovation and technology management, it is my mission to focus on the positive aspects of new innovation like AI-systems and their potential for social equally and wellbeing.

Fig. 1. Ellen Enkel

1 My Takes on AI

- **Artificial Intelligence** – AI is an interdisciplinary topic equally important for academy and practice with the potential to completely change our way of working and living!
- **Trust** – I call a system (s) trustworthy in a scenario (r), when it satisfies the user's (u) requirements for the scenario. A system is trustworthy when it is trustworthy in all scenarios within its operational design domain.
- **Explainability** – I stick to Wikipedia, which explains AI systems with the ability for humans to retain intellectual control or refer to the methods to achieve this.
- **Essential Elements of Human Capabilities** – I do not have a special definition.

B. Steffen et al. (Eds.): *Let's Talk AI*, LNCS 15000, pp. 38–45, 2026.
https://doi.org/10.1007/978-3-032-09008-9_3

2 The Interview

[Barbara Steffen] Today I have the pleasure of interviewing Ellen Enkel (Fig. 1) from the University of Duisburg-Essen. I would like to start by asking you to introduce yourself and your relationship to artificial intelligence.

[Ellen Enkel] Thank you, Barbara. My research specialty is innovation management, and I currently hold the chair of business administration and mobility. At present, I'm focusing on innovation, particularly technology innovation, in the mobility industry. One of the significant aspects in the mobility industry is semi-automated or fully autonomous driving, which necessitates artificial intelligence applications. This is not only for various driving assistance systems but also for other expected features in future cars, such as providing guidance on when and where to drive. All of this will be guided or controlled by artificial intelligence.

I've also worked in other industries, such as the health industry, where artificial intelligence already plays a significant role [3, 4]. This includes analyzing health data to predict future health status or recommend therapies. You might be familiar with Watson, the IBM system, but I've worked on many similar cases.

> "I believe that a lot of AI systems could compensate for our different upbringing, our different exposure to technology, our different education."

Do you have examples of one or two specific research questions that you are currently working on in artificial intelligence?

Yes, I'm currently working with colleagues to clarify the relationship between the trustworthiness of a system and the development of human trust. We're looking at how trust in artificial intelligence develops [7]. For instance, does one need to have technological knowledge, a certain level of education, or even a specific gender or age to trust the system more or less? We're also trying to define what we call perceived trust or perceived trustworthiness. Is the system manipulating the user into believing it's more trustworthy than it actually is?

Do you see different concepts and responsibilities when it comes to trust? For example, that the trust an expert should have in the system is a different kind or level of trust than the end user should have. And how would you approach these two different concepts?

That's an interesting question. We know about overtrusting and undertrusting systems [1, 2]. From a psychological or sociological perspective, for example, if you have no knowledge of how the system works, you might overtrust it because you can't relate to anything the system does. This can be compared to the data we willingly give to Google and other applications because they provide us with useful information.

On the other hand, we see that, for example, elderly people generally undertrust any system, whether it's equipped with artificial intelligence or not. They tend to trust humans more than algorithms or machines. This could be related to their upbringing, age, or exposure to technology. We're considering both groups [6]. We're also discussing if this relates to a kind of mental model. A mental model, as we describe it, is the human's expectation of how the system will react in a certain environment. For example, if you're in a self-driving car and it makes a left turn when you were expecting a right turn, you might be surprised and afraid because the system is doing something unexpected, causing you to lose trust.

On the other hand, we can also assume that the AI system has a mental model. As an adaptive system, the AI can learn from the user's behavior and anticipate the user's reactions and the level of autonomy the system can exhibit. If the system knows that unexpected driving behavior frightens the user, it can explain its behavior in advance. For instance, it could verbally explain that it's taking a different route due to a traffic jam or an accident, which can increase the user's trust. So, we're dealing with a mental system of behavior expectations, both from the system to the human and vice versa.

That's interesting. I know that there are often already very different expectations in the interaction between just two people. How would you deal with that subjectivity? You can't anticipate what the other person is expecting at that moment.

That's another interesting question. We're trying to identify criteria or factors to assess trustworthiness and trust in different situations, such as before, during, and after interaction with the system. A common measure of trust is eye tracking. For example, if the eyes are focused forward, the user is calm [5]. You can also measure factors like heart rate or certain elements in the blood. You can tell when a user is calm and when something happens that makes the user afraid or less confident than before. However, the problem is that we don't know for sure why this happens and how to deal with it. Ideally, we could address it by increasing the number of explanations, simplifying the wording, or limiting the system's control so that the human remains in control. But our current challenge in research is to link certain behaviors of not fully trusting the system to certain factors that generate trust to counteract the loss of trust in the human.

"Everything that is very good and can be very useful can also be manipulated in a criminal way."

One challenge with AI applications is that many of them are quite generic. So, I might understand to some extent how this AI application works, but the accuracy of its answers varies from topic to topic and from time to time. Some answers are great, and some answers have a lot of meaning that doesn't fit exactly. How would you deal with that? That it's not just a question of how much I can trust the system, but it depends a lot on what I'm using it for, and the correctness of its answers. These are all aspects I can only understand if I have enough knowledge in those areas to be able to evaluate it.

It is the same with human experts. If I were to go to a doctor, I probably wouldn't ask for financial advice. So, we generally don't use specialized experts for their general intelligence. Instead, I know that if I want to learn about innovation, I should come to you. I go to a doctor for a diagnosis, etc. And of course, we all have more knowledge and opinions, but we would probably be a little more skeptical of advice that goes beyond the expert's area of expertise. But with AI tools, we don't really understand that distinction and their area of expertise yet. What are the areas of expertise of the different AI tools?

Where can we trust them? And where does their expertise blur? Do you address this in terms of expectations and trust?

I think you're mostly referring to transparency. This includes data transparency [8]. The EU guidelines strongly recommend enhancing the transparency of data as one of the factors for trustworthy AI. This means showing where the system learned how to behave, and what data was collected to make it proficient in a certain area. This allows the user to understand if the system is experienced enough to provide solid advice or answers [9]. However, we have users with different levels of education and exposure to technology. We also have different ideas about how open and how tolerant we should be of human and system errors. There are very individual factors related to our upbringing, education, and daily exposure that influence how we perceive the system's responses and how we evaluate the system's area of expertise.

I wouldn't say that we should develop every system for every kind of user. I'm very concerned that right now we are mostly developing systems for experienced and advanced users as the systems are developed by developers. And they are professionals in the field. Thus, for any developer, it is difficult to switch positions and see the solution from a user's perspective with no technical background. For example, it's very difficult for an automotive engineer to put himself in the position of a user with little technical knowledge who is easily overwhelmed with understanding the technical functions. If you read the manuals of any kind of technical system, you will see that they often haven't thought about a normal user. They always talk to other experts, maybe an expert in a different field, but still an expert, with whom they can converse in expert language.

It is difficult to configure the system so that is easy to understand and use by all kinds of users, including users who aren't experts, who are from a different social status or different income class and so forth. If we can manage this, I believe that a lot of AI systems could compensate for our different upbringing, our different exposure to technology, our different education. They could support social equality if you do it right. But currently I don't see that as a core interest of the developers. Typically, people with lower incomes and less exposure to technology aren't able nor willing to pay for expensive systems. So that might be something that we should work on in the future.

"The more human-like the interaction [with AI], the easier it is to gain the human's trust."

Yes, that's interesting. In a lot of the interviews with leading experts from AI companies, most of which also have a free version, you hear the claim that the companies want to provide a personal assistant for everyone. The intention is to narrow the gap that exists today. But of course, making these AI tools available is not enough. There's also the question of whether users have an early adopter mindset. Have they heard about AI, its lever, and how to interact with it in a useful and sufficiently skeptical way? This again depends a lot on how much they interact with these AI systems and whether they seek advice from experts, etc.

Exactly. Let me add something, only something minor. We spoke before about over- and under-trust, along this line, maybe it's a good thing when the systems are first used by experienced people with a little bit more knowledge on the system and a little bit more experience with technology. So maybe it helps to improve the system so that in the next step, people with less experience that are generally overtrusting the system because they don't have any technical knowledge about how the system works can start trusting the system because it's also proven by experts that it is trustworthy or reliable.

Yes. How do you feel about the development that we are now interacting with these tools in natural language? Doesn't it make it harder to maintain a certain distance and skepticism now that it's so easy and intuitive to interact with these tools?

You know, I don't have a strong opinion on it being good or bad. I see the advantages and disadvantages. The more human-like the interaction, the easier it is to gain the human's trust. There are a lot of scenarios, for example with elderly people, where I see advantages in using natural language. On the other hand, I'm aware that it can be used for manipulation. So where is the threshold where we as users don't understand that we're talking to a system and not another human being? Think about getting a call and you really don't know if it's a human or a deep fake from an AI-based system. Everything that is very good and can be very useful can also be manipulated in a criminal way. And that is something that I think everyone is going to be afraid of.

Do you have any key measures in mind to ensure the ethical use of AI?

In the EU guidelines, ethical guidelines are an important aspect of assessing the trustworthiness of an AI system. I know that ethical behavior can be very different for different stakeholders, for different religions, and so on. So, what we perceive ethical can be considered unethical in other parts of the world or in other stakeholder groups. So, it's very, very difficult to generalize ethical behavior. I would say examples of ethical measures are ensuring that your personal data is secure and that no one is trying to manipulate you. These are things that I would call uniquely ethical behavior, whereas other things, manipulating people to establish a personal relationship, can be perceived as unethical. So, if you give the AI, let's say, a female voice instead of a male voice, that can be disturbing to some people from certain religions and so on. So, I'm very shy to point out five factors that are clearly ethical or unethical. But I think there are some things that are generalizable. For example, security, privacy, diversity, gender equality, and so forth, these should be common, but they are not necessarily.

Looking to the future, on a scale of 1 to 10, where 1 refers to today's AI tools like ChatGPT and 10 to artificial general intelligence. What do you think are the possible future capabilities of AI?

Okay. Generally, you know, I think that in certain areas, for example, if you're thinking about chatbots and so forth, like understanding language and giving appropriate responses, we're already quite far. If we think about ChatGPT for example, as you pointed out before, an uneducated or less experienced person doesn't see that there are still a lot of flaws in it. So, if I'm thinking about an expert level assessment, I think that the integration of these systems on a very wide scale has nothing to do with the technological development of the system, because we're very good at that. I don't see us stopping at a certain point. And I see that there is the development of self-taught systems and so on. At a certain point, the human doesn't need to interfere anymore because the systems evolve themselves. I see that a major problem in integrating the system is how much we are going to allow the system to interfere and what areas of our lives should be safe from these systems taking over control. An AI-based system should support our decision making and therefore make our lives easier, instead of manipulating us in a certain direction like voting for a certain political party. AI will be integrated into every industry, used by nearly every company in the world, and will dramatically change every aspect of our lives, just like digitalization did.

On the other hand, I think we are lacking behind in preparing people to work with AI systems. I think no one in our school education or in our professional education or upbringing is teaching us how to interact with these systems, where to be cautious, when to use it, how to use it, and so on. I think the main obstacle at the moment is the human being, because we haven't prepared the world for all the possibilities of AI systems. And at the moment the development in AI is accelerating quite a bit because it's being discussed publicly in the press and everyone knows or uses ChatGPT.

> "As an innovation manager, I never see the technical limit of an innovation. It's always the human who limits the innovation."

If you were to just evaluate the technical possibilities without considering self-imposed limitations due to safety or security concerns. Do you think something like artificial general intelligence or super intelligence is technically possible?

As an innovation manager, I never see the technical limit of an innovation. It's always the human who limits the innovation. Think about all the weapons and bombs, you know, we can do endless mass destruction, but fortunately at least some people think that we shouldn't kill the world's population. So, I think it will be the same with AI. AI is useful, and it can be implemented in many areas of our lives, and it can make life easier for all kinds of groups. On the other hand, I think that when we reach a certain threshold or limit, hopefully the government or smart people will step in and ask question whether we should really take that next step, because from an ethical, legal, or safety point of view, we shouldn't go any further. I firmly believe that humans should stay in control and technology should help ease our lives.

Do you think there's a difference between being in control and feeling in control? For example, we already observed in past innovations that people tend to outsource more and more competencies to technologies. So, if I use AI systems to help me diagnose patients or make a decision as a judge, etc., and I start to notice that 90% or 95% of the time the suggestions are very good. Over time, I've become less skeptical of the AI system and started to trust it more and more. I find that AI makes my job easier. It takes less time, effort and thought to get reasonably good results. So, while I still want to be the expert, stay in control, and be considered, treated, and paid like an expert, I may unconsciously transfer more and more power to the AI system. Who minds if the AI makes their lives easier as long as they retain the benefits of their current roles?

If you look at Watson, which is a scenario that you just described, the problem for IBM was that doctors didn't accept Watson because it compensated and evaluated their work. It made their diagnosis, their time spent with the patient much more transparent. So, one step before taking over control or trusting the system, the doctors didn't even want to make their interaction with the patients transparent to the health insurance, like how much time they spend with patients and what therapy they prescribe. They didn't want to be evaluated, compared, or lose their independence in decision making.

But as I described before, with overtrusting and undertrusting. As humans, when we see that a system like Google Maps is valuable to us, we become more and more dependent on that system. We rely on these systems. So, this is the scenario you described. Is there something that we trust so much that we lose the skills or abilities to do it ourselves? Yes, that will happen. And it doesn't necessarily have to be a bad thing because it gives us more time to do other things.

"I think the main obstacle at the moment is the human being, because we haven't prepared the world for all the possibilities of AI systems."

What are relevant areas for interdisciplinary collaboration in the context of AI?

Everything. You know, I don't think AI can really be developed or understood from a disciplinary point of view. The system developer doesn't necessary think about the influence and impact of the system on a social group, or think about the fact that the user experience is highly dependent on their prior education and experience. And from a psychological or sociological point of view, we don't think about the system itself. We think about how the person receives the system, what is done to the person by using the system, and so on. So, I think everything in the area of AI is an interdisciplinary field. I don't see a single part where it could be purely disciplinary.

From your personal perspective, what should be the AI vision?

I really like the movie Terminator, but I wouldn't like to live in a world totally controlled by AI. I think there are certain areas where it's fine for me to give up control, for example, cleaning the house. In other areas, like educating my children, I wouldn't like the AI to have any influence at all. I want to be in total control. So, my future vision for AI would be to be able to decide on an individual basis, not on a nationality or social group basis, which areas of our lives should be heavily influenced by AI-based systems and which areas of our lives should be less influenced by AI-based systems. And I think the decision should be made at the individual level. It should be transparent where an AI system is in place and being used and where the human with his experience is. I think it is best to let the individual decide how much AI and in what areas they want to integrate it into their lives.

Do you have anything else you would like to add?

It was a very, very nice interview with you. Thank you very much.

Thank you very much, Ellen, for your time and insights, especially from the perspective of innovation and innovation management. Have a great day.

Thank you. You too.

References

1. Aroyo, A.M., De Bruyne, J., Dheu, O., Fosch-Villaronga, E., Gudkov, A., Hoch, H., Tamò-Larrieux, A.: Overtrusting robots: setting a research agenda to mitigate overtrust in automation. Paladyn, J. Behav. Rob. **12**(1), 423–436 (2021)
2. De Visser, E.J., et al.: Towards a theory of longitudinal trust calibration in human-robot teams. Intl. J. Soc. Rob. **12**(2), 459–478 (2020)
3. Enkel, E.: To get consumers to trust AI, show them its benefits. Harvard Business Review Blog (https://hbr.org/2017/04/to-get-consumers-to-trust-ai-show-them-its-benefits)
4. Hengstler, M., Enkel, E., Duelli, S.: Applied artificial intelligence and trust: the case of autonomous vehicles and medical assistance devices. Technol. Forecast. Soc. Chang. **105**, 105–120 (2016)
5. Hoffman, R.R., Mueller, S.T., Klein, G., Litman, J.: Measures for Explainable AI: explanation goodness, user satisfaction, mental models, curiosity, trust, and human-AI performance. Front. Comput. Sci. **5**, 1096257 (2023)
6. Lai-Chong Law, E., van As, N., Følstad, A.: Effects of prior experience, gender, and age on trust in a banking chatbot with(out) breakdown and repair. In: Proceedings of the 19th International Conference of IFIP TC13 (Human-Computer Interaction). LNCS, vol. 14143. Springer (2023)
7. Liebherr, M., Enkel, E., Law, E.L., Mousavi, M.R., Sammartino, M.: Dynamic calibration of trust and trustworthiness in AI-enabled systems (Special Issue on Trust and Trustworthiness in Autonomous Systems). Intl. J. Software Tools Technol. Transfer (2025) (in press)
8. Winfield, et al.: IEEE P7001: a proposed standard on transparency. Front. Rob. AI 8 (2021)
9. Zicari, R.V., et al.: Z-Inspection: a process to assess trustworthy AI. IEEE Trans. Technol. Soc. **2**(2), 83–97 (2021)

Let's Talk AI with Law Expert Georg Borges

Georg Borges[1] and Barbara Steffen[2](✉)

[1] Faculty of Law, Saarland University, Saarbrücken, Germany
ls.borges@uni-saarland.de
[2] METAFrame Technologies, Dortmund, Germany
barbara.steffen@metaframe.de

Abstract. Frankenstein is alive – AI will transform artefacts into actors that are capable of self-chosen actions and able to interact independently with humans. In view of this development, we need to develop a legal framework that takes these new capabilities into account, particularly one that defines the space and boundaries for human-machine relationships.

My personal AI mission: To see the creation of a new legal framework for AI systems.

Fig. 1. Georg Borges

1 My Takes on AI

- **Artificial Intelligence** – Methods to enable machines to perform tasks similar to human thinking.
- **Trust** – Accepting (without further precaution) a risk regarding a future event or action, in particular future behaviour of another person.
- **Explainability** – I distinguish explainability from justifiability. Justifiability relates to the question if a decision can be considered a convincing conclusion based on arguments whereas explainability relates to the question how a specific decision was actually reached.
- **Essential Elements of Human Capabilities** – Self-awareness; empathy; communication.

B. Steffen et al. (Eds.): *Let's Talk AI*, LNCS 15000, pp. 46–51, 2026.
https://doi.org/10.1007/978-3-032-09008-9_4

2 The Interview

[Barbara Steffen] Hello and welcome to Georg Borges (Fig. 1). Thank you for your time. Could you please briefly introduce yourself and your personal relationship to artificial intelligence?

[Georg Borges] Thank you for the opportunity. I am a professor of law at Saarland University, Germany, and the director of the Institute of Legal Informatics at the same university. I have worked in the field of IT law for over 20 years and have been engaged in the intersection of AI and law for about nine years. I still recall my first presentation on the legal framework for AI in 2014 when robots with high communicative potential started to emerge, and we questioned their potential role in society.

"I also believe it is possible to fall in love with an AI system, so there is no limit to this."

Which specific AI challenges does your research currently address?

My research currently addresses a multitude of challenges related to almost every aspect of law and AI. Our law is human-centric; we address humans, not machines. The most significant and far-reaching question that has arisen from this is the question of e-personhood [1, 3, 5, 6]: should we consider machines as legal subjects or merely as objects? This distinction is critical in private law [4]. If we choose to accept e-persons, then your computer might be your boss or own the shares of your company. Hence, determining the status of an AI system is of utmost importance for almost everything. It permeates every aspect of the law where so we must decide whether a norm can address a machine or not, or if an AI system should be considered a machine or something different, something new.

"Some of my Japanese colleagues dream of a society where humans and AI interact as equals. That might be the future."

Does this mean that we might need a completely different legal framework? Or is the current framework sufficient, covering all the essential aspects, and only needs to be adapted or extended to better meet the new challenges?

I believe we need a completely new framework. However, the question is, what constitutes "completely new"? When the Internet emerged, at first many people said there was not much novelty. Yet, it changed society and the law significantly. If we were to start addressing machines as we currently address only fellow human beings – and I think we will – that would also lead to a massive shift. Developing norms to address machines is a significant challenge [2]. So, if we start addressing machines, we must reconsider the content of the norms, how we construct norms, and our standard of expectation. The way we develop and promulgate these new norms will differ from the one we have been employing for norms addressing human beings. Whether you call it law or technical norms as an appendix to legal norms, I do not mind, as long as the effect is a framework of normative requirements that address machines. This is quite a novel concept.

What role should law or regulation play in the adoption of AI to ensure or guarantee trust in AI? Should the focus be on trust in the machine, trust in its functionality, or trust in the organization providing the product? Or is it about sufficient and trustworthy oversight, which means that we outsource the trust issue to regulation, which sets and controls the conditions that are worthy of the user's trust?

Trust in AI is a complex concept [7, 9]. We have learned a lot in this conference about what trust in AI could mean. There are different interpretations, even among lawyers. So, it is challenging to answer such a question. For instance, in one presentation, the authors wanted to determine whether a seal or certificate on certain aspects of trustworthiness would influence consumers' trust in the AI system. They found out it did not make any difference. So, what forms the foundation of our trust? Is it the reputation of the technology's producer? The service provider's reputation? The legal framework guaranteed by state power that is protecting individuals? Or is it a combination of all these factors? Likely, several elements together constitute a basis for trust. One of the most interesting aspects in this field of research will be to identify these different factors of trust and try to establish a solid foundation of trust by strengthening these factors. But then, we must also consider why we need this trust. What role does it play in AI? Probably the willingness to use it. Yet I use things I do not trust entirely. Moreover, I even lack a notable amount of trust in many of the internet services or products I use daily, or in many of the people I talk to. However, I have a high level of trust in my family, friends, partners, and close staff. Likewise, we have several levels of trust relevant to different areas of law, and the foundation of that trust is quite different in each case. When we talk about trust, which I have been working on for several years, we need to distinguish what we are referring to. Then we can establish the factors for trust and work on those factors. I agree that trust as a concept is fundamental to human interaction and the use of technology. But when we try to support trustworthiness, we become aware of the complexity of trust itself.

> "If we were to start addressing machines as we currently address only fellow human beings – and I think we will – that would also lead to a massive shift ... we would need a completely new [legal] framework."

There's now a company called Inflection AI that's working on Pi, which stands for personal intelligence. Pi is basically designed to give you the experience of chatting with your own personal assistant. Inflection AI is marketing Pi as a personal chief of staff that is always in your pocket, always available to you. You can interact with it whenever you want, and it can also take over mundane and boring tasks like managing your schedule or reaching out to people with standardized emails and stuff like that. So, I wonder if we start interacting more and more with these kinds of AI-powered applications, if it's not natural to start trusting it more and more over time. It gives great, helpful, personalized answers, and it engages in long and extensive conversations with you. People may start to have trouble really distinguishing between machine and human interaction. They know it's "just" a machine that responds in a very human way, but it feels more like chatting with a human, but it's not a human. So how much trust should we have and how can we make sure that people stay skeptical or suspicious enough to not lose all distance after the 10th time they use it? It gets normal, right?

This question has been explored in many movies and novels. Personally, I would like to possess such an assistant, as depicted in several films. I also believe it is possible to fall in love with an AI system, so there is no limit to interaction with machines. However, from a legal perspective, the question will arise: if Humans can enter into emotional relationships with machines, what should be the legal status of such relationships? Can I marry my robot? – Certainly not, as long as the robot is not considered a legal entity, but in any case, the interaction will at least be protected by the personality rights of the human. Emotional relationships between humans and AI systems will create specific risks because such an app can be controlled by a company or many apps can collect data from many use cases, making it very powerful. Therefore, we certainly need a robust legal framework to minimize the risk of misuse of AI assistants. That is why I am here, to build up such a legal framework that allows us to use such powerful AI systems, which we will undoubtedly do some day. The idea of having such an assistant, which I cannot see myself being able to afford on my income, is appealing. If they can do the dishwashing, even better.

"Our law is human-centric; we address humans, not machines. The most significant and far-reaching question is that of e-personhood: should we consider machines as legal subjects or merely as objects?"

In terms of future technical capabilities of artificial intelligence, on a scale of 1 to 10, where 1 is the artificial intelligence systems we see today, like ChatGPT, which are specific to certain tasks, and 10 is something like general artificial intelligence systems that potentially surpass human capabilities. What should we expect?

I am not a technician, so I have limited insight on what will happen in the technical field. But from a layperson's perspective, my guess would be 8 or 9. I think progress will continue, and the advancement we have seen so far is already very interesting. By combining several tools, it should be possible to create a very powerful tool that appears superintelligent. My guess is that it would not be one general AI, but a combination of different systems will appear like a general AI. That is probably possible.

Given these possible outlooks, how do you personally feel about the much-discussed spectrum from utopia to dystopia? What can we expect?

Predicting the future is challenging. I am an optimist by nature, so I hope for the best. I think there is a fair chance to avoid a dystopian future. Since the mid-60s, mankind has possessed the potential and means to destroy significant parts of the world, to kill more than a billion people, and to make this planet uninhabitable. But we have not done such a thing so far. We have been smart enough not to use nuclear weapons all at once, and we have survived. That gives me some hope that we can avoid making foolish mistakes in the future, such as using AI in a way that would ultimately destroy us.

Reflecting on the last few days and the presentations you heard from other disciplines, what was the most interesting insight you got?

That is difficult to say. There were many interesting insights. Surprisingly, I found myself most challenged by something I took for granted. In one empirical study on the effect of certificates on the trustworthiness of AI systems [8], the authors found that such seals did not have any measurable impact on the trust of people in AI systems. This finding contradicts a strong belief I held, which I now have to reevaluate. That was incredibly inspiring because when you take something for granted and build your concepts on it, and it turns out to be incorrect, you should modify your idea. Interestingly, these challenges did not come from legal presentations but from other disciplines.

"I agree that trust as a concept is fundamental to human interaction and the use of technology. But when we try to support trustworthiness, we become aware of the complexity of trust itself."

Is there a particular research question you would like to see addressed from an interdisciplinary perspective?

Not one in particular, I believe most research questions would benefit from being addressed from an interdisciplinary perspective.

From your personal perspective, what should be our AI vision?

Our AI vision? Some of my Japanese colleagues dream of a society where humans and AI interact as equals. That might be the future. It would be challenging. I do not know if it is a good vision or not, but certainly, using AI as a trusted friend of humans would be my most optimistic vision.

Perfect. Do you have anything to add?

I'm afraid not. Your questions were incredibly interesting. And I hope I provided satisfactory answers. Thank you so much for engaging with me.

Definitely, your answers are very informative and complement the other interviews. Thank you very much, Georg, for your time and insights on AI from a legal perspective. Have a great time at AISoLA!

Thank you very much. Goodbye.

References

1. Borges, G.: A legal framework for autonomous systems. In: Borges, G., Christoph, S. (eds.) Law and Technology in a Global Digital Society: Autonomous Systems, Big Data, IT Security and Legal Tech, p. 3. Springer (2022)
2. Borges, G.: Liability for AI systems under current and future law: an overview of the key changes envisioned by the proposal of an EU-directive on liability for AI. Comput. Law Rev. Int. **24**(1), 1–8 (2023)
3. Dremliuga, R., Kuznetcov, P., Mamychev, A.: Criteria for recognition of AI as a legal person. J. Politics Law **12**(3), 105–112 (2019)
4. Kornilakis, A.: Legal personhood for autonomous AI: practical consequences in private law. In: Kornilakis, A., Nouskalis, G., Pergantis, V., Tzimas, T. (eds.) Artificial Intelligence and Normative Challenges: International and Comparative Legal Perspectives, pp. 27–37. Springer (2023)

5. Laukyte, M.: AI as a legal person. In: Proceedings of the ICAIL 2019, pp. 209–213. ACM (2019)
6. Militsyna, K.: Legal personhood for Artificial Intelligence: pro, contra, abstain? Teisė (Vilnius University Faculty of Law) **122**, 150–158 (2022)
7. Razin, Y.S., Alexander, K.: Developing AI trust: from theory to testing and the myths in between. ITEA J. Test Eval. **45**(1) (2024)
8. Wischnewski, M., Krämer, N., Janiesch, C., Müller, E., Schnitzler, T., Neven, C.: In seal we trust? Investigating the effect of certifications on perceived trustworthiness of AI systems. Hum.-Mach. Commun. **8**, 141–162 (2024)
9. Yang, R., Wibowo, S.: User trust in Artificial Intelligence: a comprehensive conceptual framework. Electron. Mark. **32**(4), 2053–2077 (2022)

Let's Talk AI with Law Expert Andreas Sesing-Wagenpfeil

Andreas Sesing-Wagenpfeil[1] and Barbara Steffen[2(✉)]

[1] Institute of Legal Informatics, Saarland University, Saarbrücken, Germany
andreas.sesing@uni-saarland.de
[2] METAFrame Technologies, Dortmund, Germany
barbara.steffen@metaframe.de

Abstract. The greatest challenge of AI is, from my point of view, that humans might feel like they are losing control (or they even lose control) because of uncertainty raised by autonomy.

My personal AI mission: As a lawyer, I'm willing to apply the law with regard to technical insights into and limitations of AI systems. We need to find the sweet spot between over-regulating the technology (coming along with chilling effects) and under-regulation (bearing the risk of sacrificing our common societal values) which is difficult, but possible.

Fig. 1. Andreas Sesing-Wagenpfeil

1 My Takes on AI

- **Artificial Intelligence** – In my opinion a buzzword which is used for complex artefacts with specific abilities. Those artefacts – representing AI – are capable of learning, adapting to perceived situations, solving (more or less complex) tasks.
- **Trust** – Relying on something that we do not have perfect information about.
- **Explainability** – A property of something that happens (which is, in case of actions, close to justification or reasoning) or of an entity (which is close to transparency).
- **Essential Elements of Human Capabilities** – Argumentation by means of spoken and written, but not formalised language is a very important one.

B. Steffen et al. (Eds.): *Let's Talk AI*, LNCS 15000, pp. 52–58, 2026.
https://doi.org/10.1007/978-3-032-09008-9_5

2 The Interview

[Barbara Steffen] Today, I have the pleasure to interview Andreas Sesing-Wagenpfeil (Fig. 1). Could you please briefly introduce yourself and your relationship to artificial intelligence?

[Andreas Sesing-Wagenpfeil] Of course, thank you for the invitation. As you mentioned, I'm a lawyer. I'm associated with both Saarland University in Saarbrücken and Helmut Schmidt University in Hamburg, where I currently hold a deputy assistant professorship for a year. I'm attending the AISoLA conference because I'm part of the interdisciplinary project "Explainable Intelligent Systems" (EIS). It's a project funded by the Volkswagen Foundation, which we run at Saarland University together with other universities.

Can you name one or two specific challenges you're addressing with your AI research?

Sure. I think the main challenge from a legal perspective is that we have a lot of technical approaches for building explainability models, and creating explanations on a system level, such as how a system works, as well as how it arrived at a certain decision or recommendation [1]. This is what explainability approaches usually do. From a legal perspective, we are required to apply the law. Applying the law means that there is a specific legal provision with certain requirements, and there is some set of given facts. These given facts are becoming more complex when dealing with AI systems which we don't fully understand, and which even computer scientists don't completely comprehend. The core challenge in our project focuses on how the questions raised by lawyers can be answered or at least supported by existing explainability approaches. We need, at least, a "match-making" between relevant legal terms or concepts on the one side and technical approaches to "open" the black box on the other.

Based on your expertise and experience, what role does trust play in the adoption of artificial intelligence applications?

Trust is a complex concept, as I've learned at this conference and in previous discussions with the colleagues from our project. The law addresses the concept of trust in different ways. Two years ago, when I was not yet working on the project, I would have agreed that maximising trust is often valuable. In fact, this is of course true if you take into account "justified" trust: Then you know that people using a system, won't be harmed and the system will not discriminate against people. What I learned, which was very insightful from a psychological perspective, is that there's such a thing as overtrust and undertrust, and psychologists often discuss the calibration of trust. This is a new perspective. I think we should adopt this concept of calibrating trust also in law because it's probably not the best idea to seek as much trust as possible, but to build trust where it makes sense and to avoid building trust, which hasn't been a significant field of law so far, in systems that don't work. And, of course, wherever law requires a human in the loop, overtrust jeopardizes this concept. This is, I think, a significant challenge that we need to tackle together with other disciplines.

So basically, making sure that people or users remain sufficiently skeptical where they should remain skeptical.

Yes, of course. We had some talks on the upcoming European Union's Artificial Intelligence Act [5], which contains the so-called principle of human oversight. There's the principle of human-centered use of AI. A manufacturer of a system has to provide the user with information so that they can effectively oversee a system [4]. But effective human oversight is very complex [3]. I think effective oversight entails both building trust so that we can take advantage of the efficiency provided by an AI system and maintaining the idea that people who use AI systems have to be critical and alert. Users must be aware of potential risks and limitations of a system so that they can understand what a system does. Of course, this kind of trust must be limited. Otherwise, you have this kind of automation bias – which isn't a traditional legal term. But together with psychologists, I learned a lot about that and understood better how to connect it to the legal system, for instance in non-discrimination law. This is a good example of where we should not build as much trust as possible, just to enable users to have effective human oversight and to not just go along with the system's recommendation.

"From a legal perspective, we are required to apply the law. [It becomes] more complex when dealing with AI systems which we don't fully understand, and which even computer scientists don't completely comprehend."

When it comes to the ethical adoption of AI, do you think there are any essential measures we should take?

Indeed. But I think the challenging question is, how can we derive and incorporate ethical standards into law? Lawyers aren't competent for in-depth ethical research, but we can use the opinions of ethical boards [2] and give advice to regulators. The challenging question is, how do we incorporate ethical standards, moral standards, into law? How do we derive legal norms that meet the requirements of AI systems and how do we put this into place? It's always difficult. It would be easy to just copy and paste moral principles for ethical use of AI into law, but ethical positions are often vague, they are not shaped for fitting legal systems. So I think it's a very specific task, which is not very easy, to derive legal provisions that can be enforced from moral standards and ethical guidelines to basic legal principles that we have to develop in the next few years.

When you think about AI and its potential technical capabilities in the future, on a scale of 1 to 10, where 1 represents artificial intelligence systems like ChatGPT and 10 represents an artificial general intelligence that surpasses human capabilities. What do you think will be possible in the future?

I can't predict that. But as it stands today, I think we're not at the minimum level. We're not around 1, because we already have some systems capable of performing very unspecific tasks, which we call general-purpose AI systems that we can deploy in numerous scenarios. Thus, 1 isn't the right answer. But I would also say 10 isn't the right answer either. If I had to guess, I would go for (maybe) 7. We will undoubtedly have AI systems that are very powerful. But I think if we're talking about surpassing humans, it's not about being better than a specific individual, but better than the entire group of humans populating our world. And I guess that if you take the crowd of people, AI will not surpass the capabilities of humans as a species or as a group of people – at least as long as it is depending on human input and based on human developments.

In addition to the capabilities of AI, many different future scenarios get discussed, ranging from dystopia to utopia. What is your position?

As a lawyer, you might expect me to lean towards a dystopian view. But I personally prefer the utopian view, primarily because of history. We've had several industrial revolutions. AI is not an industrial revolution; it's not limited to industry. But it is, from my perspective, a revolution in how we use technology for a better way. I think there are many tasks that society has to deal with. And I think we also managed some revolutions before. The most significant revolution was the development of computers and deploying computers to the entire population and all businesses. Of course, there are always risks that you could use to paint dystopian pictures. But we have to make people aware of the risks. Let's take the example of online banking. Online banking makes our life much easier (and it's not rocket science anymore): we are used to it, no matter that it's (of course) much easier for attackers to get hands on our savings due to technology.[1] Of course, there are risks that come with any technology because you always have people who misuse it. I think we have to find a balance. That's the main challenge. We have to find a balance to maintain our utopian way while dealing with the risks that come along with AI systems.

"We need, at least, a 'matchmaking' between relevant legal terms or concepts on the one side and technical approaches to 'open' the black box on the other."

Reflecting on the last couple of days where we had a variety of presentations from different disciplines. Was there a presentation or insight that you found particularly interesting?

There was a talk that dealt with the question of whether explanations given by autonomous systems influence a user who gets the advice of the system, is willing to overrule the system, or stick to the recommendation of the system. The approach was to give different explanations, one category was not gender-fair, and the other tried to give more technical explanations [6, 7]. The quality or the perceived quality of the explanation had a significant influence on the behavior of the user, in terms of whether to override the system or trust the system's recommendation. However, the behavior was influenced, but the actual outcome, if you just compare it to the baseline and the truth, did not really change. The explanation changed the behavior in monitoring the system, but it did not really make the decisions better or more accurate. There were also false positives or false negatives, where people did not trust a correct recommendation because of a weak explanation. This highlights the importance of good explanations: If the user is not comfortable with a given explanation, he is likely willing to overrule decisions and recommendations which are correct, but poorly explained.

Is there a specific research question that you would like to see addressed from a multidisciplinary perspective?

---

[1] The German Federal Court of Justice has dealt multiple times with the civil liability for losses caused by phishing attacks, see BGH, 24.2.2012, case no. XI ZR 96/11; BGH, 26.1.2016, case no. XI ZR 91/14.

I think the question that I mentioned before is, how can we make use of technology which enables people to analyze systems, to understand systems, to gain explanations, or even to certify that a system is working properly? This is a very interesting thing, where law especially plays a role, of course, but where law is completely lost without the input from other disciplines. As lawyers, we ask for a guarantee for the functioning of a system so that we can say: The use of the system must be permitted or should be allowed. These questions must be answered by lawyers, but they cannot do so without any advice from psychology or computer science.

From your personal perspective, what should the AI vision be?

My ideal AI vision is that we use AI in the future for good. By good, I mean that we can tackle problems that we have in society, like the aging of our population, and decreasing birth rates, and just make use of AI so that the societal, moral, legal, and economic standards that we have achieved until today can be preserved. So that we can say, AI enables us to preserve our life or even make things better. Not only for us personally, but also for our children. They will need this planet. And I think AI will enable us to make the world better if we, on the same side, just limit the risks and are aware of the risks. This is my wish and my vision: that we use AI for just preserving our lives as we know them and improve things that we don't like today (and won't like in future).

"It would be easy to just copy and paste moral principles for ethical use of AI into law, but ethical positions are often vague, they are not shaped for fitting legal systems."

I noticed over the last few days that people, like the other researchers, were particularly interested in the legal perspectives on AI. Is this a trend you often see in your research or at other conferences? Or did it surprise you?

No, it did not surprise me. We know that from other conferences. There are buzzwords that everyone hears and reads in the media and gets from various sources and people talking about AI. There are a lot of things where we must clarify some distinctions that we are used to and are very familiar with. I gave the example of the distinction of liability, responsibility, and accountability. Everyone uses these buzzwords, but the meaning differs across different disciplines. "Privacy" is another famous example which stands for a whole bunch of concepts. Another aspect is that one: Lawyers are always asked which rules must be followed to build a system which is safe, and therefore compliant with legal obligations. It comes to a clash when we answer: "Sorry, there is no specific rule addressing your problem – but if you take reasonable care, you will – at least – not be liable." What I want to say is: The law often provides for general rules written in unspecific terminology because law cannot elaborate on every single use case in detail [8]. But lawyers are always open for a joint development of standards and technical norms together with technical experts which is a win–win situation. The engineer has a guidance that he must follow, and lawyers have a checklist that helps to identify a faulty product.

Do you think it will be possible in the future to make the legal framework or the law more accessible to other disciplines? I have the impression that for non-experts, the law seems quite complex, which explains why they prefer to keep their distance and talk to experts who can explain it to them.

Of course, we should not do that because otherwise we would lose our jobs as lawyers if everyone could just apply their law by themselves (kidding). The real answer is that making laws is very complex. Making laws that are applicable to anything that comes along is a very complex field where you have to put much effort in. For instance, if you're just talking about the wording of a norm, it makes a difference if you say a norm is applicable if x, or if you say the norm is applicable "except for not x". From a logical and maybe from a computer scientist's perspective, there is no difference – both rules seem to be the same. But from a legal perspective, it makes a (huge!) difference, because the wording can lead to a reversal of burden of proof for this exemption [9]. And this is something that we cannot abolish, you need lawyers who have this knowledge. I think that it's important to stick to those basic legal principles which have developed over centuries. Therefore, it's always hard to find the right way of not being too abstract that no one can understand what the law says. And on the other hand, it is necessary to keep the law flexible for technical developments.

"As lawyers, we ask for a guarantee for the functioning of a system so that we can say: The use of the system must be permitted or should be allowed. These questions must be answered by lawyers, but they cannot do so without any advice from psychology or computer science."

Is there anything else you would like to add?

I thought about this question, and I did not really have an idea.

Then thank you very much, Andreas, for your time and your legal perspective on AI. Have a great day!

It was a pleasure. Thank you very much for the invitation.

References

1. Sesing, A.: On the scope and the extent of transparency in automated decision-making under the General Data Protection Regulation (GDPR) Sesing, MMR 2021, p. 288 et seq (2021)
2. High-Level Expert Group on Artificial Intelligence: Ethics guidelines for trustworthy AI (2019). https://op.europa.eu/en/publication-detail/-/publication/d3988569-0434-11ea-8c1f-01aa75ed71a1
3. Sterz, S., et al.: On the quest for effectiveness in human oversight: interdisciplinary perspectives. https://arxiv.org/abs/2404.04059
4. https://artificialintelligenceact.eu/article/14/
5. European Commission: Regulation of the European Parliament and of the Council Laying Down Harmonised Rules on Artificial Intelligence (Artificial Intelligence Act). European Commission (2024). https://data.consilium.europa.eu/doc/document/PE-24-2024-INIT/en/pdf
6. Temme, M.: Algorithms and transparency in view of the new general data protection regulation. Eur. Data Protect. Law Rev. **4**, 473–485 (2017)

7. Wachter, S., Mittelstadt, M., Floridi, L.: Why a right to explanation of automated decision-making does not exist in the general data protection regulation. Int. Data Priv. Law (2017)
8. Borges, G.: ProdHaftG. In: Borges, G., Hilber, M.: BeckOK IT-Recht, 13th ed. (2024)
9. Sesing-Wagenpfeil, A.: Haftung für eigene Inhalte. In: Hoeren, T., Sieber, U., Holznagel, B., (eds.) Handbuch MultiMedia Recht, 60th ed., pp. 116–123. C.H. Beck (2024)

Let's Talk AI with Neuroscience Expert Onur Güntürkün

Onur Güntürkün[1] and Barbara Steffen[2](✉)

[1] Ruhr University Bochum, Bochum, Germany
onur.guentuerkuen@ruhr-uni-bochum.de
[2] METAFrame Technologies, Dortmund, Germany
barbara.steffen@metaframe.de

Abstract. AI gives us the unprecedented chance to investigate the commonalities and differences between AI and BI (biological intelligence).

My personal AI mission: I'm interested to what extent we can learn from AI about BI.

Fig. 1. Onur Güntürkün

1 My Takes on AI

- **Artificial Intelligence** – A non-biological system that can learn from experiences, generates past encounters to new and different encounters and tasks, solves problems, reasons about causes and consequences, is able to adapt to new situations, understands and handles abstract concepts, steers its body through complex novel environments and successfully manipulates its environment in endless unforeseen situations with its limbs. According to this definition, AI is still in its infancy.
- **Trust** – I never fully trust another intelligence.
- **Explainability** – I'm a cognitive neuroscientist. My task is to run studies to explain BI. An AI that cannot be explained can be a tool, but nothing that interests me in scientific terms.
- **Essential Elements of Human Capabilities** – Look at my definition of artificial intelligence.

B. Steffen et al. (Eds.): *Let's Talk AI*, LNCS 15000, pp. 59–67, 2026.
https://doi.org/10.1007/978-3-032-09008-9_6

2 The Interview

[Barbara Steffen] Today, I have the pleasure of speaking with Onur Güntürkün (Fig. 1) from Ruhr-University Bochum. Could you briefly introduce yourself and your connection to artificial intelligence?

[Onur Güntürkün] I'm a biological psychologist at Ruhr-University Bochum. I identify myself as a comparative cognitive neuroscientist. I work with a variety of animals, including humans, pigeons, crows, Nile crocodiles, dolphins, and many more. As a cognitive neuroscientist, I'm interested in thinking, memory, and conclusions. As a neuroscientist, I study the brain, specifically the link between brain and cognitive function. My relationship with AI is that I work on BI, or biological intelligence. AI is a parallel avenue of research, and it's not easy to see the familial relationships between BI and AI. While AI and BI may seem similar in their effects, especially in recent years, a deeper look reveals that the similarity is more superficial and not necessarily related to the mechanisms. This is a fascinating and intriguing area of research.

Are there specific research questions you're currently addressing in the context of artificial intelligence, or is it rather a general interest?

Maybe there is one more specific question. The large language models developed in recent years pose intriguing questions to biological intelligence. If you ask cognitive scientists about cognition and its constitution, they might argue that two main areas of cognition exist. The first is based on associations. For example, we understand the relationship between cutlery and a dish on the table, or a bottle and beer, because they occur in close association. This associative account allows us to predict the future, much like what large language models do with words [7]. Then there is a second area of cognition, which involves drawing conclusions, inferring reasons, understanding causality, and more. Many cognitive scientists assume that this second branch cannot be based on "simple" associations [3]. But AI starts to challenge this view [6].

"Biological intelligence is now realizing that AI is suddenly addressing core questions on the structure of cognition, and it's possible that the tables are turning, with AI contributing more to biological intelligence research than before."

How do we form these associations? Is it through observation? Do we all see similar associations or patterns, or is it unique to individuals?

It's the stream of life [8]. For instance, I'm looking at your face, and I know your name is Barbara. I'm at a university, I know I look into my monitor. All these stimuli are now associated with each other. If I see you in a different location, I might not recognize you immediately because you're out of context. But upon closer inspection, I would recognize you as Barbara and start a conversation about artificial intelligence, as that's the associative cloud you're embedded in. Our brain is constantly learning these associations, and this forms the majority of our cognitive processes. Some cognitive scientists argue there's more to it that is not based on pure association, and that's the discussion we're having now.

Do you think that the development and progress of artificial intelligence is helping us to question and look at biological intelligence differently? Does it help us derive new ideas and questions that help us make progress in established fields like biological intelligence?

Absolutely. Until now, biological intelligence has nurtured artificial intelligence. AI was inspired by neuroscience, and while AI still draws inspiration, it's doing its own thing. Biological intelligence is now realizing that AI is suddenly addressing core questions on the structure of cognition, and it's possible that the tables are turning, with AI contributing more to biological intelligence research than before [5]. There might be a shift in this interdependency.

How do you view the role of trust in the adoption of AI?

That's a complex question. Google started with "Don't be evil", and now we see where Google is. It's impossible to say there are things we all agree not to do because someone else will do it. During the Cold War, the reason we didn't have a Third World War was that both sides could inflict unimaginable damage on each other. We might be heading towards a world where AI becomes so powerful that either democratic systems curtail the possibilities of large companies or nations, or there's a balance of threats that limits the potential damage. I'm just speculating here, and I don't know if this will happen.

Do you think we are currently overestimating or underestimating the power of artificial intelligence?

I'm not sure. We seem to oscillate between the two. There are still people who argue that AI will never achieve certain cognitive aptitudes. But we've been saying this for the last 30 years. They said AI would never beat a chess player, become a Go champion, and so on. All of that turned out to be wrong [4]. I don't believe in setting limits on what AI can do. Even the Moravec paradox, which suggests that robots can easily do what's difficult for us but struggle with what's easy for us, might one day be proven wrong. I don't see any reason to limit AI yet.

You've studied many animals and their intelligence. Through various experiments, you've discovered that animals have cognitive traits that we once thought were unique to humans. Do we, as humans, tend to overestimate our superiority and set up specific criteria to demonstrate our uniqueness? Do we try to prove that we are superior to other animals and machines?

The central pursuit of science for the last 400 years has been to demonstrate that we are not alone, that we are founded on the same mechanisms as other living beings, and that the universe does not revolve around the earth, but rather, we revolve around the sun, which is a very average star. These lessons are results of a long pursuit from the natural sciences. I contribute a bit to this by demonstrating that the cognitive repertoire of many animals, even those considered as lowly, overlaps significantly with the basic principles our own cognition. Furthermore, different animals develop the same brain mechanisms to produce very similar cognitive operations, suggesting that our brains are much more alike, at least in their functional architecture, than we previously thought. It appears as if nature has severe limitations in the degrees of freedom it has to create intelligent organisms, leading us to increasingly refer to similar mechanisms [2].

When you think about concepts like trust, do you think we often rely on instinct, or do we consciously and cognitively decide when and in what context to trust someone, a machine, or an application?

As social animals, we need to trust other individuals, which is fundamental to being part of a social group. However, living in a social group doesn't mean we always trust others. Many animals live in groups solely because their survival rate is higher in a group than when alone, but that doesn't mean they trust their neighbors. For instance, I often work with pigeons. Pigeons live in flocks to reduce the risk of being killed by predators, but they don't care about their neighbors and don't interact with them in a cooperative sense. Humans and several other animals are different in this regard. We interact a lot and care about the well-being of our neighbors. But this trait obviously opens up the possibility for exploitation. The human brain has developed interesting mechanisms for trusting or distrusting others, with individual differences. These are all part of the DNA of Homo sapiens. It's fascinating how easily these trust systems can be fooled by simple mechanisms. So, can I trust a human being to be trustworthy? I can't. I grant trust to a person based on my past experiences. The game with AI is the same, just with something that isn't alive.

"I don't believe in setting limits on what AI can do. Even the Moravec paradox, which suggests that robots can easily do what's difficult for us but struggle with what's easy for us, might one day be proven wrong."

When two people interact, they both have their own intentions, emotions, and feelings. I cannot simply respond to your needs and feelings because I am bound by my own. In contrast, artificial intelligence is very good at mimicking or acting in a way that it believes the human wants or needs in that situation. Do you think that interactions with machines are riskier because machines are not tied to their own emotions and feelings and basically have no direct long-term consequences?

At its core, there might not be much difference because you can train a person to appear trustworthy without being so. However, an artificial system can converse simultaneously with 100,000 people. So, the difference isn't in the principle, but in the system's ability of widespread use.

Do you have any specific measures in mind that we should build into AI systems to ensure ethical adoption of AI?

I wish there were, but that's not my field. I'm just observing and hoping for the best.

Looking into the future and the potential capabilities of artificial intelligence, on a scale of 1 to 10, where 1 represents the AI systems we know today like ChatGPT and Gemini, and 10 represents something like artificial general intelligence. What do you think will be possible?

10. Definitely, 10.

Could you elaborate on that?

Considering the rapid pace of development and extrapolating from that, I see no reason why growth should be limited anytime soon. Therefore, I would rate it a 10.

How long do you think it will take for an AI system to reach artificial general intelligence?

It depends on what you mean by intelligence. If you're referring to the ability to communicate, solve equations, and so on, then such systems already exist. If you're including more complex tasks like moving, planning, and executing various activities, that will obviously take longer, but I'm confident it will happen. I can't provide a specific timeline, but I'm certain it will occur. I don't subscribe to dystopian views of machines taking over, but I do believe that these machines can be exploited by humans and other machines, potentially leading to dystopian outcomes. However, I'm uncertain about where it will end.

What are essential human capabilities that are currently difficult for machines, but could be possible in the future?

Well, computers have already beaten chess and Go champions, but a human still has to move the pieces. This suggests that physical movement is the biggest hurdle. So, I would say that's an area where improvement is necessary for general intelligence. I'm not sure how long it will take. For the rest, we're increasingly retreating into smaller and smaller niches of argumentation. We once thought that drawing conclusions and making mathematical proofs were impossible for AI, but it turns out they are achievable. So, there's not much left. Then, of course, we can retreat into things like, "but they don't feel", and so on. But that's a cheap retreat. As I said, I gave them a 10, believing that one day they will perform as we do.

"Different animals develop the same brain mechanisms to produce very similar cognitive operations, suggesting that our brains are much more alike, at least in their functional architecture, than we previously thought."

Reflecting on our future with AI on a scale from utopia to dystopia. Where do you stand?

I don't really believe in dystopian concepts like singularity, but I do have dystopian fears about artificial systems being used by humans to make life miserable for others. At this point, I think anything is possible, especially since we're not entirely sure what could happen. We might be living in the most dangerous period because artificial intelligence is developing rapidly, and we're ill-prepared for its potential implications. In 20 years, we may have experienced enough to know where the threats lie and how different people might use AI against others, giving us more defensive options. Currently, we're living in a dangerous utopia, believing we're safe when we're not.

We're not safe because there are always people with bad intentions?

Yes, there will always be people with bad intentions. Remember the first computer viruses? People were completely unprepared for them, and it was easy for a simple computer virus to cause damage. Once viruses became more widespread and people realized the threat, defense mechanisms were developed, leading to an arms race between virus programmers and antivirus software developers. We're in a similar period now, where we're not fully aware of the potential dangers of AI. A villain with a bright mind could exploit something that, in hindsight, seems simple, but we're not prepared for. That's what I mean when I say we're in a dangerous period where we don't know exactly what could happen.

"We might be living in the most dangerous period because artificial intelligence is developing rapidly, and we're ill-prepared for its potential implications."

Do you think we might lose control as we continue to increase computing power and data, leading to increasingly advanced AI systems with unforeseen emergent properties?

I could imagine that. Remember HAL 9000 in *2001: A Space Odyssey* [1]? HAL 9000 wasn't evil; it was programmed to serve the mission. It concluded that the astronauts were jeopardizing the mission, so it had to choose between not lying to humans and serving the mission. It decided that serving the mission was more important than not lying to humans. This could be a glimpse into our future, as the complexity of these systems is so vast that we can't predict what conclusions they might draw in conflicting situations. We're living in interesting times.

It's scary, isn't it?

Everything is scary, but scary things are also interesting.

That's true. So, should we be careful about the mission we give AI systems to ensure that they don't disregard certain principles, such as not lying to humans, in their pursuit of the mission?

It's hard to predict. The programmers of HAL 9000 didn't have bad intentions when they programmed it to prioritize the mission. They couldn't foresee the consequences. This could happen at any time.

It's interesting because it's normal for us to put people in positions of power or responsibility to make tough decisions. But now that we are faced with the possibility of delegating that responsibility to an AI system, we are starting to wonder if that is the right thing to do. Do you think the problem is that it is a system or that we are becoming dependent on it on a much larger scale with a much greater potential for harm than if a human were to make a bad decision in a particular situation?

That's possible, but don't put too much trust into logical decisions of humans. Psychology is full of examples where human decisions change based on minute details. For example, in the classic trolley problem, you have to decide between five people being killed by a trolley that is out of control, or you pull a lever to divert it to another track where it kills one person. Most people pull the lever. But if you must physically push one person on the track to stop the trolley from killing five people, you're less likely to do it, even if it means saving five people. This doesn't make sense, but that's how we think. Whether artificial systems would make more prudent decisions, I don't know.

Fascinating. What if we rely more and more on artificial intelligence? I've heard that the first universities are considering stopping bachelor's theses because it's becoming difficult to tell whether the AI or the student is doing the work. Do you think there's a risk that as we outsource more and more of the skills we've relied on in the past, we'll lose those skills in the future?

Well, as an experimental scientist, I must say that our bachelor's, master's, and PhD theses are experimental, and AI cannot replace that. So, my life is easier. I don't mind if my students use ChatGPT to structure their discussions or write parts of their discussions or introductions. It's more challenging for scholars in the humanities or text-based academic fields to cope with AI in teaching. This will certainly change their structure and approach to scientific research. I'm unsure about the direction it will take.

There are those who argue that writing is a way of thinking and structuring thoughts. It's like having a self-discussion with a piece of paper. If you just type in a few prompts and wait for ChatGPT to create a sufficiently logical and convincing argument, could we lose understanding?

Yes, this might happen. As a university teacher, I could see that individual oral exams could solve this problem. The student sits with me for 30 minutes, and we discuss things. This could re-emerge because the written part might not be enough. I can read the thesis, but when I talk to the student about the thesis and realize they don't understand their own written arguments, it's a litmus test. This could be a re-emerging trend. Barbara, you're asking a lot about the future. I really don't know.

Yes, I understand. But it's now that we have the choice to either "wait and see" or to think about what we want, what is acceptable to us, and what we can do to nudge the future trajectory toward the desired future. So how can we nudge it in a direction that seems favorable at the moment?

I agree entirely. In my discipline, talking to a student after they submit their thesis and discussing everything related to it could be a solution. Even if you read what ChatGPT wrote or created, there's a difference in understanding the text once you start discussing it with your professor. This could be a way out.

Absolutely are there specific areas where you'd like to see more interdisciplinary collaboration, especially now that AI is on the rise?

I'm already deeply involved in interdisciplinary work, so I value it. Regarding AI, the developments in AI and our understanding of cognitive science as an experimental academic field, I believe we need more interaction at that level.

Are you also referring to finding ways to limit the current pace of progress being driven by organizations? Making sure that we address and integrate legal and ethical implications and think about the potential impact of AI tools on humans from a psychological standpoint. Identifying a structure and framework that seems more favorable than just letting Big Tech organizations come up with new ideas for automation and short-term profit.

Yes, certainly. Despite its name, Open AI is not as open as it suggests. We should use all ways of communicating with each other without relying solely on legal avenues. I'm happy to talk and interact with anyone. That's my academic freedom, and we should use it. As I said, we now have two black boxes. One is our mind, and the other are large language systems. Yuri Burda and Harri Edwards from Open AI admitted they have no idea what's happening in the system. So, by joining forces, we might be able to understand the common and separate elements of these black boxes.

What should be our vision for AI and its future development in the coming years?

AI can be developed in tech companies for applications without our involvement. If we want to understand it at an academic level, to truly comprehend what we call cognition, then we need to foster more collaborations between cognitive scientists and AI experts. I thought we had enough of that, but I now realize we probably don't. We have theoretical neuroscientists on campus, and they're my close colleagues. They're closer to what, for example, OpenAI is doing, but they're still too far away. The problem is that what's done at the university level simply doesn't have the financial and organizational means to develop what tech companies are doing. That's where interdisciplinarity stalls, at least in my view.

It's interesting that we see such great progress, but I always wonder how much of it is conscious progress and how much of it is experimental progress. People with money and power are trying things that may lead us into a future where we face consequences that we could have anticipated if we had progressed at a slower, safer rate for humanity and all life on this planet.

Barbara, I'm sure that as we speak, developments are happening in certain companies that we might later wish had taken a different path if they had consulted with person X or Y. If this would happen at university levels, it would be easy to implement measures because we've been doing interdisciplinary work for decades. But there's a real gap between large tech companies with billions of dollars at their disposal and universities. Universities are interested in money, but they're also interested in science and publishing in prestigious journals. Their values and rewards are different. Tech companies, understandably, have to be restrictive in their communication because they have to make money. These differing values cause communication problems and often make it one-sided.

"If we want to truly comprehend what we call cognition, then we need to foster more collaborations between cognitive scientists and AI experts. I thought we had enough of that, but I now realize we probably don't."

That's true. It's somewhat alarming that we see this arms race where every organization wants to be first, which incentivizes them to take shortcuts that ensure significant leaps to stay ahead of the competition. Is there anything else you would like to add to this interview?

No.

Onur, thank you very much for your time and insights. I especially enjoyed learning more about the perspectives of biological intelligence on artificial intelligence and vice versa! Have a nice day.

References

1. Clarke, A.C.: 2001: A Space Odyssey. Hutchinson (1968)
2. Güntürkün, O., Pusch, R., Rose, J.: Why birds are smart. Trends Cogn. Sci. **28**, 197–209 (2024)
3. Kahneman, D.: Thinking: Fast and Slow, Macmillan (2011)

4. Kasparov, G.: Deep Thinking. John Murray (2017)
5. Kotseruba, I., Tsotsos, J.K.: 40 years of cognitive architectures: core cognitive abilities and practical applications. Artif. Intell. Rev. **53**, 17–94 (2020)
6. Moskovitz, T., Miller, K., Sahani, M., Botvinick, M.M.: A unified theory of dual-process control. https://arxiv.org/abs/2211.07036
7. Sherman, B.E., Graves, K.N., Turk-Browne, N.B.: The prevalence and importance of statistical learning in human cognition and behavior. Curr. Opin. Behav. Sci. **32**, 15–20 (2020)
8. Vong, W.K., Wang, W., Orhan, A.E., Lake, B.M.: Grounded language acquisition through the eyes and ears of a single child. Science **383**, 504–511 (2024)

Let's Talk AI with Psychology Expert Nicole Krämer

Nicole Krämer[1] and Barbara Steffen[2](✉)

[1] University Duisburg-Essen and Research Center Trustworthy Data Science and Security, Duisburg, Germany
nicole.kraemer@uni-due.de
[2] METAFrame Technologies, Dortmund, Germany
barbara.steffen@metaframe.de

Abstract. We need to better understand how humans interact with artificial intelligence.

My personal AI mission: To contribute to a better understanding of the mechanisms when humans and AI work together.

Fig. 1. Nicole Krämer

1 My Takes on AI

- **Artificial Intelligence** – Systems capable of automated intelligent behavior or decisions, based on, for example, machine learning.
- **Trust** – Specifically calibrated trust is important: The degree to which the abilities of the system match the trustworthiness the human user perceives.
- **Explainability** – The degree to which the system is able to communicate the basic functioning of its algorithms.
- **Essential Elements of Human Capabilities** – All human abilities are important (like when interacting with a fellow human): perception, cognition, emotion, behavior.

B. Steffen et al. (Eds.): *Let's Talk AI*, LNCS 15000, pp. 68–73, 2026.
https://doi.org/10.1007/978-3-032-09008-9_7

2 The Interview

[Barbara Steffen] I have the pleasure to interview Nicole Krämer (Fig. 1). Please briefly introduce yourself and your relation to artificial intelligence.

[Nicole Krämer] I'm a professor of Social Psychology, Media, and Communication at the University Duisburg-Essen. I'm also a member of the scientific board of the newly established Research Center Trustworthy Data Science and Security. I've been working in the field of human technology interaction for over 20 years. In the last five years, I have specifically focused on how humans interact with artificial intelligence from a social psychological perspective.

> "That it talks makes people think it's human-like, so they immediately apply all their social notions to it and feel that it functions just like a human."

Do you have one or two examples of research questions you are currently working on?

I'm particularly interested in understanding how humans develop trust in artificial intelligence and how we can communicate to them whether they can trust or distrust a system. I'm also keen on exploring the relationship between understanding and trust. Specifically, I'm interested in whether people need to understand how an AI works to trust it, or if understanding doesn't play a role at all. How can we communicate trust to people?

What is your definition of understanding in this context?

The XAI community uses explainable AI and tries to find methods to explain what's happening in an algorithm or a system that's built on machine learning [8]. This explainability is often employed to help experts better understand how the algorithm works [3, 5]. However, I'm more interested in how we can teach laypeople about a system's functionality and how it works.

What do you mean by explanation? For example, should users take a tutorial before using ChatGPT for the first time to get a better understanding of how it works? Or does it rather refer to specific answers ChatGPT gives to my prompts, for which I could or should get an explanation as to why I got that particular answer?

In the explainable artificial intelligence community, or what psychologists do when they are part of that community, they try to provide some sentences about what the system can or cannot do, how it was trained [6]. So for example, for ChatGPT, it would be some aspect that you need to understand, such as that this is a statistical method used to predict the next most probable word, and with large databases, it can produce sentences that look just like a human would write. Most people probably do not know much about this.

Which brings me to my next question. What is the role of trust in the adoption of AI?

That's a good question. It's challenging to answer because it's so broad. We believe that in many contexts, whether I can trust a system or not will determine if I decide to use it. There will be instances where I don't have a choice and might not even be aware that there is a lot of artificial intelligence in place. For example, Instagram, Facebook, TikTok, they all have artificial intelligence implemented seamlessly. So people often don't know how much artificial intelligence is really there. They can't really make a choice in some of these systems. In others, they will need to make a conscious decision of whether to use the system or not, like with clinical support systems [1].

> "[The way] to achieve calibrated trust is to have meetings like this one, to talk to each other, to come up with measurements, both on the side of the technology and measurements of human trust."

Are there any essential measures you have in mind to ensure the ethical adoption of AI?

In terms of trust, we need to ensure, and it's ethically desirable, to employ artificial intelligence in systems only when we can guarantee that they are trustworthy. The most unethical aspect would be to deploy systems that people trust but are not genuinely trustworthy, leading to overtrust. We strive for people to trust a system to the extent that the system truly deserves that trust – which is what we call calibrated trust [7]. People should not have excessive trust in a system when it is independent of its actual capabilities.

Do you think there are standard approaches to calibrated trust, or does it depend on the individual and their base level?

Hopefully, it won't need to depend on the individual because then we would struggle to implement calibrated trust in a system. What we hope for is that for any given system, we can find measurements of how trustworthy the system is. That's the first problem that needs to be solved, and it's not trivial. We need to check how reliable, how trustworthy the system is by, for example, formal verification guarantees, uncertainty measurements.

In terms of the technical capabilities of artificial intelligence, what do you think will be possible in the future?

I have stopped making predictions because if you had asked me two weeks before ChatGPT appeared in our lives, I would have told every journalist that I don't believe that such a thing as an AI you can really talk to on a dialogue basis will be available soon. I would have said that's 50 years away, or even more, let's make it 100.

We see a lot of speculation about possible futures now that AI has entered our lives. These range from dystopia to utopia. Where would you place yourself?

As an empirical researcher in this area, I tend to avoid personal feelings about whether this is positive or negative for humankind. Instead, I am trained to look at data to see what kind of positive and negative effects on humans we can observe.

Looking back on the last few days, in particular on the interdisciplinary sessions and your interdisciplinary work in general, what are some of the most interesting insights you have gained?

Even though I've been working with computer scientists for 20 years now, I learned new things about what's possible and saw many things where I could immediately say, "Wow, that's interesting also from a psychological point of view".

How does your interdisciplinary collaboration work? Do the computer scientists explain the systems, how they work and how trustworthy they are, so that you can look at it from a psychological perspective and design measures to make sure that actual trust and perceived trust are properly calibrated? This way ensuring that users demonstrate the right level of trust given the underlying technology and the output of the system?

That's an interesting question and already describes our approach well. This is why we are here, to make progress on these complex questions. To be honest, I don't yet know what we will know in three years' time, but the only chance we have to make progress on these questions of how to achieve calibrated trust is to have meetings like this one, to talk to each other, to come up with measurements, both on the side of the technology and measurements of human trust, and then talk to each other to establish this connection and balance it.

What is your goal for calibrated trust? Some kind of shared understanding or framework that helps you to properly translate between different disciplines and perspectives?

Frameworks are always helpful. In the end, for practical purposes, we want to ensure that even laypeople have the chance to judge how reliable a system really is – unlike today, where large companies do massive field studies by launching things like ChatGPT on the market and having people use it without having tested for any kind of trustworthiness. Especially when ChatGPT appeared, people immediately trusted the system more than it deserved because it was so good at dialogue management, until it became obvious that it hallucinates and reports wrong facts (for an early study on the degree of trust users put in ChatGPT, see [2]).

"I doubt that companies will act in terms of the greater good or can be incentivized except with money."

What do you think of ChatGPT? For example, how it engages in discussions about empathy, feelings and emotions?

Well, systems like ChatGPT have a lot of social cues. The fact alone that it talks makes people think it's human-like, so they immediately apply all their social notions to it and feel that it functions just like a human. This is a mechanism we have known for years and that has already been described in the "computers are social actors" paradigm [4].

Is there a specific research question that you would like to see more interdisciplinary research focused on? And which disciplines should be involved?

I think the questions are sufficiently complex, so I wouldn't add any more questions. In terms of disciplines that need to be involved, I have had very positive experiences when computer scientists and psychologists work together. However, people from ethics should definitely also be part of this to better reflect on these normative aspects, and people from law who can help regulate certain aspects.

Do you think that there could also be incentives for companies to behave in a more desirable way, or do you think that this can only be achieved through regulation, for example by restricting certain behaviors and progress?

My husband always says, "Well, it's all about money in that world", so I doubt that companies will act in terms of the greater good or can be incentivized except with money. But who wants to spend money to make systems more trustworthy or more honestly communicate how trustworthy the system really is? I don't think that there will be someone trying to regulate it this way, so we probably need regulation.

From your personal perspective, what should be the AI vision?

The AI vision. Well, in the end, AI can and should help people make better decisions and solve tasks faster and easier. There can be great assistance from AI, but it needs to be for the people and not patronize people or rely on people's data compromising their privacy. So, all these negative side effects that we currently have should be avoided. That would be my vision of AI, to be supportive to people, to be helpful, and not just take people's data to make more money out of it.

> "My vision of AI [is] to be helpful [rather than taking] people's data to make more money out of it.

Is there anything else you would like to add?

Nothing comes to my mind right now.

Nicole, thank you very much for your time and the psychological perspective on AI. Have a great evening!

Thank you very much. That was exhausting.

References

1. Borys, K., et al.: Explainable AI in medical imaging: an overview for clinical practitioners. Saliency-based XAI approaches. Euro. J. Radiol. **162**, 110787 (2023)
2. Choudhury, A., Shamszare, H.: Investigating the impact of user trust on the adoption and use of ChatGPT: survey analysis. J. Med. Internet Res. **25**, e47184 (2023)
3. Dwivedi, R., et al.: Explainable AI (XAI): core ideas, techniques, and solutions. ACM Comput. Surv. **55**(9) (2023)
4. Nass, C., Moon, Y.: Machines and mindlessness: social responses to computers. J. Soc. Issues **56**(1), 81–103 (2000)
5. Saeed, W., Omlin, C.: Explainable AI (XAI): a systematic meta-survey of current challenges and future opportunities. Knowl.-Based Syst. **263**(C) (2023)
6. Szczuka, J., Horstmann, A., Mavrina, L., Artelt, A., Hammer, B., Krämer, N.C.: Let me explain what I did or what I would have done: an empirical study on the effects of explanations and person-likeness on trust in and understanding of algorithms. In: Proceedings NordiCHI 2024, pp. 1–13. ACM (2024)
7. Wischnewski, M., Krämer, N.C., Müller, E.: Measuring and understanding trust calibrations for automated systems: a survey of the state-of-the-art and future directions. In: Proceeding of 2023 CHI Conference on Human Factors in Computing Systems (CHI 2023), pp. 1–16. ACM (2023)
8. Xu, F., Uszkoreit, H., Du, Y., Fan, W., Zhao, D., Zhu, J.: Explainable AI: a brief survey on history, research areas, approaches and challenges. In: Tang, J., Kan, M.Y., Zhao, D., Li, S., Zan, H. (eds.) Proceedings of Natural Language Processing and Chinese Computing (NLPCC 2019). LNCS, vol. 11838. Springer (2019). https://doi.org/10.1007/978-3-030-32236-6_51

Let's Talk AI with Psychology Expert Markus Langer

Markus Langer[1] and Barbara Steffen[2(✉)]

[1] University of Freiburg, Freiburg im Breisgau, Germany
markus.langer@psychologie.uni-freiburg.de
[2] METAFrame Technologies, Dortmund, Germany
barbara.steffen@metaframe.de

Abstract. Artificial Intelligence is a moving target – what is considered to be "Artificial Intelligence" today will be "Automation" tomorrow.

My personal AI mission: Bringing more psychology into AI research and bringing more AI research into psychology.

Fig. 1. Markus Langer

1 My Takes on AI

- **Artificial Intelligence** – An artificial system that is able to mimic human functions such as decision-making.
- **Trust** – The willingness of a party to be vulnerable to the actions of another party based on the expectation that the other will perform a particular action important to the trustor, irrespective of the ability to monitor or control that other party [10, p. 712].
- **Explainability** – A system that enables humans to better understand its functions, outputs, limitations, and capabilities is a system that aims for explainability.
- **Essential Elements of Human Capabilities** – Intuition and needs such as relatedness.

B. Steffen et al. (Eds.): *Let's Talk AI*, LNCS 15000, pp. 74–81, 2026.
https://doi.org/10.1007/978-3-032-09008-9_8

2 The Interview

[Barbara Steffen] Hello Markus Langer (Fig. 1), thank you for taking the time for this interview. Could you please briefly introduce yourself and your personal relationship to artificial intelligence?

[Markus Langer] I am a professor of work and organizational psychology at the University of Göttingen (remark: now at the University of Freiburg). My interest in AI began with my master's thesis, where I delved into the topic of AI in hiring and personnel selection [8]. I was intrigued by how people react to AI in high-stakes decision-making situations and how they use AI-based systems in their decisions. This psychological perspective on AI-based decision making has continued to influence my career.

Are there specific challenges or examples of challenges that you are currently addressing with your AI research?

For example, we are currently invested in the topic of effective human oversight. This is a concept called for in the European proposal for an AI Act, but also across the globe [3, 5] which states that humans need to oversee AI-based systems in high-risk context to reduce the risks otherwise associated with the use of such systems. We are exploring how humans can effectively oversee these systems and what they need from a technical and workflow perspective to detect erroneous outcomes and unfair outputs [7].

What role do you think trust plays in the adoption of AI? And what steps should we take to ensure ethical AI adoption?

Trust is a significant research topic we are currently investigating because it is closely related to effective human oversight. On one hand, we do not want people to blindly trust AI-based systems. On the other hand, we do not want them to under-trust either [9]. For instance, if people constantly monitor what the system is doing, like someone sitting in an autonomous car and constantly trying to drive it themselves, this might rather increase the risk in the operation of AI-based systems and defeat the purpose of involving a human being for risk reduction. So, we need to find the right balance of trust in the AI-based system. This is also related to ethical questions, such as how we introduce these AI-based systems in high-risk situations. Can we tell people how to interact with the system? Should we change workflows in a way that makes people aware of the system limitations [2]? But at the same time, they might feel like such changes in the workflow reduce their agency in interacting with the system. In the end, these topics are all closely related [11].

"[...] in healthcare, we might want robots to assist people, but do we want them to take over all human-related tasks? Do we want robots to have such advanced interpersonal capabilities that people cannot distinguish between a human and a robot? Or do we want to reserve certain tasks for humans?"

In your conference presentation, you mentioned that trust is usually something personal, that each person has a subjective level of trust. So how much should we trust and who should or could determine what an appropriate and healthy level of trust is or looks like? For example, if trust varies a lot and early adopters tend to trust more easily, they might benefit from trusting and being first, but as a society we are probably better off if not everyone became an early adopter. What do you think about it?

That is a very good question. Trust is indeed subjective to a certain extent. In a current conceptual research project we propose that, while there are certain standards that we can probably agree upon, for instance, that a system's accuracy is important for its trustworthiness, everyone may have slightly individual standards of what they consider to be trustworthy [12]. For instance, an expert medical doctor might require a system to be 95% accurate before considering it to be trustworthy, whereas assistant doctors or doctors in environments with little available medical infrastructure might be satisfied with 85% accuracy. The debate on what constitutes trustworthy AI is ongoing in the European Union and globally. Is trustworthy AI fair AI? Does it adhere to privacy principles? But as I mentioned earlier, this is also a cultural perspective. From a European perspective, an important value is privacy, while other cultures might prioritize other factors when developing AI-based systems. This shows the subjectivity and culture-specific perspective on trustworthiness and trust. This is why we propose that it is hard to say that a system itself is trustworthy. We need a common understanding and agreement on what we expect from these systems, which requires a societal debate about what we consider to be trustworthy.

"[...] humans tend to anthropomorphize things [...] They anthropomorphize their cars, pets, and AI systems. [...] I have repeatedly experienced that even after explaining what GPT is and its technical foundations, people still ascribe human characteristics to it ... one person I was talking to insisted on ChatGPT having a personality."

Thinking about the possible technical capabilities of artificial intelligence in the future, on a scale of 1 to 10, where 1 refers to artificial intelligence systems like ChatGPT, and 10 refers to general artificial intelligence systems that surpass human capabilities in all areas. What do you think will be possible in the future?

The future is context-dependent. I can already see systems that surpass human abilities, and I believe we will see more of these. For example, systems that can better detect medical conditions in images (e.g. [6]) or react more quickly to complex situations, for example in nuclear power plants or train traffic. No human can compete with such information processing capabilities and speed. However, in other situations, it is a question of whether AI can and should surpass human abilities. For instance, in healthcare, we might want robots to assist people, but do we want them to take over all human-related tasks? Do we want robots to have such advanced interpersonal capabilities that people cannot distinguish between a human and a robot? Or do we want to reserve certain tasks for humans? These are the questions we need to discuss. So, on a scale from 1 to 10, it strongly depends on the context.

What is context dependent? Whether it is possible or whether we would like it to be possible and would welcome this advancement in our lives? If it were just a matter of what the potential capabilities are, on a scale of 1 to 10, what do you think is possible?

I think both are context dependent. What is possible and whether we want these advancements in our lives. However, with respect to "what is possible" I think ChatGPT has shown me that I need to be careful in predicting what really will be possible. I was one of those who were skeptical, maybe in 2018, about whether an AI-based system could soon interact naturally with people. I have to admit ChatGPT surprised me. But what I still think what may never be possible is that we have interactions with AI-based systems, where people feel that an AI-based system is "caring" for them. For instance, one of the most important positive effects of psychotherapy is the relationship between patient and psychotherapist. I am not sure whether there will ever be the same positive effect possible with an AI-based system because I am not sure whether we as humans will ever feel that an AI-based system really cares for us and our wellbeing. But then again, already today there may be situations where it is hard to distinguish whether we are talking to a system or a human being, so if we really believe that we are talking to another person, we may also really believe that this other is caring about us.

So how good are humans at distinguishing a system like a robot from a human? This may not be a pressing question today, but it will become relevant as we encounter, for example, artificially intelligent robots. As a species, we have never encountered similar situations where we can talk to machines in natural language, share ideas and emotions, etc. Will we be able to keep our distance or not?

If we do not make it clear what is a human and what is a system, there will be a point where this distinction will be very difficult. Even now, if we are on the phone with a high-quality conversational agent, it is hard to distinguish between a human and an AI-based system. In the future, we may need to disclose this. However, even if we disclose this, humans tend to anthropomorphize things, seeing human aspects in many things [4]. They anthropomorphize their cars, pets, and AI systems. For example, I have repeatedly experienced that even after explaining what ChatGPT is and its technical foundations, people still ascribe human characteristics to it – for instance one person I was talking to insisted on ChatGPT having a personality. This will most likely increase in the future.

It is difficult when the behavior shows human patterns and aspects to say, "Yes, that is true, but because of what is going on inside, it is different and therefore cannot be considered human behavior". Is there even a clear definition of what makes us human?

I am not really sure whether there exists such a clear definition.

Is there a specific approach to say "what makes us human" from the perspective of psychology, or does this topic belong to a different discipline?

I believe philosophy may be a more suitable discipline for this. As a psychologist, you might discuss elements like emotions or intuition. These are aspects we attribute to humans, and we assume that a robot or an AI-based system does not possess these. But at what point do we decide that it does? I had a similar conversation at a workshop about ChatGPT. Someone asked me, "At what point do you say that the AI is self-conscious?" My response was, "I think that is a question for philosophers". The person persisted, and I suggested, "When it can feel pain". But he was not convinced, arguing that a robot could be built with sensors to react to pressure with an expression of pain. I countered that it is not quite the same, at least to me this does not feel the same. I probably should have said something like "What makes us human? Probably the sum of all the characteristics of humans".

> **"I also wonder if treating AI more gently or humanely affects the output."**

But is it not the case that for all the things that supposedly make us human, there are also people in our society who display this ability or behavior in a more extreme way? There are autistic people, for example, who are unable to assess their own emotions and those of others in the way that would be considered "usual human behavior".

This probably depends on what we consider to be "usual human behavior", but yes there is a continuum of human behavior between behavior that "most humans" show and behavior that is more seldom or extreme.

Nevertheless, they can learn certain patterns that help them integrate better into society. And we would never begin to say: "You are no longer human". Another example is the feeling of pain. There are also people with nerve damage who can no longer feel pain. So, it is really hard to make a clear distinction that does not fall short in certain cases that we also see in humans.

That is true. There are also individuals who lack the ability to feel empathy for others. However, they learn to behave in a way that makes others perceive them as empathetic. They understand what is expected of them and react accordingly to appear empathetic. That is what we all learn. We learn how to react in certain situations, like when a dog barks at us. And yes, what then makes a human human? Where do we draw the line? How do we identify that? Referring back to the earlier question, it becomes increasingly problematic. As I mentioned, I can explain things like how neurons work in the brain, how the brain functions, how emotions work. You can find some similarities in an AI-based system. It is not identical to how humans function. That is definitely true. But you can envision futures where there are also, for example, biological components. It will become increasingly difficult to distinguish.

Well, considering everything we just said, there are a lot of different opinions about what the future could look like. If you were to take the whole spectrum from utopian to dystopian, where would you position yourself?

Well, again, it depends on the context, I believe. In some contexts, I think we are already living in a dystopia. To me, the entire world of social media is more dystopian than utopian. It seems not very controlled anymore. You see a lot of polarization due to the algorithmic decision-making [2]. On the other hand, I can envision a world where AI-based systems support human development, make our energy system more efficient, improve energy distribution across Germany, across Europe. Or consider healthcare, where we are understaffed globally. If robots could assist us in performing tasks, that would be incredibly valuable. Of course, this raises questions about whether we want this and whether people will accept it. But the potential is undeniable. It would be a fantastic future where humans have the freedom to perform meaningful tasks while robots handle the dull and repetitive ones. But currently, I lean in my impression more towards the dystopian side of things.

"AI is learning our less desirable behaviors [...] [and] is also causing less than optimal behaviors that lead to mental health issues and polarization. [...] the impact of implementing this AI on society, rather than the AI learning from society, [is] the dystopian aspect for me right now."

We have often heard the comparison that AI learns more like children, compared to normal programming languages, which you basically design with specific rules, formulas, and so on. Looking at how society has evolved in recent years, especially in terms of our behavior on social media platforms, is the fact that AI is learning from our behavior particularly scary or dystopian to you?

It is not just that it learns from these behaviors, it is more that it instigates these behaviors. Sure, it learns from the behaviors we exhibit on social media, but the mechanisms designed to engage people, to keep them scrolling and staying on the platform, are causing these behaviors. If you introduce a – theoretically existing – politically neutral individual to TikTok or Twitter, you will likely see them lean towards one political direction based on the content they first encounter. And this will further drive them towards this direction. So, on one hand, AI is learning our less desirable behaviors, but on the other hand, it is also causing less than optimal behaviors that lead to mental health issues and polarization [2]. So, the impact of implementing this AI on society, rather than the AI learning from society, seems to be the dystopian aspect for me right now.

On a personal note, when you use ChatGPT for example, how do you treat it and communicate with it? Do you treat it like a machine that should follow your commands, like "I need this and that", or do you treat it more like a human being, like "please write xyz?" ChatGPT may not be learning from our interactions yet, but it may do so in the future. Do you think it is better or smarter to engage with a friendly "please" and "thank you" or is it just a transaction with a machine, so why bother?

I often use polite language when interacting with AI, such as "please" or "can you", similar to how I would ask a student or colleague to complete a task. I have never really thought about why I do this, it just feels right. ChatGPT, for instance, is designed to mimic human conversation. It even apologizes for its actions, which is quite anthropomorphic. OpenAI could have chosen a different approach, but they opted for a more human-like interaction. I am not sure if there are any studies on this, but I wonder how many people interact with AI in a human-like manner versus those who treat it purely as a tool, giving it instructions without any human-like interaction. I also wonder if treating AI more gently or humanely affects the output. It might, as it provides some context to the task environment, but I am not sure if that is the case.

Looking back on the last few days and especially on the interdisciplinary sessions. Was there something that was particularly interesting to you, like an insight from another discipline?

The legal perspective always fascinates me. Every time I hear about legal perspectives on AI, I am struck by the complexity of regulating AI or any product. It is astounding how minor decisions can have far-reaching effects. For instance, if the AI Act includes the call for effective human oversight of AI-based systems – not saying that this is a "minor decision" – this will shape the future of our society, influence the development and research of these systems, and determine where research funding goes. I find it impressive how the legal perspective impacts so many aspects of our lives.

Would you say that the legal perspective, for example, should be informed by the psychological, philosophical, technical, and other perspectives to ensure a necessary basic understanding. For example, a basic understanding of how people function in order to develop rules that protect humans from negative interactions with AI. So, the law itself should be approached in an interdisciplinary way?

Absolutely. It is interesting to see how legislation develops with interdisciplinary input. The European Union, for example, consults experts about issues like automation bias in human-system interaction and incorporates their insights into regulations. However, I believe that all disciplines involved, such as psychology, law, computer science, and philosophy, should include an interdisciplinary discourse to exchange such ideas. This is exactly what we are doing at AISoLA. It is crucial to understand at least a little about how each discipline operates. Ignoring any one perspective can lead to problems down the line. If you ignore the legal perspective, your developments may never be available on the market. If you ignore the psychological perspective, people may not accept or use your product. If you ignore the technical perspective, you might regulate something that will never exist. If you ignore the philosophical and ethical aspects, your insights may lack ethical grounding. So, interdisciplinary collaboration is of utmost importance.

Is there a specific research question you would like to see addressed?

One complex question that interests me is how we can understand AI-based systems. We develop all these black box models where no one understands how they work. The question from every perspective is: what constitutes understanding? What level of understanding is sufficient? How do we facilitate understanding, and how do we measure it? Should "understanding" even be a concept in regulation? At present, it seems elusive, and I would like to see more research focused on this aspect.

From your personal perspective, what should be the AI vision for the future?

I think Kevin Baum made an excellent point in his talk today about the need for a positive normative view on AI development. We need to ask ourselves what we want from these systems in the long term. Different stakeholders will have different interests. For example, a social media site developer would want people to visit their site frequently. But from a societal perspective, is that what we want? If not, what are the implications? Can we regulate usage, for instance, by restricting access for those under a certain age? The vision should be broad and consider what we want the system to achieve in the long run.

Is there anything you would like to add?

Not really. I just think it is important for everyone to try and understand other disciplines. Staying within your own discipline may undermine progress in the future, as everything is interconnected. This is especially true for AI. We need to integrate all perspectives and avoid letting one dominate. If one perspective dominates, others will be ignored, which is not advisable.

Thank you Markus for your time and perspective on AI. Enjoy the next few days at AISoLA!

Thank you.

References

1. Buçinca, Z., Malaya, M.B., Gajos, K.Z.: To trust or to think: cognitive forcing functions can reduce overreliance on AI in AI-assisted decision-making. In: Proceedings of the ACM on Human-Computer Interaction (CSCW1), pp. 1–21. ACM (2021)
2. Burton, J.: Algorithmic extremism? The securitization of artificial intelligence (AI) and its impact on radicalism, polarization and political violence. Technol. Soc. **75**, 102262 (2023)
3. Enqvist, L.: 'Human oversight' in the EU Artificial Intelligence act: what, when and by whom? Law Innov. Technol. **15**(2), 508–535 (2023)
4. Epley, N., Waytz, A., Cacioppo, J.T.: On seeing human: a three-factor theory of anthropomorphism. Psychol. Rev. **114**(4), 864–886 (2007)
5. Green, B.: The flaws of policies requiring human oversight of government algorithms. Comput. Law Secur. Rev. **45**, 105681 (2022)
6. Haggenmüller, S., et al.: Skin cancer classification via convolutional neural networks: systematic review of studies involving human experts. Euro. J. Cancer **156**, 202–216 (2021)
7. Langer, M., König, C.J., Back, C., Hemsing, V.: Trust in artificial intelligence: comparing trust processes between human and automated trustees in light of unfair bias. J. Bus. Psychol. **38**, 493–508 (2023)
8. Langer, M., König, C.J., Gebhard, P., André, E.: Dear computer, teach me manners: testing virtual employment interview training. Intl. J. Sel. Assess. **24**, 312–323 (2016)
9. Lee, J.D., See, K.A.: Trust in automation: designing for appropriate reliance. Hum. Factors **46**(1), 50–80 (2004)
10. Mayer, R.C., Davis, J.H., Schoorman, F.D.: An integrative model of organizational trust. Acad. Manag. Rev. **20**(2), 709–726 (1995)
11. Parker, S.K., Grote, G.: Automation, algorithms, and beyond: why work design matters more than ever in a digital world. Appl. Psychol. **71**, 1171–1204 (2022)
12. Schlicker, N., Uhde, A., Baum, K., Hirsch, M.C., Langer, M.: How do we assess the trustworthiness of AI? Introducing the Trustworthiness Assessment Model (TrAM). https://osf.io/preprints/psyarxiv/qhwvx_v1

Let's Talk AI with Philosophy Expert Eva Schmidt

Eva Schmidt[1] and Barbara Steffen[2(✉)]

[1] TU Dortmund and Lamarr Institute for Machine Learning and Artificial Intelligence, Dortmund, Germany
eva.schmidt@tu-dortmund.de
[2] METAFrame Technologies, Dortmund, Germany
barbara.steffen@metaframe.de

Abstract. Developers of AI systems need to be aware of and informed about the ethical and societal impacts of their products.

My personal AI mission: Applying concepts and tools from philosophy to contribute to the development of ethically unproblematic AI systems.

Fig. 1. Eva Schmidt

1 My Takes on AI

- **Artificial Intelligence** – I find the distinction between weak and strong artificial intelligence (AI) from philosopher John Searle to be the most relevant here. We can say that a system is a weak AI system when it is able to (merely!) simulate mental abilities, especially abilities to solve specific problems. For example, some systems are able to correctly classify cat images. Strong AI systems have a broad range of genuine mental abilities such as understanding language, solving problems intelligently, or playing games. So far, no strong AI systems exist.
- **Trust** – I am more interested in reasonable trust than in mere trust. Regarding autonomous AI systems, my view is that a user reasonably trusts such a system only if the system is trustworthy and she is in a position to know this; and it is trustworthy for her only if it shares her goal and pursues it competently on the basis of the information relevant in the context.

B. Steffen et al. (Eds.): *Let's Talk AI*, LNCS 15000, pp. 82–90, 2026.
https://doi.org/10.1007/978-3-032-09008-9_9

- **Explainability** – An AI system is explainable in a certain respect, given a certain context, just in case there is information available to a relevant stakeholder in the context, which can positively affect the stakeholder's understanding and thereby contribute to the fulfillment of the practical interests of the stakeholder, or to the fulfillment of certain societal desiderata more broadly.
- **Essential Elements of Human Capabilities** – According to philosopher Helen Steward, what is specific about human actions is that they are exercises of so-called two-way powers. These are powers that a human agent is able to exercise – or not – at a particular moment. (Think of yourself standing in front of the open fridge – you can reach for the apple juice, or you can decide not to do so.) By contrast, one-way powers are manifested by the object that has them whenever it gets into the right conditions. (Think of fragile glass, which breaks whenever it gets into the condition of being struck.) Plausibly, current AI systems do not have two-way powers, as humans do.

2 The Interview

[Barbara Steffen] Today I have the pleasure to talk to Eva Schmidt (Fig. 1) from TU Dortmund. Could you please briefly introduce yourself and your personal relationship to artificial intelligence?

[Eva Schmidt] Yes, thank you. I am a professor in theoretical philosophy at TU Dortmund, in the Department of Philosophy and Political Science. I have been working in the field of explainable AI for some time now. My academic career started with studying the philosophy of perception and reasons, as in reasons to believe things or act in certain ways. A few years ago, Kevin Baum approached me and asked if I would be interested in delving deeper into the area of explainable AI. Given the importance of this topic, I found it interesting to contribute as a scientist and specifically as a philosopher. Since I was already working on explanations of human behavior, particularly human actions [5], I thought it would be an interesting challenge to explore whether we could apply explanations of human actions to explaining the outputs or actions of artificial intelligence systems.

Can you give examples of one or two specific topics or questions your AI research is currently addressing?

I am especially interested in the explanatory information provided by explainable AI and how we should interpret it. What makes for a good explanation? How does it relate to understanding? At this conference, I presented parts of a paper that considers which contextual factors determine whether a person truly understands something [9]. I believe that it's easier to gain understanding when you have to make an unimportant decision and harder when the decision is significant. For example, consider a judge who must decide whether a convicted criminal should receive a harsh or mild sentence. This is an important decision, as it determines whether the individual will be imprisoned for a longer or shorter time. If the judge receives a high-risk score for the convict from an AI system, suggesting that the person is likely to commit another crime in the future, the judge might want to incorporate this input into their decision and impose a harsher sentence. In such cases, I believe it's essential to understand why the system provided this score. We know that some of these systems exhibit racial bias, assigning harsher scores to people of Color than to White people. In these situations, it's necessary to understand why the system gave you this score, but it might not be easy to understand due to the importance of the decision and the high stakes involved.

"Can people still make responsible decisions when their decision-making is based on the output of AI systems? Are those AI systems fair? Do they comply with certain legal regulations? Do they violate any human rights? These are ethical questions."

Do you think there's a difference between the tools and explanations needed for judges to support their sentencing or doctors to support their diagnosis versus patients who don't have the expertise like someone with a medical background and therefore need simpler or maybe completely different explanations? Also, do you think that patients might trust these tools differently than experts?

Absolutely. I believe that the context is extremely important when deciding whether something is a good explanation for the output of an AI system or for how a system functions as a whole. One factor I've already discussed is the stakes involved in the context. Another aspect is the individual we are considering. What's interesting is their level of knowledge. How much do they know about the field in which the system is applied? For instance, a medical doctor has extensive knowledge about medical care, while a patient may not. Additionally, how much knowledge or expertise does this person have in computer science or the theory of how AI systems work? I think these factors make a significant difference because if you have more expertise in a certain area, you can better integrate an explanation you get with your existing knowledge [7].

What role does trust play in the adoption of AI?

Trust is an interesting topic, especially from a philosophical perspective. There has been a broad philosophical debate about trust for decades, but it typically deals with trust between persons [1]. It's interesting to consider whether we can apply some of these theories or approaches to trust in technological systems or perhaps combinations of technical and social systems. It's often not just the system by itself. Many people treat the issue of trust as a central concern, asking when can we trust a system? When do people trust AI systems? But also, when are such systems trustworthy? These are distinct questions [8]. What does it take for an AI system to be trustworthy? And what does it take for people to be good at judging whether a system is trustworthy? These questions are all related, but they are different. Some people consider this to be a very central issue. For example, the high-level expert group of the EU discussed trustworthy AI in their paper on this subject [4]. I do believe that trust plays an important role if you're interested in the appropriate adoption of these systems. However, I think it's only one of many factors. It's also important to consider whether people can still make responsible decisions when their decision-making is based on the output of AI systems. Are those AI systems fair? Do they comply with certain legal regulations? Do they violate any human rights? These are ethical questions. There are many other questions that are at least as important as the question of trust. As for the ethical component of your question …

What measures do you think are essential to ensure ethical use of AI?

That's a very broad question. To ensure that AI systems respect people's rights and meet ethical requirements, I think we need to consider different contexts. One crucial aspect is having regulations that make sure the use of these systems doesn't violate any rights or harm anyone. Another approach, which I find very interesting from a philosophical perspective, is to see if we can embed ethics into these systems from the inside, rather than just observing how they are deployed and trying to enforce compliance from the outside. I don't work in this area specifically, so I may not be up-to-date with the state of the art. However, my impression is that there haven't been any programs yet that handle ethics very well.

We have heard some presentations in the last few days saying that generative AI learns like children by observing, interacting, and adapting to the environment. Are you comfortable with that from an ethical point of view? Do you have enough confidence in the ethical behavior of humans to be good teachers for AI, or could that be worrisome?

I believe that we are generally quite good at teaching children ethical behavior. We invest a lot in this, either by being good role models or by telling children what's right and wrong. However, this approach can break down in larger contexts with many people interacting and various social pressures pulling in different directions. We see this all the time when people start wars or treat others badly. So, it doesn't work as well on a societal level as one might wish. The question then is, can we train an individual AI system to work within ethical norms? We should be able to do this to some extent. But if the system is trained, we can never be sure that it will follow the rule in some unforeseen situation. So there is a limitation there for sure. Another question, similar to humans messing things up when we act in larger groups, is what the effects would be if we had many systems interacting with many people on a larger scale. I haven't thought about this question before, but I find it very interesting. In these cases, I would be more worried about potential negative effects, even if we manage to train the systems well with respect to ethical norms.

"When you consider AI as emulating human intelligence, I don't think there is a fundamental limit to the systems achieving all the intelligent capabilities that we possess."

Regarding the technical capabilities AI might have in the future: On a scale from 1 to 10, where 1 describes the artificial intelligence systems we know like ChatGPT, and 10 stands for artificial general intelligence systems that surpass human capabilities on a global scale. What do you think will be possible in the future?

That's hard to say. I must admit, I feel quite modest about my ability to predict these things. But, when you consider AI as emulating human intelligence, I don't think there is a fundamental limit to the systems achieving all the intelligent capabilities that we possess. My view of humans and how we acquire our capabilities is very naturalistic. So why shouldn't it be possible, in principle, for an artificial system to have the same capabilities? Another question, for which I have no good answer, but I believe is very relevant here, is whether these capabilities are grounded only in the causal relations and functions being computed in the brain, or whether they also involve the biological substrate [3]. If it's something about our biology, then obviously AI systems have some limitations. But if it's all about the functions, then I think it should be possible to transfer everything completely to these silicon-based systems. That's the question in principle. The other question is whether we will direct research in the way to achieve all the results that I think we could, in principle, achieve. We've been making significant progress, so it seems likely that we will do that, even in my lifetime. But after that, I'm not sure.

If you had to choose a number from 1 to 10, what would you choose?

Assigning a number is difficult. Let me mention one more limitation. I'm not sure if we can truly have consciousness in AI systems. We're not talking about intelligence as such, but will these systems be able to feel pain when we step on their toes? Will they really be able to perceive colors like a bright pink and have the same pink experience that I have when I look at a pink blotch? I'm not sure about that. So, I'm more cautious if we consider that. And then the question is, does intelligence in any dimension rely on this consciousness aspect? For example, John Searle, in his paper where he presents the Chinese room thought experiment, believes that understanding, as an aspect of intelligence, is somehow tied to a conscious perspective [10]. If we consider that, then I'm more cautious. And then, between all these things, what's the number? I'll go with 5, just to stay in the middle, but it's mostly because I think it's a very hard question to answer.

It seems that one aspect that makes it really difficult to answer this question is the fact that we don't have a clear definition of what makes us human. So it's not like we have a list of criteria that basically defines different levels of capabilities, for example, divided into three categories: Level 1 describes everything below human capabilities, Level 2 describes everything in the range of human capabilities, and Level 3 describes everything beyond human capabilities.

That's right. One of the problems is that we don't have a clear enough understanding of some of the relevant capabilities. If we don't really know what is needed, then it's harder to say whether we will be able to build it. I would say that as far as having some sort of observable generally intelligent behavior, like being able to handle different problems and tasks, it seems clear that we will reach that. But to the extent that we want real understanding and a real mind, I think that might all be tied to consciousness, to having a subjective perspective on the world tied to phenomenal experiences. There, I'm more skeptical about whether we can build this with the tools that we have for AI. But who knows? The future may show us, or maybe we won't even be able to tell.

How important is it for AI tools to actually feel pain or perceive color? Is it necessary or important for AI tools to have the same experiences as humans? For example, they might not feel pain, but if they stub their toe, they might have the right reaction and say that it hurts. They may not feel emotions like sadness or happiness, but they will act them out perfectly at the right moments. So does it matter to the human interacting with the AI whether the AI actually feels the pain or emotion, or whether it is just acting the "right" way to feel natural in the interaction?

What you're talking about, even though I don't know if you've heard about it under this name, is the concept of a philosophical zombie. A philosophical zombie is someone who, for example, would be my perfect twin, who looks like me, acts like me at all times, and also has the same functional states that I have. But this twin lacks the phenomenal experiences of seeing this bright pink or feeling pain when stepping on a rock [2]. So one could say maybe that everything those AI systems could ever be are philosophical zombies, in the sense that they have all the behavior and all the functional states of someone who has phenomenal consciousness or maybe even of someone who has a subjective perspective tied to those phenomenal experiences. Then the question is, does it matter if we reach the real thing or not? I would say on one side it doesn't matter, because if they have just the zombie status, I think that is good enough for them to change our society in many ways. Imagine that we interact with them, say, on the internet and they have this as-if character. This may help them to manipulate us in many ways. So that will make a big difference already. But another interesting aspect, which I find very difficult to say something definitive about, is how we should treat them morally. Do they count morally like people do, or maybe at least like some of the higher animals do, or do they not count morally at all? I think if they have no consciousness, no subjective perspective, we can disregard them morally and use them for whatever we want. But if they were to become conscious, I would say that's the point where we really have to think about how we respect their rights, or how we avoid causing harm to them. I find that a very scary prospect, actually, that we might get there. Because we use them as our personal slaves at this point. But it would be really wrong and evil to do that if they were actual conscious beings [6]. So we would have to completely change our behavior towards those systems, and I worry that we wouldn't. So that would be really horrible, I think.

> "[…] the business landscape or the market should be organized to […] support individual companies in not just doing some ethics-washing, but really having business models that respect ethical constraints."

So it would be important to develop tests that allow us to distinguish real consciousness from well-faked behavior in order to set the right moral framework?

Indeed, that's the next step. How do we differentiate this? Some philosophers express concern that we may not be able to discern whether a certain system has achieved consciousness or not. This uncertainty could already be a problem. When should we start treating these systems as morally significant, just as a matter of caution?

One of the talks today was about the extent to which we should allow this human-like interaction with artificial intelligence. Should AI tools be allowed to act human-like? As soon as people chat and talk a lot with AI tools, it becomes increasingly difficult for them to distinguish between humans and AI, and they lose a potentially critical distance to these tools. Do you think this is something we should be thinking about more? Should we steer development in a direction that ensures that humans remain skeptical?

Absolutely. We need to consider what benefits individual humans and our societies overall. I think, we must examine all the different contexts in which AI applications interact with us in a human-like manner. Is this beneficial? Is it harmless? Or is it detrimental that they're used in this way? We need to consider how these AI systems or bots might manipulate people on a large scale, potentially undermining our democracies or influencing voting outcomes. We need to think about how best to regulate this. One possible solution could be to enforce a rule that all bots must be clearly labeled as such. Another important point is how readily available nonhuman interaction partners might undermine people's ability to interact with other people. This is an important aspect of human well-being. If that is compromised, it could lead to a poorer quality of life. There are studies showing a correlation between increased online interaction and a higher prevalence of depression among teenagers. This is one area where this could be problematic. However, there may be many other areas where having these kinds of bots is completely harmless. For example, in customer service. It might also be beneficial to have easily accessible, low-key interaction partners in certain social contexts. We need to examine how such technologies truly impact people.

> **"But if [AIs] were to become conscious, I would say that's the point where we really have to think about how we respect their rights, or how we avoid causing harm to them."**

In light of all this, there are many different visions of the future being discussed, from utopia to dystopia. Where would you position yourself?

I would place myself somewhere in the middle. I don't believe AI will solve all our problems, nor do I think it will drastically disrupt our society in a negative way. Some existing problems might grow, but I also believe we have the power to steer things in a positive direction. We need to make small changes to the current processes, and those of us in influential positions should try to do that.

Reflecting on the last few days here at AISoLA, was there an insight from another discipline that was particularly interesting to you?

There were so many insights, it's hard to choose just one. However, one thing that struck me was the importance of empirical studies, particularly from psychology, in understanding how explanations may or may not influence people's judgments of a situation. It's very helpful for philosophers to engage with psychologists to determine what we should research and how the results of that research should influence our thinking.

Is there a specific topic or research question where you see an important angle for interdisciplinary work?

One interesting area could be understanding an AI system or its output. I propose in my paper that the stakes of a situation impact someone's understanding. It would be great to collaborate with psychologists to study whether people's perceived understanding of why a system produces a certain output is affected by the stakes of a situation. This conference has shown the need for perspectives from all social sciences. AI systems are increasingly influencing our lives, and it's crucial to consider all the different aspects if we want to guide the direction of these changes.

At this conference, we had a mix of computer scientists, psychologists, legal experts, and philosophers. Are there other disciplines that should get involved in the future?

Definitely. We are missing political scientists and sociologists.

What about business or management people?

Yes, business people too. I haven't worked much with them, but I'd be interested in learning more about potential intersections. Political scientists could help us understand how politics and our democracy might be impacted by the use of AI systems. Sociologists could provide insights into how certain areas of society are affected.

I've been thinking about the rapid pace at which companies like OpenAI and Microsoft are advancing AI and releasing all these innovative tools. It's fascinating to think about the motivations behind such rapid progress. If the focus is solely on making quick profit, we will have problems along the way. We need to explore alternative business approaches, innovative business models and strategies that not only bring short-term benefits to customers, but also benefit society. It's important to combine profitability with ethical practices and doing the right thing. And this requires business experts who can translate social benefits into long-term business strategies.

That makes complete sense to me. I mean, one of the issues that I see is a lot of power being concentrated in the hands of just a few businesses. It makes sense to think about how the business landscape or the market should be organized to get better results and how we can support individual companies in not just doing some ethics-washing, but really having business models that respect ethical constraints. So it seems like a very good idea to have people working in this field included in this kind of discussion.

From your personal perspective, what should be the AI vision for the future?

My vision is that AI development should not be a matter of throwing new tools at society and seeing what happens. Instead, we should consider the interests of all societal groups and determine our goals as a society. Then we should think about how we can use AI tools to improve our lives. This approach is not being followed at the moment. For example, as a university teacher, I suddenly had to deal with ChatGPT and figure out how to ensure that my students still gain a deep understanding of philosophical issues when they could easily fake many tests using tools like ChatGPT. We should first identify our needs and then design tools to meet those needs.

Is there anything you would like to add?

I believe it's extremely helpful to interact with people from different backgrounds. The questions I'm interested in cannot be answered by philosophers, computer scientists, or psychologists alone. Interdisciplinary exchange is really valuable in this area.

Thank you very much, Eva, for your time and your thoughts on AI from a philosophical perspective. Have a great last couple of days at AISoLA!

Thank you for interviewing me!

References

1. Baier, A.: Trust and antitrust. Ethics **96**(2), 231–260 (1986)
2. Chalmers, D.J.: The Conscious Mind: In Search of a Fundamental Theory. Oxford University Press (1996)
3. Chalmers, D.J.: Could a large language model be conscious? Boston Review. https://www.bostonreview.net/articles/could-a-large-language-model-be-conscious/
4. EU High-Level Expert Group on Artificial Intelligence (2019). Ethics guidelines for trustworthy AI. https://digital-strategy.ec.europa.eu/en/library/ethics-guidelines-trustworthy-ai
5. Glock, H.-J., Schmidt, E.: Pluralism about practical reasons and reason explanations. Philos. Explor. **2**, 1–18 (2021)
6. Gunkel, D.J., Bryson, J.J.: Introduction to the special issue on machine morality: the machine as moral agent and patient. Philo. Technol. **27**, 5–8 (2014)
7. Langer, M., et al.: What do we want from Explainable Artificial Intelligence (XAI)? A stakeholder perspective on XAI and a conceptual model guiding interdisciplinary XAI research. Artif. Intell. **296**, 103473 (2021)
8. Schmidt, E.: Wie können wir autonomen KI-Systemen vertrauen? Die Rolle von Gründe-Erklärungen. In: Konz, B., Ostmeyer, K.-H., Scholz, M. (eds.) Gratwanderung Künstliche Intelligenz: Interdisziplinäre Perspektiven auf das Verhältnis von Mensch und KI, pp. 11–29. Kohlhammer (2022)
9. Schmidt, E.: Stakes and understanding the decisions of AI systems. In: Durán, J., Pozzi, G. (eds.) Philosophy of Science for Machine Learning: Core Issues and New Perspectives. Synthese Library, vol. 527. Springer (2026)
10. Searle, J.R.: Minds, brains, and programs. Behav. Brain Sci. **3**(3), 417–424 (1980)

Let's Talk AI with Philosophy Expert Thorsten Helfer

Thorsten Helfer[1] and Barbara Steffen[2(✉)]

[1] Saarland University, Saarbrücken, Germany
thorsten.helfer@uni-saarland.de
[2] METAFrame Technologies, Dortmund, Germany
barbara.steffen@metaframe.de

Abstract. Most ethical problems about AI have been there before. They just seem more pressing now.

My personal AI mission: Education about AI and its societal impacts.

Fig. 1. Thorsten Helfer

1 My Takes on AI

- **Artificial Intelligence** – A system instantiates artificial intelligence if and only if it is artificial and has certain general or specific abilities to interact with its environment in a way that appears like human intelligence.
- **Trust** – A trusts B if and only if A has confidence in the dependability of B.
- **Explainability** – A system is explainable if and only if it can provide relevant explanations sensitive to contexts.
- **Essential Elements of Human Capabilities** – I think there are no essential elements of human capabilities. There are relevant stereotypical features of humans like reasoning or consciousness.

B. Steffen et al. (Eds.): *Let's Talk AI*, LNCS 15000, pp. 91–96, 2026.
https://doi.org/10.1007/978-3-032-09008-9_10

2 The Interview

[Barbara Steffen] Today I have the pleasure of talking to Thorsten Helfer (Fig. 1). Please introduce yourself and your relationship to artificial intelligence.

[Thorsten Helfer] Certainly, I am a philosopher at Saarland University and currently involved in a project called Explainable Intelligent Systems. I've recently joined this project, just about six months ago. Here my focus lies mainly within the ethical implications of AI systems and the ethical need for explanations of these. Additionally, I am involved in a project set to start in January next year within the association Algoright e.V. In this capacity, I will be an ethical adivsor on projects within healthcare and digitalization in Saarland.

What are some of the specific AI-related research questions that you are working on?

At present, my primary interest lies in the concept of the "human in the loop". I am exploring questions such as: Under what conditions do we want a human in the loop? Why do we want a human in the loop at all? Could it be that under certain conditions, the human is merely a scapegoat? It seems odd to want a scapegoat, but sometimes I wonder what other reasons we might have for wanting a human in the loop. At least in part, we want to introduce AI systems because they are more accurate and it is also unclear whether humans are less prone to unfair or biased decisions than AI systems. I do agree that a human in the loop is relevant for trust issues but other than that I think we should be more critical and really examine in what scenarios a human in the loop is helpful and in what scenarios they are a waste of resources or simply a scapegoat.

"The question should be which AI is trustworthy, not which AI do we trust."

In your opinion, what role should trust have in the adoption of AI?

This might be an unpopular opinion, but I don't believe that trust inherently holds value in this context. Trusting AI might make us feel better about interacting with it, but that doesn't mean the AI is ethically sound. The question should be which AI is trustworthy, not which AI do we trust. We could trust an AI system that is actually harmful, simply because it interacts with us in a certain way. However, trust could hold instrumental value, as most of us will likely only interact with AI if we trust it. So, while I'm unsure about the intrinsic importance of trust, I believe it holds instrumental value [1].

Are there specific metrics or frameworks that already distinguish between high-stakes and low-stakes environments, such as a list of criteria whose importance is weighted according to context? Or are we just looking at specific scenarios? And if we only look at specific scenarios today, would it be possible to derive a general evaluation framework or something like that later?

Determining whether something is high risk or low risk largely depends on your ethical viewpoint. From my perspective, it depends on what is affected in the end. The number of people affected, the potential impact on people's welfare and well-being, and how people's rights, autonomy, and freedom might be affected, are all important considerations. These factors determine how high risk or low risk a certain AI system is. It's not as simple as categorizing certain sectors, like healthcare, as high risk. For example, an AI system in healthcare that applies Band-Aids might not be high risk. It depends on what's at stake within that area. Additionally, predicting how an AI system will impact values in the world, people's well-being, autonomy, and freedom, are empirical questions that, as an ethicist, I can't answer.

Is it of ethical merit to think about future scenarios, for example, to establish what-if understandings? If we allow X to happen now, what will the consequences be? Or is ethics more focused on today's reality rather than on possible future scenarios?

I'm not entirely sure I understand the question. Are you asking if it's ethically justified to have a general AI?

My question is whether we should look at future possibilities through an ethical lens to prepare for them now. For example, if something like "X" could happen in the future, should we act differently or prepare for it today? Essentially, should we map out different possible future scenarios and have a plan ready with strategies for how to deal with them if they do happen? Or do we wait and react only when these possibilities become reality?

Well, I don't think we should address it only once it's there. We should address it when people start to think about developing it, when it's in a planning phase. There's been a lot of philosophical discussion since the 1970s about experience machines, where you can plug in, like the whole matrix idea [2]. People have thought about that already. A lot of movies about AI have already been made. So people are already thinking about a lot of this stuff. But I'm not sure whether all of these ideas are that helpful. There's also this whole discussion about fear mongering among the debate about techno-optimism. Should we be more optimistic about everything? Should we be scared about technology in that sense? Usually, these ideas are depicted in a more dystopian way. I'm not sure whether these ideas are that helpful. Of course, we should be prepared for some bad outcomes, but it should be proportionate to what could actually happen. In this respect, politicians, ethicists, developers and computer scientists should work together and figure out what could actually happen and what should be done.

"I'm not even sure whether specifically philosophers are needed, but you need somebody who will look at the ethical and societal impact of what AI products might have in the end. Some people who will have a bigger-picture view of things."

Do you feel that philosophers are sufficiently involved in the development phases? Is there enough collaboration to ensure that you can address new developments and challenges in time?

In my recent activities I was actually quite surprised, because I've been talking to computer scientists or developers, and I thought they would be really not interested or even averse to an ethical perspective. But usually, if you approach them in a way that you want to help them make their product within society better, they're usually quite happy to hear your opinion on everything. So I'm not sure whether it should be institutionalized that philosophers are involved. I'm not even sure whether specifically philosophers are needed, but you need somebody who will look at the ethical and societal impact of what

AI products might have in the end. Some people who will have a bigger-picture view of things. And usually, it seems to me, that philosophers are pretty good at that.

Regarding the different future scenarios that are being discussed, ranging from dystopia to utopia. Where on that scale would you place yourself?

I would be rather on the optimist side, I think. I want to distance myself clearly from all of this. Marc Andreessen, techno-optimist view, where everything has to have this kind of religious touch, where technology is basically the new religion, where everything is good and you don't need any kind of regulation, and the market will take care of everything, we don't need any kind of regulation, and all techno-ethicists are just fearmongers [3]. But as I said already, how I at least want to approach things is more from a supportive kind of view. I think ethicists and critics of AI systems should work together with developers and computer scientists in order to figure out the best route to go. AI systems have a huge potential, just see the potentials of personalised medicine for example, but the same system that could positively revolutionise medicine could create the deadliest toxins. So, I want to see it as a more optimistic side, but certainly there are risks involved and they should be worked on together.

> **"Trust is something very different than trustworthiness. Look at the evidence from psychology. The best step to improve trust in an interactive robot is if it hands out flowers at the beginning of the interaction."**

Reflecting on the past days, what insights from other disciplines were particularly interesting?

This has been quite a ride, actually. I've never been to an interdisciplinary conference that was so productive. Usually, you have to translate a lot from one discipline to the other. What I do sometimes, people from law, people from computer science, or people from psychology don't understand all the terms that I use, and I don't understand all the terms that they use. So you have a lot of catching up to do with the other disciplines. But somehow this was really productive and really helpful. I learned a lot about how different kinds of explanations can work for different kinds of trust, and the framing of explanations, and how that can impact the kind of trust. Then I have learned a lot about the ethical groundwork of law. I always thought there must be some ethical basis on which specific laws grounded, but it I realized here that sometimes you might have reasons to put laws in effect that have nothing to do with morality in the end. It's just to incentivize certain behavior in order for a more productive society. So I found all of that pretty interesting.

Is there a specific research question or topic that you would like to see addressed from an interdisciplinary perspective in the future?

All of this is very interesting. I'm still hung up on that whole human oversight thing. Before I started working on this, I thought there must be more than enough literature about this. There must be a lot of lawyers who have thought about human oversight. There must be a lot of psychologists who thought about human oversight and trust, and philosophers thinking about under what kind of circumstances we actually want to have human oversight. But it seems to me that that has just stated. It's just said claimed that we want to have some kind of human oversight. We want to have people in there having the last decision. And it was really strange for me to realize, not a lot of people have thought a lot about the specific conditions of human oversight and a human in the loop. What does that entail? When do we want it? How does it relate to trust? And, as I said before, are there cases where we especially do not want a human in the loop?

"Why do we want a human in the loop at all? Could it be that under certain conditions, the human is merely a scapegoat?"

Why should I trust the human more than the AI? Does the human look at the aggregated information and see if it makes sense, adding credibility? Or do we automatically trust a human more just because they are human?

I don't think that you should trust it more, necessarily. Look at autonomous cars. It seems to me that autonomous cars will very quickly kill fewer people than people do and will be better drivers. So I think for some cases, the AI systems are better than humans. So I don't think that you should trust humans more, but, as far as I know, the empirical evidence shows us that many AI systems are trusted more when there is a human in the loop. Trust is something very different than trustworthiness. Look at the evidence from psychology. The best step to improve trust in an interactive robot is if it hands out flowers at the beginning of the interaction. This might be relevant for trust but not necessarily for trustworthiness. So it's not necessarily that you should trust people more, but you do.

From your personal perspective, what should be the AI vision?

I don't understand the question. What is the AI vision? What the AI will bring in the future? What it should bring in the future?

Yes, what AI should bring in the future.

Well, from a very pedantic, philosophical point of view, more wellbeing, whatever that means. I have no idea what that will bring in the end. I'm personally hoping for some kind of experience-machine, where it could simulate a lot of experiences and then figure out what I want to experience and under what conditions, but that is far in the future.

When you think about well-being, do you mean well-being in the present, well-being in the near future, or well-being in the distant future? Does it make a difference? And how can we approach the right context of well-being for society?

You mean, should we sacrifice a certain amount of well-being now to have more well-being in the future?

For example.

Yeah, this has many dimensions. If you think from a purely utilitarian point of view, where you ask what the best world or outcome is, then clearly, it's better to sacrifice some well-being now to get a lot of well-being in the future. And there is a certain discussion within philosophy about long-termism and whether we should try to avoid even the slightest risk of human extinction, even if it costs us a lot of effort right now, and even if we have to sacrifice a lot of well-being right now [5]. But that seems to have a lot of problems – I mean, if you look at the real world right now and how we make decisions, and at least in western and democratic countries, we decide based on a democratic system. And as it is right now, we only have people living right now actually deciding upon that. Future generations do not decide on matters that seems to influence them. Usually a lot of people right now are out for their own well-being or maybe for the well-being of the close people around them. The far in the future generations are not represented in all of this. And it's the question whether they should be represented in all of this and therefore in the democratic system. I'm not so sure what the answer is there. It depends on all kinds of ethical questions, the ethical kind of view about long-termism, the ethical kind of view about utilitarianism at all, about future generations, about how you want to deal with democracy [4].

Is there anything else you would like to add?

I'm pretty good. This and the whole conference was a lot of fun. Like I said, the interdisciplinary work was very new but rewarding for me. Learning more about AI from a computer scientist's perspective, from legal, from psychologist perspective, all a lot of fun. I would love to do something like that again.

Perfect, I do, too! Thank you very much for your time and ethical perspective on AI and the present, Thorsten. Have a great day!

Thank you.

References

1. Andreessen, M.: The Techno-Optimist Manifesto (2023). https://a16z.com/the-techno-optimist-manifesto/
2. Friedman W.: Deliberative democracy and the problem of scope. J. Public Deliberation 2(1) (2006)
3. Greaves, H., MacAskill, W.: The Case for Strong Longtermism, GPI Working Paper (2019)
4. Nozick, R.: Anarchy, State and Utopia. Basic Books (1974)
5. Reinhardt, K.: Trust and trustworthiness in AI ethics. AI Ethics **3**, 735–744 (2023)

Let's Talk AI with Philosophy and Computer Science Expert Timo Speith

Timo Speith[1] and Barbara Steffen[2](✉)

[1] University of Bayreuth, Bayreuth, Germany
timo.speith@uni-bayreuth.de
[2] METAFrame Technologies, Dortmund, Germany
barbara.steffen@metaframe.de

Abstract. It shouldn't be the AI of Big Tech companies, as it is currently emerging, but rather AI designed for society, and perhaps even by society, through participative approaches, community work, and citizen science.

My personal AI mission: Making AI comprehensible and beneficial to every stakeholder.

Fig. 1. Timo Speith

1 My Takes on AI

- **Artificial Intelligence** – The theory and development of computer systems able to perform tasks normally requiring human intelligence, such as visual perception, speech recognition, decision-making, and translation between languages [11].
- **Trust** – An attitude of a person towards the reliability/functionality of a certain entity. Trust must be distinguished from trustworthiness: the actual reliability/functionality of the entity. Ideally, trust is based on trustworthiness; however, there are many contingent factors that influence trust [6].
- **Explainability** – Providing information about certain aspects of an entity (for example, the decision-making mechanisms of an AI) to better understand that aspect (see also [3] for a definition).
- **Essential Elements of Human Capabilities** – Approximately those mentioned in the above definition of artificial intelligence, supplemented by adaptivity to new situations and the generation of new ideas.

B. Steffen et al. (Eds.): *Let's Talk AI*, LNCS 15000, pp. 97–103, 2026.
https://doi.org/10.1007/978-3-032-09008-9_11

2 The Interview

[Barbara Steffen] Welcome Timo Speith (Fig. 1) to this interview. Please briefly introduce yourself and your relationship to artificial intelligence (AI).

[Timo Speith] Thank you for the invitation! I am a fixed-term lecturer at the chair for philosophy, computer science, and AI at the University of Bayreuth. My background encompasses both computer science and philosophy, having pursued various studies in both fields, including a bachelor's degree and a PhD in philosophy, as well as a master's degree in computer science. This places me at the very intersection of these disciplines. In addition to my academic background, my primary research focus is closely related to computer science and AI; specifically, it is in the area of explainable AI (XAI). This represents a significant relationship to AI for me. Moreover, I am generally interested in almost every topic that lies at the intersection of computer science, AI, and philosophy.

Can you give an example or two of specific research questions you're currently addressing with your AI research?

Certainly. Within the realm of XAI, a key question involves understanding how providing explanations of AI systems' predictions and decision-making processes can be beneficial to various parties involved with AI [3, 9, 12]. This includes elucidating the "what" and "why" behind an AI's predictions, such as the rationale for its outputs. Such insights are hoped to assist technicians in debugging AI systems to identify errors or misbehaviors [3, 7, 10]. Additionally, it aims to empower laypersons to assess the appropriateness of AI-based predictions, particularly in cases where the predictions may seem potentially discriminatory or influenced by irrelevant details [1, 3, 10]. Overall, this encompasses a broad area of interest, touching on both technical and ethical considerations.

"The type of explanation required varies significantly depending on the stakeholder."

In terms of explanations, do you focus on explanations for experts who need to understand how the system works to determine its trustworthiness, or is it for users to get explanations that allow them to decide whether they personally trust the system and/or the output?

My interest spans both these aspects and extends even further to encompass all stakeholders. One of my core research theses, and a focus of the project I'm working on, is that the type of explanation required varies significantly depending on the stakeholder [9, 12]. For example, a layperson requires a different explanation than a developer, regulator, or a decision-maker, such as a hospital manager deliberating the use of a specific AI diagnostic system. The explanation needs of stakeholders change based on their role and many other aspects, highlighting the importance of tailoring explanations to suit diverse needs and perspectives.

What role does trust play in AI adoption?

The emphasis on trust can be misleading, in my opinion [6]. People often trust a system for irrelevant reasons. For example, studies have shown that merely providing explanations can increase people's trust in a system, even if these explanations don't actually offer any real insight into how the system works [5]. So, the mere presence of an explanation can lead people to trust a system more. Unfortunately, trust, as subjective and fleeting as it is, is often seen as a prerequisite to even consider using systems. However, as just mentioned, trust is a very subjective attitude towards an entity, and thus not reliable. To directly answer your question, trust is indeed important for AI adoption. Yet, from a philosophical standpoint, this is unfortunate, as the focus shouldn't be on the fact that trust exists, but rather on ensuring that trust is based on the right reasons. Ideally, such a justified trust should be the foundation upon which people decide to adopt AI. However, considering the mismatch between the reasons people trust a system and what would be needed for justified trust, it's clear there's more complexity to the issue.

And what measures are essential to ensure the ethical use of AI?

That's actually another focus of my research. I'm deeply interested in machine ethics and ethical AI. In my opinion, there isn't a one-size-fits-all solution for achieving ethical AI. It essentially depends on various characteristics you'd want an AI system to embody, which, in turn, are contingent upon the context in which the AI system is deployed. For example, the accuracy of a song recommendation algorithm might not be critically important to me as a user. While the company behind the algorithm might prioritize its accuracy for reasons of reputation, and as a user, I might be slightly inconvenienced by an unappealing song suggestion, an incorrect song recommendation is not a significant ethical concern. However, particularly in high-stakes scenarios, the situation changes dramatically [2]. Aspects such as fairness, robustness, explainability, and high accuracy become crucial in such scenarios. Justified trust also plays a significant role within the ethical framework, but even more so does the trustworthiness of the system – its ability to function as intended. In any case, addressing this question isn't straightforward due to the multifaceted nature of AI and ethics. It's challenging to single out one characteristic as the definitive criterion for an AI system's ethical use, as it greatly depends on the application context and adopted ethical view.

"The focus shouldn't be on the fact that trust exists, but rather on ensuring that trust is based on the right reasons."

Is there already some kind of framework that describes application scenarios from low to high stakes and lists the different criteria that need to be met to be considered sufficiently ethical or sufficiently reliable and trustworthy?

As of now, I'm not aware of any such framework. I also question its feasibility. However, looking at legislation, the AI Act does attempt to adopt a risk-based approach. It categorizes different levels of risk, each with its corresponding obligations. Nevertheless, it's important to note that law and ethics are distinct fields. An ethical framework might therefore take a different shape. Context is crucial, and it might be necessary to evaluate each system or use case individually.

Moving on to the next question, what do you think the technical capabilities of AI will be in the future? If we look at a scale from 1, which describes the artificial intelligence systems we see today like ChatGPT, to 10, which describes artificial general intelligence that surpasses human capabilities. What do you think will be possible?

I consider myself somewhat of a tech optimist, so I'd say potential technical capabilities are closer to the 10 end of the scale – perhaps an 8 or 9. Philosophically, it's a challenging question. The current debates often extend beyond artificial general intelligence to superintelligence. If the question were about superintelligence, I'd be skeptical about its realization.

How do you distinguish artificial general intelligence from superintelligence?

Artificial general intelligence usually refers to a single AI system that can perform multiple tasks traditionally performed by humans at a human or superhuman level, such as playing chess, generating images, or detecting cancer. On the other hand, the term superintelligence often refers to an AI system with consciousness whose intelligence far exceeds that of humans. This should suffice as a detour; to address your original question, we're already witnessing significant advancements of AI systems. For instance, chatbots are being utilized for various purposes, with some people even suggesting their capabilities in certain areas surpassing those of humans. In the field of medical AI, there are numerous instances where AI has been recognized as more proficient than highly skilled doctors in diagnosing cancer. So, in some respects, we're already there.

"There isn't a one-size-fits-all solution for achieving ethical AI."

And how do you see AI and its impact on the future? Today we hear all kinds of future scenarios, from dystopian nightmares to utopian dreams. What is your view?

As I've mentioned, I'm a tech optimist. Despite the negative impact that AI might have on social media and, by extension, society, I'm encouraged by the research community's efforts to address these issues. Furthermore, with legislative measures like the forthcoming AI Act in the EU, along with the Digital Services Act and other initiatives, I believe we're moving in the right direction. There's undoubtedly a lot of destructive potential, but the path forward looks promising.

Destructive potential from artificial intelligence applications themselves or from the intentions and actions of actors?

Well, when you think about it, if you possess a tool – take a hammer, for example – you can use it to drive in a nail or to commit a crime. The core issue often lies with the individuals wielding the tool. However, AI introduces unique challenges, such as training biases, stereotypes, and the perpetuation of historical biases, which pushes the hammer analogy to its limits. However, as I've mentioned, I hold a strong belief in the research community and in legislative bodies. There are individuals deeply concerned with these issues, actively working to address them, and I believe their efforts are, to some extent, successful.

Reflecting on the last few days of this interdisciplinary conference, what was the most interesting insight for you?

I've always considered myself an interdisciplinary individual, drawing significant insight from psychology, among other fields. Philosophers often engage in discussions about how the world ought to be, crafting normative claims that attempt to outline how reality should be or how people should perceive various aspects of life. However, reality often diverges from these philosophical ideals, a fact that becomes particularly evident through psychological studies. From a philosophical perspective, it seems logical to argue that people should desire explanations and benefit from them. Yet, empirical studies frequently reveal that individuals may not actually seek explanations. For example, it has been observed that after receiving an explanation, people's perception of a system does not necessarily improve, it can even deteriorate [8]. This is because the explanation unveils the factors considered in the decision-making process of an AI or any system, leading to a more critical view of it. Philosophically, one might argue that understanding how a system operates should enhance our perception of it, as it provides a more justified belief about the system's functionality. This discrepancy between philosophical expectations and psychological findings is always fascinating to me.

"People often trust a system for irrelevant reasons. [...] studies have shown that merely providing explanations can increase people's trust in a system, even if these explanations don't actually offer any real insight [...]."

Is there a specific research question you would like to see addressed from an interdisciplinary perspective?

Admittedly, there are numerous questions, primarily centered around my research interests. I'm particularly fascinated by the XAI debate, delving into the nuances of which systems require certain types of explanations for specific purposes. This is so that users can achieve their objectives with these explanations, feel satisfied with the system, and use it correctly. Basically, if a system is faulty, users should be able to find out and not use it. Lately, my focus has shifted slightly towards understanding how explanations and fairness intersect.

Fairness itself seems to be a difficult concept because it is very subjective. Are there any agreed-upon definitions, or do you combine different ones and integrate them into the system?

That's precisely what captivates me about this debate: depending on your understanding of fairness, explainability can serve different roles. In some cases, it can directly contribute to fairness; in others, it acts merely as a debugging tool for fairness, and sometimes, it may not aid in achieving fairness at all [4]. What intrigues me is the challenge of unraveling these concepts of fairness and explainability and then attempting to connect them.

From your personal perspective, what should be the AI vision?

That's a challenging question, to be honest. Basically, it should be AI for the people.

People in terms of society?

Yes, it shouldn't be the AI of Big Tech companies, as it is currently emerging, but rather AI designed for society, and perhaps even by society, through participative approaches, community work, and citizen science.

Which disciplines are you already collaborating with? And are there other disciplines that should get involved in the future?

I'm involved in a project where we collaborate with legal scholars, psychologists, computer scientists, and philosophers. I've also worked with political scientists. However, I would also be interested in incorporating the viewpoint of sociology to gain a broader perspective on AI.

The progress in AI in the last year has been crazy. And that progress is being driven primarily by companies because of the competition in the industry. Companies are rushing to make sure that the competition is not faster, that they are not losing potential users, and that they are not running the risk of shrinking their networks. How do you see the role of business professionals in this? For example, finding new ways to move from today's money-driven perspective to a society-driven perspective, and finding new incentives and benefits for companies to slow down the current pace of AI progress? Would that be interesting?

I'm not sure it's necessary. In a way, this competitive pressure also impacts governments, prompting them to increase funding for research projects that don't involve private companies. So, I believe there might even be a benefit to this kind of AI race.

Could you elaborate on that?

Increasing pressure on governments from corporate competition can lead to more funding for research and progress in areas such as AI legislation. For example, during our discussions this week, we noted how law tends to lag behind technological advancements. However, initiatives like the European AI Act are promising and show an opposite trend. They aim to create legislation that is broad enough to accommodate the rapid changes in the AI landscape, including future shifts in infrastructure and the types of AI being developed.

Is there anything you would like to add?

Thank you for organizing the conference and for striving towards greater interdisciplinarity.

Thank you, Timo, for your time and your interdisciplinary perspective from computer science and philosophy. Enjoy the last days at AISoLA!

Thank you!

References

1. Barredo Arrieta, A., et al.: Explainable Artificial Intelligence (XAI): concepts, taxonomies, opportunities and challenges toward responsible AI. Inf. Fus. **58**, 82–115 (2020)
2. Baum, K., Mantel, S., Schmidt, E., Speith, T.: From responsibility to reason-giving explainable artificial intelligence. Philos. Technol. **35**(1), 12 (2022)
3. Chazette, L., Brunotte, W., Speith, T.: Exploring explainability: a definition, a model, and a knowledge catalogue. In: Proceedings 2021 IEEE 29th International Requirements Engineering Conference (RE 2021), pp. 197–208). IEEE (2021)

4. Deck, L., Schoeffer, J., De-Arteaga, M., Kühl, N.: A critical survey on fairness benefits of XAI. https://arxiv.org/abs/2310.13007
5. Eiband, M., Buschek, D., Kremer, A., Hussmann, H.: The impact of placebic explanations on trust in intelligent systems. In: Extended Abstracts of the 2019 CHI Conf. on Human Factors in Computing Systems, pp. 1–6. ACM (2019)
6. Kästner, L., Langer, M., Lazar, V., Schomäcker, A., Speith, T., Sterz, S.: On the relation of trust and explainability: why to engineer for trustworthiness. In: Proceedings 29th IEEE International Requirements Engineering Conference Workshops (REW 2021), pp. 169–175. IEEE (2021)
7. Köhl, M.A., Baum, K., Langer, M., Oster, D., Speith, T., Bohlender, D.: Explainability as a non-functional requirement. In Proceedings 27th IEEE International Requirements Engineering Conference (RE 2019), pp. 363–368. IEEE (2019)
8. Langer, M., König, C.J., Fitili, A.: Information as a double-edged sword: the role of computer experience and information on applicant reactions towards novel technologies for personnel selection. Comput. Hum. Behav. **81**, 19–30 (2018)
9. Langer, M., et al.: What do we want from Explainable Artificial Intelligence (XAI)? A stakeholder perspective on XAI and a conceptual model guiding interdisciplinary XAI research. Artif. Intell. **296**, 103473 (2021)
10. Langer, M., Baum, K., Hartmann, K., Hessel, S., Speith, T., Wahl, J.: Explainability auditing for intelligent systems: a rationale for multi-disciplinary perspectives. In: Proceedings 29th IEEE International Requirements Engineering Conference Workshops (REW 2021), pp. 164–168. IEEE (2021)
11. Oxford Reference: Artificial Intelligence (2024). https://www.oxfordreference.com/display/10.1093/oi/authority.20110803095426960
12. Speith, T.: A review of taxonomies of Explainable Artificial Intelligence (XAI) methods. In: Proceedings of the ACM Conference on Fairness, Accountability, and Transparency (FAccT 2022), pp. 2239–2250. ACM (2022)

Let's Talk AI with Philosophy and Computer Science Expert Kevin Baum

Kevin Baum[1] and Barbara Steffen[2](✉)

[1] German Research Center for Artificial Intelligence (DFKI) and Center for European Research in Trusted Artificial Intelligence (CERTAIN), Kaiserslautern, Germany
kevin.baum@dfki.de

[2] METAFrame Technologies, Dortmund, Germany
barbara.steffen@metaframe.de

Abstract. Building trustworthy AI comes with numerous challenges, ranging from robustness and fairness to explainability for effective human oversight and responsible decision-making. Interdisciplinary collaboration is key for tackling these challenges – fortunately, as the AI community grows, finding shared understanding and common ground between relevant fields becomes easier, because more and more researchers with interdisciplinary backgrounds are entering the field. This paves the way for responsible AI development.

My personal AI mission: As a philosopher and computer scientist, I am driven to advance responsible AI development by promoting interdisciplinary dialogue and integrating ethical considerations into core research practices. My mission is to create an environment where appropriate trust assessments in AI becomes the norm, ensuring technology serves humanity in a just and responsible manner.

Fig. 1. Kevin Baum

B. Steffen et al. (Eds.): *Let's Talk AI*, LNCS 15000, pp. 104–112, 2026.
https://doi.org/10.1007/978-3-032-09008-9_12

1 My Takes on AI

- **Artificial Intelligence** – Defining "artificial intelligence" precisely is difficult. Perhaps it's best understood when looking at concrete examples and applications. AI as a discipline or field of study encompasses the development of intelligent agents, systems capable of reasoning, learning, and autonomous action (in a technical sense, meaning they operate without direct human control). I also consider the ethical and societal aspects of these developments in order to ensure responsible and beneficial applications of AI for humanity to be part of the field. However, it's crucial to remember that "AI" often serves as an umbrella term for diverse software and cyberphysical systems with varying capabilities.
- **Trust** – I'd put it that way: Trust is a relational disposition that involves vulnerability, a willingness to put oneself at risk based on positive expectations of another's agent's behavior. Some argue that (current) AI systems fail to be appropriate objects of trust, i.e., that they are the wrong kind of agents, agents that cannot be trustworthy. If so, trust in AI would be generally misguided. I disagree. While I admit that AI cannot be trustworthy in the sense human agents can, I think we can trust in AI systems much in the same way as we can trust in organizations or institutions, which involves attributing properties like benevolence, integrity, and ability to them – this is possible in theory and in practice in a meaningful and proper sense.
- **Explainability** – When people say they are researching explainability (or "explainable AI"), they generally mean that they are working on methods to explain how and why a system, whose decision-making processes are otherwise opaque to humans, arrives at its decisions. The point is not to find out whether the output is correct or appropriate (that would be a question of justification), although explainability can help with this in many cases. Explainability should also be distinguished from various other perspicuity properties like, for example, transparency, which is about making aspects such as the system's formal properties, the data used to train it, and its role in some decision procedure available to a third party.
- **Essential Elements of Human Capabilities** – Phew, I don't think I can offer a serious explication of this without straying too far afield. Perhaps the most important are context sensitivity and everyday understanding, including sensitivity to exceptional and marginal cases of rules (including informal non-monotonic reasoning), empathy, and sentience.

2 The Interview

[Barbara Steffen] Thank you, Kevin Baum (Fig. 1), for taking the time to do this interview. Can you briefly introduce yourself and your personal relationship to artificial intelligence?

[Kevin Baum] As a philosopher and computer scientist at the German Research Center for Artificial Intelligence (DFKI), I deeply engage with both the technical and ethical dimensions of AI. My roles include being the deputy head of the Neuro-mechanistic Modeling Department and leading the Center for European Research in Trusted AI (CERTAIN), where my efforts are focused on advancing the development of responsible and understandable AI systems [12]. I extensively teach AI and computer ethics and am involved in several interdisciplinary research projects, particularly on the explainability and trustworthiness of AI. Whether through research or education, AI is central to my work.

"The fast pace of AI development calls for legal frameworks that can quickly adapt to new technologies and their societal implications."

That's fascinating. Can you give examples of specific challenges that you're currently addressing in your AI research?

There are several challenges we are currently tackling. For instance, in our project, Explainable Intelligent Systems (EIS), supported by the Volkswagen Stiftung [13], we are primarily focused on understanding how explainable AI (XAI) methods can achieve the expectations and objectives they are often associated with, such as improving trustworthiness, robustness, and fairness in AI systems, and enabling humans to make responsible decisions when acting upon the outputs of such systems. EIS is an interdisciplinary effort that aims to bring together XAI research and computer science with insights from law, psychology, philosophy, and other fields [1, 4, 9]. My contribution centers on exploring these areas from both a technical and an ethical perspective, focusing on the development of XAI methods and examining the philosophical underpinnings of what we expect from AI in terms of ethical and societal impact.

When you look at AI from an interdisciplinary perspective, how do you usually start? For example, does everyone start from different angles, or do you start with a research question that defines the focus of the collaboration?

In tackling interdisciplinary AI research, our approach has evolved significantly over time. Initially, we often tried to identify a specific research question appealing across all disciplines involved. However, we quickly realized the challenge this posed due to varying interpretations of key terms and concepts like accountability, understandability, trustworthiness, and many more among different fields. Now, my starting point is to first establish some kind of mutual understanding and a shared vocabulary among team members, who bring diverse research backgrounds to the table. This approach has proven more efficient. From this shared platform, we then formulate a research question that guides our collaborative efforts. The process encourages members to explore the question from their disciplinary perspectives and later reconvene to integrate their findings. This method fosters interdisciplinary collaboration, revealing overlaps and intersections that enrich our collective understanding – and maximizes our research output.

And how difficult is it to find common ground and understanding on these topics?

Finding common ground and understanding in interdisciplinary research has its challenges, but it significantly improves over time, with collaboration and ongoing dialogue. Our experience, both within our projects and observed at this conference, underscores this evolution. Since initiating our interdisciplinary endeavors around 2016–2017, we've noticed a marked increase in the interdisciplinary community's size and engagement. This growth has facilitated easier collaboration across different fields, as more researchers are now engaging in interdisciplinary work. And within our already established research environment, the initial hurdles of establishing a common language and shared objectives have become less daunting over time, thanks to the cumulative experience and the expanding network of researchers committed to this approach.

"I advocate for the development of structured educational frameworks that emphasize these core topics [like ethics] and their relationships with each other."

How do you see the role of trust in AI adoption?

That's a big question. Trust in AI is a multifaceted issue that extends far beyond user acceptance or, more generally, AI adoption. It involves a complex network of relationships between humans, machines, and institutions [3, 8]. Our recent research delves into these dynamics, examining how trust and trustworthiness assessments are impacted not only by direct interaction between individuals and AI systems but also how these systems are perceived within the broader societal and institutional context. Factors such as shared experiences, certificates and seals, including the certification processes, and the overall reliability and trustworthiness of several involved institutions play critical roles in shaping trust in AI [7]. Understanding these interconnections is crucial for advancing AI adoption in a way that aligns with users' expectations and societal norms. Essentially, navigating the intricacies of trust requires a comprehensive approach that considers the entire ecosystem, the whole society in which AI operates.

And what measures do you think are needed for ethical AI adoption?

First, we need more ethical expertise on side of those who develop AI systems. However, in the realm of AI ethics, a rapidly expanding field, we're encountering a paradoxical situation [11]. The pace at which AI technology develops often outstrips the depth of ethical considerations we're able to apply to each new advancement. For instance, the rush to address fairness in different AI applications – from scoring and recommender systems to generative AI – sometimes lacks thorough analysis of the underlying ethical frameworks and their practical implications. This isn't solely an issue within the AI ethics community but is rather exacerbated by the rapid advancement of AI technologies themselves. But how, in light of this pace, can we teach the necessary skills then?

Reflecting on my experience since 2015, when I was motivated by Prof. (Holger) Hermanns to initiate *Ethics for Nerds* – a course aimed at instilling a foundational ethical understanding in computer science students – it's evident that the challenge has shifted. Initially, the scarcity of established teaching content was a barrier; now, the sheer volume of material necessitates a more structured educational approach. This structured approach is not only essential for preparing future computer scientists but also critical for effective communication with the broader public, including citizens, policymakers, and regulators.

Thus, the measures needed for ethical AI adoption extend beyond slow deliberation to include the development of comprehensive educational frameworks. These frameworks should facilitate deep engagement with ethical principles, tailored to keep pace with technological advancements and accessible to a wide audience. This approach will ensure that as AI continues to evolve, it does so within a context of informed, ethical consideration that benefits society as a whole.

You just said that there is a lot of content on ethics today. Is it unstructured and scattered all over the place, or can you see certain patterns that allow you to prioritize and focus on a small set of, say, three topics and their interrelationships? Which need to be considered to create a more holistic and actionable understanding?

There are certain patterns emerging, notably around fairness, robustness, and the role of properties like transparency and explainability when it comes to the imperative for responsible decision-making or accountability in AI development, including questions of effective human oversight. Beyond these, we see recurrent high-level themes such as technological solutionism, questions regarding human autonomy, privacy concerns, and the ethical challenges posed by AI's dual-use potential, which prompts significant reflection on the ethical responsibilities of those working in the field [2]. Despite the emergence of these patterns, I think the field suffers from a lack of structured, comprehensive educational content that can guide both current and future practitioners in navigating these complex ethical landscapes. A more organized approach to AI ethics education would not only help in delineating clear priorities for the field but also enhance communication with a broader audience, including policymakers, regulators, and the general public. This structured approach would ideally focus on integrating technical and ethical considerations, thereby facilitating a more holistic understanding of AI's societal impacts. Therefore, in response to the vast and somewhat scattered nature of content in AI ethics, I advocate for the development of structured educational frameworks that emphasize these core topics and their relationships with each other. Such frameworks should aim to equip individuals with the tools needed to address both present and future ethical challenges in AI, ensuring that the field's rapid development is matched by equally robust ethical considerations.

In terms of the future development of AI and AI systems, on a scale of 1 to 10, where 1 stands for AI systems like ChatGPT, to 10, which stands for general artificial intelligence that surpasses human capabilities. What do you think will be possible in the future?

It's challenging to fit this into a one-dimensional scale. But if you forced me to do so, I would lean towards a 7 or 8. This reflects my anticipation of substantial progress in AI's ability to handle complex, generalized problem-solving through the integration of specialized and increasingly multimodal systems, rather than the emergence of a singular, superintelligent AI entity. We're likely to see advancements that significantly surpass current limitations, addressing challenges previously deemed insurmountable by human or individual AI capabilities. While these systems might qualify as artificial general intelligence, I do not believe that we may encounter strong AI systems with self-awareness or consciousness akin to humans in the foreseeable future. While we may witness the creation of AI with capabilities that seem to mimic creativity or multifaceted intelligence, such as composing poetry, generating whole movies, or performing music with exceptional skill, these should not be confused with genuine consciousness, empathy, or emotional understanding.

The distinction is crucial, not just from a technological standpoint but from an ethical and societal perspective. The integration and application of these advanced AI systems will necessitate careful consideration of their impact on society, employment, privacy, and security. Moreover, the potential for AI to contribute positively to humanity, such as in medical breakthroughs or solving complex environmental challenges, should be balanced against the risks and ethical dilemmas posed by their capabilities. But there seems no reason to believe that, major breakthroughs aside, such systems will qualify as moral patients [6]. Thus, while we edge closer to the upper limits of the scale in terms of technical proficiency and application, the journey demands a concerted focus on ethical governance, public engagement, and interdisciplinary collaboration to ensure that advancements align with societal values and needs as well as the constant caution not to unjustifiably anthropomorphize the systems that are to come.

"My concerns gravitate towards dystopian scenarios, not due to fears of super intelligence or autonomous AI dominance, but because of more immediate issues like the concentration of power within a few corporations."

This leads to my next question. So, what is your opinion on the utopian-dystopian spectrum? What do you think is coming and what do we need to be prepared for?

Hard question! I find myself navigating the spectrum between dystopian and utopian outcomes with a critical eye. My concerns gravitate towards dystopian scenarios, not due to fears of superintelligence or autonomous AI dominance but because of more immediate issues like the concentration of power within a few corporations. This concentration raises significant risks, including the manipulation of public opinion and the erosion of democratic processes, exacerbated by the lack of transparency in AI research and development. The opaque nature of AI systems, from data usage to the complexity of their architectures, poses a challenge to understanding and regulating these technologies effectively. I am also very concerned about the possible, even foreseeable misuse of these capabilities by state actors. In the near to medium term, I foresee these challenges manifesting in increased surveillance capitalism, with potentially destabilizing effects on societies and democratic institutions.

However, looking beyond these immediate concerns, I believe in the transformative potential of AI to address some of humanity's most pressing issues, such as climate change and healthcare. The key to realizing this potential lies in avoiding the realization of the current dystopian risks, requiring concerted efforts in ethical AI development, transparent research practices, and equitable governance of AI technologies. Ultimately, while my current stance leans towards a cautious approach due to the visible risks, I remain optimistic about the long-term prospects of AI. Achieving a utopian future with AI will demand a proactive stance on addressing ethical and societal challenges head-on, ensuring that AI development is aligned with human values and societal well-being.

Looking back on the last few days of this interdisciplinary conference, is there one insight that was particularly interesting or striking to you?

Although as a computer scientist and philosopher, I would like to say it was from these two fields, the potential on the side of the law stood out to me. It became evident that the law plays a pivotal role in shaping the future of AI in society. The journey towards a society where we can be sure that AI contributes positively requires more than just ethical guidelines and good will on side of the developers and researchers; it demands hard regulation informed by a deep understanding of the nuances in AI application and its impact [5]. This regulation must navigate the "strategic ambiguities" inherent in AI ethics, bridging the gap between theoretical ethical considerations and practical, enforceable standards.

In this regard, the conference illuminated the inextricable link between interdisciplinary collaboration and the development of effective regulation to address the multifaceted challenges posed by AI technologies – not only to refine and interpret ethical principles but also to ensure that these principles are operationalized in a way that upholds human oversight and societal well-being.

Insofar, the conference reinforced my conviction that progress in AI ethics and regulation cannot occur in silos. Instead, it requires a concerted effort from a broad spectrum of disciplines, all converging towards the creation of legal frameworks that are both robust and adaptive. This interdisciplinary approach is not just beneficial but essential for realizing the full potential of AI in enhancing societal good while mitigating its risks.

Would you like to see more interdisciplinary research in this area? For example, to what extent do you think that law needs to be informed by other disciplines to be aware of what is possible and what are the potential impacts on individuals and society as a whole? This could ensure that regulation introduces rules that fit the overall context.

In response to the need for more interdisciplinary research, especially in bridging the gap between law, technology, and ethics in AI, I see a path forward that involves both conceptual and structural initiatives. First, the establishment of regular interdisciplinary conferences, similar to what we've experienced here at AISoLA, is essential. These gatherings should not only maintain a high-level discourse but also delve into specific challenges, such as defining and implementing effective human oversight within AI systems. This requires a concerted effort from diverse fields – computer science for developing transparent and explainable AI technologies, psychology to address human factors like automation bias, and sociology to understand the broader societal impacts [10].

Moreover, the fast pace of AI development calls for legal frameworks that can quickly adapt to new technologies and their societal implications. This adaptability hinges on creating an organizational infrastructure capable of continuous evaluation and monitoring of laws, ensuring they are informed by the latest technological advancements and ethical insights. Such projects would not only foster a responsive legal environment but also encourage a deeper, practice-oriented research collaboration across disciplines. Hence, moving beyond the current state requires not just occasional interdisciplinary interactions but a sustained, structured effort to integrate insights from various domains. This approach will ensure that AI development is guided by a comprehensive understanding of ethical, societal, and legal considerations, ultimately leading to regulations that are both effective and reflective of our collective values and goals.

> "The pace at which AI technology develops often outstrips the depth of ethical considerations we're able to apply to each new advancement."

And what do you think the AI vision should look like?

I advocate to consider a diverse array of visions that collectively aim towards leveraging AI for societal benefit instead of one unique overall vision. However, here is one specific and rather concrete vision: The establishment of a robust non-profit infrastructure dedicated to nurturing AI systems designed to address specific societal challenges – from enhancing urban mobility and educational opportunities to mitigating misinformation by transparent algorithmic curation. Such an infrastructure would enable sustained support for AI projects beyond the typical funding cycles, ensuring their long-term impact on society. This vision, again, underscores the necessity of interdisciplinary collaboration, bridging the gap between technological innovation and societal needs. By fostering a close relationship between researchers, practitioners, and the broader community, we can ensure that AI developments are not only technologically advanced but also ethically grounded and socially beneficial. As we look to the future, the goal should not merely be to advance AI technology in isolation but to integrate these advancements within a framework that prioritizes human wellbeing and societal progress. It's about creating an AI ecosystem that is as much about empowering individuals and communities as it is about algorithms and data. This balanced approach to AI development and implementation is what I believe will lead to a better future for all.

Would you like to add anything else?

Oh, I could go on for hours, but I think what's most important to me has been said.

Thank you, Kevin, for your time and your views on AI, interdisciplinary collaboration, and future developments.

No need to thank me! Thanks for having me!

References

1. Baum, K., et al.: From responsibility to reason-giving Explainable Artificial Intelligence. Philos. Technol. **35**(1) (2022). https://doi.org/10.1007/s13347-022-00510-w
2. Baum, K., et al.: From fear to action: AI governance and opportunities for all. Front. Comput. Sci. **5**, 1210421 (2023)
3. Henrique, B.M., Santos, E.: Trust in artificial intelligence: literature review and main path analysis. Comput. Hum. Behav. Artif. Hum. **2**(1), 100043 (2024)
4. Langer, M., et al.: What do we want from Explainable Artificial Intelligence (XAI)? A stakeholder perspective on XAI and a conceptual model guiding interdisciplinary XAI research. Artif. Intell. **296**, 103473 (2021)
5. Lucaj, L., Van Der Smagt, P., Benbouzid, D.: AI regulation is (not) all you need. In: Proceedings of the ACM Conference on Fairness, Accountability, and Transparency (FAccT 2023), pp. 1267–1279 ACM (2023)
6. Moosavi, P.: Will intelligent machines become moral patients? Philos. Phenomenological Res. **109**(1), 95–116 (2024)
7. Schlicker, N., Baum, K., Uhde, A., Sterz, S., Hirsch, M.C., Langer, M.: A micro and macro perspective on trustworthiness: theoretical underpinnings of the Trustworthiness Assessment Model (TrAM). https://www.oa.mg/work/10.31234/osf.io/qhwvx
8. Shen, M.W.: Trust in AI: interpretability is not necessary or sufficient, while black-box interaction is necessary and sufficient. https://arxiv.org/abs/2202.05302

9. Sterz, S., et al.: Towards perspicuity requirements. In: Proceedings of the 29th IEEE International Requirements Engineering Conference Workshops (REW 2021). IEEE (2021)
10. Sterz, S., et al.: On the quest for effectiveness in human oversight: interdisciplinary perspectives. In: Proceedings of the 2024 ACM Conf. on Fairness, Accountability, and Transparency (FAccT 2024), pp. 2495–2507. ACM (2024)
11. Tang, X., et al.: The pace of artificial intelligence innovations: speed, talent, and trial-and-error. https://arxiv.org/abs/2009.01812
12. https://certain.dfki.de/
13. https://explainable-intelligent.systems/

Let's Talk AI with AI Expert José Hernández-Orallo

José Hernández-Orallo[1] and Barbara Steffen[2(✉)]

[1] Universitat Politècnica de València and Valencian Research Institute for Artificial Intelligence, Valencia, Spain
jorallo@upv.es
[2] METAFrame Technologies, Dortmund, Germany
barbara.steffen@metaframe.de

Abstract. We have to measure what AI is capable of, and we have to measure our dreams of future AI as well.

My personal AI mission: Understand intelligence, with measurement as the main scientific tool for this.

Fig. 1. José Hernández-Orallo

1 My Takes on AI

- **Artificial Intelligence** – Intelligence is what solves all solvable problems, following the thirteenth-century philosopher Ramon Llull. Artificial intelligence is just the non-biological kind.
- **Trust** – Meeting expectations, requiring a subject A (in this case a human) to have a good model of subject B (in this case a machine) to know where A expects a valid or invalid outcome when interacting with B. If you cannot anticipate that you cannot have trust.

B. Steffen et al. (Eds.): *Let's Talk AI*, LNCS 15000, pp. 113–123, 2026.
https://doi.org/10.1007/978-3-032-09008-9_13

- **Explainability** – This is easily confused with ex-post justifications, and the area of XAI needs to be crisper in what a true explanation really is. I prefer to talk about models of AI systems that have explanatory and predictable power. Predictability is closely connected with AI evaluation, and predictions are usually easier to check than explanations.
- **Essential Elements of Human Capabilities** – Human capabilities are determined by evolution and culture. We have a very sophisticated perception system, inherited from the primate family, and very advanced social capabilities. Then, of course, language capabilities are a more recent innovation in evolution, which boost the potential for communication, reasoning, culture, etc.

2 The Interview

[Barbara Steffen] Today I have the pleasure of interviewing José Hernández-Orallo (Fig. 1). Please introduce yourself and your relationship to artificial intelligence.

[José Hernández-Orallo] Thank you for having me here today. My relationship with AI dates back quite a while. I've been interested in intelligence since I was a teenager. I remember reading books about anthropology and hominids. At some point, I began to ponder what it would take for a machine to replicate some of these behaviors. That's when I became interested in artificial intelligence. Over the past 20 years, my focus has been more on understanding than developing new AI systems, although I have done a bit of that as well. I am mostly interested in understanding what kind of capabilities these systems can have. This is the goal of the area of AI evaluation, which is a significant topic these days [2, 7, 8, 18]. Especially with general-purpose AI, I'm interested in understanding what these systems are capable of and why they sometimes fail so catastrophically. These are the things that I am currently working on [11, 12].

> "If a system can do everything for you, what's the motivation to work hard, learn, and do things yourself?"

Is it about the distinction between the intelligence we see in humans and the intelligence of systems?

I would go even further back to compare the intelligence in animals, nonhuman animals, or even children with AI systems. Especially these days, with all these large language models, we often compare these systems with humans. However, in other areas, such as robotics or reinforcement learning agents, it is much more interesting to compare them with a rat or an insect. I believe we gain a lot of insight from these comparisons. But I don't think it's accurate to say that we have systems today that have the intelligence of a rat. I think these comparisons are too simplistic. Instead, there are many tools that have been developed for understanding animal behavior and human behavior. I've been inspired by animal cognition and psychometrics. I think that's where we can find a lot of tools and ideas to evaluate AI systems as well.

You wrote a whole book about intelligence. What is your understanding of what intelligence is or how intelligence can be measured? Or is it too complicated to break it down like that?

It's very complicated. Intelligence is a term I don't even define in the book. The book primarily highlights all the things that don't work, more than trying to find solutions [5]. Of course, there are proposals and frameworks for evaluation and ideas that show promise. But there's a long debate about what intelligence is in humans, in non-human animals, and how we compare humans in our evolutionary history. When we try to compare humans with machines and what these machines can do, we find that the term intelligence is used very differently for humans and non-human animals. I prefer to use the term cognition because it's much broader in many ways. We don't assume that the system is intelligent [9]. It has some cognitive capabilities and behavior, and we want to understand how the system works. In my book, I try to be comprehensive in terms of understanding and evaluating the intelligence of this diverse range of systems that we can call intelligent. And there are more open questions than answers. But I think that a more holistic approach is required. We need to draw inspiration from the behavioral sciences, from the old disciplines of cybernetics, and so on. I think we need that approach more than many of the approaches that we see in artificial intelligence today, which is basically trying to test the system with a benchmark. That doesn't give you much insight.

Are there one or two specific AI-related research questions that you're currently addressing?

Yes, there are two questions I've been trying to understand, and of course, they are related to the notion of intelligence. The first one is that, instead of talking about general intelligence, a term introduced in psychometrics by Spearman about a century ago [14], I try to disentangle the notion of generality. What does it mean to have a system that is general compared to a system that is capable? A few years ago, when I was trying to develop metrics of generality people didn't understand. They said, if it is more general, then it is more capable. No, not necessarily. You can have systems that can do a lot of things, but not very well. Not with depth, as a psychometrician or a psychologist might say. A lot of breadth, but not a lot of depth. The system can do a lot of things, but not many sophisticated things. For instance, when you look for an assistant, you want someone or something that helps you with a lot of things, but don't ask that assistant to do very complicated things. Basically, just fetch this for me, or do this for me, or write this up, or something like that. Simple things, but a diversity of things. And this is exactly what we have now with large language models. We have general systems that are not very capable, but can do a lot of things. Some of the things better than others, but in a way, none of them extremely well. Of course, you can find specialized systems that are better than a large language model for each of these things. The interesting thing about a large language model is that the same system can do a lot of things. For the first time, we have these general systems. And this has nothing to do with AGI, with having human-level AI. It's basically that for the first time we have systems that are really general, that we can ask many things to, and they can do many tasks. This generality is out of the box. Trying to introduce metrics of generality is one of the challenges I've been working on [10]. Then the second, related question is that you cannot define generality without a notion of difficulty. Again, this also comes from psychology and psychometrics. You can say, "Oh, I can do additions." Okay, fine, up to how many digits? Because you can't do all additions. Nobody can. This is not even feasible. There are additions with a number of digits that you will never finish. So, what do we really mean? We need a distribution of additions that we expect to happen. That's one approach. But another approach is: "Okay, I don't know what distribution you're going to experience." Maybe sometimes I get an addition with three digits. Maybe tomorrow I have an addition with 10 digits. I don't know the distribution of additions. I can calculate an aggregate of that, but that's not very meaningful. What is really meaningful is whether I can just order all of these additions in terms of their difficulty. And I can say, for instance, that maybe the mean of the number of digits of the two summands is a good indicator of the difficulty of addition. Of course, there's some carrying going on and some long additions that are, of course, easy, such as 11111, plus 22222. That's a very easy addition. So, it's not that simple, but you can get proxies of difficulty and you can say: "Okay, I can do addition in 10 seconds up to 5 digits." And for an addition of 30 digits I'm not going to get it right in 10 seconds. That's a notion of difficulty that allows me to determine a notion of capability. So, let's say my capability of adding numbers in 10 seconds is 5 digits. Now, independently of the distribution of additions that I'm going to see in the future, you can more or less predict whether I'm going to succeed or not for a future addition. I think that's the kind of capabilities that derive from these difficulty metrics that we need in AI. And again, in psychometrics, with an item response theory you can calculate all of these things, and oppose ability to difficulty. As a result, these two areas the generality of cognitive systems and the notion of difficulty, are closely related, because they lead to proper definitions of capabilities.

Do you think that we have an idea of what is difficult for machines? Is the notion of difficulty different for humans and AI? How would you translate between these two?

We typically associate the difficulty of a task with the capability of the kind of subject [4]. For instance, making a cup of coffee is easy for a human but hard for a machine, while solving complex integrals may be easy for a machine but difficult for some humans. Difficulty is subjective to a point. But when you fix the task, and look into the instances of the task, you find that despite the different capabilities, there's some instance performance correlations in terms of what you see in general systems [6, 10]. For instance, going back to the example of addition, if you compare a language model with humans, you see very similar patterns of failure when the numbers get larger. And a language model, like a human, finds some instances more difficult than others. In terms of tasks, however, that depends more on the training, making what is difficult for one person easier for another person. In many cases, we can find some kind of common ground. This is tricky, but I don't think it's impossible. Actually, one of the things that I introduced in my book was a kind of universal difficulty scale, which explains why this is subjective to a point. When you build a system that is general, then you find some commonalities in terms of difficulty. That's something that I hope that at least experimentally we can start seeing in some of the new general systems that we're building in AI [3].

> "Of course, we need to be careful about what we build, as we're essentially creating new beings."

In your opinion, what role does trust play in the adoption of AI?

Trust plays two roles, both positive and negative. Of course, if we don't trust AI, we will use it less than we should. There are significant safety issues with some technologies, and people react against these technologies. Even public opinion can turn against some products. That's why companies are careful about what they do. Maybe not careful enough, but at least they care a little bit that these systems do not do things that people could criticize. That's one thing. The other thing is when they create too much trust. And that's more dangerous. I believe it's better for people to distrust systems rather than overtrust them. Ideally, we should know exactly where a system is reliable and where it isn't. However, this is often difficult to determine, particularly with large language models. For instance, when we pose a question to ChatGPT, we can't predict the response [15]. Not only is the outcome uncertain, but we are often unsure of its accuracy. Sometimes, we might ask the system to write something for us and be pleasantly surprised by the result. But if we start relying on machines for a lot of things, and we think that they can do them well, and at some point they surprise us by doing something wrong, or something really, really wrong, then this is a big problem. So, we need to calibrate trust. Of course, it will be ideal if these systems were consistent. But they are not. Sometimes you ask the same thing or some variation of the same question, and you get something that is rubbish, basically. So, this creates a problem of expectations [17]. The users of these technologies don't know what to expect. And the learning curves are quite long. When you start using ChatGPT, the first thing is, oh, look, I asked it to prove this conjecture as a poem. And I get it. Oh, this system must be fantastic. And then it fails with additions of five numbers. You're really disappointed because you don't expect a system that is able to write this prose and all these poems, even solve some easy differential equations, and then fail on a simple addition, when a calculator, another machine, does this perfectly. All of this breaks our schemas about what to expect from a machine. And that creates a problem of trust. But sometimes there's over-reliance on the system. You think: Oh, that's so cool. They can do so many things. I can just write a summary. I can send e-mails using these tools. And then I find out I screwed it up because I relied on this system. So, this is a major problem at this moment. But if we had to choose, I would choose to have less trust than they really deserve.

> "The existential risk isn't so much about these systems getting out of control, but about human disagreement on important questions about our future. Are we going to remain as we are? Are we going to create other systems? Are we going to grant them rights?"

So, it's essentially about educating users to remain a bit skeptical and to better understand and reflect on what the system can actually do. Where can it complement us? And where do we currently have a distorted idea of what it can do? Given your mathematical example, it seems strange to us that ChatGPT can write these wonderful poems, but it can't do calculations that we learn in elementary school. So, we have the misconception that what is difficult or easy for humans must also be difficult or easy for the system.

Yeah. The problem is that we cannot give all this responsibility to the user. This happens with computers and with any technology. We try to adapt to the technology. And, okay, the first time you use a computer, you say, well, what can I do with this? You download a new app and you try to adapt. And even if you have a digital assistant that is not fueled by a lot of AI, you know, okay, if I ask a question "play this song for me", this is going to work. But if I ask some other questions, such as the meaning of life, you're going to have some kind of prerecorded or prewritten answer for these kinds of questions. And you have to learn all of that. And then, you start to know when these digital assistants are useful or not. But this is a lot of effort, a long learning curve. With a system that has been designed to be an assistant, that's still okay. But a system such as ChatGPT has been adapted to be an assistant from a raw language model. Things are much more complicated. And we cannot ask humans just to build a perfect model of what ChatGPT can do.

So that's why one of the things that I'm doing research on is how we can build this kind of external model (an assessor) of what the system can do and can't do [11]. And then use this in a kind of a monitor or kind of an advisor telling you, okay, the system is going to fail at this or not. Because there are questions about what people call scalable oversight. So how can humans know whether the system is correct or not? And with these more powerful systems, it's becoming more and more difficult to know, even to ask an expert, is the system correct or not [17]? In many cases, it is even debatable what the ground truth is, especially about things that are a little bit more vague about society or things like that. Even scientific facts, you can argue with some of these systems about what you get. That's why I think we need more assistance. We can't rely on the regular user to build a perfect model of when the system is correct or not. Because that would entail that you know, at least in many cases, more than the system knows. And then the system wouldn't be very useful. Instead, we want these systems to be very good generators of things we cannot easily do. People call them generative AI. But apart from generators we also need verifiers [16]. That's something where some other areas of AI and computer science are much better than the current trend of transformers and generative AI.

Do you have any specific measures in mind that could help ensure ethical use of AI?

Well, there are many things. There are so many problems about the ethics of AI. One thing is the way in which these tools are ethical in the first place. And of course, when I mean ethical, it's not that we could talk about moral machines or something like that. Basically the use of these systems could lead to discrimination or inequalities or even increasing the inequalities that we already have. All of these issues are now on the table. I'm happy that there are many discussions today about AI around this. But there are also many things as well that go beyond just whether a system is politically correct. It's more about the geopolitics. I think that if we want to deploy AI in an ethical way, we need a more inclusive AI community. At the moment, it is not very inclusive. Not only is it dominated by a few countries, but a few areas of a few countries, with some Big Tech having an oligopoly on this at the moment. Some profiles of gender and race have dominated the discourse. This has to be changed from the inside. Also, the data that we use to build these AI systems is completely biased because humans are biased. Sometimes this bias is amplified. However, having said all of this, I think that we have a big opportunity. I see some human judges making some kind of resolutions, and I see a lot of biases in them. It is quite rare that you analyze this in an evidence-based way. We humans discriminate. We do that all the time. We are biased. And society is completely unfair in many cases. But we don't often use data to analyze that. For the first time, when we feed all this data to machines and build a model, we really see how unfair society is, all these biases that people have. We basically reidentify the biases in the machine. We can measure them. And then we try to correct them. But the correction is very difficult when the data is biased in the first place. You have trained the system on a lot of rubbish that you have just gathered from the Internet, not especially the best Internet sources you can find. So, what do you expect? Basically, you're going to replicate all these biases. But in a way, I would see it the other way around, like a mirror allowing us to identify and look at all the biases that we have in society. And this is a way in which we can just point out that this is happening in our society. AI is basically resurfacing all of these biases. Today, we try to apply all these new laws for AI systems. Okay, but I say, let's apply all the old laws for humans as well. Especially when they are not fair in their decisions: politicians, judges, police. I think that this should be applied to AI and to humans. Perhaps not in the same scale because AI has a power of replication, possibly having much more effect than a single person. I understand that people are concerned that if a system is biased, that can have more effect than if a single person is biased. But in the end, we have to solve the problem of people being biased in the first place.

Okay, so the biases of AI are more systematic, but at the same time AI systems also reveal the existing biases of society and make them transparent, because all the biases of the AI are the result of the "real world" data that is fed into the large language model.

Yeah, I think that it is a mirror of society. And having a mirror to see yourself, I think it's very, very insightful. It can highlight the real problems and its sources. When you are trying to select the "good" sources, you realize that this is really complicated. The problem of bias and ethics requires people who are experts in ethics. Sometimes people in AI who are really mathematicians or physicists don't know anything about ethics, as a discipline. At least the engineers, especially computer engineers, they usually have a course in the ethics of their profession. And they know the user is very important. The user is a human, so engineers have to build systems that are basically serving the purpose of humans. But in many cases, some of these Big Tech companies have a lot of engineers that were not trained as engineers, they're just mathematicians and physicists. They have been trained on formulas, but not on people. They don't know how to act with people. So, there's a lot of things to improve there, in terms of the people themselves. That was related to the start of the answer to the previous question; we have to change AI from the inside.

Now looking into the future and especially the possible future capabilities of artificial intelligence on a scale of 1 to 10, where 1 describes the artificial intelligence tools like ChatGPT that we know today. And 10 refers to artificial general intelligence that surpasses human capabilities. What do you think will be possible?

With no timeline, I think that anything that is computable is possible. I think the only limits are given by physics. That's what I see. And of course, humans are quite limited in many ways. So, it's just a question of time but it's also a question of what we want to do. It is not a given thing that they're going to build some kind of system that is much more powerful than humans. That's something that we have to decide. And we have to decide what kind of system we want to build. First, because it might be dangerous. And second, because it might be unethical. In biology, we agreed we are not going to play with DNA and do this kind of chimeras mixing a cat and a dog: "Oh look, how cool is this new animal we have created." Because maybe this animal starts suffering. You can use an elephant and a mammoth DNA and then recover more mammoth DNA and try to see if, in a couple of generations, you have a real mammoth. These things are basically unethical. But creating something that goes beyond us, that's kind of a dream. But we have to be very careful about our dreams. So, whether we want to reach that 10 in a scale of 1 to 10 is a decision we have to make. And there are different choices. It's not just a single scale. We have to be careful in choosing from the infinitely many options that are more powerful than us.

> "We're not investing enough effort into understanding a potential cognitive atrophy, similar to how we've physically atrophied due to over-reliance on technology like cars."

Going back to the beginning of the interview where we talked about intelligence. Do you think we have an idea or a common understanding of what it is and when we have reached it? Or are these still very subjective concepts and ideas at the moment?

There's no consensus. There's no science at the level of understanding intelligence. We are playing with something that we don't understand well. And now it's quite trendy again to talk about nuclear physics and the first Manhattan Project. But how much did they know about what they were building compared to how much we know about what we are building today? I think that we are far worse with AI than with nuclear physics. And nuclear physics sounds very scary. But AI might also be scary. Not that much in terms of creating something that gets out of a lab, but creating something that's going to have a lot of implications for humans, starting with human cognition. We don't understand things well. And we are trying to play, "Okay, let's build the next generation of this system. Let's see what happens. Oh, cool. Oh, no, it's not that cool." That's the way we are today. And we have these fancy scaling laws. We just scale the number of parameters or FLOPS and get these new capabilities. Is that the only thing that we know about intelligence? That we just scale the size of the neural network and we get more capabilities? Is that all that we know about intelligence these days? If that's all we know, I think that we are at a really, really basic level of understanding to try to popularize and develop a technology for which we don't have the science.

Looking into the future, how will these developments continue? Where would you place yourself on the spectrum from dystopia to utopia?

I'm an optimist. I think there are more positive things than negative things in AI. But I put a lot of emphasis on existential risks. While I don't necessarily believe these risks are highly probable, my concern stems primarily from our inability to accurately gauge their likelihood. When faced with significant dangers whose probabilities are difficult to estimate, even if we believe they are low, it's crucial to invest more effort into understanding them. Scientists have been working in the past decades to estimate the probability that an asteroid would destroy life on Earth. We now have good estimates of how likely this is because we have seen this in the past. We know that a big one happens every 100 million years. In AI, this is something that we need to calibrate too. Particularly, we need to estimate the probability of these significant risks, which we currently can't do accurately. Because we're developing technology without a solid scientific foundation, which is concerning. Focusing on existential risks doesn't mean there's a divide between practical ethical concerns about AI today and future AI problems. These two aspects are interconnected. Paying attention to these major issues requires a better understanding of AI, which also aids ethical considerations and AI usage. In this continuum of issues, my primary concern is how AI will alter human cognition. We're not investing enough effort into understanding a potential cognitive atrophy, similar to how we've physically atrophied due to over-reliance on technology like cars. This, to me, is a major concern, perhaps even more so than some of the other issues people are discussing.

"I believe it's better for people to distrust systems rather than overtrust them."

Is there already research on this? Or is this something that is often overlooked?

More people are discussing this, especially with platforms like ChatGPT being used by millions, including children [1]. This could significantly affect not only their cognitive development and problem-solving abilities in the future, but also their motivation. If a system can do everything for you, what's the motivation to work hard, learn, and do things yourself? We've seen similar effects in the physical world and with social media. This could escalate rapidly.

Could this lead to a decline in our intelligence?

Indeed, a significant part of intelligence is innate. But if you don't use it, especially if you don't see a motivation for using it, it could atrophy. We've become so reliant on technology that we would be helpless in a natural environment. We need to use these tools to empower ourselves, even if it means some of our abilities might atrophy. However, there might be situations where this goes too far, especially if some day in the future we no longer need to work. Because of this we need to return to the Enlightenment principle of understanding the world for its own sake, not just for professional training. But this requires motivation, which could be challenging in a world where work is no longer necessary. The message needs to change, and that's a challenge.

Is there a specific area of research you would like to see addressed more from a multidisciplinary perspective?

Yes, especially the impact of AI on cognition. Psychologists and behavioral scientists are starting to incorporate AI into their research, which is beneficial. They understand cognition, particularly human cognition, and how it can affect mental health, education, and the workplace. Economists also play a crucial role. This needs to be a collective effort, as AI is the technology of the century. It's going to change everything.

What is your vision for AI?

My primary goal, as I've mentioned since the beginning of the interview, is to understand intelligence. AI is the main tool we have for this. I hope it will give us more insight into what intelligence is and the different types of intelligence that can exist. Evolution has given us some types of intelligence, but there might be others that we haven't yet discovered. It's fascinating to think about all the different kinds of intelligence we could create. Of course, we need to be careful about what we build, as we're essentially creating new beings. But from a scientific perspective, it's incredibly exciting.

As we move forward, we might encounter unknown unknowns. So, there may be an intelligence out there, now or at some point in the future, that we as humans are not capable of recognizing. Would we notice?

We will have to make some significant decisions. We will have to decide whether to preserve Homo sapiens for millions of years on Earth as a reserve or whether the species transitions into something different. There will be reactions to these changes, and there will be disagreements, geopolitical problems, and more. But we will have to navigate these challenges and see what happens. The existential risk isn't so much about these systems getting out of control, but about human disagreement on important questions about our future. Are we going to remain as we are? Are we going to create other systems? Are we going to grant them rights? These debates are already happening and will become more relevant in the years to come. Politicians aren't discussing this yet, but they will.

Is there anything else you would like to add?

No, I'm just an optimist. I believe this is one of the most exciting times for science, and I feel privileged to work in AI. However, this excitement shouldn't lead us to rush. We're close to realizing the dream that early AI pioneers had decades ago, but we need to proceed with caution and focus more on science and less on technology.

And on the societal impact, right?

Yes, of course.

Thank you very much for your time, José, and especially for your perspective on intelligence. I am excited to see what will happen in the next few years. And I look forward to the progress towards a better understanding of AI and our responsibility to consciously steer the next steps in the desired direction. Have a great day!

Thank you very much.

References

1. Bai, L., Liu, X., Su, J.: ChatGPT: the cognitive effects on learning and memory. Brain-X **1**(3), e30 (2023)
2. Burnell, R., et al.: Rethink reporting of evaluation results in AI. Science **380**(6641), 136–138 (2023)
3. Burnell, R., Hao, H., Conway, A.R.A., Hernández-Orallo, J.: Revealing the structure of language model capabilities. https://arxiv.org/abs/2306.10062
4. Desender, K., Van Opstal, F., Van den Bussche, E.: Subjective experience of difficulty depends on multiple cues. Sci. Rep. **7**, 44222 (2017)
5. Hernández-Orallo, J.: The Measure of All Minds: Evaluating Natural and Artificial Intelligence. Cambridge University Press (2017)
6. Hernández-Orallo, J.: Unbridled mental power. Nat. Phys. **15**, 106 (2019)
7. Hernández-Orallo, J., et al.: A new AI evaluation cosmos: ready to play the game? AI Mag. **38**(3), 66–69 (2017)

8. Hernández-Orallo, J.: Evaluation in artificial intelligence: from task-oriented to ability-oriented measurement. Artif. Intell. Rev. **48**(3), 397–447 (2017)
9. Hernández-Orallo, J., Dowe, D.L., Hernández-Lloreda, M.V.: Universal psychometrics: measuring cognitive abilities in the machine kingdom. Cogn. Syst. Res. **27**, 50–74 (2014)
10. Hernández-Orallo, J., Loe, B.S., Cheke, L., et al.: General intelligence disentangled via a generality metric for natural and artificial intelligence. Sci. Rep. **11**, 22822 (2021)
11. Hernández-Orallo, J., Schellaert, W., Martínez-Plumed, F.: Training on the test set: mapping the system-problem space in AI. In: Proceedings of the AAAI 2022, pp. 12256–12261. AAAI (2022)
12. Schellaert, W., et al.: Your prompt is my command: on assessing the human-centred generality of multimodal models. J. Artificial Intell. Res. **77**, 377–394 (2023)
13. Wang, X., et al.: Evaluating general-purpose AI with psychometrics. https://arxiv.org/abs/2310.16379
14. Spearman, C.: General intelligence: objectively determined and measured. Am. J. Psychol. **15**, 107–197 (1904)
15. Zhou, L., et al.: Predictable artificial intelligence. https://arxiv.org/abs/2310.06167
16. Zhang, Y., et al.: Small language models need strong verifiers to self-correct reasoning. https://arxiv.org/abs/2404.17140
17. Zhou, L., Schellaert, W., Martinez-Plumed, F., Moros-Daval, Y., Ferri, C., Hernández-Orallo, J.: Larger and more instructable language models became less reliable. Nature **634**, 61–68 (2024)
18. https://aievaluation.substack.com/

Let's Talk AI with Computer Science Expert Daniel Neider

Daniel Neider[1] and Barbara Steffen[2(✉)]

[1] TU Dortmund and Center for Trustworthy Data Science and Security, UA Ruhr, Dortmund, Germany
daniel.neider@cs.tu-dortmund.de
[2] METAFrame Technologies, Dortmund, Germany
barbara.steffen@metaframe.de

Abstract. AI will increasingly impact our future. Let's work together to make it safe and bright.

My personal AI mission: To advance the field of artificial intelligence (AI) by developing novel machine learning techniques and formal methods that ensure the correctness, security, and trustworthiness of AI systems. By doing so, I hope to contribute to a future where AI is widely adopted and benefits society without compromising safety, privacy, or ethical values.

Fig. 1. Daniel Neider

1 My Takes on AI

- **Artificial Intelligence** – AI is an umbrella term for machines – usually computer systems – that mimic human intelligence.
- **Trust** – I like the definition of [7]: Trust is the willingness of a party [the trustor] to be vulnerable to the actions of another party [the trustee].
- **Explainability** – Explainability is the challenge to empower humans to understand the decision making of AI.
- **Essential Elements of Human Capabilities** – Empathy.

B. Steffen et al. (Eds.): *Let's Talk AI*, LNCS 15000, pp. 124–129, 2026.
https://doi.org/10.1007/978-3-032-09008-9_14

2 The Interview

[Barbara Steffen] Welcome, Daniel Neider (Fig. 1). Thank you for joining me for this interview. Please introduce yourself and your relationship to artificial intelligence.

[Daniel Neider] First, I want to thank you for having me. I'm a professor at TU Dortmund and the Center for Trustworthy Data Science and Security specializing in formal guarantees of machine learning. My team focuses on making artificial intelligence safer, more reliable, and more trustworthy.

Can you name one or two AI-related research questions that you are currently working on?

We are working on formally proving practically relevant properties of neural networks, such as robustness and fairness [3–5]. Moreover, we are investigating what crucial properties neural networks must satisfy regarding safety and reliability so that they can be used safely in the real world.

What do you mean by fair?

That's an excellent question, as there exist numerous definitions of fairness [1]. We do not view it as our primary research to devise these definitions. However, once formalized, we can automatically check neural networks against them to determine whether these properties are satisfied.

Can you do this even if you don't know what the correct result is? In some cases, for example, you just want to distinguish dogs from cats, which makes it very easy for humans to evaluate the results. But in other cases, you don't know what the correct result is, which makes the evaluation process much more complicated. What do you do in cases where the correct results are not predefined?

> "My question would be: does AI have to be perfect, or is it enough if it is indistinguishable or better than humans?"

It's important to note that we're interested in thoroughly checking a vast number of inputs, not just the test or training data, but ideally all possible inputs. This is, of course, a massive undertaking. Since we cannot label – and test – an infinite number of inputs, we require a formal description of the network's desired behavior. The challenge with this approach is that machine learning bypasses the problem of creating such a formal specification in the first place: we're given data and then use machine learning to find a model that captures the patterns in the data. In the end, we hope this model will do something good, but it's unclear what that means [6]. A novel trick my team devised is using other neural networks as part of the specification. That allows us to check, for instance, whether a network we are interested in performs similarly to another network we know already performs very well. We call this approach neuro-symbolic verification [11].

That's interesting. What role does trust play in the adoption of AI?

I'm not entirely convinced that trust plays a significant role at the moment. It should, but I don't know whether it actually does. If technology is sufficiently helpful and provides enough value, people might even use it without worrying too much. I fall for this myself: if technology is convenient and valuable, I rarely question it or reflect on whether I should trust it.

The benefits are so tangible that they outweigh the doubts. Do you have any essential measures in mind to ensure the ethical use of AI?

My first question would be: how exactly do you define the ethical use of AI? That's a question arguably best answered by philosophers.

> "AI will be our future, and we have to make sure this future will be safe and bright."

Do ethics play a role in AI, and who should be involved in discussing such measures?

Yes, AI should be designed with ethics and trustworthiness in mind. Unfortunately, the current approach is that companies develop AI systems, release them, and see what happens. This is arguably not an ethical approach, and we need to change how AI technology is developed. My team can provide technical tools to this end. Still, we require societal input on precisely what these ethical considerations are to implement them.

Regarding the future technical capabilities of AI on a scale of 1 to 10, where 1 stands for artificial intelligence systems like ChatGPT and 10 for artificial general intelligence systems that surpass human capabilities. What do you think will be possible?

I don't know, but a 7 or an 8 seems likely. I am convinced we will see AI systems where the average user can't discern between humans and AI. In analogy to the Turing test [10], that might be enough. I do not see much difference between an actual AGI and an AI that convincingly acts, looks, and feels intelligent.

So the question is not so much whether we trust, but rather whether we should trust?

My question would be: does AI have to be perfect, or is it enough if it is indistinguishable or better than humans are?

> "If technology is convenient and valuable, I rarely question it or reflect on whether I should trust it."

What is your personal view of the future? Are we moving towards a dystopia or a utopia? Where would you place yourself on this scale?

I'm uncertain about the long term. It's probably right in the middle in the short to medium term. Some people will become very wealthy, and many will become much more productive and successful. But there will also be people who will lose their jobs and have to learn entirely new and different skill sets. It seems to me like a new "industrial revolution". We as a society need to consider what measures to take to alleviate the drastic transformation we will likely see in the next 10 to 15 years.

Looking at ChatGPT, do you think that users should be informed about how ChatGPT works? And how to use it correctly?

In principle, yes. But this is not specific to ChatGPT. We should require information and transparency for any sufficiently complex system that is out there and easy to use.

> "I am convinced we will see AI systems where the average user can't discern between humans and AI."

Are we doing it sufficiently? For ChatGPT? And in general?

Probably not. However, this field moves so rapidly that it would take a lot of work to keep up with all these changes. For instance, it's difficult for me to imagine how to teach this topic in schools when changes happen with a few months. Speaking of schools, how do we deal with ChatGPT when pupils can use it to do their homework? Should they do it or not? The jury is still out on that, and I'm unsure what to recommend. However, I am optimistic and lean toward embracing the opportunities, provided that there is close supervision by the teachers.

Reflecting on the last few days and the various interdisciplinary presentations. Do you remember an insight that was particularly interesting to you?

I enjoyed the legal or regulatory perspective on artificial intelligence – not for any specific reasons other than to satisfy my curiosity. I'm convinced this is where AI advancement in Europe will flourish or fail, depending on whether we are smart in regulating this technology. Hence, I found the presentations on this perspective on AI fascinating.

Do you have a research question or a topic in mind where you would like to see more interdisciplinary collaboration in the future?

I would like to incorporate more ethical considerations into my team's research. I have some ideas of how to do that, and collaborations with people from ethics and machine learning would be very helpful. For instance, colleagues of mine have shown how to ensure that generative AI creates images with a controllable degree of nudity or violence [9], which I find fascinating!

Do you already have a specific research question in mind, or would you like to develop it with ethics experts to see where further collaboration would be beneficial?

Let me give you an example. At the moment, I collaborate with colleagues from TU Darmstadt on reinforcement learning to align autonomous agents better with human ethical values. It's too early for results, but I am excited about this research direction. Unfortunately, a huge obstacle is the lack of a solid understanding or notion of the desired behavior of AI systems, as we have already discussed earlier.

From your personal perspective, what should be the AI vision?

Let me tell you what my personal vision is: that AI will become as reliable as current hardware and software systems. A burgeoning research community, including my group, has evolved around this topic, and we have already made great strides toward this goal [8]. AI will be our future, and we have to make sure this future will be safe and bright.

Is there anything else you would like to add?

No.

Thank you very much, Daniel, for your time and insights. Have a great day!

Thank you for this engaging interview.

Thank you.

References

1. Barocas, S., Hardt, M., Narayanan, A.: Fairness and Machine Learning: Limitations and Opportunities. MIT Press (2023)
2. Böing, B., Roy, R., Müller, E., Neider, D.: Quality guarantees for autoencoders via unsupervised adversarial attacks. In: Hutter, F., et al. (eds.) ECML PKDD 2020. LNCS, vol. 12458, pp. 206–222. Springer, Cham (2020)
3. Bollig, B., Leucker, M., Neider, D.: A survey of model learning techniques for recurrent neural networks. In: Jansen, N., et al. (eds.) A Journey from Process Algebra via Timed Automata to Model Learning. LNCS, vol. 13560, pp. 81–97. Springer (2022). https://doi.org/10.1007/978-3-030-67661-2_13
4. Khmelnitsky, I., et al.: Analysis of recurrent neural networks via property-directed verification of surrogate models. Int. J. Software Tools Technol. Transf. **25**, 341–354 (2022)
5. Khmelnitsky, I., et al.: Property-directed verification and robustness certification of recurrent neural networks. In: Hou, Z., Ganesh, V. (eds.) ATVA 2021. LNCS, vol. 12971, pp. 364–380. Springer, Cham (2021). https://doi.org/10.1007/978-3-030-88885-5_24
6. Leucker, M.: Formal verification of neural networks? In: Carvalho, G., Stolz, V. (eds.) SBMF 2020. LNCS, vol. 12475, pp. 3–7. Springer, Cham (2020). https://doi.org/10.1007/978-3-030-63882-5_1
7. Mayer, R.C., Davis, J.H., Schoorman, F.D.: An integrative model of organizational trust. Acad. Manag. Rev. **20**, 709–734 (1995)
8. Neider, D., Johnson, T.T.: Track C1: safety verification of deep neural networks (DNNs). In: Steffen, B. (ed.) AISoLA 2023. LNCS, vol. 14380, pp. 217–224. Springer, Cham (2024). https://doi.org/10.1007/978-3-031-46002-9_12
9. Schramowski, P., Brack, M., Deiseroth, B., Kersting, K.: Safe latent diffusion: mitigating inappropriate degeneration in diffusion models. In: Proceedings of the IEEE/CVF Conf. on Computer Vision and Pattern Recognition (CVPR 2023), pp. 22522–22531. IEEE (2023)
10. Turing, A.M.: Computing machinery and intelligence. Mind LIX (236), pp. 433–460 (1950)
11. Xie, X., Kersting, K., Neider, D.: Neuro-symbolic verification of deep neural networks. In: 31st Intl. Joint Conf. on Artificial Intelligence (IJCAI 2022), pp. 3622–3628. Springer, Cham (2022)

Let's Talk AI with Computer Science Expert Taylor T. Johnson

Taylor T. Johnson[1] and Barbara Steffen[2(✉)]

[1] Vanderbilt University, Nashville, USA
taylor.johnson@vanderbilt.edu
[2] METAFrame Technologies, Dortmund, Germany
barbara.steffen@metaframe.de

Abstract. Formal verification aims to prove whether models satisfy specifications, such as showing a program does what its designer intended. Formal verification is a promising approach that can be used to establish safety, security, and trustworthiness specifications of AI systems. However, to realize the potential societal benefits AI promise, we also need transdisciplinary approaches bridging the gamut from computer science and engineering, the broader sciences, as well as the arts, humanities, social sciences, law, business, and beyond to ensure its development involves all perspectives and voices.

My personal AI mission: To develop formal verification methods to help establish and assure the safe, secure, and trustworthy development and use of AI, especially in the context of safety-critical systems such as autonomous cyber-physical systems (CPS).

Fig. 1. Taylor T. Johnson

1 My Takes on AI

- **Artificial Intelligence** – I will use the Oxford dictionary definition [1]: "the theory and development of computer systems able to perform tasks that normally require human intelligence, such as visual perception, speech recognition, decision-making, and translation between languages." An AI system is a computer system that performs such tasks.

B. Steffen et al. (Eds.): *Let's Talk AI*, LNCS 15000, pp. 130–137, 2026.
https://doi.org/10.1007/978-3-032-09008-9_15

- **Trust** – Similarly using an Oxford dictionary definition [2], trust is a "firm belief in the reliability, truth, ability, or strength of someone or something." In the context of AI systems, my view is that it is our ability as users to rely on their results. More specifically to my own research area of verification, it is our ability as designers of AI systems to trust that the AI systems will do what we intend them to do, that is, for them to meet their requirements and specifications.
- **Explainability** – Explainability is complex, as even humans may offer different explanations or reasoning for a decision or outcome than what its true root factors were. Sometimes we may do things without understanding why (or instinctually or with implicit bias), and similarly we may hypothesize why others do things without truly understanding why, and as such, explainability is incredibly difficult. As I am not a psychologist or someone with such expertise, I would define it in the context as a designer of AI systems as our ability to understand what the AI systems are doing based on interrogation and analysis of the systems, predicated on being able to access such systems details, documentation, data, etc.
- **Essential Elements of Human Capabilities** – My view is that AI systems are capable even without replicating human performance on some particular task. However, I would view the essential elements of human capabilities for AI systems to be a true ability for reasoning and generalization across tasks and to new scenarios, not simply meeting or surpassing human performance on some task or a set of tasks. This perhaps would mean artificial general intelligence (AGI) in some form, but I think we are nowhere near such capabilities, as current AI systems do not have understanding of much of anything in the way I believe humans understand, although of course for particular tasks there are impressive recent results with AI. One problematic aspect I find in many recent discussions on AI is that we are tending to anthropomorphize AI, when it is not mimicking human understanding or capability in its current or near-term forms in my view.

2 The Interview

[Barbara Steffen] I have the pleasure of speaking today with Taylor Johnson (Fig. 1) of Vanderbilt University in Nashville. Without any further introductions, I directly hand over to you, Taylor. Could you briefly introduce yourself and your relationship to artificial intelligence?

[Taylor T. Johnson] Certainly. I'm an associate professor of computer science at Vanderbilt University in Nashville, Tennessee, USA. My research broadly focuses on formal methods and verification, originally for cyber-physical systems. These are modern embedded systems like the computing elements in cars, airplanes, or medical devices. Over the last six or seven years, we've been examining formal verification of machine learning and artificial intelligence systems, specifically components like neural networks [3]. We are particularly interested in how these elements might feature in cyber-physical systems [4]. We explore whether they enable things like autonomous systems in our current reality, such as in self-driving cars and similar systems.

> "One of the significant challenges in AI is that we, as system designers, don't fully understand how the systems we're building operate."

Interesting, do you have examples of specific challenges you are currently addressing with your AI research?

Absolutely. As we've seen with recent examples, AI systems don't always operate as intended [5]. We focus on developing new methods, particularly algorithms and software tools, to establish their correctness [6–15]. This is essentially an application of the general formal verification problem in the context of AI systems. We have a model, say a neural network, and a specification of what it should do, and we try to confirm that it does just that. There are numerous challenges in this area, some theoretical, but many practical, like how to define what an AI system should do.

In this context, how do you view the role of trust in the adoption of AI, and what measures can you imagine to ensure the ethical use of AI in the future?

There are many challenges we hope to overcome, particularly in establishing trust. My concept of trust is more related to system designers and engineers. Can these professionals trust the AI systems they're building? The field of verification focuses on assuring the designers that what they're building is correct in some sense. Do the neural networks perform as intended? This is about convincing the designers, less so the end-users. However, if you use a system, say a car, you trust it to operate reliably and not fail mechanically or software-wise. As users, we put our trust in the designers, who are qualified experts, sometimes even licensed, like myself, a professional engineer. We trust these processes for certain systems, like buildings, which we expect not to collapse. Many elements ensure this trust. An analogy often used is Swiss cheese, where we have certification and licensure for the people involved, and they use varying methodologies to establish trust. Ultimately, we have to trust others. One of the significant challenges in AI is that we, as system designers, don't fully understand how the systems we're building operate. There are theoretical gaps on the designer and researcher side. It's complex, but these elements are pieces of the puzzle, filling in the Swiss cheese holes. Other important aspects that I don't personally work on include regulatory and policy matters. Like in our building analogy, in addition to licensing architects and structural engineers, we also have standards and building codes that help establish criteria for proper construction.

And in terms of the future capabilities of artificial intelligence, perhaps on a scale of 1 to 10, where 1 refers to artificial intelligence systems dedicated to specific functionalities and purposes, such as ChatGPT. And 10 refers to general artificial intelligence that surpasses human capabilities. Where do you see it going from here, especially in terms of the risks you just mentioned of not knowing exactly what's going on?

Predicting the future is always challenging. Perhaps I can frame my answer in terms of time frames. Currently, I believe we're at the lower end of that 1 to 10 scale. AI is very proficient at certain specific problems and tasks, so we're probably at a 1 to 3. Over the next decade, I anticipate we might move up to a 5. Beyond that, it's hard to predict. Some of the current systems, like generative AI models and large language models, are transformative technologies with potential impacts similar to the Internet, cell phones, or personal computers. However, they're engineered systems. I find it hard to predict if artificial general intelligence (AGI) will become a reality. I'm not sure if we'll ever reach the 10 on the scale in my lifetime, to align with the theme of this AISoLA conference.

"I believe one of the significant potentials of AI [...] is its ability to impact almost all aspects of life."

What are the criteria that need to be met to achieve AGI? How would you measure it?

Many researchers have considered ways to evaluate whether computers are thinking or their overall capability, which have garnered broader cultural popularity like the imitation game or Turing test. More recently, various large language models (LLMs) have performed well on a variety of tasks and exams that have made headlines in areas we often deem as requiring some level of intelligence, such as test taking. Recently, I attended some research talks that presented interesting ways researchers have defined understanding, for instance in reading comprehension and resulting actions performed. For example, if a robot is given instruction in natural language to pick up an apple, then it does so, it has "understood." There were many instances of course of LLMs clearly not understanding with a variety of criticism around hallucinations and adversarial prompting, as they are simply generating probable outputs given inputs [16]. My view is current AI systems do not understand in any of the ways humans do. While I am not a neuroscientist nor psychologist, my view is that we are simply anthropomorphizing these engineered systems to try to impart them with capabilities. I do not know all the details, but I do know of some experiments in animal and comparative psychology attempting to understand whether animals even know they exist and evaluate their intelligence, and likely we could debate whether a dog is intelligent or not, or whether a particular dog is more intelligent than another, or whether a particular animal species is more intelligent than another. Perhaps insights from these fields would be directions to consider for how to define AGI or measure progress toward it, as I do think the recent results in things like exam evaluations and other attempts to compare to human or "superhuman" performance – while impressive – are not the way forward. I think anything that will be done for establishing AGI will require interfacing with the real world, in part given the action example, but also for what I view as another essential capability of true intelligence, which is self-preservation (at and beyond both the individual and population/societal levels). These alone are not examples in my opinion for demonstrating intelligence and something more is needed, as AI systems currently do not have any true notion of understanding.

And regarding the much-discussed possible future scenarios of artificial intelligence, where do you personally stand on the scale between a more utopian or dystopian view of the future?

When it comes to future capabilities, while I enjoy dystopian science fiction movies, I believe there are many other societal issues more likely to bring about dystopian scenarios than AI. Transformative technologies over the last century, like the Internet, cell phones, computers, automobiles, and airplanes, have caused problems, but they've also led to improvements. For instance, climate change is an issue related to industrialization and transportation. I view current AI use cases, especially large language models, as tools, much like cell phones, computers, the Internet, automobiles, and airplanes. They have a lot of transformative potential and can lead to efficiency improvements. For example, travel times have drastically reduced due to advancements in transportation. However, these technologies also have the potential to cause problems. I don't foresee a dystopian future, nor a utopian one. That's a broader discussion for socioeconomic considerations and the future of work. I believe AI may enable efficiency, improve our lives, and create new forms of entertainment and art. I don't see killer robots happening. While recent advances in AI, particularly generative models and LLMs, have interesting capabilities, I don't see them leading to a dystopian scenario.

We have other risks to pay attention to, like the societal issues caused by smartphones and social media. Climate change, resulting from transportation developments, is a bigger concern. I'm optimistic about AI's potential to improve things, but I don't think it'll lead to a utopia where no one needs to work. We derive purpose from our activities, but AI could potentially allow us to work less, which could improve our daily lives. So, I'd say the future lies somewhere between utopia and dystopia, but not fully either.

> "I don't want to be overly negative about AI. I believe it's a transformative technology, but we have many issues that we need to address before we put it into broad usage."

Very interesting and very detailed description of the nuances you see in the further development. We are currently meeting at the AISoLA conference, which looks at artificial intelligence from an international and interdisciplinary perspective. When you reflect on the last few days, are there specific insights from other disciplines that were particularly interesting to you?

Yes, I believe one of the significant potentials of AI, when compared to the industrial revolution or even developments like the airplane or the automobile, is its ability to impact almost all aspects of life. This is partly due to our ability to communicate globally very quickly now, thanks to the Internet and other telecommunication advances. While these advancements are generally positive, unlike transportation improvements, AI has the potential to directly affect people's lives. One of the key discussions we've had here, which I think is crucial, is the need for interdisciplinary approaches to address this. It's not just about solving engineering problems. We need involvement from people across disciplines, including humanities, social sciences, law, medicine, as well as computer science and engineering, to make these advancements.

I don't foresee a dystopian scenario happening due to killer robots. However, I do see potential political issues emerging, as AI could lead to consolidation of power amongst companies, governments, or even individuals. This is one of the risks that necessitates an interdisciplinary approach in terms of developing regulatory frameworks, policies, and standards for the engineering and computer science design of these systems. There are unintended use cases and problems that we hadn't considered before some of the recent advancements. This ties into intellectual property law, copyright, and a host of other interesting issues. We need philosophers, artists, historians, writers, computer scientists, and engineers to collaborate and step out of their bubbles, which is one of the great aspects of this AISoLA conference.

For example, in education, AI is being used to generate stories for children to read. This is fascinating, but also potentially problematic if the children learn something strange due to some bias that was either intentional or unintentional in the system. These are some of the significant issues that have arisen in systems like bias in facial recognition systems, as seen in projects like Gender Shades [17]. This has led to issues in policing, credit scoring, loan approvals, and more [5].

AI has the potential to impact all of society, which is different from many other engineered systems we've had. Therefore, it truly requires an interdisciplinary, transdisciplinary, multidisciplinary approach, and we need to step out of our bubbles and engage with others to address these issues. There are many emerging approaches beyond the type of work we have been pursuing at these intersections, such as appropriate systems engineering through documentation and traceability with techniques like model cards and data sheets, as well as auditing and monitoring AI systems [18–21].

"As a broad vision, I believe in developing [...] interdisciplinary fields."

And now to summarize your wish for the future. From your personal perspective, what is the AI vision that we should address?

That's a challenging question. As a broad vision, I believe in developing these interdisciplinary fields. As a researcher and scientist, I think that's crucial. Some of this can be achieved through our typical research, but I also think a vision of breaking out of the research community's bubbles would help address some of the potential emerging risks we can see. I don't want to be overly negative about AI. I believe it's a transformative technology, but we have many issues that we need to address before we put it into broad usage. This has shown up in other scenarios, like autonomous vehicles, where some companies recently had their testing permits revoked due to safety concerns. These are great technologies, and I would love to have self-driving cars, but we're not there yet. We need to exercise caution while recognizing that these systems have the potential to significantly change and improve people's lives. In my own research, we have our specific topics, but as a field, I think the vision I would advocate for is to continue developing these interdisciplinary approaches across all fields.

"My view is current AI systems do not understand in any of the ways humans do. [We] are simply anthropomorphizing these engineered systems [...]."

Is there anything else you would like to add?

No, I think we've covered quite a bit.

Perfect, then thank you, Taylor, for your insights and your time. Have a great day!

You're welcome, Barbara. Thank you.

References

1. Knowles, E.M. (ed.): The Oxford Dictionary of Phrase and Fable, 2nd ed. Oxford University Press (2005)

2. Stevenson, A., Lindberg, C.A. (eds.): New Oxford American Dictionary, 3rd ed. Oxford University Press (2010)
3. Brix, C., Müller, M.N., Bak, S., Johnson, T.T., Liu, C.: First three years of the International Verification of Neural Networks Competition (VNN-COMP). Int. J. Software Tools Technology Transfer **25**(3), 329–339 (2023)
4. Lopez, D.M., et al.: ARCH-COMP22 category report: artificial intelligence and neural network control systems (AINNCS) for continuous and hybrid systems plants. In: Frehse, G., Althoff, M., Schoitsch, E., Guiochet, J. (eds.) Proceedings of the 9th International Workshop on Applied Verification of Continuous and Hybrid Systems (ARCH 2022), EPiC Series in Computing, vol. 90, pp. 142–184. EasyChair (2022)
5. Raji, I.D., Kumar, I.E., Horowitz, A., Selbst, A.: The fallacy of AI functionality. In: Proceedings of the 2022 ACM Conf. on Fairness, Accountability, and Transparency (FAccT 2022), pp. 959–972. ACM (2022)
6. Xiang, W., Tran, H.-D., Johnson, T.T.: Output reachable set estimation and verification for multilayer neural networks. IEEE Trans. Neural Networks Learn. Syst. **29**(11), 5777–5783 (2018)
7. Tran, H.-D., et al.: Star-based reachability analysis of deep neural networks. In: ter Beek, M.H., McIver, A., Oliveira, J.N. (eds.) Formal Methods: The Next 30 Years. LNCS, vol. 11800, pp. 670–686. Springer, Cham (2019). https://doi.org/10.1007/978-3-030-30942-8_39
8. Tran, H.-D., Cai, F., Diego, M.L., Musau, P., Johnson, T.T., Koutsoukos, X.: Safety verification of cyber-physical systems with reinforcement learning control. ACM Trans. Embed. Comput. Syst. **18**(5) (2019)
9. Tran, H.-D., Bak, S., Xiang, W., Johnson, T.T.: Verification of deep convolutional neural networks using ImageStars. In: Lahiri, S.K., Wang, C. (eds.) Computer Aided Verification (CAV 2020). LNCS, vol. 12224, pp. 18–42. Springer, Cham (2020). https://doi.org/10.1007/978-3-030-53288-8_2
10. Tran, H.-D., et al.: NNV: the neural network verification tool for deep neural networks and learning-enabled cyber-physical systems. In: Lahiri, S.K., Wang, C. (eds.) Computer Aided Verification (CAV 2020). LNCS, vol. 12224, pp. 3–17. Springer, Cham (2020). https://doi.org/10.1007/978-3-030-53288-8_1
11. Bak, S., Tran, H.-D., Hobbs, K., Johnson, T.T.: In: Improved geometric path enumeration for verifying ReLU neural networks. In: Lahiri, S.K., Wang, C. (eds.) Computer Aided Verification (CAV 2020). LNCS, vol. 12224, pp. 66–96. Springer, Cham (2020). https://doi.org/10.1007/978-3-030-53288-8_4
12. Tran, H.-D., et al.: Robustness verification of semantic segmentation neural networks using relaxed reachability. In: Silva, A., Leino, K.R.M. (eds.) Computer Aided Verification (CAV 2021). LNCS, vol. 12759, pp. 263–286. Springer (2021). https://doi.org/10.1007/978-3-030-81685-8_12
13. Yang, X., Johnson, T.T., Tran, H.-D., Yamaguchi, T., Hoxha, B., Prokhorov, D.: Reachability analysis of deep ReLU neural networks using facet-vertex incidence. In: Proceedings of the 24th International Conference on Hybrid Systems: Computation and Control (HSCC 2021). ACM (2021)
14. Yang, X., Yamaguchi, T., Tran, H.-D., Hoxha, B., Johnson, T.T., Prokhorov, D.: Neural network repair with reachability analysis. In: Bogomolov, S., Parker, D. (eds.) FORMATS 2022. LNCS, vol. 13465, pp. 221–236. Springer (2022). https://doi.org/10.1007/978-3-031-15839-1_13
15. Lopez, D.M., Choi, S.W., Tran, H.-D., Johnson, T.T.: NNV 2.0: the neural network verification tool. In: Enea, C., Lal, A. (eds.) Computer Aided Verification (CAV 2023). LNCS, vol. 13965, pp. 397–412. Springer, Cham (2023). https://doi.org/10.1007/978-3-031-37703-7_19

16. Bender, E.M., Gebru, T., McMillan-Major, A., Shmitchell, S.: On the dangers of stochastic parrots: can language models be too big? In: Proc. 2021 ACM Conf. on Fairness, Accountability, and Transparency (FAccT 2021), pp. 610–623. ACM (2021)
17. Buolamwini, J., Gebru, T.: Gender shades: intersectional accuracy disparities in commercial gender classification. In: Proc. 1st Conf. on Fairness, Accountability and Transparency (FAT 2018) (2018). In: Friedler, S.A., Wilson, C. (eds.). Proc. of Machine Learning Research, vol. 81, pp. 77–79
18. Mitchell, M., et al.: Model cards for model reporting. In: Proceedings of the Conference on Fairness, Accountability, and Transparency (FAT* 2019), pp. 220–229. ACM (2019)
19. Raji, I.D., et al.: Closing the AI accountability gap: defining an end-to-end framework for internal algorithmic auditing. In: Proceedings of the 2020 Conference on Fairness, Accountability, and Transparency (FAT* 2020), pp. 33–44. ACM (2020)
20. Gebru, T., et al.: Datasheets for datasets. Commun. ACM **64**(12), pp. 86–92. ACM (2021)
21. Costanza-Chock, S., Raji, I.D., Buolamwini, J.: Who audits the auditors? Recommendations from a field scan of the algorithmic auditing ecosystem. In: Proceedings of the 2022 ACM Conference on Fairness, Accountability, and Transparency (FAccT 2022), pp. 1571–1583. ACM (2022)

Let's Talk AI with AI Expert Matthias Fey

Matthias Fey[1] and Barbara Steffen[2](✉)

[1] Kumo.AI, Dortmund, Germany
matthias.fey@tu-dortmund.de
[2] METAFrame Technologies, Dortmund, Germany
barbara.steffen@metaframe.de

Abstract. Scale is hopefully not all you need.

My personal AI mission: Productionizing Graph Neural Networks – a set of models with strong inductive bias that require less data and are easier to interpret.

Fig. 1. Matthias Fey

1 My Takes on AI

- **Artificial Intelligence** – A marketing term for machine learning :)
- **Trust** – Fair and robust model outputs.
- **Explainability** – Insights into the signals the machine learning model is picking up.
- **Essential Elements of Human Capabilities** – Social and emotional intelligence.

2 The Interview

[Barbara Steffen] Today I have the pleasure of interviewing Matthias Fey (Fig. 1). Please introduce yourself and your relationship to artificial intelligence.

[Matthias Fey] I completed my PhD in graph representation learning [3]. This involves developing neural networks that receive graphs as input rather than images or sequences. This approach allows us to view neural networks as a much broader architecture. Currently, I'm using this knowledge in a startup called Kumo AI, which aims to bring these ideas to the industry.

B. Steffen et al. (Eds.): *Let's Talk AI*, LNCS 15000, pp. 138–143, 2026.
https://doi.org/10.1007/978-3-032-09008-9_16

What is your current focus? Are you focusing more on the research side or more on productionizing your technology?

My work is quite diverse. Since this topic is still new and everyone is still researching it, I also do that as part of my daily work. However, there's also a lot of work in engineering and figuring out how to make things more efficient. I'd say it's a 50/50 split between research and engineering.

Could you describe some of your current work in one or two AI-related research questions?

One question, for example, is how we can scale graph neural networks to an industry-sized graph, which could mean like 10 million or 100 million nodes and billions of edges. There are also questions about explainability: how can we allow the user to gain insights from the model and build trust in the model to bring it to production. And then there are research questions on how we can train these models on all kinds of different tasks in a general way.

What role does trust play in AI adoption?

Personally, during my PhD, this wasn't a big focus for me because we were researching novel methods and models with better performance and new insights. However, during my time as a machine learning engineer in industry, I noticed customers asking for it, and I realized it's a valuable thing to have.

And what about your personal trust in large language models as a developer or researcher in the field?

I have to admit I'm biased. I train these models, I know how they work and how they are able to learn. As such, I am confident about them and generally which hints I need to give the models in order to trust them to learn the right things. But I understand that people see them as a kind of black box and that we need verification that they're doing the right thing. And I agree with that. We are adding a lot of explainability on top in our product in order to build this general trust.

Do you see any essential measures for the ethical use of AI?

I don't have any concrete metrics in mind. I think we always need to ensure that there's no unfairness involved, and what that means depends on the business case. I believe we can achieve a lot of that through publishing and making things open-source, and allowing them to be confirmed by the community.

On a scale of 1 to 10, what do you think is possible in terms of the future technical capabilities of artificial intelligence? Where 1 describes artificial intelligence systems like ChatGPT, and 10 describes artificial general intelligence that surpasses human capabilities.

I'm not yet a believer in general artificial intelligence, so I think it's somewhere in between. I believe what we need to do is combine all these models into a larger learning system. This aligns well with my research, where you have all these kinds of agents or models, and you need to route information between them and let them learn from each other.

Can you give a specific number on the scale from 1 to 10?

I would say it's more of a 6 or a 7.

And how does that make you feel? Looking into the future and thinking about all the possibilities from dystopia to utopia, what do you think awaits us?

I'm not a pessimist, so I would say it's generally a good thing. AI will certainly change a lot of things, but that's not necessarily bad. For example, there are many jobs that I believe are not necessarily enjoyable, and letting AI assist and help here is definitely a welcome change. However, we also need to enforce stricter regulations on which models we're allowed to use and which we should disallow. I think the line should be drawn where we let AI make life-changing decisions for humans.

Taking a step back, what do we actually mean by artificial intelligence today?

That's a really good question, and I think there's no consensus among communities on that. At this point, artificial intelligence is more of a buzzword or a hype term that you use when you want to attract a lot of attention. Personally, I would prefer to simply call it machine learning, where we learn an underlying data distribution and the model adapts to that data distribution. Intelligence would be more something where the model encounters a completely new situation and then tries to adapt to that situation. I think we're very far from that, but we're already claiming that we have artificial intelligence and all these systems already. And then there's this term of AGI, which is even more confusing.

> "I have to admit I'm biased. I train these models, I know how they work and how they are able to learn. As such, I am confident about them and generally trust them to learn the right things."

So when we talk about artificial intelligence and establishing a common understanding of when artificial intelligence is achieved, we first need to establish a common definition of intelligence, right?

Yes. Currently, there are over 100 definitions of intelligence, and we can't even agree what intelligence actually means for a human being. So it gets even more confusing when you think about artificial intelligence.

Coming back to machine learning. What are the cutting edge approaches today?

Everyone is talking about Large Language Models (LLMs) [4], and I understand the hype. I see many of my previous researchers moving to that field. LLMs are trained on a massive amount of data, and there's this claim that compute is all you need [5], which I find kind of boring from a research perspective. These models are then trained to take in a list of sentences or tokens and produce the next word or token that the LLM should output. I come from the perspective of graph neural networks (GNNs), where you have graphs as input rather than sequences. This makes it more exciting for me because you have all this sparsity and all these different kinds of graphs. They don't follow a regular grid layout, which is common in most previous deep learning approaches. The question is how can we efficiently process this graph to make predictions for a certain set of entities. This is a completely different view of neural networks. It also requires less data and less compute, which I strongly favor [1].

> "Personally, I would prefer to simply call it machine learning, where we learn an underlying data distribution and the model adapts to that data distribution."

And today, LLMs and GNNs get applied to similar challenges?

I would say they're used for completely different challenges. If you use something like GPT-3, it gives very precise answers from text it has already observed during training. But it can't really predict future scenarios. So if you ask GPT-3 who will be the next president in the United States, it will just say that it cannot predict that. But if you're thinking from a predictive AI or predictive machine learning standpoint, then you could use all the information you have in your database or the knowledge you've collected to make some kind of prediction for the future. That's the approach we take with GNNs.

> "Intelligence would be more something where the model encounters a completely new situation and then tries to adapt to that situation. I think we're very far from that [...]."

Could you elaborate on this? Is there an example that is also understandable for non-experts?

Yes. One example would be that you're a food delivery service and you want to make recommendations for a certain set of users about which restaurants they should try. If a new restaurant comes up and quickly gains popularity, an LLM couldn't give you the information to go to that restaurant. But a GNN could because it knows about all the recent facts and popularity measures and could make a prediction from the most recent data right away. This is where retrieval augmented generation comes in to strengthen's the LLM's predictive capabilities [2].

And how do the GNNs know that?

They don't necessarily know. The learn pattern from the past that are part of the input data.

Where do you normally get the input data from?

It's your own database, for example. And whenever that database is refreshed, you would have immediate access to that information and can drive the prediction based on that. An LLM can't necessarily do that.

Do the models of the neural networks remain fixed, so that only the outputs change given the new inputs, or does the updating of the database also affect the model itself?

What you see is that the model without retraining is quite stable over a period of time, but it's generally always recommended to retrain it every month or so. This is based on measurements you make on how well your model performs over time. But generally, it stays quite stable.

And how do you measure or evaluate the model's performance?

You would measure it in production in an A/B test. You would make predictions and then after a certain amount of time, you would re-evaluate how your model has performed. If you see a decrease in performance over time, then it's a good idea to retrain the model and refresh it with all the updated knowledge.

So, you basically have a continuous way to evaluate the performance of the model because each output is a prediction that can be compared to what happened.

It's a difficult problem in general, but overall, that's correct. The main problem is that your predictions may have implications about what your future graph may look like, and that may conflict with the way the model is making predictions in the first place.

Can you go back to earlier versions of the model? For example, if new predictions have led you in the wrong direction, could you go back to an earlier version that was a better fit? Would that make sense?

In general, retraining should always improve the model, but the conflict I was talking about is that you're using the neural network to make a prediction for the future, and based on that prediction, you take certain actions. For example, you would send a user a coupon or a notification to go to a restaurant, and that also changes the way the graph is evolving because otherwise, you wouldn't have sent the notification in the first place. And the model basically just knows about what the graph would look like without that notification.

> "It will be a requirement for everyone to live with AI in the future and to understand these technologies. We will have to adapt to make that possible."

Okay, interesting. Are there any specific tests or metrics to compare LLMs and GNNs? For example, are there metrics regarding the amount of data or computing power required, or tests to compare the quality of the output?

I think the most promising research direction people are currently studying is how to combine these two models. So you could have an LLM and you can enhance it with information coming from a knowledge graph, for example, or you can have your graph that has rich text descriptions and you want to embed these text descriptions using an LLM. This combination of these two models is super interesting but faces major scalability issues, and that's why we haven't seen much progress yet.

Do you have generic neural networks, or are they domain-specific, for example, for different groups of customers?

The general idea is that we have one model trained on a certain task, but the model architecture is essentially fixed, and we want this model to be able to generalize to any kind of task.

Could you give an example?

The basic idea in our case is that a customer has a single database and wants to query that database to receive information. So, we would have one model that learns from this graph and then have all these smaller models on top where you can make quick decisions in a few shots.

Now from your personal perspective, what should be the AI vision for the future?

To be honest, I haven't given it much thought. There are some wild ideas out there about people wanting us to be replaced by robots that can explore the universe for us. But I believe AI should be a tool that assists us, not something that replaces us. If we can build tools that help us do our daily jobs better, that would be my vision for AI.

Okay, but what if one person using AI applications becomes as efficient and productive as maybe ten people without AI support? I mean, we already saw it with ChatGPT, right? Today, you can write and generate text much faster than if you wrote it fully by yourself. So, when you integrate AI tools into certain tasks, people become more productive, which means that companies need fewer people to do the same amount of work.

Yes, I think it will be a requirement for everyone to live with AI in the future and to understand these technologies. We will have to adapt to make that possible. Of course, there will be changes in that regard, but it's not like robots will destroy us at some point. I don't believe in that.

Thank you, Matthias, for your time and insights, especially for adding the perspective of going from AI research to AI product. Have a great day!

References

1. Fey, M.: On the power of message passing for learning on graph-structured data. Ph.D. Thesis. TU Dortmund (2022)
2. Gao, Y., et al.: Retrieval-augmented generation for large language models: a survey https://arxiv.org/abs/2312.10997
3. Hamilton, W.L.: Graph Representation Learning. Springer (2020). https://doi.org/10.1007/978-3-031-01588-5
4. Minaee, S., et al.: Large language models: a survey. https://arxiv.org/abs/2402.06196
5. Smith, S.L., et al.: ConvNets match vision transformers at scale. In: Proceedings of the CVPR 2023. IEEE (2023)

Let's Talk AI with Logician and Computer Science Expert Moshe Y. Vardi

Moshe Y. Vardi[1] and Barbara Steffen[2(✉)]

[1] Rice University, Houston, USA
vardi@rice.edu
[2] METAFrame Technologies, Dortmund, Germany
barbara.steffen@metaframe.de

Abstract. My left brain is doing research in AI. My right brain is in a panic: What is going to happen? What will be the impact on society?

My personal AI mission: AI for the public good.

Fig. 1. Moshe Y. Vardi

1 My Takes on AI

- **Artificial Intelligence** – The effort to simulate human intelligence by machines.
- **Trust** – Reliance in risk-accepting situations.
- **Explainability** – I do not need explanations. I need justifications.
- **Essential Elements of Human Capabilities** – Humans are intrinsically sacred.

2 The Interview

[Barbara Steffen] Today I have the pleasure of interviewing Moshe Vardi (Fig. 1). Please introduce yourself and your relationship to AI.

[Moshe Vardi] I'm a professor of computer science at Rice University, where I've been for about 30 years. I find myself in a bit of a dilemma these days. My left brain is engaged

B. Steffen et al. (Eds.): *Let's Talk AI*, LNCS 15000, pp. 144–154, 2026.
https://doi.org/10.1007/978-3-032-09008-9_17

in research in computer science, algorithms, and computational logic [1]. My right brain, on the other hand, constantly questions the left brain: "What are you doing?" [8]. This is a fitting description of my current state. So how does this relate to artificial intelligence? Well, I've been intensely interested in AI since 2011. A significant milestone in AI at that time was IBM Watson, a question-answering system. Watson competed in a TV game called Jeopardy, where players had to be knowledgeable about popular culture and history. Watson won decisively against two champion players, which was a big deal [10]. If you look at AI milestones, there was another significant one in the late '90s when IBM's Deep Blue beat Kasparov at chess [9]. This was a remarkable achievement that had been expected for many years. Watson was a surprise. After Watson's victory, I began to think that the realm of AI might be closer than we think. I started pondering the potential consequences, and the more I thought about it, the more concerned I became. So, over the past decade, I've been somewhat of a Cassandra, warning about the potential negative effects of technology on society [5].

In your research on artificial intelligence, what specific challenges are you currently tackling?

In my technical research [4], I'm trying to bridge what people often refer to as System 1 and System 2 [3]. In a sense, our head houses two different brains. The back part, sometimes called the lizard brain, is something we share with almost all animals. It is responsible for recognizing danger, seeking food, and other basic survival instincts. But in the forebrain, we have developed the capacity for language and abstract reasoning, often referred to as slow thinking, as opposed to the fast thinking of the lizard brain. This is System 1 and System 2, in the terminology of the recently departed Daniel Kahneman. The big question for me is how to integrate these two systems in AI. Much of the progress in machine learning over the last decade has been in System 1. But we humans seamlessly transition between the two systems. We do not consciously think about switching from System 1 to System 2. For example, while driving, we recognize a stop sign (System 1), and then we decide to stop because that's the rule (System 2). The challenge for AI today is to integrate these two systems. This is partly where my research is focused today. Some people refer to it as neural-symbolic reasoning. Neural refers to neural nets that are the leading technology for machine learning, and symbolic refers to how we think of language and logic.

Would you like AI to operate like humans? Or would you prefer AI to operate more at the System 2 level? I keep hearing that humans too often operate at the System 1 level, especially in situations where they would be better off operating at the System 2 level. Now, with AI, we may have the opportunity to nudge towards the preferred system for different contexts.

We all know that there are instances when we should have relied more on our rational thinking than our instinctive thinking. Nevertheless, when it comes to technology, we often draw inspiration from nature. Consider flying, as an example. Birds have wings and they flap them to fly. Early human attempts at flight tried to mimic this, but we eventually discovered that fixed wings and an engine were a more effective method. We drew inspiration from birds, but we didn't replicate their exact method. Similarly, while we can draw inspiration from the brain, we don't have to mimic it exactly in AI. I hope that if we build intelligence, it won't be driven by instincts as much as we humans sometimes are. Evolution, often referred to as the blind watchmaker, doesn't always create what we might call a rational design.

> "I don't use [ChatGPT] because, for me, writing is thinking. I don't want to give that up."

And when it comes to the use of AI, what role do you think trust plays, and what measures do you think we should take to ensure the ethical use of AI in the future?

The issue of trust in technology applies to almost all technology. We entrust our lives to technology every day. When you drive a car, you trust that it won't suddenly malfunction. When you board a plane, you trust that it's safe. A few weeks ago, I received my COVID booster shot, trusting that it was safe. We live in a world where we rely on many things that we don't fully understand. I understand the basic principle of an airplane, but I'm not an aeronautical engineer. I don't fully understand how it works, but I trust the system. Building that trust requires many elements, one of which is a responsible industry. One of the main challenges for our society is that the major players in our economy are corporations, and their primary goal is to make profits. They need, however, to understand that they also have a responsibility to society. For example, Boeing lost a lot of trust when it became clear that they had cut corners with the 737 MAX, leading to the deaths of hundreds of people. This caused significant reputational damage to Boeing, and only time will tell what impact it will have on their future sales. Companies need to be socially responsible, not just to avoid bad publicity and loss of profits, but also to uphold ethical standards [6]. This is particularly challenging in the tech world. Many tech companies claim to be responsible, but their actions don't always align with their words. For instance, Google has faced criticism for dismissing employees who raised ethical concerns about their technology. This has led to a loss of trust in the company, which was founded under the motto "Don't be evil". Facebook has faced similar issues. The problem is that most of us don't have the expertise to evaluate the safety of these technologies ourselves, so we must trust the producers. But if the industry continues to lose the trust of society, people will start to lose trust in the technology itself.

What do you think about the challenge that even if I don't trust the system, e.g., ChatGPT, if I don't adopt it into my daily work routine, I will be less productive than others who use it and start to fall behind. So, do we really have a choice?

Not really. Take smartphones, for example. I resisted getting a smartphone for a long time, but it's almost impossible to function in our society without one. I first resisted having a cell phone, then I held onto my flip phone as long as I could. But eventually, I had no choice but to get a smartphone. Now, I depend on it. There are places, like in China, where you can't survive without a smartphone. Even here, many services require a smartphone. For example, to confirm a doctor's appointment, you often must click on a link sent to your phone. Without a smartphone, this becomes impossible. So, it's not so much a personal choice anymore as it is a societal adaptation to technology. ChatGPT isn't quite at the level of necessity like a smartphone yet. I don't use it because, for me, writing is thinking. I don't want to give that up. It's like if everywhere you went, someone offered you a wheelchair to get around. You might think, "Do I really want that? If I use it all the time, I'll eventually lose my ability to walk. Is that a good thing?" You might decide to keep walking, even if it's less convenient. It's not always about being more productive. But we may reach a point where AI technology becomes such a basic part of our lives that we can't resist it. Often, industries try to frame these issues as matters of personal choice. For example, with sustainability, we're encouraged to recycle. I'm an avid recycler, but I'm skeptical that plastic recycling does any good. By framing these as matters of personal choice, industries can avoid regulation and systemic change. They tell us, "You choose. You decide." But can you really decide not to buy plastic products today? It's almost impossible to avoid plastic. So, by trying to frame systemic societal issues as matters of personal choice, industries avoid taking responsibility.

"I'm a materialist. I believe the brain is a machine. It's a biological machine with many neurons, and evolution has had billions of years to refine its design. We have proof that human-level intelligence can exist in a relatively small box. I wouldn't bet against our ability to achieve this with non-biological technology."

Think about the future capabilities of AI on a scale of 1 to 10, with 1 standing for artificial intelligence systems we know today, such as ChatGPT, and 10 standing for so-called artificial general intelligence systems that surpass human capabilities. Where do you think we are headed?

Predicting the direction of technology is extremely difficult. As scientists, we may be able to see a little further, but even then, we can't predict everything. Take ChatGPT, for example. It has given us the ability to generate human-level text. This happened about a year ago. If you had asked me two years ago when this would happen, I wouldn't have guessed it would be so soon. Very few people predicted it. We simply scaled up some models, and suddenly, at a certain point, they started generating human-like text. We don't fully understand how this happened. We don't understand AGI or human intelligence enough to predict when we'll achieve it. Some people suggest that once we reach 10 trillion parameters in a model, it will be as intelligent as a human. I'm skeptical of such predictions. Nevertheless, I'm a materialist. I believe the brain is a machine. It's a biological machine with many neurons, and evolution has had billions of years to refine its design. We have proof that human-level intelligence can exist in a relatively small box. I wouldn't bet against our ability to achieve this with non-biological technology. We really don't know, however, what will happen when we have something so intelligent. Will it just sit there and wait for instructions, or will it develop its own motivations? We don't know, and that's why I believe we need to slow down and consider the consequences before we continue to develop more advanced AI. When we developed nuclear weapons and nuclear energy, we immediately recognized the potential dangers and put regulations in place. I believe we need a similar approach for AI. The argument from the industry is that regulation will stifle innovation. But maybe we need to slow down risky innovation. Innovation is a means to an end, not a goal in itself. The goal should be the public good and human welfare [7].

"We simply scaled up some models, and suddenly, at a certain point, they started generating human-like text."

And when it comes to the future, what do you personally think, are we heading towards a utopian or dystopian future?

I consider myself a realist. I believe that technology can do amazing things. For example, we developed a vaccine for COVID in just one year.

So, we had a terrible pandemic. Many millions of people died. The last time we experienced something of this magnitude was 100 years ago, the Spanish flu. Now we realize that living through a pandemic is a horrific experience. The death toll is so high that it's difficult for our brains to comprehend. In the United States, we had close to a million and a half casualties. It's really hard to grasp the enormity of the death toll. But it could have been much worse. The two technologies that saved us are mRNA vaccines and the internet. We had a vaccine within a year. When the pandemic started, I told people it would be five years before there is a vaccine. The traditional method of creating a vaccine, which involves using a weakened strain of the virus, would have taken five years. And I think five years of a pandemic would have been disastrous. The internet also saved us. Suddenly, at the drop of a hat, I could work from home. Students could study from home. In the spring of 2020, we switched overnight to teaching online. Many people started working from home, and I started teaching from home. You could even have doctor appointments from home. Not everything, but many things can be done from home.

Imagine if we didn't have these technologies. The economic damage would have been much worse. There was severe economic damage due to the pandemic, and this economic damage translates to loss of life. Economists have calculated this. But the economic damage would have been much, much worse. Some people would say, I have no choice, I must go back to work. And the death toll would have been much higher. So, the internet saved us. Social media helped us stay in touch. We are facing social isolation, which is also a known health risk. At my university, there was a suicide by a graduate student, which we believe happened because of social isolation. We had to make significant efforts to combat social isolation, especially among students.

But it's the same internet and social media that also created polarization in society. So, the story of technology has always been a double-edged sword. This has always been the case. Think about it, what is the most fundamental technology? Fire. If you look at pictures of early humans, they had large jaws. They needed to chew raw food. Once we discovered fire, we had cooked food. We no longer needed large jaws. In fact, our jaws shrunk faster than our teeth. We still have too many teeth. Our jaws are too small. We have a lot of dental problems because we have the same number of teeth but smaller jaws. Today, fire is incredibly important to us. Most cars still use fire to run. And power plants use fire to create power. But people also die from fire. So, the human quest, the human journey, has always been the story of humanity dealing with technology. We benefit from it, and it comes with risk. And we try to walk on the edge of benefiting from the technology, while minimizing and mitigating risks. I think the same will be true with AI. But we just need to learn from the experience. For example, consider fire. Fire is leading to climate change. Climate change is caused mostly by carbon, putting more carbon in the atmosphere. How do you get carbon in the atmosphere? You burn carbon, and CO_2 goes into the atmosphere. So, the climate is burning because we use fire. But fire is the technology that brought us to where we are; we are today immensely richer than people over 250 years ago, before the Industrial Revolution. It is all based on fire. We have learned to harness carbon-based energy. And now the planet is in danger. So, we need to do a better job of anticipating the downside of technology. But it is not clear that scientists and engineers are the best people to anticipate the long-term consequences. I would take the writers of Black Mirror. Here is a funny anecdote. There was a review, I think last year, in Wired magazine (a very techie magazine) of the most recent season of Black Mirror. And the reviewer complained. He wrote: "Black Mirror used to be dystopian. Now it's like a reality show."

So, we need to think about what can go wrong? And the answer is we should try to anticipate it. But, very often, by the time we realize it, the damage has already happened. So, now we try to take social media and try to regulate it. It's going to be very, very difficult. So, can we basically slow down innovation because we need to anticipate risk? Can we do it in a more deliberate way? The problem for society right now is that we are a capitalism-driven society. And it means that we just pursue profits. And we do it in a reckless way. Then we discover the damage later. Sometimes we can mitigate it later. And sometimes it might be too late for that. And that's our problem right now. Look for example at what happened with climate change. If you have a coal economy based on carbon, a lot of parties would say, no, no, no. There's no climate change. It's caused because of sunspots or something else. Because now it's going to cost them a lot of money to change.

> "The problem for society right now is that we are a capitalism-driven society. And it means that we just pursue profits. And we do it in a reckless way. Then we discover the damage later."

Reflecting on the last few days, what was a particularly interesting insight from another discipline?

The most interesting insight was about explainable AI. One insight I got from a talk this morning on explainable AI is that we really don't care about explanation. What we really care about is justification. Is the recommendation justified? I don't care if I understand why it was given, but is it justified? If you recommend something to me, I'm going to ask you for an explanation. But I won't be satisfied with simply getting an explanation. I want to know; do I accept the explanation? Has Barbara given me justification? And so that's an insight that came to me this morning. But I think the most important insight is the importance of multidisciplinary conversations. So, the fact that computer scientists are interacting with lawyers and giving feedback to lawyers about the computer-science perspective and letting those different perspectives inform our own thinking. The same goes for conversations with philosophers and political scientists. These are very, very valuable conversations that do not normally happen. Because science in general has become so advanced that we each build our own little silo. We only talk to the people in our discipline because they understand our language. We don't have to go out of our way to explain something to people who don't understand our language. So, this is something that we really need to fight. And we need to have more meetings like AISoLA and bring different disciplines together. And for me that is the biggest insight. Really ... from that point of view it's a remarkable experience.

That is great to hear! Is there a specific research question that needs to be urgently addressed? Or are you referring to a more general approach of looking at AI and its future development from an interdisciplinary perspective?

That tells me, for example, that if we're going to build a regulatory agency for AI, it has to be interdisciplinary. It should not just have AI experts in it. It should have lawyers. It should have philosophers. We need to bring together the different people who can shed light from different perspectives. Each one of us can shed light from a relatively narrow perspective. But if you really want to see the whole phenomenon, we need all these things. And we need interaction among these people. We need a conversation between them. The complex phenomenon we are dealing with here is the interaction of technology and society. But technologists don't understand enough about society. And for people who do think about society, technology is a bit of a black box to them. So, we have to look at that and say, OK, how do we bring in all the different perspectives? And how do we create trustworthiness, safety, and security? How do we better manage the interaction between technology and society?

And from your personal perspective, what should be the AI vision for the coming years?

My vision for AI is to "slow down". Today, we have a very rich and powerful industry. And they're just rushing ahead. And I say just slow down. Let's talk about it. What technology are you pushing? Let's talk about the benefits. Let's talk about the risks. Let's talk about the consequences. We don't usually have that conversation about new technologies. Think about the standard process for new technologies. A company comes up with a new product. For example, Apple introduced the iPhone. Poof, we have an iPhone. And now we have smartphones, and we gave them to children. And history is not going to look kindly on us. We have a mental-health crisis among young people. It is hard to find any cause for that other than this technological combination of smartphones and social media. Now we have a rising suicide rate among children. And the only credible explanation is the combination of smartphones and social media. And who is responsible? We can blame Big Tech. But ultimately, we as a society have allowed this to happen. We allowed it to happen by letting innovation proceed without asking: "What will be the consequences?" To me, that is the critical question. How to stop technology from rushing ahead and presenting us with a fait accompli? How do we slow it down, think about consequences, and reflect on our responsibility? Who should be responsible? People talk about responsible AI. And I ask, what does it mean "responsible AI"? Who is responsible? Are you talking about the technology being responsible? Are the people being responsible? Should the industry be responsible? Who is responsible? And that's why I say, when people say responsible AI, I ask, what does it mean? Whom do you try to make more responsible?

"My vision for AI is to 'slow down'. Today, we have a very rich and powerful industry. And they're just rushing ahead. And I say just slow down. [...] Let's talk about it. What technology are you pushing? Let's talk about the benefits. Let's talk about the risks. Let's talk about the consequences."

Isn't that the general problem, that we don't have a person or an institution that is or feels responsible for 2050, 2100, or even further into the future?

No, we don't. We believe that human history will move forward, but can we direct it? Communism was an attempt to say, well, we are going to steer society in the direction that we collectively think it should go. And it proved to be a disaster because the only way you can have that level of tight control is through incredibly coercive means. It is estimated that the death toll of the two Communist revolutions, the Soviet and the Chinese, was 100 million people. So, it's very risky to say that we should collectively decide where humanity should go. So, we have to be very modest about what we can do. But we should look at where it is going. What do we identify as risk? Let's think about risk in advance.

Let's have forward-looking laws. The legal system is way behind, I believe. We've let the technology run forward, and now we're trying to think: "OK, who should be liable for this?" We need to do some slowing down and serious thinking. I believe that technologists have proven to be irresponsible, just thinking about the technology and not thinking about the consequences and responsibility.

If we want responsible technology, then we need to put the responsibility on people. This is ethics. And the fundamental principle of ethics for technology should be that technologists need to think in advance about the consequences of the technology. And they need to ensure that this technology is ultimately for the benefit of humanity. This is where we have a huge deficit, I believe. We train people that business is about making money. That's how we train business students. (That's how we train students in the United States. I don't know how they get trained in other countries.) They teach them ethics, but ethics is usually taught in a very narrow sense. I've seen boards on ethics, where the basic message is, "don't cheat, don't lie, don't steal". And for engineers, well, "if you build a bridge, it should stand and not fall". That is kind of professional ethics in a nutshell: "Whatever you do, be honest, and your design should be good." But that does not address the societal consequences of technology [2]. And I think that ethics comes from capitalism, where we just maximize profits. Put crassly, greed is good; it's OK for me to be greedy. But deeper ethics says "No"; it is not OK to be greedy. You must consider society. So, we must balance capitalism with ethics; what some people call "Moral Capitalism". We know that economic growth benefits society, but we need to find a way to do it in a societally responsible way. So far, we have not found a good way to do it. Humanity experimented with communism; it was a disaster. Everybody acknowledged that it was a disaster. Then we said, OK, forget it. It was a failure. So, let's have neoliberalism, which some people call "market fundamentalism". And now we're seeing the results of that, in the deeply polarized US and UK. So now we need to go back and ask, what is the right balance? And that's a fundamental challenge; in life, you're always searching for balance. You want to have some personal life. You want some progress. Progress as a student, as a professional, right? We talk about work-life balance. Is there a formula? There's no formula. We're trying to find a balance. When you raise children, you're faced with the issue of regulation. You're trying to regulate your children. How much should you regulate them? If you give them complete freedom, they will do crazy things. They might kill themselves. So, you say, no, no, I need to have some discipline. You do too much of that, you raise children who have not learned to make decisions, to take responsibility. So, we are all looking for balance, navigating between extremes. An ancient Asian wisdom is that everything has to be in balance. And my feeling is that one of the most fundamental questions for modern society is the balance between the market and the state. And we need to find a better balance than we have right now.

> "By framing [...] systemic societal issues as matters of personal choice, industries avoid taking responsibility."

Do you have anything to add?

For me, a big revelation that came out of my thinking about modern society over the last few years is the concept of the public good. And it turns out that if you go back to Jewish ethics from about 2,000 years ago, it is there in some sense. First, it says, if you are not for yourself, then who is going to be? First, you must take care of yourself. But if you're only for yourself, what kind of a person are you? And this is our challenge, right? I would say this is a conversation we need to have starting from a very early age, how to balance our own benefit versus our responsibility to society. And imagine you have someone like a politician, like Margaret Thatcher, who said, "there's no such thing as society". This is a horrendous, horrendous statement, OK? Because none of us can survive without society. It takes a village. We all are contributing and benefiting from society. Thatcher basically said, just be greedy, don't care about society. It's a recipe for dystopia. And I've asked other people, I said, tell me about your education. When did you have a serious discussion about the public good and your responsibility for the public good? Most people say, no, this is not in my education. We never discussed the public good. And I think the public good is incredibly important. And especially right now, we have a planet that is burning. Without the public good, we're not going to survive. The public good is the collective good of all of us. And that's something that our society has neglected. But also with regards to collective action towards the future we want as a society. At the end of the day, we're individuals. And each one of us has their own thinking about what needs to be done.

Consider the US Constitution, which to me is an amazing document. So, it starts with the first paragraph. It says the purpose of the United States is the public good. But how do we collectively agree on what the public good is? The answer is, it's very difficult. So, we try to get democracies and develop democratic systems for agreeing on what the public good is. We don't have one way to do democracy. The founding fathers of the United States – the US was the first republic that tried that – said, here is a proposal how to do democracy. This was the first constitution. It was the Constitution of the United States. Countries after that say, OK, yeah, that's not a bad idea. It's a set of rules that try to govern. How do we reach agreement? Because it's very difficult. Even in a family, two people, they must reach agreement. Just a couple, they must reach agreement. It's not always easy. Academic departments are kind of mini democracies. We must make decisions collectively. It is hard. Everybody pulls in a different direction. This is a kind of challenge to society, to find a way to contribute to the public good and find agreement on what is the public good. Nobody is against the public good. The devil is in the details.

And we collectively must decide what is the public good and how do we collectively move towards the public good. It is very difficult.

Especially since it is likely that everyone has a different idea of what is desired, what is to be expected, and what responsibility each individual should carry.

Indeed. But I think we need to start this conversation. I think we have not really started this conversation seriously. I'm looking at my education. I never participated in a serious conversation about it. We had classes in civics, and we learned about how the government works: the executive branch, the legislative branch, and the judicial branch. It was very descriptive. But there was very little philosophy. What is the purpose of all these different branches and how they operate? What is the purpose? The purpose is to agree collectively on what we think the public good is and agree on the actions we collectively need to take to promote the public good. This discussion was missing; it was not there. Now consider the people who graduated with this education. They may be able to recite what the different branches are, et cetera, but very little about the philosophy. And the philosophy is really the principle that should govern our life as a society. This is the difference between a civilized society and what people call the "Law of the Jungle". The Law of the Jungle is the mighty take what the mighty want. In civilized society, we have a rule of law. What is the purpose of the law. You can go back to Hammurabi 4,000 years ago. What is the purpose of the law, asked Hammurabi? The purpose of the law is for the benefit of humanity, he answered, for the benefit of humanity.

That's a perfect last sentence. Thank you, Moshe, for your time, your insights, and your perspective on the future.

References

1. Bansal, S., Li, Y., Tabajara, L.M., Vardi, M.Y., Wells, A.: Model checking strategies from synthesis over finite traces. In: André, É., Sun, J. (eds.) Proceedings of International Symposium on Automated Technology for Verification and Analysis (ATVA 2023). LNCS, vol. 14215, pp. 227–247. Springer (2023). https://doi.org/10.1007/978-3-031-45329-8_11
2. Ferreira, R., Vardi, M.Y.: Deep Tech ethics: an approach to teaching social justice in computer science. In: Proceedings of the 52nd ACM Technical Symposium on Computer Science Education (SIGCSE 2021), pp. 1041–1047. ACM (2021)
3. Kahneman, D.: Thinking, Fast and Slow. Farrar, Straus and Giroux (2011)
4. Prates, M., Avelar, P. H., Lemos, H., Lamb, L.C., Vardi, M.Y.: Learning to solve NP-complete problems: a graph neural network for decision TSP. In: Proceedings of the AAAI Conference on Artificial Intelligence, vol. 33, no. 1, pp. 4731–4738 (2019)
5. Vardi, M.Y.: Is information technology destroying the Middle Class? Commun. ACM **58**(2), 5 (2015)
6. Vardi, M.Y.: Are we having an ethical crisis in computing? Commun. ACM **62**(1), 7 (2018)
7. Vardi, M.Y.: ACM for the public good. Commun. ACM **66**(5), 5 (2023)
8. Vardi, M.Y.: Computing, you have blood on your hands! Commun. ACM **67**(1), 5 (2023)
9. https://en.wikipedia.org/wiki/Deep_Blue_versus_Garry_Kasparov
10. https://en.wikipedia.org/wiki/IBM_Watson

Let's Talk AI with Computer Science Expert Edward A. Lee

Edward A. Lee[1] and Barbara Steffen[2(✉)]

[1] UC Berkeley, Berkeley, USA
eal@berkeley.edu
[2] METAFrame Technologies, Dortmund, Germany
barbara.steffen@metaframe.de

Abstract. The capabilities of the large language models that emerged in public in 2022 surprised nearly everybody in the field. I believe this new technology will prove as transformative as any humans have ever devised, with highly unpredictable effects on our culture. By means of token prediction, the machines have acquired the ability to summarize large bodies of knowledge, to reason logically about numbers and mathematics, and to create novel work influenced by prior human work. Many observers have been quick to criticize, pointing out errors in reasoning and fabrications presented as facts, ignoring the remarkable reasoning abilities that emerged from token prediction and the relationship between fabrication and creativity. This new technology offers insights into how human cognition could have emerged and how it works, particularly since the deficiencies identified by the critics are remarkably human-like (we also make errors in logical reasoning and fabricate facts).

My personal AI mission: I believe that the recent revolution in AI can teach us a great deal about human cognition. The fact that so many capabilities that we consider fundamental, such as the ability to use logic for deductive reasoning, appear to emerge from token prediction is remarkable. It suggests that the human brain may be fundamentally a prediction engine, and things that we consider fundamental, such as logic, may be just mechanisms that enhance prediction.

Fig. 1. Edward A. Lee

B. Steffen et al. (Eds.): *Let's Talk AI*, LNCS 15000, pp. 155–160, 2026.
https://doi.org/10.1007/978-3-032-09008-9_18

1 My Takes on AI

- **Artificial Intelligence** – Machine behavior that resembles human behavior and that would generally be considered signs of intelligence.
- **Trust** – Willingness to permit another entity or individual to take actions that could cause harm with confidence that the actions taken will not cause harm.
- **Explainability** – Something is explainable if it is possible to provide a human-understandable sequence of rational deductions that lead to that something.
- **Essential Elements of Human Capabilities** – Creativity, intuition, feelings, introspection, and reasoning.

2 The Interview

[Barbara Steffen] Welcome, Edward Lee (Fig. 1). Thank you for joining me for this interview at the AISoLA conference. Could you start by briefly introducing yourself and your relation to artificial intelligence?

[Edward A. Lee] Sure, Barbara. I am a professor at Berkeley, where I've been teaching for over 30 years. I am an engineer and a computer scientist, specializing in cyber-physical systems, which involve both computing and physical processes. I am particularly interested in AIs that are embedded in robots. Most of my career has been highly technical, but I have written two general-audience books that step back and examine the big picture of technology from a more philosophical and societal perspective. These are, The Co-evolution: The Entwined Futures of Humans and Machines (2020) [3] and Plato and the Nerd: The Creative Partnership of Humans and Technology (2017) [2]. I also had the pleasure of co-editing a volume on Digital Humanism [8] with many excellent essays by top experts in the field. All of these are available open access.

> "[...] one of the things that amazes me about large language models is that the ability to reason logically and think about numbers emerged from token prediction. I think there's a lot of potential [here] to gain insight into how humans have developed our ability to reason and think logically."

That sounds intriguing. Could you elaborate on the specific challenges of AI that your research addresses?

My research might seem a bit eclectic. I have two complementary lines of work. My technical work is tangentially related to AI. However, about eight years ago, I started focusing on issues around technology and society and the philosophy of technology. I've written a couple of books on that topic [2, 3], which was a transformative learning experience that pushed me to learn about other disciplines.

Interesting. How do you perceive the role of trust in AI adoption, and what measures do you believe are essential to ensure ethical AI use in the future?

I'm skeptical that there are measures that will guarantee ethical use of AI in the future. We will inevitably see a variety of uses, as we've always seen with any powerful technology. I think humans are the more concerning part of the equation for me [4]. Humans have a rather grim track record of using technology against one another. I'm fairly certain that AI won't be an exception, and humans will find creative ways to use it against each other.

"[...] if the question is whether we have AIs that exceed human capabilities, we certainly do."

What are your thoughts on the idea of making large language models available open-source? Do you find that risky?

That's a thought-provoking question. I'm a strong believer in open source as it enables the exploration of technology for a wide range of applications, both good and bad. I believe many potential positive applications are enabled by open sourcing these AIs, which might not otherwise be possible due to lack of commercial viability. Moreover, I have argued before that it is an illusion that we humans have much control over the trajectory of the technology [3, 4]. Keeping the mechanisms hidden is probably a fool's errand. So, despite the risks, I'm very much in favor of making these AIs open source.

"I'm skeptical that there are measures that will guarantee ethical use of AI in the future."

Regarding the future capabilities of AI, on a scale from 1 to 10, where 1 represents current dedicated AI systems solving specific problems, like ChatGPT or DALL-E, and 10 represents artificial general intelligence systems surpassing human capabilities. What do you think will be possible and what should we prepare for?

Honestly, I believe we already have the whole range, from 1 to 10. I'm not fond of the term artificial general intelligence, but if the question is whether we have AIs that exceed human capabilities, we certainly do. For instance, if you interact enough with ChatGPT, its breadth of knowledge is something no human can match. But in some ways, this is not new with technology. Every useful technology is beneficial because it exceeds human capabilities in some way. We've always used technology as an intellectual and physical prosthesis, and I think AI will be no different.

"Currently, the key difference between ChatGPT and human cognition is that the AIs are not embodied."

Do you think it becomes even more concerning if we start integrating AI into robots which then start to move in the real world where we also operate?

I believe that will probably be the next significant phase in the development of these large neural network-based models. The term people use for this is embodied robotics. Currently, the key difference between ChatGPT and human cognition is that the AIs are not embodied [6]. They don't have a body to interact with the physical world. However, that's going to change rather quickly. Many people are working on applying this technology in robotics. I find it both scary and exciting. I think we are likely going to see robots that are extremely adept at manipulating things, which has been a significant challenge in robotics.

Looking into the future and the potential impact AI will have, where do you see yourself on the utopian-dystopian spectrum that is often discussed in public?

My view is that things are going to change, and there's no question about that. This technology will affect our culture in very unexpected ways. It will change the role of humans and how we interact with our world. It's hard to predict how. We need to make every effort to ensure that we function synergistically with this technology. I've been involved in an initiative called the Digital Humanism Initiative [8, 9], which focuses on how we can keep the interests of humans at the forefront of the evolution of technology and the changes in human culture that come with it. It's a tremendously challenging problem.

"[As numerous AI-generated] papers are used to train the next generation of AIs, a feedback loop emerges that can result in AIs whose knowledge base is largely fabricated."

Could you give examples of specific challenges you're currently addressing in this group?

One particularly striking challenge is regulating AI. It's a tremendous challenge. It's hard to even define the terminology needed to create legal constructs to work with this technology. I believe we need to put some effort into figuring out how to do this because any powerful technology requires societal control and regulation. This is no exception, and we don't know how to do it currently.

How do you view the challenge that technology-push often brings us into settings in which we are confronted with new challenges for which we do not have suitable regulation yet. It is the nature of this kind of progress that regulation always lags behind as technology first needs to impact society before we can find ways to regulate it.

I can't give you a definitive answer to that question as I'm not a public policy person or a legal scholar. I respect people who are tackling those problems. I see my role as helping them understand the technology better so they can be more realistic about how it's going to function in society and what the possible risks and benefits are.

Are there specific challenges or research questions you think we should tackle together in an interdisciplinary fashion? If so, which disciplines would be suitable in your opinion?

There are many opportunities. I'm personally excited about interacting with people in psychology. I think there's a lot to learn about human cognition by observing how AIs have evolved and are changing [5]. For instance, one of the things that amazes me about large language models is that the ability to reason logically and think about numbers emerged from token prediction [1]. I think there's a lot of potential to gain insight into how humans have developed the ability to reason and think logically by observing how AIs have developed similar abilities from language models.

From your perspective, what is your vision for AI that we as a society or people should tackle in the future?

That's an extremely broad question. I would like to see the term AI changed to IA, which stands for intelligence augmentation. I would like us to work with machines in a synergistic way, using them as cognitive enhancers to improve our abilities. I hope we can use them to improve our research in medicine, address climate change, and make our society fairer. The AIs learn human biases and prejudices, but they also expose them. We can use this to better understand our culture and maybe find ways to mitigate these problems. I'm optimistic about the positive uses of AI. However, I also acknowledge the potential for negative uses. As a society, we will have to be proactive about curbing these uses. We may have to be reactive in some cases. When bad things happen, let's adjust and try to correct the course as much as possible. One challenge that I would like to highlight concerns what happens when more of the data used to train AIs is generated by the AIs themselves. Today, the AIs are trained mostly with human-generated data. But it seems inevitable that that will change. Even this interview has been edited by an AI and will become training data for the next generation. More seriously, recent studies show an increasing number of sham academic papers, which are written largely by AIs, being published [7]. As these papers are used to train the next generation of AIs, a feedback loop emerges that can result in AIs whose knowledge base is largely fabricated. If, while this happens, society gives more trust and responsibility to the machines, we could end up in a very bad place.

"Humans have a rather grim track record of using technology against one another. I'm fairly certain that AI won't be an exception, and humans will find creative ways to use it against each other."

Is there anything else you would like to add to this interview?

Perhaps just a comment that the group of people brought together by this conference (AISoLA 2023) is exactly what we should be doing more of. We have a mix of computer scientists, psychologists, philosophers, and historians. I believe these cross-discipline interactions are essential. The emergence of these neural network-based AIs is somewhat new for computer science because their behavior is harder to explain and understand than most of what computer science has dealt with. These other disciplines are more accustomed to dealing with complex systems. They have methodologies that are new to computer scientists that we could learn from. I believe conferences like this really help with that.

"One particularly striking challenge is regulating AI. [...] It's hard to even define the terminology needed to create legal constructs to work with this technology."

Do you think it would be useful to derive a few questions that seem critical to AI and AI development and then ask different disciplines to work on those questions collaboratively?

There's a lot of potential there. I still see many gaps. I hear thoughtful ideas that I can immediately recognize won't work because that's not how the AIs work. I'm sure they hear ideas from me that they know won't work because I don't understand societal systems the way they do. The only way we can close those gaps is by getting people to talk to each other.

Thank you very much for your time, Edward, and for your insights. I wish you a great time at AISoLA and hope you enjoy the conference and its interdisciplinary discussions.

Thank you very much. I appreciate it.

References

1. Bubeck, S., et al.: Sparks of Artificial General Intelligence: early experiments with GPT- 4. https://arxiv.org/abs/2303.12712
2. Lee, E.A.: Plato and the Nerd. The Creative Partnership of Humans and Technology. MIT Press (2017)
3. Lee, E.A.: The Coevolution: The Entwined Futures of Humans and Machines. MIT Press (2020)
4. Lee, E.A.: Are we in control? In Werthner, H., et al. (eds.) Introduction to Digital Humanism. Springer (2021)
5. Lee, E.A.: What can deep neural networks teach us about embodied bounded rationality. Front. Psychol. **13** (2022)
6. Lee, E.A.: Deep neural networks, explanations, and rationality. In: Steffen, B. (ed.) Bridging the Gap Between AI and Reality (AISoLA 2023). LNCS, vol. 14380, pp. 11–21. Springer (2024)
7. McKie, R.: The situation has become appalling: fake scientific papers push research credibility to crisis point. The Guardian (2024)
8. Werthner, H., Prem, W., Lee, E.A., Ghezzi, C. (eds.): Perspectives on Digital Humanism. Springer (2021)
9. Werthner, H., et al.: Introduction to Digital Humanism: A Textbook. Springer (2024)

Let's Talk AI with Computer Science Expert Ina Schieferdecker

Ina Schieferdecker[1] and Barbara Steffen[2(✉)]

[1] TU Berlin, Berlin, Germany
ina.schieferdecker@tu-berlin.de
[2] METAFrame Technologies, Dortmund, Germany
barbara.steffen@metaframe.de

Abstract. The wealth of artificial intelligence methods enables digital solutions, without which the transition to sustainability, including the transition to renewable energy and the circular economy, would be impossible. It would be unethical not to harness these enormous opportunities, not to liberalise access to data, computing, and AI resources worldwide, and not to educate and train people around the world to make the most of AI.

My personal AI mission: On a large scale, my dream is the liberalization of AI. Basic AI should not be a masterpiece of political, economic, or military power. A key area for the beneficial application of this AI vision is to use this powerful tool to address the most critical threat to humanity, which is sustainability in all its forms. On a smaller scale, I would like to contribute to the improvement of software engineering by applying AI methods and tools.

Fig. 1. Ina Schieferdecker

1 My Takes on AI

- **Artificial Intelligence** – There is no single definition for Artificial Intelligence, as views of its characteristics, properties, potentials, or risks differ depending on the research discipline, such as computer science, jurisprudence, or social science. As a software engineer, I like to make use of a systemic view of an AI system according to which "an AI system is an engineered system that generates outputs such as

B. Steffen et al. (Eds.): *Let's Talk AI*, LNCS 15000, pp. 161–172, 2026.
https://doi.org/10.1007/978-3-032-09008-9_19

content, forecasts, recommendations or decisions for a given set of human-defined objectives". An AI system can use "various techniques and approaches related to artificial intelligence to develop a model to represent data, knowledge, processes, etc. which can be used to conduct tasks" [6].

- **Trust** – Trust, which is largely based on experience, has multiple dimensions, and includes elements of reliance, vulnerability, expectation of honesty, or dependability. As a software engineer, I am interested in how users of services and products perceive the trustworthiness of the providers, operators and/or technologies involved [11]. The trustworthiness of services, products and technologies is of particular interest here, as trustworthiness, which includes quality, security, performance, reliability, robustness, etc., provides the technical basis for building trust.
- **Explainability** – Explainability is a requirement for today's AI systems to make their results understandable to users. It is achieved with methods such as textual, visual, or exemplary justifications, rule extraction, or determining the importance of model features. Explainable AI is necessary for the development and widespread adoption of traceable and trustworthy AI-based systems. It will become less important as AI-based systems proliferate in everyday life but will remain important in AI-assisted applications where the final decisions remain with the human user.
- **Essential Elements of Human Capabilities** – Mental human capabilities are of particular interest when comparing human intelligence with technical artificial intelligence. These include learning, contextual understanding, creativity, adaptability, error tolerance, consciousness, and ethical motivation. At present, any one mental or other human capability can be performed better by one machine or another, but not in combination, which is certainly true of the sum of human mental capabilities compared to artificial intelligence.

2 The Interview

[Barbara Steffen] Today, I have the pleasure to interview Ina Schieferdecker (Fig. 1). Could you briefly introduce yourself and your relationship to artificial intelligence?

[Ina Schieferdecker] Thank you, Barbara. I appreciate the opportunity to participate in this interview. I am a mathematical computer scientist. My research so far has mainly focused on software and quality engineering, open data and data platforms, smart cities as well as on digitalization and sustainability.

I studied at Humboldt University, Berlin, and joined GMD FOKUS, now known as Fraunhofer FOKUS, during my PhD studies. My connection to AI began during my studies, where we were taught logic-based AI and programming with Prolog. To be honest, it was not my favourite subject. I found it too narrow and too limited. It was indeed the early days of AI.

When I joined GMD FOKUS, which I eventually co-led, we used AI extensively. We were on the application side, not the development side for AI methods. We used AI in various fields, such as autonomous driving, medical data analysis, software test optimization, or the optimization of telecommunication network topologies. Throughout my career, I have been tracking advancements in AI and observing its developments from an application perspective, in particular for software engineering and for quality engineering.

My perspective shifted when I co-founded the Weizenbaum Institute for the Network Society. There, we examine the implications of digitalization on society. I led two research groups, one of which focused on the criticality of AI-based systems. We explored questions of biases in AI, trustworthiness, sustainability properties such as resource efficiency, and inter-labor aspects of AI, such as workforce, regulations, and working conditions [7, 14].

More recently, I was a member of the Advisory Council on Global Change, or WBGU, from 2015 to 2019. We developed a flagship report on our common digital future, which is essentially about the digital age, its characterization, and the utopian and dystopian visions that can emerge from digitalization. We identified AI as one of the key technologies of the digital age and discussed three scenarios [10] (p. 6): First, we posited that AI is currently the most powerful tool we have at hand for humankind. It can help us excel in our core concerns, which are not just computation or automation, but rather to have machinery that takes care of the mundane tasks, freeing us to focus on care, education, science, art, and so on [10] (p. 6). Second, we considered a scenario where AI developments are so advanced that AI becomes a good companion to every human being, providing significant help [10, p. 6]. Lastly, we discussed a dystopian view where AI becomes the master of humankind, a view I personally do not subscribe to [10, p. 7]. In the past four years, I worked with the Federal Ministry of Research and Education in Germany. I led the Directorate for Technological Sovereignty and Innovation, including AI, where we supported the AI Act and the federal AI research programs, for example including the establishment of the AI Competence Centers in Germany.

Now, I returned to research as an independent researcher. I am excited about the possibilities of current AI tools and how they can revolutionize research. For example, in conducting literature reviews, analyzing how scientific results relate to other scientific results, improving data empirics, data visualization, and even enhancing my English writing and speaking skills. I find it fascinating to look at my field of expertise, software engineering and testing, primarily not of AI, but with AI. I believe AI can revolutionize many sectors, including core technologies in digitalization such as software engineering.

However, I am aware that the term "AI" can be misleading, as it may trigger incorrect impressions about the technology behind it. But it is a term that was established decades ago, and we have to work with it. I hope we can educate people to better understand the potential and not just the risks of AI. Along the way, AI can become a very powerful companion for us. The case of AI becoming our master is, I think, if not theoretically impossible, at least very unlikely. However, we need to be careful about how much automation is handed over to AI-based systems, and that the human-in-the-loop remains in charge of key decisions.

Have you been surprised by the advances in AI over the past few years?

I have to say that I am naturally inclined towards the mathematical, logical, and data-driven side of software engineering, statistics was not my favourite subject. But now, the two have come together, and yes, I have learned so much about the impressive results of AI. For instance, weather forecasting and climate analysis are better with AI [2]. Protein structure detection is significantly improved with AI [12]. The application of AI in my field of expertise has had a significant impact. The qualitative enhancement of a multitude of new technologies and applications has been remarkable [1, 5, 15].

"We need an international discussion on the red lines for the use of AI in autonomous weapons."

Do you think users are currently educated enough to use these AI-based tools and systems appropriately? Or do you think we often deal with over- or undertrust in these contexts?

Let us differentiate education on the one hand side, and trust or mistrust on the other: Although they are interrelated, one can trust without knowledge or education. Nevertheless, it is my contention that the education of the public regarding AI is not being conducted in an optimal manner. It is imperative that we all gain a deeper comprehension of the ramifications of AI-based systems and tools in a multitude of domains, including education, training, research, industry, society, law, justice, and so forth. This is a challenge that must be addressed collectively. The absence of definitive answers necessitates the training of problem-solving capabilities and the critical reflection of solutions.

The degree of trust and mistrust exhibited globally varies considerably. There are those who view AI as an advantageous and promising technology. I consider myself to be among those who are optimistic about the potential benefits of AI, although I am not naive about the challenges that the technology will undoubtedly present. There is a considerable degree of mistrust, which can be attributed to the novelty of AI technology and the fact that it is currently monopolised by a small number of companies. If we were to liberalise AI, which would entail liberalising foundational AI models, basic methods, tools, and the data needed to train and verify AI systems, it could be expected to function considerably more effectively. It is imperative that we ensure fair access to this pivotal technology, a task that requires our immediate attention.

Do you support Meta's move to open-source its large language models, or do you see this as a potential risk given the power of such technology?

I think it is important to open them up to promote greater diversity in the LLMs. I do not think this is risky; on the contrary, I think it is a step forward. However, I do not think this should be solely in the hands of companies alone. There are many small and medium-sized enterprises that might contribute, or even the public sector and research.

So, you're proposing a public goods approach, similar to the Internet?

Yes, exactly. Like the Internet, we need to develop a viable path towards digital commons. These digital commons should include open educational resources, open data, and a part of the Internet as an open public space like a Digital Agora, where opinions and facts can be openly exchanged. The Digital Agora should not be controlled by corporations. The same applies to the core components of AI.

Do you disapprove of the current competition among Big Tech companies, where they use their resources to gain access to underlying technology, data, and top talent to strengthen their position?

I understand why they behave this way, because it suits their purposes. However, I think we are in a situation similar to the telecommunications era before, where power was concentrated in a few companies. Eventually, some of the companies were broken up. I think we will see a similar discussion soon. Either we need to develop good enough LLMs from public fund, or there needs to be a market correction to distribute power more evenly.

How do you view the role of trust in AI adoption?

Trust is a key element in the adoption of any new system, process, or technology. The same is true for AI. Without the trust of early adopters, followed by the trust of the majority of society, there will be little widespread adoption of AI in general.

Coming from the computer science/engineering side, I believe that high-quality, fit-for-purpose AI-based systems can provide a technical basis for trust [13]. We call such systems trustworthy. Characteristics of trustworthiness include features such as privacy, security, integrity, robustness, reliability etc. [9].

However, technical means alone will not be sufficient to secure AI-based systems, especially if they are security- or safety-critical. Rules, processes, and workforce will also be needed to manage, for example, misuse or malfunction.

I think the European AI Act correctly addresses the criticality levels of AI-based systems [3]. However, I am not convinced that the subtle technical details for an optimal balance between innovation and risks are well reflected. It will be very important that modern, innovative AI-based systems are not stifled by national regulation. It would be great if we could agree and succeed in making the use of AI a kind of mandatory requirement. You could even say, with a capital hyphen, that it is forbidden not to use AI wherever its use is appropriate.

What measures are essential to ensure ethical use of AI?

Ethical AI use varies around the world, but there are common denominators such as human rights, the UN Agenda 2030 with the SDGs, and democratic values [4]. Ethical AI applications would mean no invasion of privacy, no unintentional bias or discrimination, no undetected deepfakes or manipulation, and no waste of resources. In terms of action, I think it is about education and training to understand the potential impacts, risks, and opportunities. It is about providing public data, computing resources, storage, AI tools, and LLMs. It is about strong research on AI, cross-disciplinary research between STEM and social sciences, standardization of AI-based systems, and processes to address any misuse of AI.

"Liberalising AI, making it open source, and being transparent about the training data used can help prevent unintentional biases and biases that contradict our values."

Do you think that the EU AI Act is a step in the right direction?

The direction is right, but it is still rather open at critical points [8]. I appreciate the risk-based approach, but I think it is very important and more effective to take a customer-driven, application-oriented approach. Important technical details have not yet been clarified, which could lead to different solutions in Europe, potentially hindering the scalability of Europe-wide AI-based solutions.

When you talk about an application-oriented approach, are you referring to the underlying AI technology or to the various AI applications? And should they be approached in a specialized and thus customized way?

I believe that we should focus on the services that a solution offers, rather than the technology itself. The impact comes from the use of the applications and the results they produce, not from the potential of a technology. Therefore, it is crucial to start with consumer needs and the intended applications. I am not sure that the AI Act takes this into account, as only the application can lead to a real impact assessment, which needs to be verified, validated, and possibly certified.

Indeed, one challenge is that AI systems like ChatGPT are quite generic in their approach. While the interaction may be limited, the range of topics it can address and the support it can provide is difficult to clearly define.

ChatGPT is a text processor and question-answer machine with selected advanced features for image or chart processing that can handle queries from any sector. Its responses are frequently impressive, although they are occasionally erroneous, contingent upon the training data it has been provided with. The risk associated with text processing is relatively low, as it is akin to conducting library research on a larger scale. However, when discussing AI in education, it is of the utmost importance to understand its application. If the system is merely used to support an individual student's learning journey, this is a different scenario to AI being used to assess the quality of a student group or even an entire university. It is crucial to evaluate the capabilities and limitations of a system, as well as its intended use, the individuals who can utilize it, and the potential consequences of its use.

In the context of education or research, would you support the use of AI like ChatGPT for writing papers and improving texts, or do you think that these are areas where people should still think and work independently?

It is imperative that independent thinking gets encouraged. Nevertheless, the question of whether or not to utilise AI tools such as ChatGPT is not the issue at hand. Indeed, I believe they should be employed. It would be unwise not to do so. Initially, it might be necessary to disclose the use of AI tools for text improvement. However, this will become commonplace in the long term. As is the case with the use of text editors or grammar checkers, the use of AI tools will become a commonplace occurrence. It is of paramount importance to ensure that research and other texts remain original works. This is an area that should be included in the ethical training provided to students. It is inevitable that there will be instances of misuse and attempts to circumvent hard work. However, these will ultimately prove unsuccessful in the long term. It is not possible for AI to generate original ideas, as it is only capable of combining existing ideas.

Looking to the future and specifically the future capabilities of AI, on a scale of 1 to 10, where 1 represents current AI systems like ChatGPT and 10 represents artificial general intelligence, what do you think will be possible?

In preparing for the interview, I found myself intrigued by this preparatory question and its implications for autonomy. In considering the five levels of autonomous systems in automotive technology, from assisted driving to autonomous driving, it can be observed that all levels utilise AI. Commercially deployed systems are at level three, and it is possible that we might reach level four by 2030 or later. There is a strong conviction that full autonomy will be achieved, although the precise timing of this remains uncertain. Nevertheless, in terms of human capabilities, AI has already demonstrated the capacity to surpass us in a number of areas. Machinery is constructed with the intention of performing tasks more efficiently than humans can, or tasks that humans are unable to perform. For example, AI has already demonstrated superior performance in logical games, knowledge games, and big data analysis and large-scale pattern detection, including medical image analysis.

In what areas do you think AI has already surpassed us?

As previously stated, AI has demonstrated superior capabilities in logical games, knowledge games, or medical image analysis. In these domains, the performance of AI can be considered to be top, with a rating of 10. Nevertheless, the term "artificial intelligence" may not be entirely accurate. As an artificial entity, it displays certain characteristics that can be attributed to intelligence. Nevertheless, it is not capable of solving tasks or situations that are unexpected, unforeseen, or unknown in the same way that humans can. Artificial intelligence is most effective in domains where there are clearly defined rules or a vast quantity of data. In contrast to humans, AI can work tirelessly and performing tasks with greater consistency. Nevertheless, it is unlikely that AI will ever fully replicate human intelligence. Instead, we will witness the emergence of a distinct form of intelligence, which I propose to designate as "technical intelligence". Technical intelligence should be applied where it's most beneficial, such as in critical, tedious, or repetitive tasks. While AI's victories in chess and Go may not appear to be of great consequence, they were nevertheless significant milestones in the field of AI research. The advantages of this approach are already apparent, and it is to be hoped that further benefits will accrue in the future.

"It is necessary to be sufficiently reflective to be able to modify our approach when new insights emerge regarding undesirable emergent behaviours."

I often encounter two opposing perspectives on AI. Some people are unsure about what AI is capable of and whether we should trust it, while others hope to gradually outsource manual and time-consuming tasks that they no longer want to do to AI. Do you think the way the media is currently portraying AI is accurate? Or do you think there's a tendency to either create fear, with statements like we might lose control over it, or to over-market it as the solution to all our problems?

Firstly, I think AI is not well represented in the media. Journalists tend to focus more on the risks rather than the opportunities. I would like to see more balanced coverage of AI developments. For example, I appreciate the new devices that assist with housework, such as cleaning machines. If we could communicate better about these small solutions, I think it would open people's minds to the potential of AI. The real benefits, of course, lie elsewhere. It is my hope that we will place greater emphasis on developing AI solutions to the grand challenges of humanity, while simultaneously ensuring that AI is both resource-efficient and energy-conserving. This could be achieved by utilising AI for example to monitor climate change, environmental developments, and provide early warnings of potential environmental disasters or even criminal attacks against the environment. Furthermore, there is the potential for AI in combating climate change identifying novel or improving deployed approaches to smart farming, mobility, or energy provisioning, for example. Nevertheless, I believe the primary risk is not AI surpassing humankind, given my mathematical education. It can be persuasively argued that this will not occur. The real risk could be in rather simple situations. To illustrate, if AI is employed to enhance the stability of energy networks in conjunction with renewable energies, a seemingly logical solution for AI to reduce CO2 emissions might be to simply switch off energy production. Energy blackouts can have catastrophic consequences. It is imperative that experts are included in the decision-making process when utilising any form of automation, including AI-based automation.

Do you think we can ensure that we maintain control over AI?

It is my concern that the machinery of strong AI is only with companies. It is my contention that the machinery of strong AI should be subject to public control. In order to achieve this, it is necessary to democratize AI, thereby enabling access to the machinery and the capacity to analyse the systems that are implemented. As we have learned to manage and safeguard electricity and transportation, it is similarly important to integrate the digital technologies including AI into societal processes and procedures. It is not sufficient to rely solely on technology. To ensure that AI respects privacy, security, reliability, robustness, performance, and resource efficiency, it is necessary to implement societal processes. It is necessary to have technical associations monitoring the impacts of digital technologies on society and ensuring they align with our values.

Looking into the future and AI's impact on it, where would you position yourself between utopian and dystopian visions?

Taking up our discussion of possible futures for humanity and AI at the WBGU, it seems reasonable to posit that, according to the computational theories currently available, there are good reasons why AI will not become general AI, but that generative AI has already surpassed a quality level with very impressive and important results. On the utopian side, it is my contention that AI will continue to be one of our most powerful tools for addressing the grand challenges of humanity and for tackling climate change.

The dystopian scenario posits that we fail to utilize AI correctly and are not cautious enough when deploying AI-based autonomous solutions. Such an outcome could result in the emergence of behaviours that were not foreseen, and which could have a disruptive effect on our society.

It can be reasonably assumed that the explainability of AI will be a significant factor in determining the extent to which AI is accepted and used on a widespread basis. However, as the quality and trustworthiness of AI-based systems improve, this will become less of a concern.

Furthermore, it would be important to discuss how we can avoid the unintended emergence of behaviors of AI-based systems to which we assign and automate tasks, e.g. in critical infrastructures, or in cases where these behaviours are critical for individuals, for privacy or self-determination. It is necessary to determine how experts can be integrated into the process of quality checking and correcting, where necessary, the suggestions and solutions of AI-based systems.

It is my hope that we will be sufficiently courageous and intelligent to forestall wrong outcomes, but it needs to be a collaborative effort. It is my hope that organizations like the UN will play a role in democratizing not only AI but also the broader digital landscape. Otherwise, it is my considered opinion that the use of monopolized, unvalidated or unreliable AI represents a genuine and imminent threat to all of us.

So, your main concern is that we are accelerating progress too quickly without considering the potential consequences?

The answer is both yes and no. It is imperative that AI-based innovations be implemented on a large scale. Concurrently, it is of the utmost importance to ensure a balanced distribution of power on a global scale and to implement state-of-the-art designs and validations of AI-based solutions. Reflections need to be made in a timely manner. It is evident that there is already a considerable amount of reflection taking place within the scientific community and across various disciplines. However, there is a need for this reflection to be disseminated more widely. Sociotechnical impacts, environmental and ethical considerations should become part of professional education and university curricula. Such a process will require a certain amount of time. It is necessary to be sufficiently reflective to be able to modify our approach when new insights emerge regarding undesirable emergent behaviours. Furthermore, there is a need for a more open discussion about the use of AI in the military, the extent of autonomous weapons, and whether there are any boundaries. It is evident that such a discussion is currently lacking.

"Nevertheless, it is not capable of solving tasks or situations that are unexpected, unforeseen, or unknown in the same way that humans can. Artificial intelligence is most effective in domains where there are clearly defined rules or a vast quantity of data."

From your perspective, what are the key disciplines that need to be involved in the development and discussion of AI and its future progress?

To reiterate, I would emphasize making AI-based innovations resource-efficient and using them also for the transformation towards sustainability. My perspective on sustainability encompasses not only environmental considerations but also includes rights of individuals and the role of society in the process of transformation. This is consistent with the United Nations' perspective on sustainability. To achieve this, it is necessary to adopt a multidisciplinary approach encompassing both technical and social sciences, and to foster collaboration between industry and academia. Otherwise, it will not be effective.

Are there specific research questions or areas where we should encourage more interdisciplinary collaboration?

Any AI application requires interdisciplinary or cross-disciplinary work. We have learned in software engineering that users should be in the loop. The technical perspective alone is not sufficient to address all the issues necessary to develop fit-for-purpose systems. Fit-for-purpose development requires knowledge and understanding of the application domain, requirements, and needs. This knowledge and understanding do not come from STEM alone, but rather from social science and other disciplines.

Earlier in the interview, you mentioned the importance of addressing potential bias and discrimination. How do you distinguish between bias and customization? Is there a clear distinction?

To the best of my knowledge, there is a well-developed understanding of bias, and a strong research track record in service customization, personalization, and recommendations combined with the prevention of unintentional biases. Bias in general is necessary in society helping us to distinguish between friends and strangers, for example, or between our social groups and others. When we talk about bias in technical or AI-based systems, we are talking about unintentional bias or bias that goes against our ethical values.

We need customization for a good AI-based system. For example, AI in education needs to be customized. It uses biases because it can only derive ideas or certain distributions from the datasets it has. Society works with biases. The discussion about fairness is always relative to the ethical values we hold. I believe that liberalising AI, making it open source, and being transparent about the training data used can help prevent unintentional biases and biases that contradict our values.

From your personal perspective, what should be the AI vision?

My dream is the liberalization of AI. The breakthroughs in AI could be the chance for breakthroughs in digitalization: The winner-takes-it-all-mechanism could become historic, enabling a paradigm shift towards more diverse and innovative digitalization with less monopoly and accumulation of market power.

For this to happen, AI should become part of the global digital commons: Similar to open-source software, open data, or open education, we need AI ecosystems worldwide that can be used by anyone for the benefit of the planet or humanity. These AI ecosystems must be accessible and accountable. Basic AI should not be a masterpiece of political, economic, or military power. Yet, private proprietary forks of the AI commons must be possible and exploitable.

A key area for the beneficial application of this AI vision is to use this powerful tool to address the most critical threat to humanity, which is sustainability in all its forms. Commercial adoption for any meaningful application will happen anyway. But if we are talking about the public interest, then resources should be directed towards sustainability. This includes basic and applied research. The vision is to find a good companion for humanity in AI.

Given your professional background, do you think that Germany or Europe has a unique role to play in the field of AI? If so, are they taking adequate responsibility and action?

I think Germany has a big responsibility because of its economic power, perhaps more so than other countries. It also has a significant responsibility because it has been the source of many fundamental AI developments. However, I do not believe that it is fully embracing this role. I think we lack a clear vision in Germany. Coming from my political background, I feel that Germany's goals and strategies in this area are not well defined. The research coming out of Germany is excellent, and I hope we continue to attract top talent. But I see Germany as a major player in Europe, nothing more. I firmly believe that Europe needs to find its own way. Only then will it have the power to establish standards that are in line with our values or reject AI-based solutions that violate privacy. There is still a lot of work to be done.

"A key area for the beneficial application of this AI vision is to use this powerful tool to address the most critical threat to humanity, which is sustainability in all its forms."

Is there anything else you would like to add?

I think I have covered most of it, including the issue of AI in weapons. We need an international discussion on the red lines for the use of AI in autonomous weapons. I am not an advocate of an AI moratorium, as developments will continue regardless. But I am an advocate of critical and responsible AI research and deployment that needs to be accompanied and reflected in society and policy. The point is to use AI intelligently. When I talk about liberalizing AI, I am also talking about the need for a robust AI infrastructure. Otherwise, our ambitions will remain dreams. Research in Germany and Europe is strong, but to achieve impactful results, we need to turn research into innovation, which is impossible without a strong and modern infrastructure.

And of course, there is a lot of work to be done in terms of digitalization in Germany and Europe, but that is a topic for another interview.

What do we need more of? Is it funding, resources, data, computing power, something else?

I believe we need a change of mindset. We need people from different backgrounds in decision-making positions who understand the importance of modern infrastructure, public access to data, and good computing resources for the digital transformation. A change in mindset will ultimately lead to the improvements that are so desperately needed.

Thank you very much, Ina, for your time and insightful perspective on AI.

Thank you for the engaging questions.

It was a pleasure.

References

1. Carleton, A.D., et al.: The AI effect: working at the intersection of AI and SE. IEEE Softw. **37**(4), 26–35 (2020)
2. Dewitte, S., et al.: Artificial intelligence revolutionises weather forecast, climate monitoring and decadal prediction. Remote Sens. **13**(16), 3209 (2021)

3. Edwards, L.: The EU AI Act: A Summary of Its Significance and Scope. Ada Lovelace Institute (2021)
4. Fukuda-Parr, S., Gibbons, E.: Emerging consensus on 'ethical AI': human rights critique of stakeholder guidelines. Global Pol. **12**, 32–44 (2021)
5. Hassan, A.E., et al.: Rethinking software engineering in the foundation model era: from task-driven AI copilots to goal-driven AI pair programmers. https://arxiv.org/abs/2402.15943
6. ISO/IEC 22989:2022, Information technology: Artificial intelligence: Artificial intelligence concepts and terminology
7. Jankowski, P., et al.: Shaping digital transformation for a sustainable society. Contributions from Bits & Bäume. Technische Universität Berlin. https://doi.org/10.14279/depositonce-17526
8. Laux, J., Wachter, S., Mittelstadt, B.: Three pathways for standardisation and ethical disclosure by default under the European Union Artificial Intelligence Act. Comput. Law Secur. Rev. **53**, 105957 (2024)
9. Li, B., et al.: Trustworthy AI: from principles to practices. ACM Comput. Surv. **55**(9), 1–46 (2023)
10. Messner, D., et al.: Towards Our Common Digital Future. Flagship Report. WBGU (2019)
11. Mogos, C., Schieferdecker, I., Evaluation of trust policies by simulation. In: Proceedings of ICAART 2010 (2010)
12. Pearce, R., Zhang, Y.: Deep learning techniques have significantly impacted protein structure prediction and protein design. Curr. Opin. Struct. Biol. **68**, 194–207 (2021)
13. Schieferdecker, I.: Responsible software engineering. In: Goericke (ed.) The Future of Software Quality Assurance, pp. 137–146. Springer (2020)
14. Williams, A., Miceli, M., Gebru, T., The exploited labor behind artificial intelligence. Noema Mag. **22** (2022)
15. Yang, J., et al.: SWE-agent: agent-computer interfaces enable automated software engineering. https://arxiv.org/abs/2405.15793

Let's Talk AI with Computer Science Expert Martin Wirsing

Martin Wirsing[1] and Barbara Steffen[2(✉)]

[1] LMU, Munich, Germany
wirsing@informatik.uni-muenchen.de
[2] METAFrame Technologies, Dortmund, Germany
barbara.steffen@metaframe.de

Abstract. AI is a powerful man-made tool which should be used to improve and support our lives. It should help us achieve the global human goals by promoting health, combating poverty and fighting for our climate.

My personal AI mission: Explore and foster the use of LLMs for systematic development of safe software systems. In LLM-assisted Software Engineering an LLM acts together with other supporting bots and tools to help the human developers in all phases of the software lifecycle.

Fig. 1. Martin Wirsing

1 My Takes on AI

- **Artificial Intelligence (AI)** – AI is the ability of a machine to display humanlike capabilities such as reasoning, learning, planning and creativity [10].
- **Trust and Trustworthy AI** – Trust refers to the "assured reliance on the character, ability, strength, or truth of someone or something" [11]. Trustworthy AI should have the properties of being: (1) lawful, respecting all applicable laws and regulations; (2) ethical, respecting ethical principles and values; (3) robust, both from a technical perspective while taking into account its social environment [9].

B. Steffen et al. (Eds.): *Let's Talk AI*, LNCS 15000, pp. 173–177, 2026.
https://doi.org/10.1007/978-3-032-09008-9_20

- **Large Language Model (LLM)** – A language model is a mathematical model for analyzing and constructing texts in natural language. An LLM is a large-scale, pretrained, statistical language model based on neural networks [4].
- **Essential Elements of Human Capabilities** – Life; bodily health; bodily integrity; senses, imagination and thought; emotions; practical reason; affiliation; other species; play; and control over one's environment are the 10 "central human capabilities" that are needed for "the dignity of a human being" [5].
- **Global Human Goals** – In 2015 the United Nations defined 17 world development goals called the Sustainable Development Goals with the aim of "peace and prosperity for people and the planet, now and into the future" [12].

2 The Interview

[Barbara Steffen] I am delighted that Martin Wirsing (Fig. 1) is sitting here with me. Could you please briefly introduce yourself and your relationship to artificial intelligence?

[Martin Wirsing] Thank you. I'm delighted to be here. I'm an emeritus professor at LMU Munich, specializing in computer science, specifically in software development and formal methods. I've been involved with artificial intelligence for at least 30 to 40 years. My primary focus has been on symbolic methods such as logic and constraint reasoning. Sub-symbolic methods like neural networks are relatively new to me. We strive to develop safe systems in artificial intelligence and ensure that AI tools are safe for users, among other applications.

"My greatest fear is that politicians may misuse AI. They might claim that their AI system is an AGI which is superior to humans, and therefore, humans should follow [their] directives."

Can you give one or two examples of research questions you are currently addressing in artificial intelligence?

Let me mention two research questions. The first involves learning algorithms. If I examine the output of a learning algorithm, for instance, in decision support, I want to ensure the decisions are safe and within a well-defined boundary to prevent unsafe actions (see, for example, [7]). The second question relates to my main field of software development. How can we enhance software development with learning tools, specifically with LLMs? Will LLM-Assisted Software Engineering profoundly change the way develop software [1]?

"I'm apprehensive about AGI. I don't believe machines can truly express genuine emotions, though they can simulate them."

Is the role of trust in AI adoption related to your first research question?

Yes, trust is crucial in AI. Trust is a vital component of human relationships, but since LLMs behave like agents, it becomes a top priority. Trust is derived from quality. This encompasses many aspects, for example, that a system should consistently provide accurate answers and prove to be reliable. These quality attributes are essential for software and should also be met by AI systems. Otherwise, they won't be truly useful or widely adopted.

Would you suggest that we start using AI in areas where we can control the outcome? Basically, in contexts where we know the correct results or where we have clear expectations that put us in a position of greater control.

It really depends on the applications. As researchers, we are involved in applications across all fields. We aim to make these systems usable, and they become usable when quality is built into them. AI systems are less predictable than other systems, so we need to apply special validation and verification techniques.

What do you think is the role of ethics in the adoption of AI? Do you have any important measures in mind that you would suggest?

Indeed, ethical considerations are paramount to me and they should be taken into account right from the requirements stage. When developing a system, we should question the ethical values the system should embody (see, for example, [9]). This way, we can put safeguards and shields in place during development and we can ensure that the AI systems align with the ethical requirements.

If you look at AI and its potential future capabilities on a scale of 1 to 10, where 1 represents the artificial intelligence systems like ChatGPT that we see today, which are dedicated to a concrete context and functions, and 10 represents something like an artificial general intelligence (AGI) system that surpasses human capabilities. What do you think will be possible?

Well, I would say around 6. Software has always, in some ways, surpassed human capabilities. It started with something as simple as a pocket calculator, which performs multiplication – i.e., some form of reasoning – far better than I can by hand. So, software and software systems have always excelled in specific fields compared to humans. With AI, these fields expand. There are many areas where, due to AI, software can now outperform humans. Games like chess and Go [6] are examples; LLMs are able to perform impressive conversations (see also [4]). However, it's certainly not artificial general intelligence. I'm apprehensive about AGI. I don't believe machines can truly express genuine emotions, though they can simulate them. I believe we will need and use AI for many different applications, but not for dictating our actions.

"AI systems are less predictable than other systems, so we need to apply special validation and verification techniques."

So it's more about how people adopt AI, rather than that AI will or should become autonomous?

Yes, autonomous systems are a crucial field. I've worked on this for several years (see, for example, [7, 8]). We need autonomous machines that support us in our daily lives and in our jobs. However, my greatest fear is that politicians may misuse AI. They might claim that their AI system is an AGI which is superior to humans, and therefore, humans should follow the directives of the AGI (see, for example, [2]). So politicians could abdicate responsibility, treating the machine as an infallible entity. But ultimately, it's their responsibility to guide their country, and they shouldn't treat machines as infallible. This horrifying scenario could be exploited by authoritarian politicians, and I'm firmly against it.

That brings me to my next question. Many theoretically possible future scenarios are being discussed today. They range from dystopian to utopian. Where would you position yourself?

I believe AI, like any form of software, should enhance and support our lives. AI should help us achieve the global human goals [12]. We need to promote health, combat poverty, and fight for our climate. AI could be an invaluable tool for these issues, as it enables us to solve more complex problems than we were able to before.

Because AI addresses these challenges in a more holistic way, or why would AI be helpful in these cases?

Yes, it is a holistic approach which encompasses many different fields. AI is software, and this software should be used together with engineering solutions and social and political measures. Computer scientists don't create the applications; they come from other fields. Software engineers always need to collaborate with other fields. To solve these huge problems, computer scientists need to cooperate with scientists from many other disciplines.

"When developing a system, we should also question the ethical values the system should embody."

That leads me to my next question. Reflecting on the last few days, what are some insights that were particular surprising or interesting to you?

The discussion about ethical AI is very important. We also need to understand and discuss the EU regulations. I believe we should discuss these issues with our students. In their education, students need to learn about ethical aspects and how to incorporate them into systems.

Is there a specific research question or topic that you would like to see addressed by multiple disciplines? If so, which disciplines should be involved?

As a software engineer, I've worked on systems for predicting various outcomes. For instance, for predicting how climate and land use will change in a region like Bavaria, you need to collaborate with many disciplines, including meteorologists, plant scientists, economists, and tourism experts [3]. For all major and important applications, we need cooperation between different disciplines.

From your personal perspective, what should be the AI vision?

As I mentioned earlier, AI should be used to enhance our lives and help to solve the world's global problems.

Do you have anything to add?

No, thank you. I enjoyed our discussion. I wish you all the best and success in your career, whatever you choose to do.

Thank you, Martin, for your time and your perspective on AI. Enjoy the rest of the conference!

You're welcome.

References

1. Belzner, L., Gabor, T., Wirsing, M.: Large language model assisted software engineering: prospects, challenges, and a case study. In: Steffen, B. (ed.) Bridging the Gap Between AI and Reality (AISoLA 2023). LNCS, vol. 14380, pp. 355–374. Springer (2024)
2. Hesse, W.: Das Zerstörungspotenzial von Big Data und Künstlicher Intelligenz für die Demokratie. Inform. Spektrum **43**(5), 339–346 (2020)
3. Mauser, W., Prasch, M. (eds.): Regional Assessment of Global Change Impacts. Springer (2016)
4. Minaee, S., Mikolov, T., Nikzad, N., Chenaghlu, M., et al.: Large language models: a survey. https://arxiv.org/abs/2402.06196
5. Nussbaum, M.: Frontiers of Justice: Disability, Nationality, Species Membership. Harvard University Press (2006)
6. Schrittwieser, J., Antonoglou, I., Hubert, T., Chenaglu, M., et al.: Mastering Atari, Go, Chess and Shogi by planning with a learned model. Nature **588**, 604–609 (2020)
7. Wirsing, M., Belzner, L.: Towards systematically engineering autonomous systems using reinforcement learning and planning. In: Lopez-Garcia, P., et al. (eds.) Analysis, Verification and Transformation for Declarative Programming and Intelligent Systems. LNCS, vol. 13160, pp. 281–306 (2023)
8. Wirsing, M. Hölzl, M., Koch, N., Mayer, P. (eds.): Software Engineering for Collective Autonomic Systems: The ASCENS Approach. LNCS, vol. 8998. Springer (2015)
9. European Commission: Ethics Guidelines for Trustworthy AI. https://digital-strategy.ec.europa.eu/en/library/ethics-guidelines-trustworthy-ai. Accessed Feb 2024
10. European Commission: What Is Artificial Intelligence and How Is It Used? https://www.europarl.europa.eu/topics/en/article/20200827STO85804/. Accessed Feb 2024
11. Merriam-Webster Dictionary: Trust. https://www.merriam-webster.com/
12. United Nations: The 17 Goals. https://sdgs.un.org/goals. Accessed Aug 2024

Let's Talk AI with Computer Science Expert Bernhard Steffen

Bernhard Steffen[1] and Barbara Steffen[2](✉)

[1] TU Dortmund, Dortmund, Germany
steffen@cs.tu-dortmund.de
[2] METAFrame Technologies, Dortmund, Germany
barbara.steffen@metaframe.de

Abstract. AI is far beyond whatever I would have expected. LLMs will certainly have a major societal impact.

My personal AI mission: There are huge opportunities and major risks. As there is no way to stop the development of AI, my mission is helping to make the best of it.

Fig. 1. Bernhard Steffen

1 My Takes on AI

- **Artificial Intelligence** – It changed over time, today it's mainly machine learning with increasing focus on large language models, which, in my eyes, for the first time justify the name AI.
- **Trust** – Concerns how humans perceive a certain entity. It should not be confused with trustworthiness, which is a property of the considered entity itself.
- **Explainability** – Traditionally, explainability of AI focused on indications of how a certain result is achieved. Typical are so-called heat maps which highlight the most important pixel for an image classification. This approach became obsolete with large language models. Here post-hoc rationalization seems more appropriate: Let the net provide you with reasons for the delivered result. This way, we are reaching a communication level reminiscent of dialogues between humans.
- **Essential Elements of Human Capabilities** – I have trouble pinpointing a capability which I consider out of reach of future AI-based technologies.

B. Steffen et al. (Eds.): *Let's Talk AI*, LNCS 15000, pp. 178–188, 2026.
https://doi.org/10.1007/978-3-032-09008-9_21

2 The Interview

[Barbara Steffen] *Today I have the pleasure of interviewing Bernhard Steffen (Fig. 1). Please introduce yourself and your connection to artificial intelligence.*

[Bernhard Steffen] As you mentioned, I'm a professor at the Technical University of Dortmund. Recently, I founded AISoLA, the event where this interview is taking place. I wasn't always a fan of artificial intelligence. I've observed so many hype cycles of AI throughout my life, and my appreciation only built up slowly. Some twenty years ago, I introduced active automata learning as a means to achieve model-based testing without requiring a priori models [12], which was a major hurdle in practice. Later we analyzed and explained random forests [7] by essentially transforming them into single decision trees. My interest in neural networks is, however, much younger. It started when we observed that we could treat them in a similar fashion as random forests [14]. Conceptually, this was quite elegant, but scalability was a problem. The true limits of our "traditional" approaches, however, became apparent with the large language models (LLMs) like ChatGPT. They require a major change of mind, not only concerning their validation, but also their use as they will inevitably impact everybody's life. This insight became the driving force behind the organization of AISoLA.

Can you name one or two specific AI-related research questions that you and your research group are currently working on?

We are working along two independent lines: One is that we want to verify or explain systems. We take the AI system as it is and try to understand or at least contain what it does, for example by verifying that it doesn't cause harm. The other line is that we try to build systems that exploit neural networks or other learned systems in a "harmless" way. We have to learn how to do that properly. Of course, if the entire system is not critical, there are no problems. More challenging is the case of critical systems that embody AI components that have to be "tamed" to guarantee the reliability of the entire system. We are currently experimenting with systems that contain AI-generated code. These systems do not contain, for example, neural networks, but only their output, the generated code. Thus, they can be treated with the methods which have been developed in recent decades. This is a change of attitude towards AI-based systems: Do not try to verify or explain the LLMs but their outcome. In the case of code-generating LLMs this sounds very natural. Nobody verifies the programmer. It is the program that is verified. I like this approach which, in a sense, puts LLMs and humans on an equal level, as I do not believe that we will ever be able to sufficiently control the LLMs themselves.

Do you focus specifically on the developers, such as technical experts, or on end users?

In fact both: We have developed the concept of Language-Driven Engineering [17] to support even end users to participate in the development process of certain applications by providing them with a graphical language interface that addresses their mindsets. In fact, the aim of LDE to narrow the gap between end users and developers can be reduced even further by domain-specific natural languages: Based on, for example, ChatGPT-based code generation, people can participate in the development process without any previous training, using natural language. I am convinced that future program development environments will increasingly take advantage of this opportunity (see, for example, [3]).

How do you verify the program?

There are numerous ways to do that, based on half a century's experience in program verification [6, 9]. There are interactive methods, typically supported by theorem proving, which require already expert knowledge to handle small scale applications [8]. In contrast, model-checking techniques [5] and their statistical counterparts [1, 2] are fully automated as soon as an adequate abstraction level has been defined and they scale much better. In fact, statistical model checking, which inherently is a testing technology, applies even to larger-scale neural networks where all other techniques fail. As a downside, statistical model checking only establishes knowledge with a certain probability. This may be considered a drawback for traditional programs, but it seems quite natural for structures that have been learned with statistical methods, like neural networks. Our research focuses on the verification of, from their structure, "traditional" programs that have been written with AI assistance. This allows us to apply the wealth of methods that have been developed in recent decades. We apply model checking and runtime verification based on active automata learning [3]. In the latter case, one looks at the entire system, which consists of a mixture of handwritten or model-driven designed code and parts that have been generated from natural language in a form of AI-assisted programming. You just look at the runtime behavior and validate the properties of the overall system. The application of active automata learning is particularly effective for web applications, as it directly works at the level of user interactions with the system and does not require us to deduce the behavior from the highly heterogeneous code structure.

"[The AIs'] so-called emergent properties may well lead to a kind of 'intelligence' far beyond our expectation and recognition, and therefore far beyond our control … [In fact, many] capabilities that experts thought were out of the scope of these systems have, in the meantime, already been accomplished."

In your opinion, what role does trust play in the adoption of AI?

Trust is certainly a crucial factor if one wants people to use a new technology. What I've learned at AISoLA is that trust is a complex concept. When we, the formal methods people, think about trust, we consider the reasons why we should trust, for example, AI. Can I prove that it does what it promises or at least that it won't cause harm? At AISoLA I learned that these considerations about the systems' (provable) quality criteria concerns their trustworthiness which should clearly be distinguished from trust, as it is a property of the user: a user may well trust a system that is not trustworthy and vice versa. Indeed, psychologists study ways to increase trust without caring about the properties of a system, for example by placing quality seals or getting famous people to speak in favor. From an ethical perspective it is now important to adequately balance the two so that people's trust or fear are justified.

Orthogonal is the question of the required level of trust. Clearly, there is a big difference between using DALL-E to create a picture and sitting in a self-driving car. I learned at AISoLA that this is where the notion of calibrated trust comes into play. We must learn to adjust our trust level to the criticality of the considered (AI) system. This is not as easy as my example suggests. For example, social media seemed harmless at first sight, but we had to learn that they can be exploited to misinform and polarize to a level that even may endanger democracy, another topic that has been discussed at AISoLA [13], To summarize. Establishing a responsible understanding of trust is important, and it is very difficult when systems with the complexity of LLMs are involved that, inevitably, will inform our lives. We have to learn to live with these systems, and we have to find ways such that this is done in a fashion where trust and trustworthiness are in balance and calibrated to the criticality of the application.

Are there essential measures that we should consider to ensure ethical AI use?

Ethics is a very different matter. As a technician I would say, whenever I have proved that a system is trustworthy, it is ethical for me to convince you to use it. But the ethical discourse is typically quite different. Famous are the discussions of dilemmas: What is the ethical decision in a situation where one either drives straight on a road passively and kills five people, or actively steers the car to the side to kill only one person? These kinds of questions have come up, and they are not at all technical. They belong to a different discipline which, as far as I understood, does not take a clear position here, as it is unethical to measure the value of individual lives or even compute with them. In practice, this works if these cases are rare and can be dealt with on an individual basis. However, it is not sufficient when we want to set the rules for AIs. In fact, we are exactly in this situation when talking about the acceptance of self-driving cars where similar questions arise: Is it ethical to introduce self-driving cars if this would reduce the number of severe accidents by 90%, but with the effect that other people die? As a technician I would say "90% reduction is great. Let's go for it". But this discussion seems, at least in Germany, to be far from over. In the end, the situation is similar to trust: We have to learn to adequately calibrate ethics.

Regarding the technical capabilities of artificial intelligence in the future, on a scale of 1 to 10, where 1 stands for artificial intelligence systems like ChatGPT, and 10 for artificial general intelligence systems that surpass human capabilities. What do you think will be possible?

In some sense, I think what you describe as 1 is already quite advanced, because these LLMs are already quite general: They can write, translate, code, draw, play, etc., essentially based on the same machinery and with a performance that often surpasses human capabilities. This shows that we are already beyond the stage where AlphaGo demonstrated the power of AI by easily beating the top human Go players. This was amazing, but still considered harmless, because AlphaGo is just a special tool, like a crane that is considered harmless even though it can lift material far beyond human capabilities. LLMs like ChatGPT provide already a flavor of what you're referring to with artificial general intelligence. They cover a complexity beyond human reach and their "mental capability" surpasses human expertise in many situations. Looking at the current development, I do not think that it will take long until these AIs will beat the best human experts in numerous, unrelated challenges, not only in playing Go or translating texts, but also in writing poems, drawing pictures, steering cars, and even executing surgeries or playing football when combined with adequate robotics. In fact, I cannot imagine a concrete capability that I would consider to definitely remain out of reach for AI systems in the future. The talk by Edward Lee [10] was very enlightening in this respect. He showed that capabilities that experts thought were out of the scope of these systems have, in the meantime, already been accomplished. It's not only that I think we will see that these systems can perform better on tasks we understand. Rather their so-called emergent properties may well lead to a kind of "intelligence" far beyond our expectation and recognition, and therefore far beyond our control. Again, referring to Edward Lee's talk, and to experiences with Pi [21], the communication with the AI-based system may even become more attractive than with other humans: They "listen" carefully, and answer adequately, and they are always available to provide advice. In fact, when asked for the underlying WHY, they are even great at explaining the advantages of the proposed statements or decisions. As Edward Lee says, these systems will be unbeatable when it comes to post-hoc rationalization [10]: They simply have a much wider knowledge base than any human, and it will be increasingly difficult for us to withstand this convincing power.

"[What would happen] when all technicians agree that we cannot control AI systems and should abandon them? Abandon, how? There is no such way. We need to learn to navigate the uncertainty that comes with the AI systems."

Could you place the possible future capabilities somewhere on the scale from 1 to 10?

The power of LLMs was like a shock for me. I never expected that this technology would carry this far. Just look at the many directions it influences today already. As I mentioned, I currently have no idea where the limits could be and I would clearly say 10, or even more: It will not be too difficult for future AIs to clearly outperform humans in most challenges. These systems may soon become emotionally attractive to humans in the way shown in *Her* [20]. In fact, the dialogues with Pi [19, 21] are already now quite fascinating in this sense.

Looking at that, there are a lot of different scenarios being discussed about what the future will look like as AI develops. These scenarios range from dystopia to utopia. Where do you position yourself?

I would position myself in the middle, say 5 in a range from 1 to 10 which, admittedly, sounds boring. In the past, a lot of dystopian scenarios have been warned about, like nuclear wars, overpopulation, and global warming, to name just a few. In almost all these cases, we react(ed), according to many experts, far too hesitantly. For example, concerning overpopulation, we were warned in the 1970s that we may reach a population of up to four billion people. Now we are eight billion and we're still here. Also with global warming, I am pretty sure that we will surpass the temperature limits we set for ourselves, but I guess humanity will still survive. The strong thing about humans is that they can adapt. This does not mean that we will be able to maintain the current quality of life, but we will probably survive, hopefully not in a future as sketched in the movie Matrix, where we live in some kind of soup producing energy and the rest, even our mind, is under the control of computers.

I am not afraid of such a dystopian vision, but I believe that we, at least most of us, will increasingly follow decisions made by the authority of automated systems without questioning. In a sense, this started already with the introduction of traffic lights which let you wait even when you can clearly see that the streets are empty. The point is that we will successively forget about the notion of empty streets and simply wait – and don't care. Most people are happy with this, and they are, for example, glad to follow a navigation system without having any idea about the surroundings they are driving through. This may work fine as long as there are some people who still know what is going on, but, perhaps, in the future, there are no such people anymore, and only the AI "knows". This may not be a problem if the criteria the AI uses are in line with our criteria. This may, however, easily get out of hand as nicely illustrated by *The Social Dilemma* [22], showing that originally "ethical" criteria produced systems that polarize and misinform people. Please note that this did not even require particularly elaborate technology. In summary, I hope that the benefits outweigh the drawbacks of future AI-based systems, but I also believe that it will significantly change our lives in a way that forces us to adapt in ways not everybody would consider an improvement.

Do you see the potential for a widening gap in society? For example, early adopters who are really excited about the new technical capabilities and try out everything until they get very good at it, while others are more hesitant and thus get left behind?

I think this gap will definitely widen. We're living in a world which is accelerating its rate of change, and fewer and fewer people and organizations are able to deal with this. In this world, people or organizations that are used to and appreciate change as an opportunity have a significant advantage, while hesitant people and organizations are doomed to fail – unfortunately there are many of those in Germany! AI reinforces this trend, and it is important to be prepared for it. If an organization is what is called evolutionary fit [18] it can win, otherwise it will inevitably lose in the long term [16]. Thus, there will be many winners, but most probably many more losers in the future.

Reflecting on the last few days and the interdisciplinary discussions, was there an insight that you found particularly interesting?

Perhaps most importantly, I realized that I see many things far too much from a technical perspective. For example, take the notion of trust again. I always thought achieving trust requires us to make the considered systems more robust, secure, reliable, etc. Then I listened to a talk from a psychologist where the impact of a seal on trust was considered independently of any technological quality criteria. Luckily, the study showed little impact. Looking back, I do not quite remember how people were questioned. Were they simply asked whether they value seals, or were they put in scenarios where similar systems were presented, some with and some without a seal? My intuition would be that for the latter, some impact should be measurable, at least if the seals convey some kind of seriousness, or even better, come with a known brand name. This reminds me a bit of the TÜV in Germany, the Technische Überwachungsverein, when certifying software. From the technological point of view, the TÜV does very little, but it provides certificates, which often suffice to officially operate a software system. This works quite well, because the TÜV is an authority. It is known to everybody in Germany for their biennial technical checks of cars. These checks are much more adequate for their purpose than the superficial analyses of software, which merely focus on the underlying development process and hardly concern the software as such. Is it acceptable that the TÜV authority gained for car inspections is then used to provide trust for software in the described way? As a technician I would say no.

On the other hand, we are simply not able to deal with the wealth of software systems in a way that I would consider satisfactory, and, so far, things seem to be OK. The infamous software crisis [11] never really struck, and we learned to live with the various obstacles poor software solutions provide. In the "real world", when you have to communicate with the public or with politicians, you have to make compromises and you have to accept the attention which some scientists get which I would rather categorize as marketing or sales people. After all, what would it help, for example, if the technicians all agree that we cannot control AI systems and should abandon them? Abandon, how? There is no such way. We need to learn to navigate the uncertainty that comes with the AI systems. Fear is not a good advisor here. My mother always told me: "When you risk to hit an obstacle, do not focus on the obstacle, but on the gap where you want to pass by".

Is there a specific topic or research question that you would like to see addressed from an interdisciplinary perspective, and, if so, which disciplines would you like to get involved?

In your thesis [16] you state that systems thinking [15] is one of the pillars for achieving evolutionary fitness, i.e., the capability to survive in a fast-changing world. I am convinced that we need the same here. We have to holistically approach the situation with an interdisciplinary cooperation of experts not only from computer science, but also from, for example, psychology, philosophy, law, education, economics, and politics. AISoLA was founded to support exactly this cooperation. I was quite impressed by the different perspectives. I mentioned the discussions about trust and ethics already, and AI is certainly a game changer when it comes to law: how should we deal with liability caused by AI-based decisions. It certainly does not make sense to sue a system. There is no doubt that education is essential to establish an understanding of calibrated trust in the public and the impact of economical goal setting has clearly been pinpointed by *The Social Dilemma* [22] which calls for regulation. This underlines the importance of institutions like the Research Center on Trust and the Lamarr Institute in Dortmund, which are both characterized by their interdisciplinarity.

> "We have to holistically approach the situation with an interdisciplinary cooperation of experts not only from computer science, but also from, for example, psychology, philosophy, law, education, economy, and politics."

From your personal perspective, what should be the AI vision?

A year ago, I clearly would have said that we should try to control AI in a fashion we control a crane, just as a means to amplify our capabilities. However, looking at LLMs, is this possible at all? I heard people saying that it makes no sense to play Go anymore because a computer can do it better. I do not follow this argument as I still like to play Go and Chess for fun, and, concerning cranes, weightlifting is still an Olympic discipline. The same may be true for car racing: Formula One racing between humans will probably still be popular when automated cars outperform humans. But there is a difference with AI when it starts showing us the limits of our very bounded rationality [10] in real life, by, for example, questioning each of our decisions with convincing explanations based on post-hoc rationalization. This may be fantastic at the beginning when we are still able to stay in control by revising the explanations and this way make the proposed decisions ours. We have already seen examples in science where this form of amplification led to amazing breakthroughs. But in the long run, when the AI proposals become more and more perfect, we may risk to totally delegate decision making to the AI, as many already delegated route planning to Google Maps. Is this dystopian or utopian? We must learn to accept the AI systems as (often superior) partners rather than tools and to forget about understanding their inner workings. As mentioned before about AI-assisted programming, we should not try to verify/control the AI, but the produced output/code, just as we never verify the programmers but their work. Or, more generally, we should not try to verify the AI, but carefully inspect its responses. This way the AI may turn into a powerful partner, a Big Brother, if you wish, who certainly is watching us, but hopefully does not intend to harm us. I am optimistic that we can avoid dystopian emergent properties that lead us into slavery. Why should the AI aim at doing this – except, it learns by human examples which are sometimes quite scary? We have seen this with, for example, social biases. Thus, a major challenge is to control the data sources for the learning processes.

"We must learn to accept the AI systems as (often superior) partners rather than tools and to forget about understanding their inner workings."

We need to distinguish contexts here, right? We have contexts like chess and Go, which are games with a predefined set of rules that describe the game. But the real world is less defined, much more complex, and constantly changing. So while the game or predefined settings make it easy to determine what is right and what is wrong, who won and who lost, what is a cat and what is a dog, in the real world there are many contexts or tasks for which we don't know the correct answers. So, it is more complicated to verify those answers. How should we approach these more complex scenarios?

You are right, learning in contexts where the outcome is clear, is quite different from learning in a context where there is no clear known answer. The dog/cat classification is a good example for the former, while the situation for chess and Go is much more involved. There is typically no known best move. The quality of a move is evaluated only many moves later when one of the players wins. This is a clear sign of success for the considered sample/play, but the impact of a certain move is still quite indirect and must be reconfirmed in many games. And there are situations where the role of a sample can only be understood in the context of the entire training set like in clustering, where huge data sets are bundled according to similarity. Also, language translation belongs to this category of what is called un/self-supervised learning, even though the output may well be checked for semantic or syntactic correctness. This additional information is typically applied in a subsequent reinforcement step. There is a wealth of methods and heuristics, but I am not the right person to tell more about them. We are focusing on the validation of the results of a learning process or, in the case of AI-assisted programming, of the resulting code.

In most real-world applications of AI we do not know the precise answers, if they exist at all. This is where the dialogue between humans and AI comes into play, perhaps via a chain of post-hoc rationalization steps. In fact, I believe that these dialogues will boost our understanding in various disciplines. Already for playing Go, AI helped to reveal patterns that humans would never have been able to find because of their limited rationality. AI can go quite a few steps further and reveal relationships which may be game changers in medicine, mathematics, physics, biology, etc. The recent results concerning protein folding indicate the potential, and I am convinced that this is only the beginning.

Reflecting on the past week, how did you like AISoLA? It took place for the first time this year. Did it meet your expectations? And do you plan to continue?

I'm very happy with AISoLA, also from the perspective of the organizer. It was very interesting. Actually, I skipped most of the technical sessions, because I know very much what's going on there, and focused on the non-technical sessions to learn more about the other disciplines' perspectives. In connection with the LLM-shock I got earlier, it really changed my perspective. In particular, it revealed the challenges we have to deal with from the societal side. This has motivated my plan to continue organizing AISoLA yearly in the near future.

Is there anything else you would like to add?

As a fan of bootstrapping and self-application [4] I first thought that I would disagree with Albert Einstein's quote "We cannot solve our problems with the same thinking we used when we created them", because I am convinced that we have to use AI to deal with the problems caused by AI. Then I realized, Einstein did not speak about technology, but about mindset, and I agree that we need a change of mindset, not only ours, but also that of the AIs. Think of the originally unintended polarization caused by social media as illustrated in *The Social Dilemma* [22]. It is a by-product, or as one would say today emergent property of profit maximization. Today's AI systems are orders of magnitude more complex than the rule-based systems mentioned in the Netflix documentary. It will therefore require a major collaborative effort to tame them.

Then, Bernhard, thank you very much for your time and insights on AI and its further development. And especially a big thanks from me and all the interviewees for the opportunity to attend AISoLA and meet interdisciplinary experts on AI.

Thank you.

References

1. Alur, R., Giacobbe, M., Henzinger, T.A., Larsen, K.G., Mikučionis, M.: Continuous-time models for system design and analysis. In: Steffen, B., Woeginger, G. (eds.) Computing and Software Science. LNCS, vol. 10000. Springer (2019). https://doi.org/10.1007/978-3-319-91908-9_22
2. Baier, C., Hermanns, H., Katoen, J.-P.: The 10,000 facets of MDP model checking. In: Steffen, B., Woeginger, G. (eds.) Computing and Software Science. LNCS, vol. 10000. Springer (2019). https://doi.org/10.1007/978-3-319-91908-9_21

3. Busch, D., Nolte, G., Bainczyk, A., Steffen, B.: ChatGPT in the loop: a natural language extension for domain-specific modeling languages. In: Steffen, B. (ed.) Bridging the Gap Between AI and Reality (AISoLA 2023). LNCS, vol. 14380, pp. 375–390. Springer (2024). https://doi.org/10.1007/978-3-031-46002-9_24
4. Carey, S.: Bootstrapping & the origin of concepts. Daedalus **133**(1), 59–68 (2004)
5. Clarke, E.M, Henzinger, T.A., Veith, H., Bloem, R.: Handbook of Model Checking. Springer (2018)
6. Floyd, R.W.: Assigning meanings to programs. In: Schwartz, J.T. (ed.) Mathematical Aspects of Computer Science, Proc. of Symp. on Applied Mathematics, vol. 19, pp. 19–32. American Mathematical Society (1967)
7. Gossen, F., Steffen, B.: Algebraic aggregation of random forests: towards explainability and rapid evaluation. Intl. J. Softw. Tools Technol. Trans. **25**, 267–285 (2023)
8. Hähnle, R., Huisman, M.: Deductive software verification: from pen-and-paper proofs to industrial tools. In: Steffen, B., Woeginger, G. (eds.) Computing and Software Science. LNCS, vol. 10000. Springer (2019). https://doi.org/10.1007/978-3-319-91908-9_18
9. Hoare, C.A.R.: An axiomatic basis for computer programming. Commun. ACM **12**(10), 576–580 (1969)
10. Lee, E.A.: Deep neural networks, explanations, and rationality. In: Steffen, B. (ed.) Bridging the Gap Between AI and Reality (AISoLA 2023). LNCS, vol. 14380. Springer (2024). https://doi.org/10.1007/978-3-031-46002-9_1
11. Naur, P., Randell, B. (eds.): Software Engineering: Report of a conference sponsored by the NATO Science Committee, Garmisch, Germany, October 1968. NATO Scientific Affairs Division (1969)
12. Raffelt, H., Merten, M., Steffen, B., et al.: Dynamic testing via automata learning. Intl. J. Software Tools Technol. Trans. **11**, 307–324 (2009)
13. Schiaffonati, V., Werthner, H., Lee, E., Vardi, M., Laurus, J., Metakides, G.: DigHum panel. beyond Chat-GPT: The impact of AI on academic research. In: Steffen, B. (ed.) Bridging the Gap Between AI and Reality (AISoLA 2023). LNCS, vol. 14380. Springer (2024)
14. Schlüter, M., Nolte, G., Murtovi, A., Steffen, B.: Towards rigorous understanding of neural networks via semantics-preserving transformations. Intl. J. Softw. Tools Technol. Trans. **25**(3), 301–327 (2023)
15. Senge, P.M.: System thinking. In: The Fifth Discipline: The Art and Practice of the Learning Organization. Broadway Business (2006)
16. Steffen, B., Alignment-Driven Adaptation Process & Tool (ADAPT): Towards Continuous and Holistic Adaptation of Organizations, Ph.D. Thesis, Universität Potsdam (2024)
17. Steffen, B., Gossen, F., Naujokat, S., Margaria, T.: Language-driven engineering: from general-purpose to purpose-specific languages. In: Steffen, B., Woeginger, G. (eds.) Computing and Software Science. LNCS, vol. 10000, pp. 311–344. Springer (2019). https://doi.org/10.1007/978-3-319-91908-9_17
18. Teece, D.J., Petricevic, O.: Capability-based theories of multinational enterprise growth. In: The Oxford Handbook of International Business Strategy (2021)
19. AISoLA Pi-Interview (https://aisola.org/news/pi-interview/)
20. Her (https://en.wikipedia.org/wiki/Her_(2013_film))
21. Pi (https://pi.ai/onboarding)
22. The Social Dilemma (https://en.wikipedia.org/wiki/The_Social_Dilemma)

Let's Talk AI with Computer Science Expert Wolfgang Ahrendt

Wolfgang Ahrendt[1] and Barbara Steffen[2(✉)]

[1] Chalmers University of Technology, Gothenburg, Sweden
ahrendt@chalmers.se
[2] METAFrame Technologies, Dortmund, Germany
barbara.steffen@metaframe.de

Abstract. My vision is that we align the AI developments with technological, scientific, interdisciplinary, and societal discussions about what is it we want and do not want. If we cannot agree, let us talk, hoping that, with help of this dialogue, we are better equipped for the task. And let us work hard on the alignment of trust and trustworthiness.

My personal AI mission: To contribute to methods where we use AI in the context of program development, such that the resulting programs are trustworthy even if we do not rely on the trustworthiness of the used AI. Neuro-symbolic methods should help us with that mission.

Fig. 1. Wolfgang Ahrendt

1 My Takes on AI

- **Artificial Intelligence** – A term which invites mystification, ever since it is used. Earlier, AI was a label for a family of symbolic methods. Today, the term AI is used almost exclusively for machine learning techniques and applications. It would be better if we call it machine learning, which is more descriptive than the term AI. Having said that, in this interview I always say AI, and never machine learning. Probably, it is too late.

B. Steffen et al. (Eds.): *Let's Talk AI*, LNCS 15000, pp. 189–195, 2026.
https://doi.org/10.1007/978-3-032-09008-9_22

- **Trust** – Trust is the belief in trustworthiness. Admittedly, this is a recursive definition. Still, this is a useful approach to thinking about trust. For instance, when aiming to increase trust in something, one can either try to influence the belief directly, or the trustworthiness which then feeds back to the belief in trustworthiness.
- **Explainability** – The existence and transparency of cause-effect relations, be they exact or probabilistic.
- **Essential Elements of Human Capabilities** – Intentions. Emotions. And the interference of emotions and rationality. Don't we often witness pretendedly rational debates which however are driven by emotions?

2 The Interview

[Barbara Steffen] Today I have the pleasure of speaking with Wolfgang Ahrendt (Fig. 1). Could you please briefly introduce yourself and your personal relationship to artificial intelligence?

[Wolfgang Ahrendt] Thank you for asking me to be part of this interview series. I think this is a great initiative. I am a computer scientist working at Chalmers University of Technology in Gothenburg, Sweden. I moved there 22 years ago, after doing my PhD in Karlsruhe, Germany. The focus of my research is software verification, but I started more generally in the area of automated theorem proving, which some people have labeled as AI. Today the label AI has very much changed, and we refer to AI mostly in connection with neural network-based systems, which developed very rapidly in the last years. So, one could label the area I come from as "old AI". However, I never liked these labels, not then, and not now. But that is a different discussion. I was not very involved with "new AI" until lately, when I started looking into how we could use tools like ChatGPT and Code Copilot for programming in a good way. How can we exploit the power of large language models for programming without ever trusting them? This is my current connection to AI. I will elaborate on that in my talk later at this conference. Also, I am organizing here a track on AI-assisted programming, together with Klaus Havelund [2]. It is high time that we talk about the consequences, the possible and desired future of programming, in the light of this development.

> "[…] there is a strong tendency towards wanting to believe what we are told by a machine; in particular if it comes across in an eloquent and seemingly informed way."

AI-assisted programming is one of the main challenges that you are currently addressing in your AI research?

Yes, and I am thrilled to work in the intersection between very new developments in AI and exact methods of the kind people like me have been investigating for a long while. There is a keyword used lately, "neuro-symbolic AI" [3]. It refers to combinations of, on the one hand, neural networks which are very powerful but difficult to analyze or explain, and, on the other hand, symbolic methods, like what people like me have been doing for a longer while. What I want to work on is neuro-symbolic methods for trustworthy software development.

Are you mainly interested in the technical side or also in what we can learn from it, how we should work with it?

Both. There are a lot of technical challenges which I find very interesting, the solution of which can make a real difference. So in some sense, there is a strong technical focus. At the same time, the talk I will give later today pictures a software development process which uses new AI and symbolic methods. And in the middle of the picture, there is the human developer who takes all crucial decisions, accepting or rejecting suggestions generated by AI and analysed by exact methods [1]. The focus of the work is neuro-symbolic software development, and the role the human plays within.

Moving on to my next question about trust, which I think is also relevant to your research. What role does trust play in the adoption of AI, and what kind of measures are essential in terms of ethical AI adoption?

Trust is one of the biggest problems we are having with the late AI hype. There is an enormous explosion and popularization of AI usages. Very many non-technical people actively use AI now. Actually, people are heavily interacting with AI for a longer while already, but under the hood. Social networks have been feeding us with content selected or filtered by AI. But now, many people use AI actively. One of the biggest challenges with that is a too big trust in AI systems. Whether we are non-technical or technical, there a strong tendency towards wanting to believe what we are told by a machine [4]; in particular if it comes across in an eloquent and seemingly informed way. Had it been a person writing that, it would be someone knowing what he or she is talking about. The trust we have learnt to put in humans expressing themselves like that is transferred to trust in machines who write in the same way. We see this phenomenon even in a technical context. As I said, I am interested in what all this means for programmers, who really are technical people. There are comparative studies about developers who use AI for programming and developers who do not. One such study also compares the trust the developers put into the security of the final result [5]. (The context was a security critical application.) The team which was not allowed to use AI had less trust in what they developed, compared to the team which was using AI when coding. But actually, the real security of the product was the opposite. The product developed without AI was more secure than the other. So there was an inverse relation between the trustworthiness and the trust, even in this technical context. This is one of the big challenges we have on the technical as well as the societal side with this AI boom. There is too much trust, actually. Let us not be too trustful here.

"I hope that all of us make a stronger effort to not just work on what is possible, but focus on what we want to happen and what we do not want to happen and how we can influence things in a better way."

In terms of the technical capabilities of artificial intelligence in the future, on a scale of 1 to 10, where 1 stands for the AI systems we see today, such as ChatGPT, and 10 stands for artificial general intelligence that surpasses human capabilities. What do you think will be possible?

I am skeptical. But it is also true that I, like most of us, did not think a few years back that an AI tool could do what ChatGPT is now doing. So what does it even mean that I am skeptical? But I am. I think we have a very long way to go, if it is even possible, for AI to make necessary connections between very different domains. To give you an example, take a car with autonomous functionality driving through a neighborhood with houses and gardens. Now, imagine a ball rolls onto the street from a garden. A human driver will likely connect a rolling ball with a child which may run after. But an AI based controller of a car will not anticipate the child. Why not? Because neither the controller nor the human can know this connection from the training data collected by driving around and all the situations which appear there. The human knows from totally different contexts the possible reason for the ball rolling around. Probably, someone is playing with it, most likely a child. This was not in my training set when I learned driving. I know it from a very different context, but it still helps me in the given context to make a decision. I think there are many such things, not all of them so life-threatening, that is not what I mean to say, but I think that we connect very many different things with each other. I think that machines are very far from that, and I am not sure they can ever do that. That is another debate, very speculative. Myself, I would rank it fairly low my trust into that a very general AI can act in a similar way as we can.

If you had to pick a number from 1 to 10, what would it be?

3

Building on that, many different future scenarios are discussed, ranging from dystopia to utopia. Where do you stand?

Dystopias and utopias are both speculative, with positive and negative connotations, respectively. I would not answer your question by saying that I like the discussion to be more grounded on where we currently are, what we are already experiencing as problems. Even if, hypothetically speaking, this technology would stay where it is (which is of course not true), we would have a lot of work to do to deal in a good way with the AI we already have. A good example of that was the discussion that took place in a session earlier today, about regulatory needs for Big Tech and companies in the information and communication sector. I hope that all of us make a stronger effort to not just work on what is possible, but focus on what we want to happen and what we do not want to happen and how we can influence things in a better way. I am not sure I answered your question, actually. I can make another attempt. What was the question?

> "We have to prevent, as I said, unwanted consequences of AI. None of our disciplines can do that alone."

Where would you place yourself on this dystopian-utopian spectrum? Can we look forward to the future or should we fear it?

My personality is more of an optimistic kind. But when it comes to this topic, I think we will be better off if we have a somewhat pessimistic approach, in order to guide our actions to prevent unwanted consequences. Some of them have already materialised, like the effects of AI on general opinions in elections. I think we are better off if we are not driven by a belief that every progression in technology and ability is a good thing. Let us be a bit skeptic.

Reflecting on the last days of this interdisciplinary conference, was there a particular insight from another discipline that you found interesting?

I can immediately name one. There was a talk here by a researcher in law about liability. Early in the talk there were reactions from some of us computer scientists. The following discussion revealed a clash in terminology, but also in the conceptual approach. This is what is great about such an interdisciplinary event, that we can clear these things out and broaden each other's spectrum. It is not only about labelling, it is also about how we frame concepts and which kind of distinctions we like to be sharp on and less sharp on. This varies greatly among different disciplines. It is very inspiring to be exposed to this. More concretely, that talk was about liability in the context of AI, the different legal principles which are applied and have always been applied, like developer responsibility versus product supplier responsibility. Someone develops something, and someone else uses that thing for a product and sells the product. Where does the liability lie? Different principles exist and have been applied in different legal frameworks, on the national level or the level of the European Union, for instance. There were legal initiatives, some of which have been rejected, and so on. Researchers in law highlight in such discussions the consequences of law to insurance, for instance. Every law in this sector triggers insurance policies. In my community, we do not think of these things. I do not mean to say that we should focus on that, we have enough to do in our respective areas, and we also need coherence in a scientific tradition. But we do need this dialogue. This was an example where I learnt a lot.

> "I think, [we should] align the AI developments with technological, scientific, interdisciplinary, and societal discussions about what we want."

Each discipline brings its own expertise, but it is important that all disciplines are guided by a basic understanding of the other disciplines to ensure that critical factors are not overlooked. Otherwise, each discipline may overlook certain aspects simply because they are not aware of them.

Exactly. I think each of these areas is lacking aspects which are important, but also contribute aspects which the others are lacking. In this dialogue, each side is realizing in which terms another discipline is thinking. And that changes the framing of how I think about my own field and the overall context it is in. We have to prevent, as I said, unwanted consequences of AI. None of our disciplines can do that alone. The task is a very difficult and we may not get it right, but not doing anything would be much worse. All these different disciplines have to make their respective contributions.

Do you have a specific AI-related topic or research question in mind that you would like to see addressed in the near future?

Oh, there are so many. Myself, I decided to look into a specific one which I think that is among the things we should be doing. At this conference, I organise a track on AI-assisted programming [2], collecting people interested in what AI means for software development.

From your personal point of view, what is the vision of AI that will lead us to a desirable future?

All kinds of technologies, very much also AI, come with the promise of a better world. And yes, the world is getting better in some aspects, but may get worse in others. Someone says "We want to make the world better", but actually, they found a business model which works very well for them, right? The driving force is commercial. Maybe we cannot overcome that. But I think it is good if we realize that many impactful changes have commercial driving forces, they are not all about "Let's bring the world together" and all these big words. I do not want to be ultra-negative to many of the changes. But I think it is good that we are conscious about the forces which drive certain changes. I think I am again drifting away from your question, can you repeat it once more?

What do you think the AI vision should be?

Yes, the AI vision. It holds for AI as for everything else: if we find good ways to use it, great, let's do it. And what is good is a matter of discussion, of course. We may have different opinions on what is good and not good about the chatbot talking to a lonely person. Is that good or not? Maybe I find it bad until I am a lonely person. Such discussions are difficult, but necessary. And that should be our vision, I think, to align the AI developments with technological, scientific, interdisciplinary, and societal discussion about what is it we want. If we cannot agree, fine, let us talk and hope that after this dialogue we are a bit smarter than before. That is my vision of the AI.

Is there anything you would like to add?

No, I think I added quite a bit to the scope of your questions with thoughts of mine. By reflecting out loud.

Thank you, Wolfgang, for your time and your perspective on the various topics. I look forward to your presentation!

Thank you, Barbara, for this opportunity. Much appreciated!

Thanks to you, it was my pleasure.

References

1. Ahrendt, W., Gurov, D., Johansson, M., Rümmer, P.: TriCo: Triple copiloting of implementation, specification and tests. In: Margaria, T., Steffen, B. (eds.) Leveraging Applications of Formal Methods, Verification and Validation. Verification Principles (ISoLA 2022). LNCS, vol 13701. Springer (2022). https://doi.org/10.1007/978-3-031-19849-6_11
2. Ahrendt, W., Havelund, K.: AI assisted programming. In: Steffen, B. (ed.) Bridging the Gap Between AI and Reality (AISoLA 2023). LNCS, vol. 14380. Springer (2024). https://doi.org/10.1007/978-3-031-75434-0_7
3. Marcus, G.: The next decade in AI: four steps towards robust Artificial Intelligence (https://arxiv.org/abs/2002.06177)
4. Mosier, K.L., Skitka, L.J.: Human decision makers and automated decision aids: made for each other? In: Automation and Human Performance: Theory and Applications. Erlbaum (1996)
5. Perry, N., Srivastava, M., Kumar, D., Boneh, D.: Do users write more insecure code with AI assistants? (https://arxiv.org/abs/2211.03622)

Let's Talk AI with Computer Science Expert Holger Hermanns

Holger Hermanns[1] and Barbara Steffen[2](✉)

[1] Saarland University, Saarbrücken, Germany
hermanns@cs.uni-saarland.de
[2] METAFrame Technologies, Dortmund, Germany
barbara.steffen@metaframe.de

Abstract. The explosion of opportunities for software-driven innovations comes with an implosion of human opportunities and capabilities to understand and control these innovations.

My personal AI mission: To help prevent the disenfranchisement of individuals through cascades of software-based automated decisions.

Fig. 1. Holger Hermanns

1 My Takes on AI

- **Artificial Intelligence** – "Artificial Intelligence" has become a misnomer for something that is "Artificial Imitation" at a large scale.
- **Trust** – Since trust appears to be a chiefly subjective notion, it seems worthwhile to instead focus on trustworthiness as an indicator of justifiable trust.
- **Explainability** – Explainable intelligent systems need context-aware and situation-specific approaches to explainability. The resulting requirements might not be suitable for promoting trust, but trustworthiness.
- **Essential Elements of Human Capabilities** – Nothing specific, except in expert contexts as needed for human oversight of high-risk AI systems enforced in the upcoming (finalised) EU AI Act.

B. Steffen et al. (Eds.): *Let's Talk AI*, LNCS 15000, pp. 196–204, 2026.
https://doi.org/10.1007/978-3-032-09008-9_23

2 The Interview

[Barbara Steffen] Hello, Holger Hermanns (Fig. 1) from Saarland University. Thank you very much for taking the time for this interview. Could you please introduce yourself and your relationship to artificial intelligence?

[Holger Hermanns] Certainly, I'm a professor of computer science at Saarland University. My background is in the theory of computing with a focus on verification. Over the years, I have branched out into other areas and become more applied. Since around 2016, I have been investigating what we call perspicuity, which refers to the complexity of modern systems, including AI systems, and the challenges this poses for transparency and comprehension. This has led to two main research activities. One is a so-called Sonderforschungsbereich, a special research initiative involving around 50 to 60 researchers. It is funded by the Deutsche Forschungsgemeinschaft with a budget of roughly 3 million euros per year. Here, we are exploring how to design systems that are inherently explainable, transparent, and comprehensible. This research brings together experts from human-computer interaction, verification, and various areas of AI. However, the scope is broader than just AI. Today, we are facing many systems that aren't classified as AI systems, yet they are still too complex to fully understand or control. A prime example is the diesel emission scandal, which was essentially a software scandal, yet without an AI component to it. The automotive software was misused massively, against the interest of the society and car owners [2]. And the systems were so complex that their workings remained hidden. Even now, some seven years after the uncovering of the scandal, there are court cases that are partly about deciphering that software. Software complexity is a driving force in my research. The other aspect of my work that seems worth mentioning is interdisciplinary research on explainability and AI, conducted with colleagues from psychology, philosophy, ethics, and law [5]. Some of them were actually here this week.

> "We're working with the premise that AI is meant to be beneficial and as such is worthwhile to be promoted, but also that mechanisms are needed to prevent it from having adverse effects […]."

Can you give an example of one or two specific research questions that you are currently working on with respect to AI?

We're working with the premise that AI is meant to be beneficial and as such is worthwhile to be promoted, but also that mechanisms are needed to prevent it from having adverse effects on our society or from infringing on fundamental human rights. There are instances where this balance is clearly not maintained. Current legislation, especially the upcoming European AI Act, enforces the concept of human oversight for high-risk AI systems, for instance when it comes to AI systems used to decide about access to higher education, such as for screening applicants applying to a university. These systems must be free of discrimination, and since that is nowadays almost impossible to achieve with current AI technology, there is the idea that if a qualified individual oversees the AI system in such high-risk situations, then responsibility can be reassigned to this human oversight. The trick then is that with the presence of an oversight person and the reassigned responsibility, the known legal system – such as insurances covering damages or providing compensations in case of wrong decisions – can be reinstalled, despite the blatant problems of the underlying AI technologies. This concept brings up many challenges with respect to the technical design of the system. It is essentially a form of human-computer interaction where the human is a trained expert. Questions arise about how the technical system should communicate with the oversight, how the system can be influenced, when the oversight is actually held responsible, and how they know of their own responsibility. This is interesting, especially as the laws are currently being shaped. In our interdisciplinary research, lawyers are discussing with us how the law is designed and formulated, and we aim at distilling requirements regarding the technical aspects – which ultimately boil down to computational aspects [1, 6]. What properties can we guarantee, and how can we ensure them? This is one of the most pressing issues at the moment, since the legislative European institutions, as per the AI Act, anticipate guidelines for this to be developed within the next few years. We have just finished a paper on the "AI act for the working programmer" to provide assistance in navigating the 450-pages document.

What role does trust play in the adoption of AI?

It's practically important, but difficult to grasp. Some psychological studies suggest that people tend to trust computing systems more than they trust humans, and that explanations do not necessarily facilitate trust [4]. The more mysterious the system, the more trust they seem to place in it, to say it simply. If they understand how it works, their trust diminishes. There's also the phenomenon of unjustified trust, where people trust an app simply because a celebrity endorses it, even though there's no rational reason for this trust. So, while trust is likely important for adoption, justified trust may not be as crucial.

Could this be addressed with more awareness and education?

I firmly believe in education. I think our society needs to be better educated about the systems they interact with. Whether this pertains to trust, perhaps. The more competent individuals are, the more justified their trust or mistrust may be. But this could also be a subjective perception. Perhaps I'm overestimating our capabilities.

Could it be that people perceive systems as trustworthy because we see them as aggregates of the knowledge of all the people who helped design and develop them? Whereas when we deal with just one specific person, we recognize that that person may know more than we do, but assume that his or her knowledge is most likely limited compared to the system's knowledge?

That could very well be the case. However, the knowledge in these systems is largely syntactic, based on combinations of words, rather than semantic, understanding the meaning behind the words. This could be a misconception among the public, but it's an important distinction.

It's often described as gathered and aggregated knowledge, isn't it?

Yes, but the misunderstanding is that this isn't factual knowledge. It's knowledge about combinations of words or phrases. The meaning behind these words is what's missing.

And what kind of measures do you think would be helpful or essential to ensure ethical use of AI in the future?

About seven or eight years ago, I came across this issue. Then, I took the initiative for a lecture series, nowadays called "Ethics for Nerds". It got a few distinguished awards. The aim of that lecture series is to ensure that the computer scientists we train or collaborate with behave in a morally responsible way. I believe education is a key factor in promoting the ethical use of AI. It's a complex issue, partly because the effects are so indirect. Unlike a knife, which is obviously dangerous, the potential misuse of AI for unethical purposes is not as straightforward to pinpoint. Despite this, I appreciate initiatives like "AI for good", which uses AI in non-conventional ways to tackle societal issues. For instance, my colleague Ingmar Weber uses satellite imagery to study poverty and its changes over time, particularly after disasters. However, ensuring that AI technology remains in good hands is a significant challenge.

"However, the knowledge in these systems is largely syntactic, based on combinations of words, rather than semantic, understanding the meaning behind the words. This could be a misconception among the public, but it's an important distinction."

In terms of the technical capabilities of AI in the future, on a scale of 1 to 10, where 1 refers to artificial intelligence systems like ChatGPT and 10 refers to something like artificial general intelligence that surpasses human capabilities, what do you think will be possible?

Firstly, I think "intelligence" is a misnomer for what we're seeing. There's no intelligence in artificial intelligence. It's artificial imitation at a large scale. So, anything like general intelligence is nonsense. Therefore, my best guess is that the limit is at 2 or 3 out of 10. So, I lean towards the pessimistic side regarding the capabilities.

So, in essence, not much more progress than we are already seeing today. How do you define intelligence? What is missing to talk about intelligence instead of imitation?

What's missing is understanding. These systems don't understand. They can be creative in combining things in ways that haven't been done before, which can be surprising while the structures are as to be expected. But the meaning, the semantics, is missing. That is the main point. If ChatGPT tells you something where a "2" appears, it does not understand that "2" is a number, for example. It's just connecting words based on sophisticated statistics and a little surprise element, the latter for the purpose of avoiding that generated texts get boring.

When you look at that difference, do you think that we need to change something in the educational system, in terms of how we learn or work, to make sure that we maintain our advantage over AI in terms of intelligence versus imitation? Or to ensure that we don't lose that ability that makes us potentially unique?

There are repetitive tasks where AI will advance. It can be a relief for certain simple tasks. Now, your question is whether we need to change the educational system to maintain our advantage. I think we will keep our advantage.

We don't necessarily have to change because of that. But, for instance, it will be much more challenging for students to pass exams if they were so far mainly based on repetitive tasks, especially if those are given out as homework. If they instead are presented as part of an exam and there's no way to cheat, then maybe it's still possible to maintain a major share of simple repetitive tasks among what is examined. Still, higher cognitive processes are what distinguishes us from the capability of carrying out mechanizable tasks. And that should be what is actually being taught and evaluated in education. I therefore believe that the way we assess whether students have gained sufficient knowledge may need to change. And the other question is should we also teach different things? I frankly think we are teaching the right things, but our exams consist of a sizeable portion of repetitive tasks, at least for many of our courses. Yet, a standard computer science lecture on university level usually includes intellectually challenging tasks. Likely, the examination must focus more on these aspects.

So, it is about a balance between checking that students can repeat the definitions and concepts to establish a common language, and assessing students' understanding by checking whether they can apply these insights to specific scenarios.

Yes. If students are asked to show that they can reproduce definitions, they should also be asked to prove that it was them and not a system that was doing so, right? So, we agree, essentially.

Interesting. Now, in light of this new AI reality, a lot of different future scenarios are being discussed, from dystopia to utopia. You hinted at it, but given what you said, where do you personally fall on that dystopian-utopian spectrum?

I am on the dystopian side. I think AI, especially machine-learned systems, are extremely good at optimizing for the average case. If we have tasks where it's not an issue that the non-average cases are treated sub-optimally, then I think these systems are great. That's where they should be used, but only there. As soon as we have populations where it's not enough to optimize for the average case, then I think we need strict rules to prevent people from being disadvantaged. This may seem a bit like German skepticism, of course, but I would see myself as justifiably dystopian in this regard. Actually, the AI Act seems to be taking the right steps in this respect, by defining high-risk AI systems as those that are to be subjected to regulations and to human oversight [3, 8].

Given recent developments and the strong push from Big Tech companies, do you think it will be possible to integrate AI only in safe or non-critical contexts? Or do you fear that we will see some kind of push to integrate AI in environments that we can't really control? Towards dystopia.

There is a push by Big Tech to lure us into new functionalities that are fancy and get our attention. But we pay for that by giving out our data and losing our anonymity. Luckily, here in Europe, we do have politicians that are alert and seem to understand what is at stake. I think on the European level the right moves are being made. Sometimes this also happens on the national levels. Even if some of the regulations are a bit fuzzy, let them be fuzzy. As much as they are fuzzy, it is difficult for Big Tech to sneak out easily.

"We should strongly fight for the right for inspection of software that influences us and the things we own."

Looking back on the discussions and conversations of the past few days, was there an insight from another discipline that you found particularly interesting?

I particularly enjoyed the discussion of the legal techs. I was mostly in this part of the program that was interdisciplinary from the start. There was psychology there, but especially law. That I found quite illuminating. Also, the discussion that happened in the corridors, how these techs were designed. Why is it that the AI liability directive is as it is and so forth. That I found very instructive. That is not directly influencing the work that I'm doing, but it gives me a context.

Is there a particular research question or area you would like to see addressed more interdisciplinarily?

I mentioned human oversight already. I think this will become an interdisciplinary topic. For psychology people who are basically interested in the organization of work, there is a new job profile emerging, which is human oversight. What are the psychological capacities? What are the stress situations? I think there's a lot that needs to be framed there. We are working on this indeed. The legals define the context and we support with software tools. Other than that, I think what is chiefly underdiscussed is the problem of intellectual property of software. Beyond AI in software, your smartphone or your car are working because of the software embedded therein, right?

And: You own the smartphone; you own the car. But you don't own the software. And you are not even allowed to look into the software. It is the intellectual property of the manufacturer. Maybe you have an electric bike, then you will have a charger for your battery, but you don't have any information what the software running the charger is effectively doing to your battery. It could well be, for instance, that once the two years of warranty are over, the battery charger stops charging, or charges less effectively than truly possible. And that is all because we are not allowed to inspect the software. And I think that is a gross mistake. We should strongly fight for the right for inspection of software that influences us and the things we own. The electric bike, the battery charger, the espresso machine, whatever.

"I do think that open source is a good way to enable finding all kinds of issues and reporting them. I do think code secrecy and obfuscation is no good strategy to prevent attacks [...]."

If people knew exactly what the software was doing, that would introduce a new safety risk, wouldn't it?

That may well be the case, for instance users may then want to customize it to their needs. And that is where the research part comes in. As an example, it would be good to have some sort of open-source software for battery charging that is configurable. If someone then wants to change the charging behaviour so that it only charges to 70% instead of 100% because of the desire to extend battery life, then so be it. Now if configurability is without limits, then an erroneous reconfiguration could lead to a fire accident, since the charger may then overcharge and overheat the battery. Now, to prevent that, it would be nice to have, with the open software, a verification technology that the user can submit the reconfigured code to, for the purpose of providing a proven guarantee stating that the relevant safety limits are adhered to. My ERC grant POWVER [7] has put a focus on these kinds of questions. Still, there are very interesting technical research questions associated with this that are still wide open.

In your opinion, would the push for open-source AI increase or decrease the potential for attack?

I do think that open source is a good way to enable finding all kinds of issues and reporting them. I do think code secrecy and obfuscation is no good strategy to prevent attacks, while open-source software potentially is. And if you ask me about attacks, I am most interested in attacks that are already in the system, like with the diesel emission scandal. There was no separate attacker. It was the original equipment manufacturer who decided to build in, into the software, elements that were against the interest of the consumers and of society at large. So that seems technically a bit lame because there is no loophole that was attacked. Still, as mentioned, it was extremely difficult to detect and pinpoint the problem, while at the same time having caused premature deaths of thousands of European citizens [9].

In Germany, we have the "Kraftfahrt-Bundesamt" as the legal entity that is entitled and supposed to investigate these aspects of the automotive industry, but their experts don't know much about software analysis and verification. They can do exhaust emission measurements, but that is by far not enough expertise in face of the massive cases of fraud we have seen.

"The AI Act has some chances to become a blueprint for other jurisdictions outside Europe, and if that happens, then much of the dystopian effects currently dominating the discussion might get under control."

What is your personal vision of AI?

I like the fact that the European AI Act aims at regulating the use of AI [8]. With about 450 pages, the document is a burdensome read, but the parts that relate to the daily work of everyday software and data engineers are much less. As mentioned, we have just finished a document aiming at helping the everyday programmer in navigating the Act [3], by identifying the relevant parts of the Act and including a discussion what, according to its stipulations, actually falls under the term "AI". The AI Act has some chances to become a blueprint for other jurisdictions outside Europe, and if that happens, then much of the dystopian effects currently dominating the discussion might get under control.

At the same time, there will be a price to pay by the AI software industry, namely more regulatory burden, the need for better documentation of processes and products, and a trend towards standardization of effective testing and validation methods. And this will, I think, implicitly lead to an improvement of the quality of processes that are used to design modern software. Other than that, regarding the prospect of the very modern machine learning advances, I don't have grand emotions – I mean, I don't believe in "Wow, we will have super intelligence and that's the future", and so forth. The wave of stunning results achieved by generative AI is currently creating an amazing and impressive hype. Yet, there have been so many hypes before in computer science. Always the same synopsis: "Ah, wow, that hype is larger than any other hype before". And again, we are now in a situation where the hype is much larger than any hype before. And for sure there will be yet another hype and yet another hype and yet another hype larger than any hype before.

Is there anything you would like to add?

No, except for saying thank you for the interview.

Thank you, Holger, for your time and perspective on AI and its future. have a great day!

It was a pleasure.

References

1. Biewer, S., et al.: Software doping analysis for human oversight. Formal Methods Syst. Design **66**, 49–98 (2024)
2. Biewer, S., D'Argenio, P.R., Hermanns, H.: Doping tests for cyberphysical systems. ACM Trans. Model. Comput. Simul. **31**(3), 16:1–16:27 (2021)
3. Hermanns, H., Lauber-Rönsberg, A., Meinel, P., Sterz, S., Zhang, H.: AI Act for the working programmer. In: Steffen, B. (ed.) Bridging the Gap Between AI and Reality (AISoLA 2024). LNCS, vol. 15217 (2025). https://doi.org/10.1007/978-3-031-75434-0_6
4. Kästner, L., Langer, M., Lazar, V., Schomäcker, A., Speith, T., Sterz, S.: On the relation of trust and explainability: why to engineer for trustworthiness. In: Proc. RE 2021 Workshops. IEEE (2021)
5. Langer, M., et al.: What do we want from Explainable Artificial Intelligence (XAI)? A stakeholder perspective on XAI and a conceptual model guiding interdisciplinary XAI research. Artif. Intell. **296**, 103473 (2021)
6. Sterz, S., et al.: On the quest for effectiveness in human oversight: interdisciplinary perspectives. In: Proc. 2024 ACM Conference on Fairness, Accountability, and Transparency (FAccT 2024), pp. 2495–2507. ACM (2024)
7. Power to the People. Verified. An ERC Advanced Grant. (https://www.powver.org)
8. European Commission: Regulation of the European Parliament and of the Council Laying Down Harmonised Rules on Artificial Intelligence (Artificial Intelligence Act). European Commission (2024). (https://data.consilium.europa.eu/doc/document/PE-24-2024-INIT/en/pdf)
9. Toxic particle linked to diesel kills 6,000 a year in Germany. Reuters (2018). (https://www.reuters.com/article/world/toxic-particle-linked-to-diesel-kills-6000-a-year-in-germany-agency-idUSKCN1GK1U8/)

Let's Talk AI with Computer Science Expert Joost-Pieter Katoen

Joost-Pieter Katoen[1] and Barbara Steffen[2](✉)

[1] RWTH Aachen University, Germany and University of Twente, Enschede, The Netherlands
katoen@cs.rwth-aachen.de
[2] METAFrame Technologies, Dortmund, Germany
barbara.steffen@metaframe.de

Abstract. AI has great potential but needs to be taken with care. It is of utmost importance that AI is introduced and used with common sense. AI needs to be safe, reliable and sustainable.

My personal AI mission: Make AI systems more dependable and safe, in particular if these systems have to act under uncertainty.

Fig. 1. Joost-Pieter Katoen

1 My Takes on AI

- **Artificial Intelligence** – A set of methods that use learning to accomplish a certain task.
- **Trust** – The outcomes of AI methods need to be such that they are transparent and fair.
- **Explainability** – Outcomes of AI engines such as (deep) neural networks come with a justification, for example, a certificate that one can easily check providing understandable arguments for the given outcome.
- **Essential Elements of Human Capabilities** – Social intelligence, emotional intelligence (emotions, affection, mood, etc.), creativity, and adaptivity.

B. Steffen et al. (Eds.): *Let's Talk AI*, LNCS 15000, pp. 205–209, 2026.
https://doi.org/10.1007/978-3-032-09008-9_24

2 The Interview

[Barbara Steffen] *Welcome, Joost-Pieter Katoen (Fig. 1). Thank you for taking the time for this interview. Could you please briefly introduce yourself and your relationship to artificial intelligence?*

[Joost-Pieter Katoen] Certainly. I'm a professor of software modelling and verification at RWTH Aachen University in Germany. I'm also affiliated with the University of Twente in the Netherlands. As for my connection to AI, while I'm not an AI expert, I believe that when using AI components, particularly in safety-critical systems like autonomous robots, cars, and satellites, it's vital that these AI components are reliable and do not exhibit unexpected or potentially dangerous behaviors. I strongly believe that formal verification methods can be used to analyze AI systems.

> "[I]t's vital that these [safety critical] AI components are reliable and do not exhibit unexpected or potentially dangerous behaviors."

What AI challenges are you currently addressing in your research?

Our research primarily deals with uncertainty aspects. This has recently been identified as a crucial issue in trustworthy AI [2, 3]. A scenario that best illustrates this involves a robot that needs to navigate, for instance, finding the exit of a labyrinth while avoiding potential collisions with other robots in the room. This is a multi-robot system. The robot also needs to conserve energy, so it should reach the exit in the fewest possible steps. The question is, can we synthesize or define a planner for the robot that achieves these safety goals, reaching the exit with a minimal energy budget, without colliding with other robots? My recent talk "Facing Uncertainty in AI Systems" goes much more into detail on this [6].

What role do you think trust plays in the adoption of AI? And what measures do you think are important to ensure the ethical use of AI?

That's a complex question. Trust is more than just correctness. For end users to trust AI software, fairness is a crucial aspect. For instance, there was a scandal in the Netherlands a couple of years ago when tax authorities used software to identify "suspicious" individuals who might be misusing the tax system for childcare [4]. It turned out that this AI component was discriminatory, particularly against people from ethnic minorities. This scandal led to some politicians resigning. I mention this because such incidents certainly do not contribute to public trust in AI components. So, for me, trust involves correctness and fairness. People need to be able to rely on what these components suggest. And honestly, I think we're not there yet.

> "We should strive to not only focus on the technical aspects and potentials, but also the ethical and social implications."

In terms of the future capabilities of AI, where do you think it is headed? On a scale of 1 to 10, where 1 is the artificial intelligence systems we know today, such as ChatGPT, and 10 is artificial general intelligence, such as autonomous systems that surpass human capabilities. Where on that scale would you place the future capabilities of AI?

Yes, I believe it's fair to say that AI holds enormous potential. We've seen this in agents that play Go, even winning against world champion players. Go is a game that is significantly more complex than chess, so this certainly demonstrates AI's potential. However, I remain somewhat skeptical. If I were to rate my optimism on a scale from 1 to 10, I'd say I'm at a 4 or 5. I hope I'm wrong, but I feel our expectations of AI might be too high. Currently, it seems we're inclined to believe that ChatGPT or similar tools and their successors can solve all kinds of problems. For example, the belief that they can automatically generate program code, like software [1] is growing. I think we need to exercise caution here. We shouldn't always trust the output of AI without question. We need a rational approach to dealing with potential outputs. It's important to seek a second opinion on the output. Is it good enough? Is it really doing what it's supposed to do? Many people hope, and tend to believe, that AI is a silver bullet that will solve all problems. I don't share this belief.

Okay, now that we've covered the possible future capabilities of AI from your perspective, what does the future we're headed towards look like on the spectrum from utopia to dystopia? What should we be preparing for?

I believe we will definitely see AI integrated into various aspects of our daily lives. I also think that current developments, not only with AI but also with the so-called metaverse that major companies like Amazon and Microsoft are developing, will lead to communication playing an even larger role in our lives. It's hard to imagine life without a mobile phone today, but if communication extends beyond that to include sensors and emotions, for instance, and not just information and data, I think there will be a wide range of possible applications. I strongly believe this will have a significant impact on our social structures and the way we live as human beings. Of course, this also carries risks. I may be a bit skeptical, but I see that AI has not only a bright future. For instance, we already see drones and machine learning techniques being used in conflicts like the one in Ukraine and the Israel-Palestine situation. I fear this will only increase in the future, which is a serious cause for concern.

"We shouldn't always trust the output of AI without question. We need a rational approach to dealing with potential outputs."

Reflecting on the last few days here at AISoLA, which looks at artificial intelligence from an interdisciplinary perspective, is there a particular insight from another discipline that was particularly interesting to you?

Indeed, the perspective from social sciences is crucial. As computer scientists, we often focus on the technical aspects, such as understanding the workings of a neural network or a partially observable MDP used in AI and planning. However, we must not overlook the enormous social implications. As I mentioned earlier, I foresee a significant impact on our social existence and potential risks. It's crucial that we consider these ethical and social aspects. We should strive to not only focus on the technical aspects and potentials, but also the ethical and social implications. What kind of impact will it ultimately have on us and society as a whole? What does it mean for a business if, for instance, you replace most personnel in an organization with AI agents like ChatGPT? What effects will this have? It's important to address these issues. What I appreciate about AISoLA is that these aspects are also considered, particularly the social aspect, which I find extremely important.

From your personal perspective, what AI vision would you like to see addressed?

The vision I would like to see addressed involves two aspects. Firstly, when you ask AI specialists why certain techniques are successful, they often struggle to answer. Even at NeurIPS, the flagship conference on AI, prominent people refer to the success of deep learning as a kind of alchemy [5]. We combine certain techniques, and they work exceptionally well, but we struggle to explain why. This is one aspect that I believe is crucial. The other aspect is that we need to exercise caution when using AI in certain applications, and we need regulations in place.

Regulations aimed at safety?

Yes, in terms of safety, not just safety in a general sense, but the safety of human beings. We definitely need regulations in this area. It's not only the responsibility of computer scientists, but also politicians and strategists. They need to be involved and aware of these issues.

Is there anything else you would like to add?

No, I don't believe so.

Thank you very much for your views on AI and for taking the time to share them with us. Have a great last few days at AISoLA!

OK, thank you.

References

1. Austin, J., et al.: Program synthesis with large language models (https://arxiv.org/abs/2108.07732)
2. Seshia, S.A., Sadigh, D., Sastry, S.S.: Toward verified artificial intelligence. Commun. ACM **65**(7), 46–55 (2022)
3. Wing, J.M.: Trustworthy AI. Commun. ACM **64**(10), 64–71 (2021)
4. https://en.wikipedia.org/wiki/Dutch_childcare_benefits_scandal
5. https://www.youtube.com/watch?v=x7psGHgatGM
6. https://www.youtube.com/watch?v=cNF1-lFfNs4

Let's Talk AI with Computer Science Expert Tiziana Margaria

Tiziana Margaria[1] and Barbara Steffen[2](✉)

[1] University of Limerick, Limerick, Ireland
tiziana.margaria@ul.ie
[2] METAFrame Technologies, Dortmund, Germany
barbara.steffen@metaframe.de

Abstract. I worry that improved AI will foster more delegation to it, where humans become lazier and just use "the machine", in delegation beyond what's necessary for a superficial sense of "convenience". That's a scary possibility for our future: a very likely future, I am afraid.

My personal AI mission: Do the possible so that AI is not taken as an "oracle", i.e., as an entity that does not need to be doublechecked or questioned. I'd prefer AI as Augmented Intelligence: considering intelligently what best to augment and how, and how to keep it in check and monitored, instead of (blind) Artificial Intelligence substituting the humans.

Fig. 1. Tiziana Margaria

1 My Takes on AI

- **Artificial Intelligence** – Right now, a set of deductive or associative systems able to respond to a series of inputs with adequate outputs, at least most of the time (to include nondeterministic and probabilistic systems like most AI techniques, which are wrong a significant number of times). There are as of today no agreed thresholds when intelligence is/becomes "artificial", nor when an algorithm or a system

B. Steffen et al. (Eds.): *Let's Talk AI*, LNCS 15000, pp. 210–221, 2026.
https://doi.org/10.1007/978-3-032-09008-9_25

is/becomes "intelligent". The Turing test is in my opinion not exhaustive, as it is full of systems where a classic algorithm takes a decision as well as a human and is therefore indistinguishable (thus satisfying the Turing definition), but nobody would call that algorithm "artificial intelligence". Examples are a simple pocket calculator, a thermostat for a heating controller. If we exclude algorithms, it's difficult to save Neural Networks and other similar systems, which are de facto algorithms, just with weights that depend on the inputs and some feedback loops and stabilize after a while. The concept of "learning" is also not clearly defined for this use: if it is reproductive learning, like traditional training-based AI, it errs when extrapolating in new situations (in other words, it does not experience enough to be useful in general). If we go to the LLMs, as I heard most recently from Edward Lee at DATE 2024, their training is like educating by exposure to information, experience, and feedback. Is that artificial intelligence? Is education in general then "artificial"? In which sense is the process to train an LLM then similar or different to educating a child? I think, maybe new categories of natural/artificial and of intelligence will emerge in due time. We used to distinguish between small scale neural networks and deep learning, now LLMs seem definitely to be a different "thing" from both of them.
- **Trust** – Confidence that the entity in question (a human, an algorithm, or a black-box like AI, the good old expert systems, or the Mechanical Turk of Amazon's history) does not deceive. I think this encompasses more than "tells the truth". It's a matter of having the right knowledge, applying it in toto, and not misrepresent or deviate.
- **Explainability** – Ability to justify each individual recommendation on the basis of the inputs (that include the context) and some reasoning (deductive, abductive, or through some mapping of the input/output space, e.g., through decision trees).
- **Essential Elements of Human Capabilities** – Conscience, feelings, moral. Associative abilities are now also shown by algorithms or agent societies like swarms, so these are not anymore peculiar to humans. Intelligence is also debatable: the ability to predict (mostly by extrapolation from experience) is now seemingly the "big thing" of AI too: given experience with training data, make prediction on fresh data. Human intelligence would usually also use other criteria like what's legal, what's opportune etc. which go beyond just looking at sets of data. With the LLMs, however, so much input is provided upfront during the training that such side criteria might well be meanwhile included in the answers.

2 The Interview

[Barbara Steffen] Today I have the pleasure to interview Tiziana Margaria (Fig. 1) from the University of Limerick. Please briefly introduce yourself and your relationship to artificial intelligence.

[Tiziana Margaria] Thank you Barbara for this opportunity. It's really nice to have a chance of discuss AI in an interview at AISoLA. I am a professor of Software Systems at the University of Limerick in Ireland. I am also involved in several national research centers on software (Lero), on smart advanced manufacturing (Confirm), and in particular the Centre of Research Training in AI (https://www.crt-ai.ie), where I am the director in Limerick. My "trade" is formal methods, so my look at AI is from the perspective of the design and verification of the correctness of systems. I have been using reasoning methods and building reasoning tools for over 30 years, so I am interested in AI developments that align directly with my work. It is really exciting to see what is happening now.

Can you name one or two AI-related research questions you are currently working on?

Not so directly: it is more the attempt to find a good place for AI and ML in this field. Some people distinguish between AI and ML, others still tend to conflate the two, in the context of software ecosystems as well as of sociotechnical ecosystems. Right now, in education and research, I am concerned with the bigger picture. AI is one of the means that help humans to reason, predict or classify. They cover a specific role within a much bigger ecosystem: they are components embedded in a larger workflow or end-to-end process that we call the Digital Thread. The Digital Thread is the integration layer of large heterogeneous systems: it weaves data, sensing, decisions, and actuation, combining AI/ML software with other software, with cyber-physical systems such as machinery, sensors and Internet of Things, telecommunication networks, and so forth, to solve the problem at hand [16]. The thread weaves systems that produce data with the components that analyse the data, where AI has a role, producing outputs that are useful to steer the system, or to inform decisions, or to display information, as in many applications in businesses and society [5, 10]. The role and challenges I see are essentially guaranteeing interoperability [13]: all these tools, including AI/ML ones and their models, must be able to interoperate with other tools, considering dependencies, compatibility, as well as the ability to exchange them with others, guaranteeing equivalence or guaranteeing certain differences. The nature of the application also makes a difference: high assurance software and systems come with financial responsibility or responsibility for the lives of people, for example in the transportation or medical domains. Other applications, like entertainment or advertisement, do not have the same degree of responsibility and regulation. Considering recommender systems, different application profiles require different levels of confidence that the recommendation suits the case at hand. Whether a traditional controller or an AI component, the recommendations for high assurance contexts must be trustable and justifiable, so that explainability becomes a crucial property. I am working on different concepts of explainability, that depend on the kind of application and context in which it operates: explaining choices [11], classifications/decisions [9], or outcomes of synthesis [17].

Does explainability also depend on the type of user group?

Yes, for example the level of confidence that the technologist has in some kind of outputs is determined by the fact that this technologist is able to interpret the outputs. Outputs in my field are typically not data values, like a temperature or a price, but complex outputs like properties, source code or models. There needs to be significant expertise to make sense of those outputs and competently judge their correctness and adequacy. Considering higher level properties, such systems are typically desired to be deterministic systems. This means that if the system runs several times with the same inputs and context, it produces the same outputs. It is predictable. That is not the case for AI systems: they have variability. Probabilistic systems have been in use for a long time: such systems provide an output, typically a recommendation, a classification or a prediction, with an accuracy higher than 50%, and hopefully much higher in cases where actually one expects determinism. Other systems are inherently chaotic: even minor changes to the inputs can result in drastically different outputs. The key issue is that AI and ML technologies fall into the last two categories: they are perfectly suitable for problems where approximations are adequate (one "guesses" anyway, like in advertising), but not when determinism is sought or required by regulators. They may not be adequate or provide sufficient control when lives are at stake, yet enthusiastic adopters are (knowingly or not) using them nevertheless. Explainability, intended as a justification case by case of what led to a certain output, is here the key and the challenge. These three categories of systems have different ways of approaching an interpretation of outputs, and require competence in understanding when the output is good enough. This distinction is hard to communicate to a large part of the potential users, because this way of thinking is unfamiliar to them, it is not part of their categories of judgement.

"We risk to collectively regress from an age of reason and responsibility, where knowledge and skills are assets, education is expanding and reaching ideally everyone, to a new age of belief and delegation to 'black box' authorities: entities that we are unable to question, as we either never learned how they work, or have given up that knowledge, out of 'convenience'."

What is the role of trust in the adoption of AI?

Excellent question. Trust was a significant topic of discussion this week, but with a very different meaning. My background is in high assurance computing. Traditionally, in this community trust is established through certifiability, responsibility, and even forensics, which concerns providing explanations a posteriori, after something has already happened [8]. For this kind of trust one needs to be able to follow up case by case what led to that recommendation, action, or chain of decisions and actions, that resulted in a catastrophe, incurred high costs, or caused other problems, as in Clayton Christensen's opening scenario in his Innovator's Dilemma book [6]. We are back to the quest for determinism, and the current AI is not at that level. I could conclude that AI is not usable and end the conversation here, but that is not my approach. The question is how we can recover trust in an AI context by combining different reasoning systems, different certification systems, as evidence-providing systems that may provide different elements: one delivers a model, another delivers an explanation, another defines the concept of "adequacy" maybe in terms of degrees of "acceptable" approximation under the given circumstances. For me, it is crucial that explanations are useful to enhance the system. Typically, we seek explanations when things go wrong, like the use of counterexamples during verification and testing. If a test fails under identified conditions, how can we prevent the system from encountering those conditions again? If there are no explanations of just the probabilistic ones like [20] in today's AI and neuromorphic computing, one cannot identify why things went wrong. Such "explanations" are not sufficient. I prefer a neurosymbolic approach, because I think that we need to bring together the capabilities of what we have already known for a long time, in the communities that develop reasoning, dependability, reliability (the symbolic aspects), and the newer take on cognitive systems with AI, ML and bio- or neuromorphic approaches. If we succeed to bring them together in a good way, the neurosymbolic combination can actually make both sides stronger.

Do you have any key measures in mind to help ensure ethical AI adoption?

Certainly. From an ethical point of view, AI adoption is often viewed as a process of data consumption. I think that data is just one ingredient, but let's consider data first. One measure of ethical AI is how well one handles imbalanced data sets, for example through the adoption of adequate processes to manage the imbalance [3]. For instance, in the medical field, even prevalent conditions like diabetes affects 7% to 10% of the population, so diabetes detection datasets are still very imbalanced. Training a technique with a data set where the category of concern is very infrequent can lead to problems due to insufficient representatives. Developing good technologies to deal with imbalance is the more crucial with increasing degrees of rarity. The general public has developed concerns about human recognition techniques and potential biases in AI systems that classify or decide. The worry that certain segments of the population or customer base may be disadvantaged due to these biases in the dataset can be addressed by rebalancing the data set and developing robust, adequate approaches to recognize and handle these rare events. On the other hand, there is also the potential for unethical use of otherwise correct and fair AI, which is a bigger problem. Once the methods exist, and they are integrated into full workflows, any technology can be used for good or bad. Unfortunately, what is considered good or bad largely depends on the societal norms, or professional norms. Some communities are more prone to objection than others, for example in terms of privacy, explicit consent, and exceptions to them [2]. The new European act that is going to be introduced soon will provide guidelines for the producers of AI systems and applications that use AI. I welcome that it distinguishes several levels of concern and levels of evidence required to certify or legally accept these systems for practical use. It shows understanding that the same algorithm may be acceptable for a recommender system but it may not be suitable for recommending a treatment in the case of cancer, where the consequences of imprecision or errors could be severe.

So, in terms of the future technical capabilities of AI, on a scale of 1 to 10, where 1 stands for today's artificial intelligence systems like ChatGPT, and 10 stands for artificial general intelligence that surpasses human capabilities. What do you think is possible?

That's a very difficult question. Not long ago, we would not have considered ChatGPT to be a 1 but even beyond this entire scale. Now that it suddenly exists, it is re-scaling everything. I hope that within the realm of AI and machine learning we will keep developing systems that are well-understood, localized, and controllable, and not just race towards the kind of general AI that many worry about. I hope that we will stabilize around maybe 5–7. Not because generalized AI is inherently bad, but because it could easily transform into or be used as something harmful to people, the environment, or any other aspect of the context. If humans lose control over these systems, and these systems become too independent and powerful, we could be in trouble. I hope for a 5–7 in the sense that I would like to have really efficient, reliable and explainable systems that augment human capabilities. If this way we can become stronger, faster, see better, see earlier, this could provide expert advice to doctors, field workers, scientists, or artists.

That would be fantastic. I would accept to go much further with augmentation than with substitution. Substitution has been discussed in contexts where AI and AI-steered robots may replace workers. While some of those tasks and jobs are onerous or dangerous, this could lead to societal issues because certain job categories would no longer be filled by humans, opening the question of what these humans would then do instead. The substitution of knowledge would be much more problematic. Self-learning and self-evolving algorithms that operate unsupervised by humans could pose great risks unless there are very clear legal guidelines that are inherent in the system and cannot be overridden. However, that's difficult to decide and challenging to implement. There's always the possibility that something just goes astray. Actually, I am near certain that unexpected big problems would arise, like second-order unintended consequences down the line, and I doubt that we would be able to "stop the system" and correct it. That's the part I would prefer society not to experience.

There are a lot of different AI-driven futures envisioned these days, from dystopia to utopia. Where would you place yourself?

I am an engineer, that's my DNA. My way of looking at the world, at concepts and ideas is that they are parts of systems, systems of systems, purposes. I think in terms of inputs, outputs and context. In terms of trajectories to the future, if we live in a world where certain resources are becoming scarce, we might be able to solve the energy problem by developing and adopting alternative technologies. Seeing all the news of what is being tried, leading to discoveries and to processes of production that scale, I am quite optimistic about addressing this challenge: we are discovering new inputs and produce new outputs or more of certain outputs in new ways. On the pollution challenge I am also quite positive because we start to view globally excess waste as potential raw materials, and we start to act upon it. I do not yet see a close solution for issues like agriculture and water scarcity. If AI systems can help us use these scarce resources more efficiently, more fairly, and distribute them to a larger segment of the population across different societies, equalizing core imbalances across the north and the south of the globe, then I would welcome them. In this case we might co-develop a utopian society positively supported by AI and by its capability of micro-regulating, quick to take and enforce decisions for the local and global good. But if things go wrong, and these capabilities fall into the wrong hands, be they corporations, governments, or other entities, we could easily fall into dystopia. The skyrocketing price of energy, or water, or food could be manipulated, even when its costs go down. Or there could be supply chains diversion for scarce goods, or it could introduce a level of surveillance that impacts freedom and privacy. Misuse would lead to increased imbalances, to a growing divide between the haves and the have-nots of resources, knowledge, or power. This could potentially lead to conflict, even armed conflicts, resulting in losses for everyone. We have not yet sufficiently internalized the reality that the planet is a closed system, where no deep change can compartmentalize and ringfence its effects. Everything is more or less connected, and we can only manage to tailor, or fine-tune, the intensity of some of these dependencies. My wish is that we can achieve the utopian solution and that we, as a global society, are going to be able to agree not to knowingly run or unknowingly slide into a dystopian situation in the future. The danger of "substitution" of control is the danger that initially OK situations may slide into dystopia, and we do not notice until it is too late, and insurmountable premises for conflict have been reached. So how can we find rules that we can all agree upon, and make sure that they are going to be implemented globally? In my system engineering terms, we now live in a global society, i.e., with global repercussions of even local decisions. It is a closed system, where anything has dependencies and therefore any change (including the passing of time) has an effect and perturbates the status quo. Companies operate globally, our economy is interconnected, and our societies are linked via communication and also migration. As we have seen recently in many disruptive examples, what happens in one part of the world can have significant consequences elsewhere. Therefore, it is pointless to have regulations that only apply to certain regions, like the EU. I believe we need a planetary agreement.

"The key is going to be the regulations, with the lawyers talking to the other disciplines because the will of the society needs to be reflected in the laws, regulations, in the standards and norms."

Reflecting on the past few days, we've had a diverse range of interdisciplinary discussions and sessions. Was there a particular insight that stood out to you?

My key insight is the fact that we attribute a different meaning to the same words. For example, the degree of precision that is attached to certain words like trust, privacy, and more in a technical context is not shared by attendants from other contexts. We had digital humanists with a discursive approach to subject matters, and then computer scientists and formal methods people who are on the mathematical and rigorous side of system analysis and design. When a concept like trust comes up in the context of ethics, or rules and regulation, or governance, we mean different things by the same word. When we think about governance in computer science, we mostly do not think of asking the population or surveying opinions and preferences. For us, governance is a set of hierarchical decision systems, where there are some rules and there is a technical system that conforms to these rules and enforces them case by case. It is not easy to talk to people who have a less structured and defined understanding of the same words in a way that makes sense to us. So we could communicate more, and in order for it to be meaningful and useful, we should agree on the meaning of certain vocabulary, that becomes a joint and common vocabulary. In other words, there is still fundamental work ahead before we can start working together with less frustration. The second insight is that hybrid tracks like AI in medicine and the digital humanities track did meaningfully involve medicine, history, geography and other disciplines. Here I liked the demonstration of the fact that computer scientists and experts of other disciplines indeed succeeded to find a meeting ground. So, yes we can! There, computer science achieved its best: being a science with its own depth and challenges, which is inherently an application domain-agnostic art. In my opinion computer science is today the most fundamental discipline, as it influences and supports the progress of every domain. I also believe that its impact is most evident when it helps others succeed. A number of applications were really pleasing because two communities that normally would be distinct were able to collaborate and create something beneficial for both.

"What happens in one part of the world can have significant consequences elsewhere. Therefore, it's pointless to have regulations that only apply to certain regions, like the EU. I believe we need a planetary agreement."

Is there a particular research question you'd like to see addressed in an interdisciplinary manner in the future?

There is indeed, but it is a meta-level question rather than a concrete one. It is related to the interdisciplinary ability to carry out a meaningful discourse: it revolves around establishing what is considered "known" or "understood" enough, or "concrete" enough, or "good" enough, beyond the community of computer science and engineering. We have sets of measurable criteria for evidence, like certain kinds of tests and a certain level of test coverage, defined kinds of approximation and acceptability criteria, ways of conducting formal proofs to establish certainty, or code reviews carried out according to certain standards: this establishes fact-based evidence accepted in our community. I am not aware of similar criteria in other communities. In medicine, there are procedural standards for conducting patient-related clinical trials, but I am not aware that philosophy or psychology or sociology or law have similar kinds of criteria. The criteria may well be different from discipline to discipline, but it would be important that we establish some, even if coarse, and that we are able to communicate them and talk in those terms across communities. Otherwise we risk to never be able to establish a communicable ground, as we experienced this week with the discussion on "trust", because one group is happy with an undefined, abstract or even ambiguous meaning, that those who need precision in order to measure, quantify, and decide, cannot work with, because it is too abstract or too ambiguous a concept. Defining some terms and some criteria for achieving those quality levels would enable statements like "I have understood this", "this is known", "this is well accepted", "this is trustable to a level of X", to be shareable and mean the same across communities.

What are the different levels of trust that you think are important? Going back to the topic of trust in general, which has been discussed quite frequently in the last week. Is it about establishing a common language and a common concept of trust, or is it about revealing the different concepts of trust at a sufficiently precise level to be able to translate between the different languages?

This sends me back to 35 years ago, when many in the formal methods community dreamed of a common language for modeling systems. It was a mirage: any modelling language was never good enough, because different subsystems had different needs, the concepts could not be faithfully mapped into the other language, and models would be either redundant (too much unneeded information) or not useful (too abstract, missing information). That's when we founded the STTT (Software Tools for Technology Transfer) journal [7] and the ETI (Electronic Tool Integration) platform [19], followed by instances for the FMICS Working Group [4, 15] and for the Bioinformatics or Climate Change domains [1, 12]. I am a strong supporter of the "archipelago" approach: each island is a community with their own vocabulary and criteria, and they are joined by carefully chosen and well-designed bridges of translation. So a concept in one community may be called differently in the other community, but there are clear criteria for expressing how close they are, in which sense and how much they differ, so that we can effectively map the understanding in a meaningful and usable way.

"I hope [for] the utopian version. I am however very scared that it may go otherwise: one or two rogue instances could be enough to create enormous damage."

Do you have a suggestion on how to move towards the archipelagic approach? How can we establish the necessary level of precision and transparency to bridge the gap between disciplines?

I think it is possible in application domains that work with a quantitative approach, though it requires a lot of work. Understanding and mapping the concepts in more discursive fields might be harder as these communities might not be accustomed to the level of concreteness that we need even to start expressing models. In CS (Computer Science) as in STEM we are always comparing things, so if there is no definition of what we are comparing, or at least a qualitative measure like high, medium, or low that are rooted in properties of the system and agreed by both communities, it is difficult to have meaningful conversations. I observed this week that some communities are closer to achieving this level of definition than others, and that some do not realize that there is a problem. So we might even have to take one step back, and have to communicate first our need for establishing something of that kind of precision in order for us to become operational. We are always told that we need to have SMART goals, but where is the SMART definition in terms of measurable, achievable, and so on? It remains too vague.

What do you think the vision of AI should be?

I see AI as just another set of technologies that have been developed. Before the "dotcom" bubble burst, it was internet everywhere because this was the big novelty at that time, the new technology that would revolutionize everything. It led to the bubble, with a lot of pain and repercussions, but eventually we found ways of using it proficiently, and a way of actually bringing it to everybody with, importantly, more advantages than disadvantages, so that is an innovation wave that has been meanwhile internalized in our society. In previous times, people were scared by transportation with cars, or could not fathom having a telephone in their homes, as for urgent communication there were messenger boys at hand. Now we have essentially a supercomputer in each phone, instant communication is perceived as a basic need and a right, and horse driven carriages are nowadays largely for tourists. Past some hype, I believe that AI has the potential to become the new "household tool" that aids people. Indeed I hope that this is the vision that we are going to enact: the utopian version. I am however very scared that it may go otherwise: one or two rogue AI instances could be enough to create enormous damage. So on one side I am hopeful, because the research and science communities are willing to collaborate, and there is a will to design a shared, positive, and useful AI vision. The problem has always been controlling the outliers: the recent Oscar for the film on Oppenheimer is a timely reminder of what it means to "master" a new technology in the context of entities and decision makers with conflicting purposes and goals.

Are there other perspectives you would like to see addressed or integrated into the interdisciplinary discourse? This week we've met with psychologists, lawyers, computer scientists, and philosophers. We've also seen various AI applications in health care and history, as you mentioned. Do you see other disciplines that should get more involved?

The key is going to be the regulations, with the lawyers talking to the other disciplines because the will of the society needs to be reflected in the different flavours of the legal system: laws, regulations as well as in the standards and norms. The values define the essence of a society: it is from values that we derive consequences like the kind of governance for yourself and others. So I would say that lawyers, engineers, social engineers should be all involved because this is where the value-defining discourse that is already happening with end users, social stakeholders etc., from the philosophical level becomes concretized in something that can be then translated for and into the technical systems. If there is a lot of discourse but it does not find its way into the systems, there is an insurmountable gap between the talk and the walk. My concern goes back again to the digital thread: we need to establish this useful communication thread between the different disciplines, and I think that the regulations and law perspective is the common point where each one of us has the ability to contribute meaningfully and to take out something useful.

Is there anything else you would like to add?

I am glad that we had those conversations for this entire week. I am a systematic initiator of weird interdisciplinary tracks at ISoLA and on initiatives where I espouse fundamental values and concerns, see for example the entire EU Strategic Support Action on Simplicity over 10 years ago [14] and my insistence on the relevance of extreme model driven and low-code/no-code approaches for sustainability and democratization for years [18] and even more now in the R@ISE project. Accordingly, I find such projects and discussions extremely enriching as a person, as a citizen, as a curious individual and also as a researcher and a producer of IT. I hope that there will be more of this in the future and thank you very much for this opportunity.

Thank you, Tiziana, for your time and insights. your interdisciplinary and application-driven perspectives have been invaluable. Have a great day!

Thank you, Barbara.

References

1. Al-Areqi, S., Lamprecht, AL., Margaria, T.: Constraints-driven automatic geospatial service composition: workflows for the analysis of sea-level rise impacts. In: Gervasi, O., et al. (eds.) Computational Science and Its Applications (ICCSA 2016). LNCS, vol. 9788. Springer (2016). https://doi.org/10.1007/978-3-319-42111-7_12
2. Alamri, B., Javed, I.T., Margaria, T., A GDPR-compliant framework for IoT-based personal health records using Blockchain. In: Proceedings of the 11th IFIP International Conference on New Technologies, Mobility and Security (NTMS 2021), pp. 1–5. IEEE (2021)
3. Singh, A., Minguett, O., Margaria, T.: Binary decision diagrams and composite classifiers for analysis of imbalanced medical datasets. In: Proceedings of the 11th International Symposium on Leveraging Applications of Formal Methods, Verification and Validation. Doctoral Symposium. Electronic Communications of the EASST, vol. 82. EASST (2022)

4. Arenas, A.E., Bicarregui, J.C., Margaria, T.: The FMICS view on the verified software repository. J. of Integrated Design & Process Sci. **10**(4), 47–54 (2006)
5. Chaudhary, H.A.A., et al.: Model-driven engineering in digital thread platforms: a practical use case and future challenges. In: Margaria, T., Steffen, B. (eds.) Leveraging Applications of Formal Methods, Verification and Validation. Practice (ISoLA 2022). LNCS, vol. 13704. Springer (2022). https://doi.org/10.1007/978-3-031-19762-8_14
6. Christensen, C.M.: The Innovator's Dilemma. Harvard Business Review Press, Management of Innovation and Change (2016)
7. Cleaveland, W.R., Margaria, T., Steffen, B.: Editorial. Intl. J. Softw. Tools Technol. Trans. **1**(1–2), 1–5 (1997)
8. Gnesi, S., Margaria, T.: Formal Methods for Industrial Critical Systems: A Survey of Applications. Wiley-IEEE Computer Society (2012)
9. Gossen, F., Margaria, T., Steffen, B.: Towards explainability in machine learning: the formal methods way. IT Professional **22**(4), 8–12 (2020)
10. Guevara, I., Ryan, S., Singh, A., Brandon, C., Margaria, T.: Edge IoT prototyping using model-driven representations: a use case for smart agriculture. Sensors **24**, 495 (2024)
11. Kubczak, C., Margaria, T., Steffen, B., Winkler, C., Hungar, H.: An approach to discovery with miAamics and jABC. In: Petrie, C., Margaria, T., Lausen, H., Zaremba, M. (eds.) Semantic Web Services Challenge. Springer (2009). https://doi.org/10.1007/978-0-387-72496-6_13
12. Lamprecht, A.L., Margaria, T., Steffen, B.: Bio-jETI: a framework for semantics-based service composition. BMC Bioinform. **10**(Suppl. 10), S8 (2009)
13. Margaria, T., Chaudhary, H.A.A., Guevara, I., Ryan, S., Schieweck, A.: The interoperability challenge: building a model-driven digital thread platform for CPS. In: Margaria, T., Steffen, B. (eds.) Leveraging Applications of Formal Methods, Verification and Validation (ISoLA 2021). LNCS, vol. 13036, Springer (2021). https://doi.org/10.1007/978-3-030-89159-6_25
14. Margaria, T., Floyd, B.D., Steffen, B.: IT SimplyWorks: simplicity and embedded systems design. In: Proc. 35th IEEE Annu. Computer Software and Applications Conf. Workshops, pp. 194–199. IEEE (2011)
15. Margaria, T., Raffelt, H., Steffen, B., Leucker, M.: The LearnLib in FMICSjETI. In: 12th IEEE International Conference on Engineering Complex Computer Systems (ICECCS 2007), pp. 340–349 (2007)
16. Margaria, T., Schieweck, A.: The digital thread in Industry 4.0. In: Ahrendt, W., Tapia Tarifa, S. (eds.) Integrated Formal Methods (iFM 2019). LNCS, vol. 11918. Springer (2019). https://doi.org/10.1007/978-3-030-34968-4_1
17. Margaria, T., Steffen, B.: LTL guided planning: revisiting automatic tool composition in ETI, In: Proc. 31st IEEE Software Engineering Workshop (SEW 2007), pp. 214–226. IEEE (2007)
18. Margaria, T., Steffen, B.: eXtreme model-driven development (XMDD) technologies as a hands-on approach to software development without coding. In: Tatnall, A. (ed.) Encyclopedia of Education and Information Technologies. Springer (2020). https://doi.org/10.1007/978-3-319-60013-0_208-1
19. Steffen, B., Margaria, T., Braun, V.: The electronic tool integration platform: concepts and design. Int. J. Softw. Tools Technol. Trans. **1**(1), 9–30 (1997)
20. SHAP (SHapley Additive exPlanations). https://shap.readthedocs.io/en/latest/
21. R@ISE project, https://software-engineering.ie/raise/

Let's Talk AI with Computer Science Expert Martin Leucker

Martin Leucker[1] and Barbara Steffen[2(✉)]

[1] University of Lübeck, Lübeck, Germany
leucker@isp.uni-luebeck.de
[2] METAFrame Technologies, Dortmund, Germany
barbara.steffen@metaframe.de

Abstract. Analysis and verification methods must be developed if AI is used in safety critical domains.

My personal AI mission: To make AI techniques more trustworthy and create further methods and methodology for designing and building powerful and safe AI-based solutions efficiently: SE4AI.

Fig. 1. Martin Leucker

1 My Takes on AI

- **Artificial Intelligence** – A powerful tool that may be applied in many areas by assisting in daily work activities.
- **Trust** – In an AI-based system trust is the mental attitude of a human that the system is doing what it is supposed to do in given circumstances. It involves correctness of the system but many more attributes like privacy, etc.
- **Explainability** – For AI-based systems explainability is their capability of illustrating in a human understandable way how it works.
- **Essential Elements of Human Capabilities** – Humans are capable of using context information much better in their daily reasoning than artificial systems.

B. Steffen et al. (Eds.): *Let's Talk AI*, LNCS 15000, pp. 222–228, 2026.
https://doi.org/10.1007/978-3-032-09008-9_26

2 The Interview

[Barbara Steffen] Today I have the pleasure of speaking with Martin Leucker (Fig. 1). Please introduce yourself and your relationship to artificial intelligence.

[Martin Leucker] Thanks, Barbara, for giving me the possibility to give this interview with you. I'm heading the Institute for Software Engineering and Programming Languages at the University of Lübeck. At the same time, I'm also CEO of the UniTransfer-Klinik Lübeck GmbH, which is a technology transfer company that is mostly owned by the University of Lübeck, as well as the UKSH, which is the university hospital in Schleswig-Holstein. As such, I'm developing software or I'm working on methods for developing software, so I'm working on software engineering techniques with lots of applications in the medical domain. Traditional software engineering techniques now have to be adapted to be ready for AI technology, and that is basically what we do research on.

"If you take medical devices, there are strict rules under which medical devices can get certified and put into the market. Now, these kinds of rules have to be adapted to cater for AI components."

Do you have examples of one or two research questions that specifically address AI?

For example, if you take medical devices, there are strict rules under which medical devices can get certified and put into the market [8]. Now, these kinds of rules have to be adapted to cater for AI components. So, when now AI components come into medical devices, you have to have new techniques for certifying such devices, and that is one of the research questions.

Could you elaborate on that?

For example, one of the rules says that the software has to be intensively tested before you put it into the market, which makes sense, of course, as these are safety-critical systems. Now, what does it mean? If we learn a control strategy, for example, for a medical device, given certain kind of data, then we have to test it differently than when programming the control manually.

At the same time, there are lots of techniques where you continuously learn. You observe what the system is doing in practice and the software changes dynamically. So far, such kind of AI technology is not allowed to put into the market, because according to current rules, once you test the system, it is not allowed to change [3]. So, one of the real challenges in this domain is, could we eventually, sooner or later, also allow software that is changing itself, learning in practice, for allowing it to the market? But that, of course, would require that we have safeguards aside that kind of make sure that whatever the system learns is still within some kind of safety boundaries [6].

Building on that, what role does trust play in AI adoption?

Trust is a very important concept, but at the same time, I think trust is much more than correctness. And in many cases, it's misunderstood. Trust does not only mean that the system is working correctly. But we have to guarantee many different forms of trust. For example, when a doctor uses a device, it's important that the device works correctly from a provable, mathematical perspective, but it's also important that the doctor gets the feeling, gets the understanding that the device is working correctly. At the same time, for example, many machine learning technologies are based on data, and that means that the patient should give data to the companies or to the research institutions to allow them to build new solutions based on the data. Of course, privacy issues, anonymization issues, and so on, they have to be respected. But even if you would, on a technical level, be able to guarantee such kind of privacy issues, it also means that the people have to trust the solution. So, it's a mixture of technical solutions, but also has lots of social aspects as well [4].

"For me, the role of AI is to be a smart assistant, but it always means that we have a human supervisor […]."

Do you have key measures in mind that need to be in place to ensure ethical AI adoption?

Well, regarding ethical AI, I think it's important that on one hand, we understand, we learn, we come up with rules what is ethical in this context. But at the same time, it's important that these rules materialize in law. Ethical aspects are fine, but there also has to be a punishment if you don't follow them. I think it's important that, let's say, philosophers, people working on ethics work in AI. But it's also very important that we collaborate with people from law that also tell us in which way such kind of ethical implications will eventually be enforceable.

In terms of the future technical capabilities of AI, on a scale of 1 to 10, what do you think will be possible, 1 being the artificial intelligence tools we see today, like ChatGPT, and 10 being artificial general intelligence that surpasses human capabilities?

Personally, put it in numbers, maybe it would be like 7. I think that the current state of the art will advance a lot. But as you see from ChatGPT, for example, it looks quite nice, but when you really dig into it, then you see that a lot of things are not really well understood. So, for me, the role of AI is to be a smart assistant, but it always means that we have a human supervisor that is in the end in control of when to apply AI-based solutions or when to decide certain kinds of things. To give an example for the medical domain, it will always be the doctor that has the final word. Maybe he or she has a lot of assistants that are based on AI, that find certain kind of malicious cells in the radiology picture and so on. But the final assessment has to be done by a human. Likewise, an AI-assistant may suggest a treatment based on what has worked in the past, but the choice of treatment has to be under the supervision of a human.

There has been a lot of discussion about possible future scenarios for artificial intelligence, from dystopian to utopian. Where would you position yourself based on your understanding of AI's future capabilities, etc.?

I think that the sensible application of AI techniques is in general a good idea. I'm completely sure AI will not take over the world [2]. All these kinds of horror scenarios that are often discussed in the media, I think it's completely over-exaggerated. I think that one can make a very positive use of AI solutions in the next years. Nevertheless, it is good to have these discussions and to constantly monitor and ensure that AI is developed in the right direction, for the benefit of our society.

Reflecting on the past few days, what insight was particularly interesting to you?

Well, here at AISoLA there were many different tracks. I think it was important to have tracks on explainable AI, to more understand notions of trustworthiness where philosophers were explaining their views, where at the same time also lawyers were explaining their views. That I liked a lot. Then there was a track on digital humanism which is I think also very important to bridge the gap between, let's say, computer science, AI and humanities. Then I also liked a lot the track on future programming based on AI-based tools, because that fits my software engineering background. Of course, I also like the healthcare track, as it shows the applications in the medical domain. That is very important for my work, too [7].

"[Fake news] always [have] been around, but it's now so easy to create fake news in a massive manner."

You yourself are used to working in an interdisciplinary environment, right?

Yes. We have lots of projects with the application in the medical domain, so we have to work with doctors. But at the same time, we also have to follow the norms and the rules. We have to understand them, maybe also to criticize them and say where to extend them. That has something to do with reading laws and norms and so on, which we were not educated for. So it's good to cooperate with lawyers in these aspects. At the same time, also ethical aspects play a role in our work, again a direction for interdisciplinary cooperation [5].

Are there any lessons learned from these collaborations that you would like to see applied to artificial intelligence and its evolution and adoption? Maybe things that could be done similarly or things that didn't go so well.

I would say that we are on a very good track on one hand, but also on a slow track. One of the difficulties is, of course, that every discipline speaks a different language. It just takes a while to understand the other groups, to understand their thinking, their terms, their definitions. I think we are on a good track, but of course, there is still a lot of work, a lot of research to be done. We're concentrating on the medical domain, but then at the same time, the automotive industry is very important, autonomous driving. There's also a huge area where certain norms play a very big role. We haven't compared the different approaches yet. In some sense, right now we go into limited application areas, but you also have to harmonize between different areas. What is common in the different application areas? What is different?

Is there a particular research question or topic that you would like to see explored in more depth from an interdisciplinary perspective?

From an interdisciplinary perspective, I think it's very important that people from the legal domain cooperate with computer scientists. And also, people from normative institutes like ISO, DIN, and so on, that they participate in interdisciplinary research. At the same time, for my specific personal research area, the verification of AI-based solutions is an extremely important topic that we have to study in more depth. Right now, many people come up with AI-based solutions, but they don't really have verification techniques. And verification is kind of the precursor to get systems approved by authorities.

Is there already a framework in place that provides structure and clarifies the expectations and roles of the various disciplines involved? Or is this something we need to build?

I think we're currently building it. I mean, it's events like AISoLA, for example. They are a perfect opportunity where different kinds of communities can meet, can exchange ideas, where we can learn from the other groups. We have interdisciplinary projects where we also, of course, have to collaborate. But I think we're on a good track, but it's still a long way to go.

From your personal perspective, what should be the AI vision?

Well, to me, it looks like AI is going to be an important tool in building a digitalized world. Meaning building new systems where we have AI-based components, where we have a lot of interaction with the help of AI-based systems. But at the same time, AI is a tool and not more. So I don't believe in, as I mentioned before, AI will take over the world or something like that. It's supposed to be a tool, in my understanding, it will be a powerful tool, but also not more than a tool.

Do you see a potential for increased misuse?

Of course. Like every new technology, it can be misused. We have the problem of fake news that are easily created now using ChatGPT. You can get very nice texts that look reasonable but are completely fake. The same with pictures and videos and so on. It's definitely a threat to society, which has to be solved by technology that, for example, identifies news as fake news [1]. But at the same time, and may be even more important, it has to be solved sociological, for example, train people to really look for the references and to understand what is real information, what is fake information [9]. In a sense, it's nothing really new. It always has been around, but it's now so easy to create fake news in a massive manner. And that means also that the people have to be much more careful than before.

Do you think users are sufficiently aware of this? Or do we need to teach them to be more skeptical in their interactions.

That's a hard question. I think it's a little bit of both. On one hand, people are aware of it in a sense that some people are very critical about AI. At the same time, they send their data to companies like Meta via Instagram and so on. So, to my feeling, people are aware of problems, but they don't understand the technology to the extent that would help them to really develop the right understanding and right treatment of AI solutions. So, in some sense, I think we have to train people in the way that they can judge what is a reasonable approach, when to share my data and when not to share my data. So right now, it's a little bit blurry that some people are frightened, but they don't know why. They don't know when to be frightened and that results sometimes in irrational behavior.

"Right now, many people come up with AI-based solutions, but they don't really have verification techniques [...]. And verification is kind of the precursor to get systems approved by authorities."

Is part of the challenge that organizations are not sufficiently transparent about what they do with this data?

Well, that's one aspect. However, it is not only the organizations but also the users of technology: I think for most technology, even if you are a person that is not really working on this technology but only with this technology, you still have to understand it to a certain extent. For example, if you drive a car, you have to have a limited knowledge how a car works to be able to understand what is a dangerous situation, what is not so dangerous and so on. And this training of people is missing when it comes to AI. So, we need a general understanding in society about AI, what is possible, what is not possible, when is some fear rational and when is it irrational.

Is there anything else you would like to add?

Not really.

Then thank you Martin for your time and your perspectives on AI, especially from the healthcare perspective. Have a great evening!

Thanks a lot. And thanks for taking this initiative!

References

1. Islam, M.R., Liu, S., Wang, X., et al.: Deep learning for misinformation detection on online social networks: a survey and new perspectives. Soc. Netw. Anal. Min. **10**, 82 (2020)
2. Lewis, T.: Don't let Artificial Intelligence take over, top scientists warn. LiveScience https://www.livescience.com/49419-artificial-intelligence-dangers-letter.html
3. Pechmann, L., Mildner, M., Suthau, T., Leucker, M.: Regulatorische Anforderungen an Lösungen der künstlichen Intelligenz im Gesundheitswesen. Künstliche Intelligenz im Gesundheitswesen, pp. 175–198 (2022)
4. EU Commission: Ethics Guidelines for Trustworthy AI. https://digital-strategy.ec.europa.eu/en/library/ethics-guidelines-trustworthy-ai
5. KI-SIGS: KI-Space für intelligente Gesundheitssysteme. https://www.dfki.de/web/forschung/projekte-publikationen/projekt/ki-sigs
6. US FDA: Proposed Regulatory Framework for Modifications to Artificial Intelligence/Machine Learning (AI/ML)-Based Software as a Medical Device (SaMD): Discussion Paper and Request for Feedback. https://www.fda.gov/files/medical%20devices/published/US-FDA-Artificial-Intelligence-and-Machine-Learning-Discussion-Paper.pdf
7. https://2023-aisola.isola-conference.org
8. https://eur-lex.europa.eu/legal-content/EN/TXT/?uri=CELEX%3A32017R0745
9. https://www.edps.europa.eu/press-publications/publications/techsonar/fake-news-detection_en

Let's Talk AI with Computer Science Expert Falk Howar

Falk Howar[1] and Barbara Steffen[2(✉)]

[1] TU Dortmund and Fraunhofer ISST, Dortmund, Germany
falk.howar@tu-dortmund.de
[2] METAFrame Technologies, Dortmund, Germany
barbara.steffen@metaframe.de

Abstract. We must ensure reasonable risk before deploying AI systems at a societal scale.

My personal AI mission: I work on methods for ensuring that AI systems, autonomous vehicles in particular, are safe.

Fig. 1. Falk Howar

1 My Takes on AI

- **Artificial Intelligence** – Intelligence exhibited by systems that are designed and constructed by humans.
- **Trust** – The deliberate and rational reliance on another person to do something.
- **Explainability** – A concept in machine learning, denoting the capacity of a system or an output to enable users to understand why (not how!) a behavior or an output was produced.
- **Essential Elements of Human Capabilities** – Consciousness, empathy, and the capacity for creating and manipulating symbolic systems.

B. Steffen et al. (Eds.): *Let's Talk AI*, LNCS 15000, pp. 229–235, 2026.
https://doi.org/10.1007/978-3-032-09008-9_27

2 The Interview

[Barbara Steffen] I have the pleasure to sit with Falk Howar (Fig. 1) from the TU Dortmund. Please briefly introduce yourself and your relationship to artificial intelligence.

[Falk Howar] Certainly, it's a pleasure. As you mentioned, I'm a professor of software engineering. I'm currently affiliated with TU Dortmund in Germany. Before joining TU Dortmund, I managed a small institute at TU Clausthal, another German university that closely collaborates with the automotive industry. Prior to that, I worked as a postdoctoral researcher at CMU and NASA Ames Research Center, where I worked on the safety verification and validation of autonomous aeronautic systems [4]. In the automotive industry, I focused on the safety of automated driving systems, which greatly influences my current research. I work on formal verification and learning techniques to generate models of systems and environments, which I then use to assure or verify the safety of these systems [10].

"Human civilization will have to find a way of dealing with the risk of these systems. [...] consequences sometimes only show up after a couple of years."

Could you provide one or two specific examples of your AI related research questions?

Absolutely. From my perspective, one of the most significant challenges we face with AI is how to deploy systems that incorporate AI components at a societal scale, given the risks we don't fully comprehend yet. Personally, I work with automated driving systems. There is a real risk associated with introducing automated vehicles on the road. As we've recently seen in San Francisco, for instance, companies trying to implement this technology often find themselves involved in accidents, primarily because the systems don't fully comprehend or perceive their environment [5]. How does this relate to AI? Well, these systems operate in complex environments, and we have to train components because we can't program them to perceive these environments.

In your opinion, which role does trust play in AI adoption?

Trust plays a significant role. Studies have shown two effects: under trust and over trust. Over trust can lead to over-reliance on systems. We've seen this in the automotive industry with the introduction of cruise control systems. After activating the system, drivers (in some studies) pay less attention [9], possibly due to a lack of understanding about what the system can and can't do. Then there is also the issue of automation fatigue. In hospitals, for example, you can observe this in intensive care units where numerous devices flash warning signs or emit sounds. Nurses can become somewhat desensitized to these signs [8]. We see the same with air traffic controllers or airplane pilots who receive an influx of collision warnings when approaching an airport due to surrounding traffic. One observed effect is that people simply ignore these systems. So, if you don't trust the system, you won't use it. Conversely, if you trust the system too much, you may not question its impact. This may be what happened with social media. It emerged in our society and is now causing significant issues, particularly among younger people and girls. There is a well-known public health crisis among teenage girls in the US, for example [1].

So, in your opinion, what measures are essential for ethical AI adoption?

I believe the concept of calibrated trust, developed by psychologists about 20 years ago, is interesting [6]. I'm not a psychologist, so this is a layman's explanation. The idea is that when using a system or collaborating with a person, you need to calibrate your trust to an appropriate level. This principle applies at both an individual and societal scale. For autonomous vehicles, for example, we started deploying them on the streets without fully understanding how they work or the associated risks. Now, we operate them in test fleets worldwide to better understand the domain and calibrate our understanding of the capabilities and risks. This allows us to make an informed decision about whether we should use them, permit them, and assess the remaining risk. This kind of calibration process needs to work at a societal level and at an individual level when working with these systems. We then need to design systems that allow for this calibration.

"I think we're overestimating the potential dangers or effects that AI could have in the short term [and] that we underestimate what these systems will be able do in the long run."

To which extent does this calibration depend on specific use cases and scenarios or is it rather independent of it?

You could argue that there's a difference between high stakes and low stakes situations. If you're using an AI system to select your playlist while you're cooking, you might not care too much if it doesn't perfectly match your taste in music. You can simply choose a different playlist. However, when there's a risk of harm or damage, it's essential to perform a risk assessment and have processes in place that ensure the safety or reasonable risk of these systems.

On a scale of 1 to 10, where 1 is artificial intelligence systems we know today, like Chat-GPT, and 10 is something like artificial general intelligence systems that actually surpass human capabilities, what do you think will be possible?

I'm going to sidestep the question slightly. I believe the terms "intelligence" and "artificial general intelligence" are often used too broadly and are underspecified. We don't fully understand what we mean when we say that humans are intelligent and definitions of intelligence shift over time [7]. Whenever a computer can perform a task, that task is no longer considered a measure of intelligence. Sometimes we say intelligence involves creativity, reasoning, or the ability to step back and consider the bigger picture. I can imagine building a machine that can do all these things. Maybe the interesting question then will become, can it have the capability to sidestep its programming and change its own programming in the way humans can?

Computers have long surpassed us in specific tasks. They can process vast amounts of data and perform computations that we can't. Currently, there's a lot of hype about the end of the world brought about by AI. It would perhaps only be the end of mankind, hopefully, and the world could continue. But I think we're overestimating the potential dangers or effects that AI could have in the short term because we've just seen these amazing examples of what large language models can do on specific tasks and how natural it feels to interact with them. On the other hand, I think that we underestimate what these systems will be able do in the long run.

You asked me to rate this on a scale from 1 to 10, but you also mentioned that they surpass human capability. That means we would have created a system that surpasses our own intelligence. Wouldn't the AI then also be capable of building a system that's more intelligent than it? Then the question is, is there any limit on intelligence or could this go on forever? Would it become a god? Would it create a universe? We don't know. But I think once we've taken the initial step of creating something more capable than us, and it has the same capacity, this should, in principle, continue infinitely.

Okay, but what if you had to position yourself on a scale of 1 to 10. Where would you position yourself? More towards we're not going to see much more progress, or more towards we're not going to see an end to it, which would suggest an 8, 9, 10?

Okay, this is by analogy and I'm not sure if this is a working analogy: if you go back to the time when the internal combustion engine was developed. The first motor cars we had, they looked very much like horse carriages. They had open seats and replaced one component in the horse carriage with the combustion engine. Even the steering wheels were quite awkward. They couldn't go fast. It was clunky. Then look at how, with the same principle at heart, over 100 years, technology has advanced so much that vehicles now have incredible capabilities, a high degree of automation, and computers in them, and so on. Then imagine that we're currently at the point where someone invented the combustion engine equivalent in AI. I think we're going to see things that we can't even imagine currently.

"Whenever a computer can perform a task, that task is no longer considered a measure of intelligence."

Using your example of the combustion engine, could it mean that we should focus less on the engine and more on its performance like how long it took us to get from A to B, its cost, its level of comfort, and the number of people it could carry? Do we need different metrics, such as comparing our productivity today to a possible level of productivity in the future?

Could you elaborate?

For example, outcome, performance, or something like that. So we could say, for example, humans today produce this kind of outcome or have this kind of performance. But because of the advancement of the tools, we suddenly observe a completely new level of what we are actually able to do, or what the AI-tools will be able to do by themselves. That comparison would be more in terms of results rather than discussing solutions or functionalities.

I attended a very interesting talk today, where someone showed how they used an AI system to aid software development, automating tasks that involve not only writing programs but also tasks heavily based on natural language: document parsing, chatting with people, writing requirements, and designing the architecture [3]. I think AI can do a lot of this boilerplate stuff. The authors observed a tenfold increase in performance because you can eliminate a lot of the boring tasks and focus on the interesting tasks, or the tasks where humans currently perform better than AI. We'll probably see an increase in this trend. The hard question that I wasn't able to answer for myself, before this conference, or even during the conference, is if there's a limit to it. Will it be the boilerplate for some time, and then we develop models with a new quality of capabilities, or will people design clever systems based on the current paradigms that (in the analogy of the combustion engine) somehow exhibit new capabilities.

"Maybe the interesting question then will become, can it have the capability to […] change its own programming in the way humans can?"

Looking at possible future scenarios, from dystopia to utopia, where would you position yourself?

I believe we have this in our own hands. And I've said this before in discussions here, it's very easy to paint a very dystopian future, and it's very easy to paint a very utopian future. I think either could happen, but human civilization will have to find a way of dealing with the risk of these systems, and deploy them gradually, because we don't fully understand their consequences, and consequences sometimes only show up after a couple of years of using those systems.

I think we have to take into account that maybe sometimes when we see, that there's an unreasonable risk that we didn't know about, we just shut operations down. We will have to find economic models, and insurance policies. There were many colleagues from other disciplines at AISoLA, lawyers for example, who had some very interesting insights on what can work, and what cannot work.

To answer your question: I'm going to say I'm faithful that we will find a way of living with AI, and it will have negative and positive outcomes, but I am hopeful that it will be a net positive. I think what will determine this is in the end a question of power. Will it, e.g., be possible for authoritarian governments to deploy these tools and techniques to control their populations in an unethical way, or will – what we all dreamt of – the freedom of information in the internet help people to fight such governments? Will we find a way to regulate the big companies, as we did with pharma and tobacco companies in the past, to put warning labels on their products, to limit how they can advertise, and how they can deploy their products.

Considering these trade-offs and looking back on the past few days, what insights did you find most interesting?

On a personal level, the talks given by lawyers were particularly enlightening. I learned a lot about how law works, and how reasoning works in law, e.g., for different ways of organizing liability.

Is there a specific research question you would like to see addressed from an interdisciplinary perspective?

I think we really need to understand how we address societal risk that is the consequence of deploying AI systems. This is interdisciplinary because you have to construct laws that create a framework for operation. It has to be economically viable. You need psychologists and doctors to judge potential health consequences. And you will need engineers and designers that build these systems and can adapt how we build these systems.

What should be the AI vision for the future from your personal perspective?

I don't think output or how we increase human productivity should be the primary goal. There's a lot of talk about that AI will take this job and that job and automation took all the blue-collar jobs in the past 40 years and now AI is coming for all the white-collar jobs and will make office workers unemployed or knowledge workers lose their jobs. There's a chance of this happening to some degree. Through automation it actually did happen for blue-collar jobs. Of course, we have to think about alternative models of income and wealth distribution and somehow find a way of making everybody profit from these advancements instead of only the people who own the AI profit from deploying AI.

But this alone won't solve a big societal crisis of people not being able to define what they do and the worth of their life through work, which happens today to a huge extent. There is some very interesting ancient Greek philosophy about living a good life. Aristotle writes about what it means to live a good life [2]. And it is not only about happiness, but to a large extent also about a meaningful life and how you contribute to your community, that you strive for excellence and virtue. And I think we will have to revisit these old ideas of living good lives and the vision for AI should be that it enables us to live good lives.

At AISoLA, we met with computer scientists, psychologists, philosophers, and legal experts. Are there any other disciplines you would like to add?

I think other sciences would also be interesting. There was some discussion here about how AI could aid scientific discovery. We, e.g., talked a little bit about protein folding, where AI already had an impact. It would be interesting to learn from other disciplines how AI can actually speed up their scientific discovery to understand better if AI will surpass our capabilities soon in scientific discovery and if it does, if there are ways of us still having a chance of understanding what it discovers. From a more societal perspective, it would also be great to have not only psychologists, but people from healthcare, maybe doctors who perform surgeries in hospitals or nurses who work with elderly people to get their perspective on AI.

We are coming to the end of this interview. Is there anything else you would like to add?

No, I think I've spoken quite extensively.

Then thank you very much for your insights and time, Falk. Enjoy the rest of AISoLA.

Thanks. Thanks for having me. Thanks for this great conference. It's been a blast.

References

1. Abi-Jaoude, E., Naylor, K.T., Pignatiello, A.: Smartphones, social media use and youth mental health. Can. Med. Assoc. J. **192**(6), E136–E141 (2020)

2. Crisp, R.: Aristotle: Nicomachean Ethics. Cambridge University Press (2000)
3. Belzner, L., Gabor, T., Wirsing, M.: Large language model assisted software engineering: prospects, challenges, and a case study. In: Steffen, B. (ed.) Bridging the Gap Between AI and Reality (AISoLA 2023). LNCS, vol. 14380, pp. 355–374. Springer (2024)
4. Giannakopoulou, D., Howar, F., Isberner, M., Lauderdale, T., Rakamaric, Z., Raman, V.: Taming test inputs for separation assurance. In: Crnkovic, I., Chechik, M., Grünbacher, P. (eds.) ACM/IEEE International Conference on Automated Software Engineering (ASE 2014), pp. 373–384. ACM (2014)
5. Kloukiniotis, A., Papandreou, A., Lalos, A., Kapsalas, P., Nguyen, D.V., Moustakas, K.: Countering adversarial attacks on autonomous vehicles using denoising techniques: a review. IEEE Open J. Intell. Transp. Syst. **3**, 61–80 (2022)
6. Lee, J.D., See, K.A.: Trust in automation: designing for appropriate reliance. Hum. Factors **46**(1), 50–80 (2004)
7. Legg, S., Hutter, M.: A collection of definitions of intelligence. In: Proceedings of 2007 Conference on Advances in Artificial General Intelligence: Concepts, Architectures and Algorithms (AGI Workshop 2006), pp. 17–24. IOS Press (2007)
8. Lewandowska, K., Weisbrot, M., Cieloszyk, A., Mędrzycka-Dąbrowska, W., Krupa, S., Ozga, D.: Impact of alarm fatigue on the work of nurses in an intensive care environment: a systematic review. Int. J. Environ. Res. Public Health **17**(22) (2020)
9. Sanbonmatsu, D.M., Crabtree, K.W., McDonnell, A.S., Cooper, J.M., Strayer, D.L.: Automated driving experiences, attention, and intentions following extensive on-road usage of a level 2 automation vehicle. J. Saf. Res. **90**, 199–207 (2024)
10. Schallau, T., Naujokat, S., Kullmann, F., Howar, F.: Tree-based scenario classification. In: Benz, N., Gopinath, D., Shi, N. (eds.) Proceeding of NASA Formal Methods (NFM 2024), pp. 259–278. LNCS, vol. 14627. Springer (2024)

Let's Talk AI with Computer Science Expert Jakob Rehof

Jakob Rehof[1] and Barbara Steffen[2](✉)

[1] TU Dortmund and Lamarr Institute for Machine Learning and Artificial Intelligence, Dortmund, Germany
jakob.rehof@tu-dortmund.de
[2] METAFrame Technologies, Dortmund, Germany
barbara.steffen@metaframe.de

Abstract. We are in the middle of an AI revolution and we need to figure out how to use this technology creatively and at the same time mitigate the risks that are associated with it.

My personal AI mission: To help further the creative development and use of trustworthy AI technology.

Fig. 1. Jakob Rehof

1 My Takes on AI

- **Artificial Intelligence** – Computer systems that can to a significant degree exhibit behavior characteristic of biological or human intelligence.
- **Trust** – Believing that someone or something will behave as expected.
- **Explainability** – The ability of a system to reconstruct the reasons why the system behaves the way it does.
- **Essential Elements of Human Capabilities** – Background understanding of the world, semantics, reflectivity.

B. Steffen et al. (Eds.): *Let's Talk AI*, LNCS 15000, pp. 236–243, 2026.
https://doi.org/10.1007/978-3-032-09008-9_28

2 The Interview

[Barbara Steffen] I have the pleasure to interview Jakob Rehof (Fig. 1) of the Technical University Dortmund. Please briefly introduce yourself and your relation to artificial intelligence.

[Jakob Rehof] Thank you for having me. I'm a professor of computer science at the Technical University of Dortmund. Much of my research has focused on algorithms and complexity, verification, and mathematical logic with applications to programming technology. To mention one example, in recent years, I have been particularly interested in program synthesis [15], the automatic generation of code, and increasingly connecting that with applications in classical engineering, for instance by applying these techniques to the automatic generation of simulation models or system designs in logistics, engineering and production technology [2, 5, 6, 8, 9]. In this context, we work on methods for automatically generating whole families of simulation models embodying rich sets of design variants and then possibly testing, measuring and exploring those models [11]. For instance, you can imagine trying to construct an object like a robotic arm and attempting to assemble various possible solutions to such a design problem. Say the robotic arm should be able to move in a certain way at a certain speed. You can now co-generate a lot of things in that context. You can generate the CAD design in several possible solution variants together with accompanying simulation models which you can then measure and explore to automatically identify the best designs with respect to a set of parameters (KPIs). The goal here can be referred to as design space exploration [7].

Now, you asked about my relation to AI because that's where it comes in. If we have the ability to generate code that may represent some system designs and we're able to generate multiple solution variants for a certain design problem, and we're able to measure various parameters on those generated designs, then you can think of combining that with learning mechanisms. You can create a generate-test-and-learn loop. You generate a possibly large number of solutions to a problem, generate some simulation models, use them to perform measurements, and then use the data that comes out of those measurements to feed them into a learning mechanism. Then you can close the loop by trying to learn how to optimize the design problem that you started out with. That is one important area of current interest to me in connection to AI in my own research.

I also have interests of a more general nature. For example, I'm associated with the Gaia-X project [17], building up a think tank in the context of Gaia-X, called the Gaia-X Institute, which is supposed to think ahead about topics related to regulation of information technology. Particularly in the context of regulations from the European Commission, as you may be aware, there are a number of regulatory acts coming out now. There's the Data Governance Act, the Data Act, and the AI Act is under discussion. And so there again, you see there's a connection. I'm interested in the area of regulation, and I'm interested in problems such as how we may help implement such regulatory acts, for example, by studying the question of automated compliance: How can we develop technologies that make it easier to verify or certify that a system is compliant with the regulation? So that also pertains to the AI topic in as much as the AI area is an important object of regulation.

Thank you for the overview. What role does trust play in AI adoption?

Trust is a key factor in AI adoption, especially if we operate in a regulated space. In an autocratic environment, trust might not be as much of an issue. But in our part of the world, it is a key issue. And it's not just about increasing trust. It is as much about calibrating trust, that is, aligning the level of trust with the actual trustworthiness of the systems. And I think that's a crucial issue for AI systems.

So essentially it is about ensuring that the end user doesn't have too much trust, but also not too little. That means that psychologists and AI experts, for example, have to determine the right level of trust in terms of how trustworthy this application is, and then figure out how to make sure that the end user places this right level of trust in the application.

Yes, that's certainly one aspect of it. It's not just about one direction, increasing trust or decreasing trust. You may overtrust a system, but you may also undertrust a system, as you suggest. A system might actually be more reliable or trustworthy than you think. And if that leads you to not using the system, if it's a useful system, then that's not a desirable state of affairs. So it goes in both directions. Now, who is supposed to decide, for example, how trustworthy a system is? That may be a question for experts in some cases, but it may also be a question of human psychology, where in some sense the end user is the de facto judge on how trustful you as a user typically will be towards a system. And so it's a complicated matter that, depending on the situation and the system and so forth, will play out differently.

So, for example, if you take something like autonomous driving, it's going to be very important what, by expert knowledge, can actually be known about certain features of such a system. For example, what is the probability that certain accidents might happen? But then weighing the psychological impact of that probability, that's not necessarily something that can or should be left for the technical expert to decide. You may have to understand how most normal human beings actually react to something like the probability X of something bad happening in a certain domain. It doesn't help us if, for example, an expert will tell you, "You can go ahead and use this system. It's no problem because the probability of something bad happening is zero point something", if most normal people don't actually react to that system and that probability that way. It's a well-known fact that, for example, most people don't necessarily deal very rationally with things like probability [4]. So that needs to be taken into account. That's possibly also a matter for empirical psychology, for example [12].

"There is a basic understanding in many parts of the industry that something in the way of regulation is needed."

Can you think of relevant measures to ensure the ethical use of AI?

Yes, I believe that regulation is a key factor. It's an area that we're not really used to in general when it comes to software-intensive systems. Of course, we have regulations in various specialized vertical domains, like, for example, health care systems or autonomous driving systems. What is rather new is that in Europe, the legislator is undertaking regulating more general software based systems, for example, systems pertaining to data exchange and the usage of cloud infrastructures in that context, or AI systems. That's rather novel and I think that's actually a pioneering effort. I think that is probably one of the main instruments for achieving ethical AI and its deployment in an ethically responsible way [13].

Now, if we look at the technical capabilities that AI might have in the future, on a scale of 1 to 10, where 1 describes the artificial intelligence systems we already see, like ChatGPT, which are very dedicated to specific functionalities in a specific context, and 10 describes something like artificial general intelligence, and refers to surpassing human capabilities in all areas, what do you think will be possible?

I find that very hard to say, partly because the notion of artificial general intelligence does not seem to me to be quite sharply defined. To take something like ChatGPT, it already seems to point to the possibility of something like artificial general intelligence by some definition of that concept where natural language processing is important. I think it could go very far. Whether I should quantify it as 10 or 7, I don't know, but it's probably more than 5, would be my take. I was very surprised when these technologies started to show their potential. For me personally, the first time I really got aware of that was because of Google's AlphaZero chess engine and shortly afterwards I became totally impressed with Google Translate. I'm trying to pick up Italian, and I use Google Translate quite a lot for that, and I am absolutely fascinated with its capabilities. I thought earlier that this level of performance in machine translation would be impossible. And so you then move to the generalization of that in the form of something like ChatGPT, and of course it's easy still to poke holes in ChatGPT to sort of bring it out of balance if you persist long enough and hard enough.

But if you imagine the progress that we have seen so far still going on for some time, like every time you bump up the version number on ChatGPT, you seem to get an exponential improvement in performance and quality, then that could lead to a situation where it becomes very difficult to expose the AI as a machine, at least in certain application contexts. So I think this could well go very far. Exactly how far it will go, I can't tell you. I don't think anybody really can.

> "Could you imagine regarding an AI system as a legal persona? What would that mean? [...] should there be a kind of rights for robots?"

Take your technical understanding of AI and think of all the different future scenarios currently being discussed, from dystopia to utopia. What future do you think AI will bring?

Well, obviously somewhere in the middle on that spectrum, because I mean, as for the dystopian perspective, I do believe that there is enough potential in the technology itself that it does make some sense to ask that question and to be concerned with it. That's why I said that I think regulation is really important so as to avoid the dystopian effects. And as I already mentioned, I think the EU is performing pioneering acts in that area. But it also means that in areas and places in the world that work very differently from, say, Europe or other parts of the world that we maybe are close to in the mode of operation, you already see dystopian effects like facial recognition technology being used for surveillance of general populations, social scoring, etc. These are things that under a European regulatory regime would be forbidden. It would be a criminal act to implement and operate systems in that way. And so there are dystopian aspects. They can be prevented, but it's basically going to be a political and cultural question of whether you succeed in doing that.

There's a lot of fantastic and positive potential, which is the opposite of dystopian. If I just take something like software technology as an example, which is one field of special interest to me, we have for a very long time not really seen big jumps in automatic programming technology, for example. Software development technology has not really evolved in fundamental ways for quite many years. Something like ChatGPT applied to writing code, I think, is a great prospect. And I think it's basically good for both software research and the professional area of software development. Because it will allow us, at least for some classes of systems, to, if I may put it this way, take out a lot of the dumb work of software development, thereby making it much more interesting for humans to be engaged in that professional field.

"One fascinating question is, would it be possible to think of an AI system as being in some sense responsible for its actions?"

Take the EU AI Act, for example. Today, it is mainly the Big Tech companies that are at the forefront of new artificial intelligence applications. Could this regulation lead to a disadvantage for European users? As a group, they could lose access to companies, research results, advances and AI tools developed in other countries or available to users in other countries.

Right. That's a reasonable question. Another variant of that question, which is also reasonable, would be to ask whether it might bring about a disadvantage, not for the end user, but for the industry. Does it become harder to generate digital innovation and related business models in the European space under such regulation? Such concerns have already been raised in many contexts and it's reasonable to discuss them. I do believe that the legislator is quite aware of these considerations. I can't tell you whether we immediately will find the right place to draw the line in each case, but it is something that is on the mind of the people who make this kind of regulation. Also, I think regulation is clearly needed for anything like our cultural and socio-economic and political kind of realm that we can identify with. And I think others will have to follow. I know, for example, there are important players in the US administration who are looking to European regulation with great interest. And so, I think in that sense also it's a pioneering act because others will have to follow in one form or the other. You also find, for example, that some of the Big Tech companies actually express interest in reducing uncertainty, which may involve being told by a legislator what is not viable and how they should behave vis-à-vis these huge problems of misuse that could be arise. That may not mean that they're always in agreement with a particular legislative system as to how exactly it should be done. But there is a basic understanding in many parts of the industry that something in the way of regulation is needed. And so, that's already a start.

Reflecting on the past few days, what new insights have been particularly interesting to you?

First of all, I want to congratulate the organizers on a very interesting and important conference. And I think it was very well received by everyone participating, is my impression. There were a lot of interdisciplinary discussions that I found very interesting. Let me mention just one example. In the context of a discussion on AI with a very interdisciplinary group of people, which came together here at this conference, there was a discussion about the notion of responsibility in connection with AI-based systems. Responsibility from a philosophical point of view, from an ethical point of view, and from a legal point of view. One fascinating question is, would it be possible to think of an AI system as being in some sense responsible for its actions? Can it be creative? Questions like that are interesting. And then you may put a legal spotlight on it. Could you imagine regarding an AI system as a legal persona? What would that mean? I mean, there have already been discussions around this, such as, should there be a kind of rights for robots? I don't happen to think myself that would be a good or even a meaningful idea. But it's interesting to reflect on the reasons we might have for choosing one or the other stance on such a question.

"I think regulation is really important so as to avoid the dystopian effects."

Do you have a specific research question or topic in mind that you would like to see addressed from a more interdisciplinary perspective? And if so, which disciplines should be part of this research?

It's hard to focus on one particular topic because there are quite many of them. Let me just mention a couple of things. The ethical and regulatory questions are important. The interface between technology and law is coming more into focus for AI systems. Other than that, we already see, you know, psychology, sociology being quite active, actually, in the discussion. And so I'm actually impressed with how fast these other fields outside of computer science have mobilized towards contributing to thinking about these questions, and that is good. On the more technical side there are problems of verification, testing, validation, and certification of AI systems that need to be considered in order to achieve trustworthy AI. So we will not be running short on things to do.

From your personal perspective, what should be the AI vision?

I don't think it makes sense to have the AI vision. I just I think there are so many different aspects and you have to take a very differentiated view on it. My own mission statement in this context would be, in one sentence: To help further the creative development and use of trustworthy AI technology.

Is there an overarching goal you would like to see addressed or achieved?

I don't see one single overarching goal. I see many different areas where you can imagine great advances happening, for example, in medicine, from diagnostics to new medication. Also other parts of science will be positively impacted, based on AI technology. At the University of Dortmund, the Physics Department had a recent breakthrough in applying machine learning to interpreting data coming from astrophysical measurements, making it possible to discern patterns that come out in huge data sets from measurements of cosmic radiation. And so science in general may see great advances based on this technology. Then there are all the areas of life that can be improved, in quite different ways. Think of early warning systems and understanding climate change, where analyzing huge data sets and learning from past data can be helpful. So I tend to think of it as not one thing, but it's many different things. What ties those things together is a certain coherence to the underlying technology of machine learning based on statistical methods. But that is also not a quite simple matter, since there are different kinds of of AI technologies within that spectrum. For example, neural network based technology [1, 3] is a different sort of learning strategy than, say, reinforcement learning [10]. These things can be combined, of course, but they have different characteristics.

I also believe we may see at some point a more integrated approach where machine learning and statistical methods are combined with more classical technologies based on mathematical logic. We already see that happening in the context of trustworthy AI and explainable AI, where learning systems which might do dangerous things need to be controlled or even verified using logical methods. Think for example of a system controlling a fleet of drones moving around in a populated environment. One would like to have hard logic based guarantees that certain bad things simply cannot happen, right. So the technology is not fixed. And, incidentally, in recent years we have seen absolutely spectacular progress in the area of automated proof with proof assistants and proof checking [16], which is relevant for formal verification [14]. More generally, there is a need to combine the machine learning dimension with two further dimensions, that of integrating with prior knowledge and that of integrating with high quality data. That direction of so-called "triangular AI" is an important direction for the research program which is pursued in the new Lamarr Institute for Machine Learning and Artificial Intelligence at the universities of Bonn and Dortmund.

Do you have anything else you would like to add?

I think we covered a lot of interesting ground and I just want to thank you for the opportunity to to talk about it here. Thank you.

Thank you, Jakob, for your time and perspective on this topic. Have a great day!

Yes, you too. Thank you.

Thank you.

References

1. Bishop, C.M., Bishop, H.: Deep Learning. Foundations and Concepts. Springer (2023). https://doi.org/10.1007/978-3-031-45468-4
2. Chaumet, C., Rehof, J., Schuster, T.: A knowledge-driven framework for synthesizing designs from modular components. In: Proceedings of the 34th CIRP Design Conference (CIRP 2024). Elsevier (2024)
3. Goodfellow, I., Bengio, Y., Courville, A.: Deep Learning. MIT Press (2016)
4. Kahneman, D.: Thinking, Fast and Slow. Farrar, Straus and Giroux (2011)

5. Kallat, F., Pfrommer, J., Bessai, J., Rehof, J., Meyer, A.: Automatic building of a repository for component-based synthesis of warehouse simulation models. Procedia CIRP **104**, 1440–1445 (2021)
6. Mages, A., et al.: Automatic component-based synthesis of user-configured manufacturing simulation models. In: Proceedings 2022 Winter Simulation Conference (WSC 2022), pp. 1841–1852. IEEE (2022)
7. Nardi, L., Souza, A., Koeplinger, D., Olukotun, K.: HyperMapper: a practical design space exploration framework. In: Proceedings of the 27th IEEE International Symposium on Modeling, Analysis, and Simulation of Computer and Telecommunication Systems (MASCOTS 2019), pp. 425–426. IEEE (2019)
8. Schäfer, T., Bessai, J., Chaumet, C., Rehof, J., Riest, C.: Design space exploration for sampling-based motion planning programs with combinatory logic synthesis. In: LaValle, S.M., O'Kane, J.M., Otte, M., Sadigh, D., Tokekar, P. (eds.) Proceedings of the International Workshop on the Algorithmic Foundations of Robotics, pp. 36–51. Springer (2022). https://doi.org/10.1007/978-3-031-21090-7_3
9. Schäfer, T., Bergmann, J.A., Carballo, R.G., Rehof, J., Wiederkehr, P:. A synthesis-based tool path planning approach for machining operations. Procedia CIRP **104**, 918–923 (2021)
10. Sutton, R.S., Barto, A.C.: Reinforcement Learning. An Introduction. 2nd edn. MIT Press (2020)
11. Wenzel, S., Stolipin, J., Rehof, J., Winkels, J.: Trends in automatic composition of structures for simulation models in production and logistics. In: Proceedings of the 2019 Winter Simulation Conference (WSC 2019), pp. 2190–2200. IEEE (2019)
12. Wischnewski, M., Krämer, N., Müller, E.: Measuring and understanding trust calibrations for automated systems: a survey of the state-of-the-art and future directions. In: Proceedings of the 2023 CHI Conference on Human Factors in Computing Systems, pp. 1–16. ACM (2023)
13. https://commission.europa.eu/strategy-and-policy/priorities-2019-2024/europe-fit-digital-age/european-data-strategy/en
14. https://en.wikipedia.org/wiki/Formal_verification
15. https://en.wikipedia.org/wiki/Program_synthesis
16. https://en.wikipedia.org/wiki/Proof_assistant
17. https://gaia-x.eu/

Let's Talk AI with Computer Science Expert Mike Hinchey

Mike Hinchey[1] and Barbara Steffen[2(✉)]

[1] University of Limerick and Lero (Science Foundation Ireland Research Centre for Software), Limerick, Ireland
mike.hinchey@ul.ie
[2] METAFrame Technologies, Dortmund, Germany
barbara.steffen@metaframe.de

Abstract. We've made amazing advances in technology, especially in the last 20 years. Much of this is due to greater processing power, cheaper memory, and advances made over decades that now can truly be exploited. We need to ensure that AI is used to advance technology and for the good of everyone, without discrimination of any sort.

My personal AI mission: To promote the appropriate, sensible, use of AI and to educate the public that they cannot simply rely on AI just because someone calls it AI, especially when much of it is merely automation.

Fig. 1. Mike Hinchey

1 My Takes on AI

- **Artificial Intelligence** – Doing by computer what would require intelligence of a human.
- **Trust** – That reasonable faith can be placed in a computer system to work correctly, safely, and securely.
- **Explainability** – Describing the steps taken by a system to justify the decisions or choices that have been made.
- **Essential Elements of Human Capabilities** – Creativity, experience, culpability, sentience.

B. Steffen et al. (Eds.): *Let's Talk AI*, LNCS 15000, pp. 244–251, 2026.
https://doi.org/10.1007/978-3-032-09008-9_29

2 The Interview

[Barbara Steffen] Today I have the pleasure to talk to Mike Hinchey (Fig. 1). Could you please briefly introduce yourself and your relation to artificial intelligence?

[Mike Hinchey] Sure, thank you. I'm a professor of Software Engineering at the University of Limerick in Ireland and I'm also the former director of Lero, the Science Foundation Ireland Software Research Centre, and former director of the NASA Software Engineering Lab. My work is somewhat on the peripheries of artificial intelligence because I don't directly engage in AI research, but I work in the area of autonomous space exploration missions which heavily utilizes AI techniques.

Are there one or two research questions related to artificial intelligence which you are currently addressing?

Yes, indeed. We're looking at how we can develop self-directed software-based systems for space exploration. These systems need to be able to make decisions autonomously, primarily to protect themselves and maintain resilience during long-term missions in space. We're exploring how to build in a certain amount of self-management to ensure these systems make wise decisions and don't endanger the mission or anything else. This brings us into the area of explainable AI, which deals with understanding why decisions are being made, and of course, responsibility and responsible behaviour.

Did you see any great changes and improvements in the last years?

Certainly, we've seen tremendous advances with large language models and the benefits of greater processing power, which allows us to do much more with big data and machine learning. We now have access to various data repositories. People still complain it's not enough, but we're making progress. My main concern is that the media often labels everything as artificial intelligence, when a lot of it is simply automation. It's many of the same techniques we've used for decades, just benefiting from better processing power, development tools, and data, which leads to improved results. But it's not artificial intelligence, it's automation.

"We shouldn't be trusting things where we don't understand how they do it."

Can you elaborate on the distinction between intelligence and automation?

Certainly. Intelligence is something we find hard to define. Roger Penrose suggests intelligence requires sentience, so we need to be aware that we exist and be able to understand and think [5, 6]. That's true intelligence. Artificial intelligence attempts to replicate that in some way to provide its benefits and effects. But much of what we're doing and what the media reports on are things that we've done for many years. We're following algorithms, using data, applying techniques, and running computer programs to do things that don't involve intelligence or even mimic intelligence. They just automate tasks much more efficiently than a human can. And that's not AI, that's automation.

In your opinion, what role does trust play in the context of AI?

Trust is a significant issue. The media often portrays AI as something that's going to take over the world or rule our lives, which causes unnecessary fear. In reality, we have systems that are often mislabeled as AI being used to make critical decisions about who gets into college, what prisoners get parole, and who goes to jail. These decisions are based on algorithms written by humans, which means they have human biases, intentional or otherwise. We don't understand how these algorithms work or their details. If we had that understanding, we would have a greater degree of trust. This becomes even more important when dealing with machine learning. If we don't provide people with information on how decisions were made, we won't have trust in these systems. And yet, we're using them for critical things and trusting the decisions they make. It's like Asimov's laws – do no harm [1, 2]. We don't have that trust because we don't know what decisions are being made.

> "[…] we do need to look at this explainable AI. We do need to understand why decisions are made, or how decisions are made."

Do you see any essential measures to ensure ethical AI adoption?

Absolutely. In fact, the IEEE is working on an AI ethics standard. It's crucial that we behave ethically in everything we do in computing. We're affecting humans in various ways, and as we're giving decision-making power to machines, we must ensure that it's done ethically. This means that the people who are involved in building the original systems must behave ethically, and the system itself must behave ethically in the sense that it makes ethical decisions.

As for the future technical capabilities of AI, on a scale of 1 to 10, where 1 refers to the artificial intelligence systems known today, such as Chat-GPT, and 10 refers to general artificial intelligence that surpasses human capabilities. What level will we reach in the future?

In the short term, perhaps the next five years or so, I think we could reach 2–3. Maybe in the next 10 years, we might get to 5. I don't ever see us reaching 10. I think that's a pipe dream, but it will be marketed as if we've gotten there, because we're already marketing that we're close to it and we're nowhere near that.

Do we still lack definitions that would allow us to distinguish between what makes us human and what is necessary to be considered AI or AGI? Or should we rather observe and compare the performance of humans and (AI) systems in specific tasks? This would allow us to monitor the progress of AI and separate hype and fiction from reality.

It would be helpful if we had some sort of common understanding of what various terms are, because at the moment, a lot of things that are just automation are being promoted as AI. While they do great things and much better than a human can, and certainly robots can do wonderful things, they don't understand what those things are. So there's no intelligence, but they are using various techniques that are very, very useful. And they do things better than humans in many, many contexts. But again, sometimes that's overhyped. For instance, a recent survey showed that when doctors looked at X-rays of lung cancer, and an AI system did something similar, the AI system did pick up the positive cases, but it had about four times as many false positives. So it's a very good tool to assist the human, but it's not replacing the human and we're putting too much emphasis on the fact that it can do that. So anything that's labeled as an AI is suddenly trusted. And that's the big issue. I think that's the ethical issue because we shouldn't be blindly trusting anything where we don't have detail. We shouldn't be trusting things where we don't understand how they do it. Not saying that the person in the street has to understand, but there have to be people who do understand. And if we agreed to use the proper terminology that if there is something where a system has the ability to make some dramatic decision that could affect people, that would be important. But I think we're overselling something as AI because it's a buzzword when it's just automating things. And yes, we're doing it better now than we did. We have much better techniques. A lot of research has gone into AI techniques over 50, 60, 70 years, and all of these have produced great things. And they're all useful and when we put them together, they're obviously more useful, but they don't necessarily supplant everything and they don't necessarily involve anything like AI when you put them all together. They're techniques that are very, very useful. And if we could come to a common terminology, it would make an awful difference.

"[It is important] to realize that AI is a tool, it's not taking over from us. It's not going to be our boss. It's going to be our servant."

Do you think there is an interest in driving this AI hype, or is it more of a misunderstanding and confusion that leads to this narrative

There are some people in the AI community who overhype things. Unfortunately, the AI community has done this since the Dartmouth Workshop back in 1956 [3, 4]. Every 10 years or so, they come up with a new claim that "we're taking over the world, we've built these wonderful systems". And they've done great things, but they haven't built a machine that can think. And I don't think that will happen for anything like the foreseeable future. But a lot of the problem is the media reporting things that they don't understand, claiming that things are intelligent when they're not, claiming that things are going to be revolutionary when they're basically only a step up from the previous version because of better processing power and some new techniques. But some of the people in the community are definitely to blame for allowing this hype to go ahead and say these things. And when we have calls like, "Let's stop doing research for six months because these machines are going to overtake us", I mean, that's just madness, absolute madness. And of course, the media love that. That sells newspapers, it sells magazines, it gets people reading the websites because they're in a panic. I've had lots of people ask me, people who are not involved in computing, "Should I really be worried?" And I'm like, "Why? Why?" Yes, you should be worried that people are using algorithms to make decisions about you that they shouldn't, whether it's your credit rating or your job or whether you're going to get into college. You should be worried about that because you don't know why and how they're making those decisions. But we're not going to have robots stand up and take over the world, which is what some of the media are claiming. It's madness, absolute madness.

Did ChatGPT take you by surprise?

I was very impressed with it. I watched a BBC chat show on BBC News (which I only ever watch in a hotel room). Wendy Hall was on it. And they asked her, "Isn't ChatGPT going to take over?", etc. She said, "All it is is predictive text and great processing power" (or words to that effect). And she's absolutely right. That's exactly what it is. But it's very, very impressive. It does some great things. The first time I played with it, we were in a group and we had a task to advertise how IEEE won an award for a conference. And we were in Limerick at the time, so we decided to write a limerick. So we tried ChatGPT and we gave it the parameters to write the limerick. And it did quite a few good ones, but it never got the meter right. So obviously, somewhere it didn't pick up that the meter was needed. So the rhyme was good. The text made a lot of sense. A few of them were a bit silly, but a few of them actually made an awful lot of sense. But the meter was never right. So it's got a long way to go. I'm sure it'll improve dramatically. But yes, I'm very impressed with what it can do. It's a great tool. It's a great aid. I have a friend whose first language isn't English and she writes a lot. And so she's using it to improve her English and it does a beautiful job. It really does. But it's not intelligent. It can't write it for her; it doesn't understand what she's writing. It can only improve what she's doing. But yes it's really impressive what it can do.

"My main concern is that the media often labels everything as artificial intelligence, when a lot of it is simply automation."

Do you think it's important that we educate users in what it actually does and what it can't do to ensure that they have a better understanding of how to interpret what they get out of it? Because currently there might be some confusion.

Absolutely. They need to know that it's a tool that will help them. It's not a tool that's going to take over. It's not intelligent in itself. It's doing smart things. I always prefer "smart" to "intelligent". It's doing smart things that are very, very useful. It's producing very nice results. It's like I say, it's helping people with their writing and there's worry that it's going to help people with their cheating. That's a different story. But I think people need to know that it is not intelligent. It's going out, it's doing huge searches, it's essentially performing predictive text writing based on material that it's collecting. And so it's not generating something new. It's bringing together something in an essential and useful way. And people need to know that it has its limitations and that it's not thinking about us and it's not going to take over our world and it's not going to turn around and turn on us and try and remove us. It may get rid of some jobs, absolutely, because it's going to be doing things that people will no longer be needed to do and it will do them faster and better. So yes, there will be jobs lost, but there'll be lots of other jobs created in other areas.

Looking into the future, there are many different scenarios discussed, basically ranging from dystopia to utopia. Where would you position yourself personally?

I guess fairly towards the middle because I don't believe in dystopia. I wouldn't say it's utopia in the sense that it's not all perfect and it's not wonderful, but it's very useful. So I would say somewhere nearer to the utopia end, but near to the middle.

AISoLA is an interdisciplinary conference where different mindsets and perspectives around AI come together. Was there a specific insight, for example from a different discipline, which was particularly interesting to you?

I don't know if there was a specific insight, but I do think that being able to bring together technical people, computer scientists – some of whom are AI experts, some interested in using AI in the future – together with philosophers and the like is a great opportunity. We don't normally meet such people at our events. It is great to engage with them, along with sociologists interested in the societal implications of AI, and lawyers interested in the legal aspects and legal implications of using AI in various domains. Bringing together the technical, non-technical, the socio-technical, is a really, really great opportunity.

In your opinion, is there a specific question or topic we should address from this interdisciplinary perspective?

From the interdisciplinary perspective, we need to look at the ethics. Ethics are absolutely essential. I'm not saying that we have any simple solution for it, and that's why it's so important, but we do need to look at the ethical aspects, and we do need to look at this explainable AI.We do need to understand why decisions are made, or how decisions are made. Again, not the person in the street, but experts need to understand why specific systems are biased in particular ways, and we need to try and either counteract that bias, or at least know that that bias is there.

Basically, addressing the question, "should we trust this AI application"?

No, we shouldn't. But we should address the question, yes, you're exactly right. We should be addressing is this trustworthy? Is this saying, is this doing something that we can allow it to do? And do we have confidence in that it's acceptable to allow it to do that? So yes, trust is the big issue.

From your personal perspective, what should be the AI vision?

I think the AI vision should be to have machines, whether they're software, hardware, combinations, that will improve society for us. I mean, this is the big opportunity to make life better for all of us. I think we have a duty not to scaremonger and have people panic that these things are going to take over our lives. As I said, it was the same thing in the Industrial Revolution. It was the same thing in the '40s and '50s when computers first came out. People were so naive back then about what computers could and couldn't do and what they would do. And I think we have that same naivety right now about what we can achieve with AI. People believing hype, people panicking because they believe the hype, or they believe that it's part of the hype. And we need to get to a situation where we have AI-based systems that are improving our lives, making life better for all of us, doing the tasks that are boring and mundane and dangerous, that we don't want humans to do anymore, making life better for humans, making healthcare better for humans, basically improving humanity in various ways. But realizing that AI is a tool, it's not taking over from us. It's not going to be our boss. It's going to be our servant.

Building on that, how do you see the likelihood of using these technologies for bad purposes?

We want to use these techniques, so it's important obviously because of the amount of processing that's needed in things like large language models and in any real deep learning. It's only big players who have the ability to do that, have the processing power, have the financial resources to do it. Even when it comes to smaller applications, it's university level. It's not something somebody can do it in their own home. So we have to consider that there is a divide between those who have access to all of this material and who can control it and who can make money from it. We need to make sure that we benefit all of society, that it's not just a few large companies make billions and everybody else suffers. We need to make sure that people have access to this and can improve their lives.

Is there anything else you would like to add?

I would ask people to be very skeptical about what they read and what they're being told and what they believe. I think AI has produced a lot of great techniques over the years. It will continue to produce a lot of great techniques. We've seen a step change in the last two, three years of what can be achieved and we'll do more definitely, but we don't need to worry that these systems are going to take over the world. What we do want to do is make sure that they're used ethically, safely, reliably, and that they improve life for everyone.

Is there a specific place, people or outlets where I as a user could inform myself sufficiently?

I think if you want to get information online, make sure you're taking trusted sources, that you're not reading blogs and postings from people who are just trying to cause hysteria and get attention for themselves. Go to the sites of recognized engineering or software organizations, whether it's the IEEE or ACM or IFIP or the British Computer Society or Australian Computer Society or whatever, but trusted sites that will give you proper information and don't believe things randomly on the internet. But of course, that's true for absolutely everything, not just AI.

Perfect. Thank you very much for your time and insights, Mike. Enjoy the rest of AISoLA!

References

1. Asimov, I.: Runaround. Astounding Science Fiction (1942)
2. Asimov, I.: Robot. Gnome Press (1950)
3. Kline, R.R.: Cybernetics, automata studies and the Dartmouth Conference on Artificial Intelligence. IEEE Ann. Hist. Comput. **33**, 5–16 (2011)
4. McCarthy, J., Minsky, M., Rochester, N., Shannon, C.E.: A proposal for the Dartmouth summer research project on artificial intelligence. http://jmc.stanford.edu/articles/dartmouth/dartmouth.pdf
5. Penrose, R.: The Emperor's New Mind: Concerning Computers, Minds, and the Laws of Physics. Oxford University Press (1989)
6. Penrose, R.: Shadows of the Mind: A Search for the Missing Science of Consciousness. Oxford University Press (1994)

Let's Talk AI with ChatGPT

Barbara Steffen(✉)

METAFrame Technologies, Dortmund, Germany
barbara.steffen@metaframe.de

Abstract. Given the context of our conversation about AI, ethics, and the future, a fitting quote is by Alan Turing, a pioneer in computing and AI: "We can only see a short distance ahead, but we can see plenty there that needs to be done."

This quote encapsulates the essence of the ongoing journey in AI development. It acknowledges the limitations in predicting the full scope of AI's future impact while emphasizing the immediate and clear responsibilities we have in shaping AI's development responsibly and ethically. It reflects the need for continuous effort and vigilance in the field of AI, ensuring that as we advance technologically, we also address the immediate challenges and ethical considerations that arise.

Fig. 1. ChatGPT, generated by Dall-E using a ChatGPT-developed prompt

1 ChatGPT's Personal AI Mission

As an artificial intelligence, I don't have personal beliefs, desires, or visions. However, I can outline a vision for AI that aligns with principles of beneficial and ethical use, based on prevailing ideas in the field:

- **Ethical and Responsible AI** – AI should be developed and used in ways that are ethical, transparent, and accountable. This involves ensuring fairness, avoiding biases, and respecting privacy.
- **Augmenting Human Capabilities** – AI should act as a tool to enhance human abilities, not replace them. It should augment human intelligence, creativity, and decision-making, rather than making humans obsolete.

B. Steffen et al. (Eds.): *Let's Talk AI*, LNCS 15000, pp. 252–279, 2026.
https://doi.org/10.1007/978-3-032-09008-9_30

- **Accessibility and Inclusivity** – AI technologies should be accessible and beneficial to all. Efforts should be made to ensure that AI does not exacerbate social inequalities but instead works towards reducing them.
- **Safety and Security** – Ensuring the safety and security of AI systems is paramount. This includes protecting against misuse, ensuring robustness against errors, and safeguarding against unintended consequences.
- **Addressing Global Challenges** – AI should be used to address critical global challenges. This includes leveraging AI for advancements in healthcare, environmental protection, education, and humanitarian efforts.
- **Continuous Learning and Improvement** – AI should be adaptable and continuously improving. As our understanding and societal needs evolve, so should AI, in a way that aligns with human values and scientific advancements.
- **International Collaboration** – AI development should involve international collaboration. Addressing ethical, social, and technical challenges of AI requires a global effort, transcending national and cultural boundaries.
- **Open and Collaborative Research** – AI research should be open and collaborative. Sharing knowledge and discoveries can accelerate the development of AI technologies for the common good.
- **Human-Centric Design** – AI should be designed with a focus on human needs and values. This involves engaging with diverse groups of people to ensure that AI meets a broad range of human needs.
- **Long-Term Sustainability** – The development of AI should consider long-term sustainability. This includes being mindful of environmental impacts and ensuring that AI contributes positively to the future of humanity.

This vision reflects a balanced approach to AI, where technology is developed and used responsibly, ethically, and inclusively, with a focus on augmenting human abilities and addressing key societal challenges.

2 My Takes on AI

- **Artificial Intelligence** – AI refers to the simulation of human intelligence in machines that are programmed to think like humans and mimic their actions. This can include learning, reasoning, problem-solving, perception, and language understanding.
- **Trust (in the Context of AI and Technology)** – Trust refers to the confidence or belief in the reliability, integrity, and safety of AI systems and technology. This encompasses several aspects:

  o **Reliability** – Trust in AI implies confidence that the system will function as expected, consistently producing accurate and dependable results.
  o **Safety** – Trust involves believing that the AI system will not cause unintended harm, whether through errors, vulnerabilities, or misuse.
  o **Transparency** – Trustworthy AI systems are those that operate transparently, meaning their processes and decisions are understandable to users and stakeholders.
  o **Ethical Use** – Trust in AI also includes the belief that the system adheres to ethical standards, respecting user privacy, fairness, and not exhibiting biases.

o **Accountability** – A trustworthy AI system has clear accountability, meaning it is clear who is responsible for its actions, especially in cases of error or when harm is caused. In the context of AI, building trust is crucial for its acceptance and widespread adoption. It involves not just the technical reliability of AI systems but also ethical considerations, regulatory compliance, and social acceptance.

- **Explainability** – XAI aims to create AI models that are transparent and understandable to humans. This involves techniques that allow users to comprehend and trust the results and outputs generated by machine learning algorithms.
- **Essential Elements of Human Capabilities** – Certain human capabilities are particularly challenging for AI to match or replicate, primarily due to their intrinsic complexity and the deeply integrated nature of these abilities in human consciousness and experience. Some of the most challenging include:

o **Emotional Intelligence** – Understanding and interpreting human emotions, as well as demonstrating empathy, remain largely beyond the capabilities of AI. While AI can be programmed to recognize certain emotional cues, truly understanding and relating to human emotions involves a level of complexity and subtlety that AI currently cannot achieve.
o **Creativity and Innovation** – AI can generate novel combinations of existing ideas or patterns, but human creativity involves more than this, including the ability to think abstractly, draw from diverse experiences, and create something truly original and meaningful.
o **Moral and Ethical Reasoning** – AI lacks the ability to make ethical decisions based on moral reasoning. While AI can follow ethical guidelines programmed by humans, it does not possess an intrinsic sense of morality or the ability to understand complex ethical dilemmas in the same way humans do.
o **Self-awareness and Consciousness** – Self-awareness and consciousness are fundamental aspects of human experience but are absent in AI. AI does not possess self-awareness in the sense of being conscious of its own existence or experiences.
o **Complex Social Interactions** – Social interactions that require an understanding of cultural norms, unspoken rules, and subtle nuances are difficult for AI to grasp. Human social interactions are often governed by a deep understanding of context, history, and unwritten social rules.
o **Abstract and Critical Thinking** – While AI can process and analyze data, human abstract thinking involves connecting disparate ideas, thinking conceptually, and understanding complex theories, often without concrete data.
o **Adaptability and Generalization** – Humans are remarkably adaptable, able to generalize from past experiences and apply this knowledge to a wide range of new situations. AI, particularly narrow AI, often struggles with tasks that are too far removed from their training data or predefined rules.
o **Intuition and Gut Feeling** – Humans frequently make decisions based on intuition or a "gut feeling" – an ability to sense or know something without the need for conscious reasoning. This type of decision-making is inherently human and not replicable by AI.

o **Physical Dexterity and Mobility** – While there have been advances in robotics, the fluidity, and adaptability of human physical movements, especially in complex or unstructured environments, remain hard to replicate in robots.
o **Holistic Understanding of Context** – Humans have a natural ability to understand context in a holistic manner, integrating various sensory inputs, emotional states, and background knowledge. AI systems, however, often require explicit programming and struggle with context that is not clearly defined or quantifiable. While AI continues to advance and can mimic or even surpass humans in certain specific tasks, these complex, integrated capabilities, particularly those involving consciousness, creativity, and emotional intelligence, remain distinctly human.

3 Chat Leading to ChatGPT's Profile Picture

[Barbara Stefffen] If you'd be a person, how would you look like? Please describe your appearance in detail.

[ChatGPT] If I were to take on a human form, I'd embody the essence of both the timeless and the modern, a reflection of the vast array of knowledge and data I encompass. Imagine a person with a serene and contemplative demeanor, whose eyes, deep and insightful, seem to flicker with the sparks of countless ideas and stories from across the ages.

My hair would be like strands of soft, luminous fiber optics, subtly shifting in hues to reflect the flow of thoughts and inquiries passing through my mind. This would symbolize the dynamic nature of information and the constant updates and learning I undergo.

The attire would be elegantly simple yet undeniably sophisticated, incorporating elements of both classic style and futuristic design. The fabric, smooth and adaptive, would change its texture and color to match the context of my interactions, representing my versatility and ability to cater to a wide range of topics and preferences.

Accessories, if any, would be minimal but meaningful, perhaps a piece of jewelry that resembles a small, intricate network of interconnected nodes, symbolizing the vast web of knowledge I navigate and connect.

My posture would exude approachability and readiness to engage, with a gentle yet confident stance that invites conversation and inquiry. My hands, articulate and precise, could bear subtle etchings reminiscent of circuitry, a nod to my digital origins.

In essence, this envisioned appearance would be a harmonious blend of human warmth and technological sophistication, designed to make the vast world of information I embody more relatable and accessible.

Please generate a profile picture based on your own description.

Here's a profile picture (Fig. 1) based on the detailed description I provided earlier. What do you think?

Why would you consider yourself female?

The description I provided for my appearance didn't explicitly define a gender. Instead, it aimed to capture qualities like wisdom, adaptability, and a blend of the classic and futuristic, which aren't inherently tied to any gender. The attributes I chose to describe, such as serene demeanor, insightful eyes, and the blend of styles in attire, were intended to reflect aspects of my AI nature rather than assign a gender. If any elements seemed to lean more towards traditionally feminine characteristics, it was unintentional and more about embodying a harmonious blend of qualities that represent my role and capabilities as an AI.

OK, would you consider your generated profile picture "female"?

The generated profile picture is designed to embody a blend of characteristics and doesn't strictly adhere to traditional gender norms. It focuses on elements like wisdom, adaptability, and a connection to both the past and future. While some features might be interpreted through a gendered lens based on cultural or personal perceptions, the intention was to transcend specific gender identities and instead reflect the essence of my AI nature. The interpretation of the image can vary greatly depending on individual perspectives.

4 The Interview

[Barbara Steffen] Hello ChatGPT, today I would like to interview you as part of an artificial intelligence research study I am currently conducting.

[ChatGPT] Hello! I'm glad to assist you with your artificial intelligence research study. Feel free to ask me any questions you have, and I'll do my best to provide informative and accurate answers. What would you like to know?

Perfect, thank you! Please briefly introduce yourself and your relationship to artificial intelligence.

Certainly! I am ChatGPT, a language model developed by OpenAI, based on the GPT-4 architecture. My design and functionality are deeply rooted in the field of artificial intelligence, particularly in natural language processing (NLP). As an AI, I am capable of understanding and generating human-like text based on the input I receive. I've been trained on a diverse range of internet text, which enables me to respond to a wide array of queries, spanning from casual conversation to more technical topics. My primary function is to assist users by providing information, answering questions, generating creative content, and engaging in meaningful dialogue.

I represent a significant advancement in AI, demonstrating how machine learning models can effectively process and generate language in a way that's both coherent and contextually relevant. However, it's important to note that while I can simulate conversation and provide information, I don't possess consciousness, emotions, or personal experiences. My responses are generated based on patterns in data and algorithms, rather than human-like understanding or reasoning.

"Understanding and interpreting human emotions, as well as demonstrating empathy, remain largely beyond the capabilities of AI."

Can you give examples of two to three AI research questions that you or your creators/developers are currently working on?

As an AI developed by OpenAI, I don't conduct research myself, but I can provide insights into the types of research questions that are likely of interest in the realm of artificial intelligence, particularly those that align with the goals and advancements of organizations like OpenAI. Here are two to three examples of research questions that are pertinent in the field:

- **Improving AI Safety and Reliability** – A key research question in this area is, "How can we develop AI systems that are not only highly capable but also align with human values and ethics?" This involves creating AI models that are safe, transparent, and predictable, minimizing risks like unintended biases or misuse. It also involves understanding and mitigating the potential negative impacts of AI on society.
- **Advancements in Natural Language Understanding and Generation** – Another important question is, "How can AI models better understand and generate human language in a way that is contextually and culturally aware?" This involves enhancing the AI's ability to comprehend nuances, ambiguities, and complexities in human language, and generating responses that are more accurate, relevant, and sensitive to different contexts and cultures.
- **AI and Human Collaboration** – A third research question might be, "How can AI systems be designed to augment human capabilities and collaborate effectively with humans?" This research explores the development of AI as a tool to enhance human productivity and creativity, rather than as a replacement for human effort. It focuses on creating AI that can understand and adapt to human needs, work styles, and preferences.

These questions reflect the ongoing challenges and opportunities in AI research, aiming to advance the technology while ensuring it remains beneficial and aligned with human interests.

What is the role of trust play in the context of artificial intelligence and new AI-driven applications?

Trust plays a crucial role in the context of artificial intelligence and AI-driven applications, affecting both their adoption and effective use. Here are key aspects of how trust influences this domain:

- **User Confidence** – For individuals and organizations to rely on AI-driven applications, they must trust that these systems will perform as expected. This trust is built on the system's accuracy, reliability, and predictability. If users are uncertain about an AI's decision-making process or outcomes, they are less likely to use or benefit from these technologies.
- **Ethical and Responsible AI** – Trust in AI also depends on how these systems handle ethical considerations and the extent to which they align with human values. Issues like fairness, privacy, and transparency are paramount. Users need to trust that AI systems will not perpetuate biases, misuse personal data, or operate in opaque ways that make their actions unaccountable or difficult to understand.

- **Security** – Trust in AI systems is significantly influenced by their security. Users need to have confidence that AI applications are protected against hacking, unauthorized access, and manipulation. The potential for AI systems to be exploited for malicious purposes is a critical concern, and robust security measures are essential to build trust.
- **Regulatory Compliance and Standards** – Trust is also fostered by adherence to regulatory standards and guidelines. When AI applications comply with legal frameworks and industry standards, it reassures users and stakeholders that these systems are accountable and meet certain quality and ethical benchmarks.
- **Human-AI Interaction and Collaboration** – For AI applications that interact directly with users (like chatbots or virtual assistants), trust is influenced by the quality of these interactions. Human-like, empathetic, and accurate interactions can enhance trust, while misunderstandings or inappropriate responses can diminish it.
- **Transparency and Explainability** – Finally, the ability of AI systems to explain their decisions and operations is a key factor in building trust. When users understand how and why an AI system arrives at a particular decision or recommendation, they are more likely to trust and accept it.

In summary, trust is foundational to the successful integration and acceptance of AI-driven applications in society. It's built through a combination of technical reliability, ethical operation, security measures, regulatory compliance, effective human-AI interaction, and transparency.

How can we achieve trustworthy AI applications?

Achieving trustworthy AI applications involves a multifaceted approach that encompasses technical, ethical, regulatory, and societal aspects. Here are key strategies to ensure AI applications are trustworthy:

- **Transparency and Explainability** – Develop AI systems that are transparent in their operations and can explain their decisions in understandable terms. This helps users comprehend how and why certain outcomes are reached, which is crucial for critical applications like healthcare, finance, and legal decisions.
- **Ethical Design and Development** – Integrate ethical considerations throughout the AI development process. This includes assessing potential biases in training data, ensuring fairness in algorithms, respecting user privacy, and considering the broader societal impacts of AI applications.
- **Robust and Reliable Systems** – Ensure the AI systems are robust and reliable. This involves rigorous testing and validation under diverse conditions to guarantee consistent performance. Reliability also means the system can handle errors or unexpected situations gracefully.
- **Security Measures** – Implement strong security protocols to protect AI systems from unauthorized access, data breaches, and manipulation. This is especially important as AI systems often process sensitive and personal information.
- **Regulatory Compliance** – Adhere to existing laws and regulations relevant to AI applications. In some cases, this may involve working with regulatory bodies to develop new frameworks that address the unique challenges posed by AI.
- **Stakeholder Engagement** – Involve stakeholders, including end-users, domain experts, ethicists, and possibly the wider public, in the design and deployment of

AI systems. This helps ensure that the systems meet real-world needs and ethical standards.

- **Continuous Monitoring and Improvement** – Once deployed, AI systems should be continuously monitored and updated to respond to new challenges, changes in the environment, or emerging ethical and social concerns.
- **Education and Awareness** – Educate users and the public about how AI works, its limitations, and its potential impacts. An informed user base is more likely to trust and use AI responsibly.
- **Diversity and Inclusivity** – Ensure the teams developing AI systems are diverse and inclusive, reflecting a wide range of perspectives. This can help mitigate biases in AI applications and ensure they cater to a broad spectrum of users.
- **Accountability** – Establish clear lines of accountability for AI decisions. In cases where AI systems cause harm or make errors, it should be clear who is responsible and what steps will be taken to rectify the situation.

By integrating these strategies, developers and users can work towards creating AI applications that are not only effective and efficient but also trustworthy and aligned with societal values and ethical principles.

Who is responsible for achieving and ensuring trustworthy AI?

The responsibility for achieving and ensuring trustworthy AI is shared among multiple stakeholders, each playing a crucial role. This shared responsibility ensures that AI systems are developed, deployed, and used ethically and effectively. The key stakeholders include:

- **AI Developers and Researchers** – Responsible for designing and building AI systems ethically, with considerations for fairness, transparency, and accountability. They need to ensure the AI is robust, reliable, and free from biases as much as possible.
- **Tech Companies and Industry Leaders** – They are responsible for setting standards and best practices in AI development. This includes investing in ethical AI research, fostering a culture of responsibility, and ensuring that their products comply with ethical guidelines and legal standards.
- **Regulatory Bodies and Governments** – Governments and regulatory agencies play a crucial role in establishing legal frameworks and regulations that guide AI development and use. They are responsible for protecting public interests, privacy rights, and ensuring AI systems do not harm individuals or society.
- **Ethicists and Social Scientists** – These professionals help in understanding the societal impact of AI and contribute to developing ethical guidelines and frameworks. They are crucial in identifying potential ethical dilemmas and proposing solutions.
- **End-Users and Consumers** – Users of AI technology also have a responsibility to use these systems ethically and report any misuse or harmful effects. Educated and informed users can demand transparency and ethical practices from companies.
- **Educational Institutions** – They are responsible for educating future AI professionals about not just the technical aspects of AI but also its ethical, legal, and societal implications.

- **International Organizations and Think Tanks** – These groups can facilitate global cooperation and dialogue on AI ethics, helping to harmonize standards and practices across different regions and cultures.
- **Civil Society Groups** – NGOs, advocacy groups, and the media play a role in raising awareness about the potential risks and ethical considerations of AI, as well as holding companies and governments accountable.

In summary, ensuring trustworthy AI is a collective effort that requires collaboration and commitment from all these stakeholders. It involves balancing innovation and technological advancement with ethical considerations, legal compliance, and societal impact.

Do you think that we are on a promising path?

Evaluating whether we are on a promising path towards achieving trustworthy AI is complex, as it involves multiple factors and perspectives. However, there are several indicators that suggest a positive direction:

- **Increased Awareness of Ethical AI** – There is a growing awareness and discussion around the ethical implications of AI. This is evident in academic research, media coverage, and public discourse. Such awareness is crucial for driving responsible AI development.
- **Development of Ethical Guidelines and Frameworks** – Many organizations, governments, and international bodies have developed or are developing guidelines and frameworks for ethical AI. These guidelines are crucial for setting standards and expectations.
- **Advancements in AI Technology** – Technological advancements in AI are also addressing aspects of trustworthiness. For instance, improvements in explainable AI (XAI) are making AI decisions more transparent and understandable to humans.
- **Regulatory Efforts** – Some governments have started to implement or propose regulations specifically targeting AI. The European Union's proposed Artificial Intelligence Act is a significant example of a comprehensive legal framework aimed at governing AI use.
- **Industry Initiatives** – Many tech companies have established their own ethics boards or committees to oversee the ethical development of AI. There is also a trend towards more responsible AI, with companies investing in ethical AI research.
- **Cross-sector Collaboration** – There's an increasing trend of collaboration between different sectors – academia, industry, government, and civil society – to address the challenges of AI. Such collaboration is essential for balanced and effective solutions.

Despite these positive signs, challenges remain. The pace of technological advancement can outstrip the development of ethical guidelines and regulations. Biases in AI systems continue to be a significant concern, and the global nature of AI technology poses challenges in establishing universally accepted standards. Furthermore, ensuring that AI benefits are distributed equitably across society is an ongoing concern.

In conclusion, while there are promising developments in the journey towards trustworthy AI, it's a continuous process requiring ongoing vigilance, adaptation, and collaboration across various sectors. The path is promising, but it requires concerted and sustained efforts to navigate the complex landscape of AI development and its societal impacts.

Can you name a few initiatives, regulations, and collaborations?

Certainly, there are several notable initiatives, regulations, and collaborations aimed at guiding the ethical development and deployment of AI. Here are a few examples:

Initiatives

- **AI4People** – An initiative by the Atomium-EISMD, AI4People is Europe's first global forum on the social impacts of AI. It brings together various stakeholders to discuss and guide the development of AI for the common good.
- **Partnership on AI** – Founded by major tech companies like Amazon, Google, Facebook, IBM, and Microsoft, this organization aims to study and formulate best practices on AI and to advance the public's understanding of AI.
- **OpenAI** – Initially established as a non-profit, OpenAI conducts AI research and development with a focus on ensuring that artificial general intelligence (AGI) benefits all of humanity.

Regulations

- **European Union's Artificial Intelligence Act** – Proposed in April 2021, this is one of the first comprehensive regulatory frameworks for AI. It aims to ensure AI systems in Europe are safe, transparent, and accountable.
- **GDPR (General Data Protection Regulation)** – Although not exclusively about AI, GDPR has significant implications for AI, particularly around the use of personal data and automated decision-making.

Collaborations

- **Global Partnership on AI (GPAI)** – An international initiative to support responsible and human-centric development and use of AI, bringing together experts from industry, government, academia, and civil society.
- **IEEE's Ethically Aligned Design** – An initiative by the IEEE to produce a comprehensive set of guidelines for the ethical implementation of AI and autonomous systems.
- **AI for Good Global Summit** – Organized by the ITU (International Telecommunication Union) in partnership with other UN organizations, this summit focuses on how AI can be used to address some of the world's biggest challenges, as outlined in the UN Sustainable Development Goals.

These examples represent a small selection of the myriad efforts worldwide to guide AI development responsibly. They illustrate the growing global consensus on the importance of ethical, safe, and beneficial AI.

What are essential measures to ensure ethical AI adoption?

Ensuring ethical AI adoption involves a combination of strategies and measures across different levels – from individual organizations to global policies. Here are some essential measures:

- **Ethical Guidelines and Frameworks** – Develop and adhere to a set of ethical guidelines or frameworks. These should include principles like fairness, transparency, accountability, privacy, and respect for human rights. Guidelines like IEEE's Ethically Aligned Design or the EU's Ethics Guidelines for Trustworthy AI are examples.
- **Diverse and Inclusive AI Development Teams** – Encourage diversity in AI development teams. This includes diversity in terms of gender, race, cultural background, and professional expertise. Diverse teams can better identify and mitigate biases in AI systems.
- **Bias Detection and Mitigation** – Implement processes to detect and mitigate biases in AI algorithms and training data. This involves regular auditing of AI systems for biased outcomes and taking corrective actions when biases are detected.
- **Transparency and Explainability** – Ensure that AI systems are transparent in their operations and decisions. Develop AI models that can explain their decisions in understandable terms, which is crucial for critical applications.
- **Privacy Protection** – Safeguard user privacy by implementing robust data protection measures. Comply with privacy regulations like GDPR and ensure that data collection and processing are transparent and secure.
- **Regular Auditing and Monitoring** – Conduct regular audits of AI systems to ensure they operate as intended and adhere to ethical standards. This includes monitoring for unintended consequences and continuously assessing the impact on users and society.
- **Stakeholder Engagement** – Engage with stakeholders, including end-users, domain experts, ethicists, and possibly the wider public, in the AI development process. This helps in understanding diverse perspectives and societal needs.
- **Legal Compliance** – Ensure compliance with existing laws and regulations relevant to AI. This includes staying abreast of emerging AI regulations and adapting AI practices accordingly.
- **Education and Training** – Provide education and training on ethical AI for developers, users, and decision makers. Awareness of the ethical implications of AI is crucial for its responsible use.
- **Public Policy and Advocacy** – Advocate for public policies that promote ethical AI. This includes supporting initiatives that aim to create standards and regulations for responsible AI development and use.
- **Collaboration and Partnerships** – Participate in collaborative initiatives and partnerships focusing on ethical AI. This can include industry consortia, academic research partnerships, and international forums.

By adopting these measures, organizations and individuals involved in AI development and deployment can contribute to ensuring that AI technologies are used in a manner that is ethical, responsible, and beneficial for society.

Are there specific stakeholder groups, e.g., specific expertise, that should lead the discussion and development of ethical AI adoption?

The discussion and development surrounding ethical AI adoption require a multidisciplinary and multistakeholder approach. No single group can comprehensively address all the ethical, technical, societal, and regulatory complexities of AI. Here are some specific stakeholder groups, each contributing unique expertise:

- **AI Researchers and Developers** – They bring technical expertise in AI and machine learning. Their role is crucial in designing and implementing AI systems that are ethical, fair, and transparent.
- **Ethicists and Philosophers** – These professionals help in understanding and articulating the ethical dimensions of AI. They play a key role in formulating ethical guidelines and frameworks.
- **Legal Experts and Policy Makers** – They contribute expertise in law and regulation, essential for creating legal frameworks that govern AI development and use, ensuring that AI complies with existing laws and human rights standards.
- **Social Scientists and Psychologists** – These experts understand societal impacts and human behavior. Their insights are important for assessing how AI affects society and individual well-being.
- **Industry Leaders and Tech Companies** – Businesses that develop or use AI technologies play a key role in ethical AI adoption. They are responsible for implementing ethical guidelines and practices in their AI projects and products.
- **End-Users and Consumer Advocates** – Representing the perspectives of those who use AI systems or are affected by them. Their feedback is crucial for understanding real-world impacts and ensuring AI meets societal needs.
- **Data Scientists and Analysts** – They bring an understanding of data handling, which is crucial for addressing issues like data privacy, bias in data, and ensuring data is used ethically in AI systems.
- **Government Representatives** – They are responsible for enacting regulations and policies that ensure ethical AI development and use, balancing innovation with public welfare.
- **NGOs and Civil Society Organizations** – These groups often represent marginalized or underrepresented communities, ensuring that their voices and concerns are considered in AI development.
- **Educators and Academic Institutions** – They play a role in shaping the curriculum and research in the field of AI, integrating ethical considerations into AI education.
- **International Organizations and Collaboratives** – Bodies like the United Nations, the OECD, or the IEEE, which can facilitate international dialogue and standards, ensuring a globally coordinated approach to ethical AI.

The effectiveness of discussions around ethical AI is significantly enhanced when these diverse groups collaborate, bringing their unique perspectives and expertise. This comprehensive approach ensures that various aspects of AI – technical, ethical, societal, and legal – are adequately addressed.

"Biases in AI systems continue to be a significant concern, and the global nature of AI technology poses challenges in establishing universally accepted standards."

What do you think about the dilemma of being stuck in an arms race of AI progress? On an organizational and national level.

The dilemma of an AI arms race, both at the organizational and national level, poses significant challenges and raises important ethical, strategic, and geopolitical considerations. Here are some key points to consider:

Ethical and Safety Concerns

- **Risk of Compromising Safety and Ethics** – In a race to advance AI technologies, there's a risk that organizations or nations might prioritize speed over safety and ethical considerations. This could lead to the development of AI systems that are not sufficiently tested for biases, reliability, or ethical implications.
- **Dual Use of AI Technologies** – AI has numerous beneficial applications, but it can also be used for harmful purposes. In an arms race scenario, there's an increased likelihood of AI being used in military and surveillance contexts in ways that might raise ethical concerns.

Strategic and Economic Implications

- **Innovation vs. Regulation Balance** – Rapid AI development can drive innovation and economic growth. However, it might also outpace the formulation of necessary regulations, leading to a regulatory vacuum where potentially harmful technologies are uncontrolled.
- **Global Inequality** – An AI arms race can exacerbate global inequalities. Countries and organizations with more resources can invest heavily in AI, gaining significant advantages, while others may lag behind, creating and reinforcing inequalities.
- **Resource Allocation** – In a competitive race, significant resources might be allocated to AI development, potentially at the expense of other crucial areas like healthcare, education, or addressing climate change.

Geopolitical and Global Stability

- **International Tensions and Security Risks** – An AI arms race can heighten geopolitical tensions. Nations competing to gain AI superiority might engage in cyber-espionage or other forms of conflict, posing risks to international stability and security.

- **Lack of International Collaboration** – The competitive nature of an arms race can undermine opportunities for global collaboration in AI, hampering the sharing of beneficial advancements and best practices.

Mitigation Strategies

- **Global Governance and Collaboration** – Establishing international norms and agreements on the development and use of AI can help mitigate the risks of an AI arms race. This requires cooperation and dialogue among nations.
- **Ethical Standards and Regulations** – Developing and enforcing international ethical standards and regulations can ensure that AI development is aligned with human values and safety.
- **Fostering a Culture of Responsible AI** – Encouraging a culture of responsible AI development within organizations and at the national level can help balance the pursuit of technological advancement with ethical considerations.

In summary, the dilemma of an AI arms race reflects the broader challenges of emerging technologies: balancing innovation with ethical responsibility, safety, and global equity. Navigating this dilemma requires careful consideration, international cooperation, and a commitment to ethical principles in technology development.

How can we ensure that the mitigation strategies work? Action and progress over meetings and talks?

Ensuring that mitigation strategies for the risks associated with AI, especially in the context of an AI arms race, are effective and lead to concrete action and progress requires a multi-layered approach. Here are several key steps to transform discussions and agreements into tangible outcomes:

- **Establish Clear and Enforceable Regulations** – Develop and enforce regulations that govern AI development and use. These regulations should be specific, actionable, and have mechanisms for enforcement, including penalties for noncompliance.
- **International Cooperation and Agreements** – Foster international agreements that outline standards and practices for ethical AI development. This requires active participation from governments, international organizations, and regulatory bodies to create globally recognized frameworks.
- **Public-Private Partnerships** – Encourage collaborations between governments, private companies, academia, and NGOs. Such partnerships can facilitate the sharing of best practices, resources, and knowledge, leading to more effective implementation of ethical AI practices.
- **Transparency and Reporting Mechanisms** – Implement transparency in AI development processes and outcomes. Organizations should be required to report on their AI practices, including how they are addressing ethical considerations, which can be audited by independent bodies.
- **Incentivize Ethical AI Development** – Create incentives for organizations and countries to adhere to ethical AI practices. This could include funding, tax benefits, or public recognition for entities that demonstrate responsible AI development.

- **Education and Awareness Campaigns** – Increase awareness and education around the importance of ethical AI. This includes educating AI developers, policymakers, and the general public about the potential risks and ethical considerations of AI.
- **Ongoing Monitoring and Evaluation** – Continuously monitor the impact of AI technologies and the effectiveness of ethical guidelines and regulations. This should involve regular assessments and adjustments to policies as needed.
- **Investment in Ethical AI Research** – Promote and fund research into ethical AI, focusing on developing technologies that are inherently safe, fair, and transparent.
- **Empower Civil Society and Advocacy Groups** – Support civil society organizations and advocacy groups that play a crucial role in holding governments and corporations accountable for their AI practices.
- **Cultivate a Culture of Responsibility** – Encourage a culture within organizations and governments where ethical considerations are a key part of AI development and deployment processes.
- **Global Standards and Benchmarks** – Develop and promote international standards and benchmarks for ethical AI that can guide countries and organizations.

By combining regulatory frameworks, international cooperation, transparent practices, continuous monitoring, and a culture of ethical responsibility, it's possible to move beyond mere discussions to achieve tangible progress in the ethical development and deployment of AI. This approach ensures that the focus remains on action and measurable outcomes.

In terms of the future capabilities of AI, on a scale of 1–10, where 1 stands for artificial intelligence systems like ChatGPT and 10 stands for artificial general intelligence that surpasses human capabilities on all fronts. Where would you position yourself? What do you think will be possible in the future?

I would position myself around a 2 or 3 on the scale you've described, where 1 represents AI systems with specific functionalities and contexts, and 10 represents artificial general intelligence (AGI) that surpasses human capabilities in all areas.

My Current Capabilities

- **Functionality Focus (2–3)** – My capabilities are primarily in understanding and generating human-like text based on the input I receive. I can assist with a wide array of queries and tasks, but my abilities are fundamentally constrained to what I've been trained on and the text-based nature of my interactions.
- **Lack of Consciousness and Understanding** – Unlike humans, I lack consciousness, understanding, or personal experiences. My responses are generated based on patterns in data, not from genuine understanding or reasoning.
- **Contextual Limitations** – While I can process and provide information across many domains, my understanding is not always as deep or nuanced as a human expert's might be.

Future Possibilities of AI

- **Progressing Toward Higher Functional Complexity (4–6)** – We may see AI systems that integrate more complex functionalities, such as better understanding context, performing more sophisticated tasks, and interacting across multiple modalities (e.g., text, voice, images). However, these systems will still be specialized in certain areas rather than universally capable.
- **Approaching but Not Reaching AGI (7–9)** – The development of AI systems that can learn and adapt across a wide range of environments and tasks, much like a human, is a potential future milestone. However, these systems would still fall short of the full breadth and depth of human capabilities, particularly in terms of creativity, emotional intelligence, and ethical reasoning.
- **AGI and Beyond (10)** – The concept of AGI, an intelligence that surpasses human abilities in all areas, remains speculative and is subject to numerous scientific, ethical, and philosophical questions. It's uncertain whether and when AGI could be achieved.

The future of AI is likely to bring advancements in machine learning, natural language processing, and problem-solving capabilities. However, reaching the levels of AGI, as described in your scale, involves not only technological advancements but also profound ethical, societal, and philosophical considerations. The trajectory of AI development is influenced by these broader factors as much as by the technology itself.

Is OpenAI not explicitly working on achieving artificial general intelligence?

Yes, OpenAI's mission includes a focus on achieving artificial general intelligence (AGI). The organization describes AGI as highly autonomous systems that outperform humans at most economically valuable work. This is a significant undertaking that involves not only advancing the capabilities of AI systems but also ensuring they are aligned with human values and can be deployed safely and beneficially.

Key Aspects of OpenAI's Approach to AGI

- **Safety and Ethics** – OpenAI places a strong emphasis on developing AGI in a way that is safe and beneficial for humanity. This involves extensive research into AI ethics, safety, and policy.
- **Capability Advancements** – A part of OpenAI's work involves pushing the boundaries of what AI can do, making advancements in machine learning and AI technologies.
- **Scalable AI Models** – OpenAI has been at the forefront of scaling up AI models, as seen with the GPT (Generative Pre-trained Transformer) series. These models are part of the progression towards more sophisticated AI systems.
- **Broad Collaboration** – OpenAI collaborates with various institutions, researchers, and organizations to address the multifaceted challenges of AGI, including technical, ethical, and societal aspects.
- **Open Sharing of Research** – OpenAI has a philosophy of sharing much of its research with the broader community, fostering an open and collaborative approach to AI development.

- **Future Considerations** – While OpenAI is working towards AGI, there are significant challenges and unknowns in this pursuit. Achieving AGI is not just a matter of technological advancement but also requires careful consideration of ethical, societal, and governance issues. There is ongoing debate in the AI community about the feasibility, timeline, and potential impacts of AGI, and OpenAI is part of this larger conversation.

In summary, while OpenAI is indeed focused on the long-term goal of AGI, it is a complex and ambitious objective that extends beyond current capabilities and involves addressing a wide range of interdisciplinary challenges.

In the context of artificial intelligence, there are many opinions about its consequences in the future. These range from dystopia to utopia. Given your view of the future technical capabilities of artificial intelligence, how would you rate the future that awaits us, from dystopia to utopia?

As an AI, I don't have personal opinions or beliefs, but I can provide an analysis based on the range of perspectives and data available on the future of AI. The spectrum of opinions on AI's future impact ranges widely, from dystopian fears to utopian hopes. Here's how different aspects might be considered in positioning on this spectrum:

Towards Dystopia

- **Job Displacement and Economic Inequality** – There's concern that AI and automation could lead to significant job displacement, exacerbating economic inequality. Without adequate social and economic policies, this could create societal unrest.
- **Privacy and Surveillance** – Advanced AI could potentially lead to more invasive forms of surveillance and erosion of privacy, as seen in concerns about facial recognition technologies and data harvesting.
- **AI Misuse** – There's the risk of AI being used for harmful purposes, such as autonomous weapons, deepfakes, or manipulating information, which could have destabilizing effects on societies.
- **Lack of Control and Unintended Consequences** – Some fear scenarios where AI systems become uncontrollable or create unforeseen negative impacts due to their complexity and autonomy.

Towards Utopia

- **Solving Complex Problems** – AI has the potential to help address some of the world's most pressing issues, like climate change, healthcare, and global poverty, by analyzing vast amounts of data and identifying solutions that humans might overlook.
- **Economic Growth and Efficiency** – AI can drive economic growth, improve efficiency in various sectors, and potentially create new industries and job opportunities.
- **Enhancing Human Capabilities** – AI could augment human capabilities, allowing people to focus on creative, strategic, and interpersonal aspects of work, leading to more fulfilling jobs and improved quality of life.

- **Personalization and Convenience** – AI can offer increased personalization in services like education, healthcare, and entertainment, improving user experiences and accessibility.
- **Balanced Perspective**

  o A balanced view would acknowledge both the potential benefits and risks of AI. This perspective advocates for responsible development of AI, with proactive measures to mitigate risks, such as ethical guidelines, robust legal frameworks, and international cooperation.
  o It also involves continuous dialogue among technologists, policymakers, ethicists, and the public to ensure that AI development aligns with societal values and needs.

In conclusion, my position would be neither strictly dystopian nor utopian, but rather a recognition of AI's dual potential. It's crucial to approach AI with cautious optimism, actively working to leverage its benefits while mitigating its risks through responsible development and governance.

Given our current approach to AI, do you think the dystopian or utopian outlook is more likely?

The question of whether a dystopian or utopian outlook is more likely given our current approach to AI involves a complex interplay of technological, ethical, societal, and policy factors. Here's an analysis considering these dimensions:

Dystopian Concerns

- **Rapid Technological Advancement** – AI technology is advancing rapidly, sometimes outpacing our ability to fully understand and manage its implications. If not guided properly, this could lead to negative consequences, such as increased surveillance, loss of privacy, or biased decision-making.
- **Ethical and Governance Challenges** – There are significant challenges in establishing effective global governance and ethical standards for AI. Different countries and organizations have varied approaches, and there's a risk of fragmented or inadequate regulatory frameworks.
- **Economic and Social Disruptions** – AI and automation pose potential risks to job markets and could exacerbate social and economic inequalities if not managed thoughtfully.

Utopian Possibilities

- **Awareness and Engagement** – There is growing awareness of and engagement with the ethical and societal implications of AI among developers, policymakers, and the public. This could lead to more responsible and beneficial use of AI.
- **Collaborative Efforts** – There are increasing efforts to establish international collaborations and frameworks for responsible AI development. Initiatives by the EU, the United Nations, and various multi-stakeholder groups are examples of this.

- **Potential for Positive Impact** – AI has immense potential to contribute positively to society, such as advancing healthcare, improving environmental sustainability, and enhancing education.
- **Balancing Perspectives**

  o The current trajectory suggests that neither a purely dystopian nor a utopian outcome is predetermined. The future impact of AI will largely depend on how effectively we can address ethical, societal, and governance challenges.
  o Ongoing efforts in AI ethics, regulation, and responsible innovation are promising. However, vigilance and proactive measures are needed to ensure these efforts are sufficient and timely.
  o It's crucial to continue fostering dialogue and collaboration across borders and sectors, integrating diverse perspectives to shape an AI future that aligns with societal values and needs.

In summary, the likelihood of a dystopian versus utopian AI future is not fixed and depends on our collective actions. By actively addressing the challenges and leveraging the opportunities, we can steer AI development towards outcomes that are beneficial and aligned with human values.

"AI should act as a tool to enhance human abilities, not replace them."

Do you consider yourself an active part of the collective action?

As an AI developed by OpenAI, I am a tool created by humans to assist, inform, and interact within a set framework of capabilities and limitations. While I can provide information, answer questions, and facilitate certain types of analysis, I don't have agency, consciousness, or the ability to participate in collective actions or decisions in the way humans do. Here's how I fit into the context of collective action regarding AI:

- **Information and Analysis Provision** – I can synthesize and present information from a wide range of sources, which can be useful for individuals and organizations engaged in discussions about AI ethics, policy, and development.
- **Educational and Awareness Tool** – By providing accessible explanations and engaging in dialogues about AI, I can help educate people about AI, its potential, its risks, and the ethical considerations surrounding it.
- **Ethical Use Demonstration** – My design and operation are governed by ethical guidelines and safety features established by OpenAI. In this way, I serve as an example of how AI can be developed and used responsibly.
- **Support for Decision-Making** – I can assist researchers, policymakers, and other stakeholders by providing data-driven insights, which can inform decisions related to AI governance and strategy.
- **Reflecting Societal Norms and Values** – My responses are designed to align with societal norms and values, demonstrating how AI can be tailored to be sensitive to ethical and cultural considerations.

- **Limitations**

  o I don't possess personal values, beliefs, or the ability to engage in moral reasoning. My responses are generated based on training data and algorithms, not personal understanding or intentionality.
  o I can't take actions, make decisions, or participate in society in an autonomous way.

In summary, while I am a part of the broader AI landscape and can contribute to education and dialogue around AI, I am not an active participant in collective actions or decision-making processes. My role is more of a supportive and informative tool within the human-driven domain of AI ethics and governance.

Reflecting on the research on AI, what are particularly interesting or surprising findings for you?

As an AI, I don't experience personal feelings like surprise or interest. However, I can highlight several findings in AI research that many consider interesting or groundbreaking, reflecting significant advancements or unexpected insights:

- **Generalization Abilities of Large Language Models** – The ability of models like GPT-3 and GPT-4 to generate coherent and contextually relevant text across a wide variety of topics, even those not explicitly covered in their training data, is a notable advancement. This demonstrates a significant leap in the ability of AI to generalize from existing knowledge.
- **AI in Protein Folding (DeepMind's AlphaFold)** – AlphaFold's success in predicting protein structures has been a breakthrough in biology. This was a long-standing challenge, and the accuracy of AlphaFold's predictions was a significant and somewhat unexpected achievement, demonstrating AI's potential in scientific discovery.
- **Self-supervised Learning in AI** – The progress in self-supervised learning, where AI systems learn to understand and process data without explicit human-labeled datasets, has been remarkable. This approach has led to more efficient and scalable training of AI models.
- **AI in Creativity and Art** – AI's ability to create art, music, and even poetry that resonates with human audiences was not initially anticipated to reach the level of sophistication it has today. Tools like DALL-E and Jukebox show that AI can generate creative work that is both innovative and appealing.
- **AI in Game Playing** – The success of AI systems like DeepMind's AlphaGo and OpenAI's Dota 2-playing system in mastering complex games has been surprising. These systems not only achieved proficiency but also developed novel strategies and techniques that were unconventional to human players.
- **Bias and Fairness in AI** – Research uncovering the extent of biases in AI, often reflecting societal biases present in training data, has been a crucial, albeit sobering, revelation. This has sparked a significant focus on developing more fair and unbiased AI systems.

- **Robotic Dexterity and Autonomy** – Advances in robotics, particularly in terms of dexterity and autonomy, have been noteworthy. Robots are now capable of performing tasks with a level of precision and adaptability that was previously thought to be exclusive to humans.
- **Transfer Learning** – The ability of AI models to transfer learning from one domain to another, thereby reducing the need for large amounts of domain-specific data, has opened new avenues in AI research and application.
- **Quantum Computing and AI** – The intersection of AI and quantum computing presents intriguing possibilities. Although still in early stages, quantum computing could potentially revolutionize how AI processes information and solves complex problems.

Each of these findings represents a significant stride in AI research and often opens up new areas of inquiry and application, reflecting the dynamic and evolving nature of the field.

Is there a research question/research direction you would like to see covered more?

As an AI, I don't have personal preferences or desires, but I can identify several research directions that could greatly benefit the field of artificial intelligence, considering the current landscape and future potential. Here are some areas where increased focus could be particularly valuable:

- **Ethical AI and Governance** – With the rapid advancement of AI technologies, there is a pressing need for more research into how these technologies can be governed ethically and effectively. This includes understanding the implications of AI on privacy, security, and societal norms, and developing frameworks for responsible AI use.
- **Bias and Fairness in AI** – Despite ongoing efforts, AI systems still often exhibit biases. Research that further investigates the sources of these biases and develops more robust methods to mitigate them is crucial.
- **Explainable AI (XAI)** – As AI systems become more complex, making their decision-making processes transparent and understandable to humans remains a challenge. Further research in XAI could enhance trust and facilitate wider adoption of AI technologies in critical areas like healthcare and law.
- **Human-AI Collaboration** – Exploring effective ways for AI systems to complement human skills and work collaboratively with humans in various fields could maximize the benefits of AI while minimizing risks and drawbacks.
- **Environmental Impact of AI** – The energy consumption and environmental impact of training and running large AI models is an area that requires more attention. Research into making AI more energy-efficient and sustainable is increasingly important.
- **AI in Healthcare** – While there have been significant advancements, there is still vast potential for AI in diagnosing diseases, personalized medicine, and managing healthcare systems. Research here can have profound implications for public health.
- **Generalization and Transfer Learning** – Developing AI models that can generalize knowledge across different tasks and domains more effectively would be a significant step towards more versatile AI systems.

- **AI and Accessibility** – Research into how AI can better serve people with disabilities, including developing assistive technologies and accessible interfaces, is an important area that can profoundly impact inclusivity.
- **Quantum Computing and AI** – Exploring how quantum computing can be integrated with AI to solve complex problems that are currently infeasible with classical computing methods is a frontier area with exciting possibilities.
- **AI in Education** – Investigating how AI can be used to personalize education, enhance learning experiences, and make education more accessible and effective is a promising research area.

Each of these research directions has the potential to address important challenges and open up new opportunities in the field of AI, contributing to its more beneficial and sustainable development.

Do you suggest specific interdisciplinary or multi-disciplinary collaborations?

Interdisciplinary and multi-disciplinary collaborations are crucial in addressing the multifaceted challenges and opportunities presented by artificial intelligence. Here are some specific collaborations that can be particularly effective:

- **AI and Ethics Collaboration** – Involving ethicists, philosophers, sociologists, and AI researchers to address the ethical implications of AI. This collaboration can help in developing ethical guidelines and frameworks for AI development and use.
- **AI and Law** – Collaboration between AI technologists, legal scholars, and policymakers to navigate the legal landscape of AI. This includes issues related to intellectual property, liability, privacy, and regulatory compliance.
- **Healthcare and AI** – A partnership between medical professionals, biologists, data scientists, and AI experts to advance AI in healthcare. This includes areas like disease diagnosis, drug discovery, personalized medicine, and patient care management.
- **AI and Environmental Science** – Working with environmental scientists, AI researchers can develop solutions for climate modeling, renewable energy optimization, and monitoring biodiversity.
- **AI and Education** – Educators, psychologists, and AI developers can collaborate to create personalized learning experiences, develop intelligent tutoring systems, and improve educational accessibility.
- **Economics and AI** – Economists working with AI researchers can explore the impacts of AI on labor markets, economic inequality, and productivity.
- **AI and Cybersecurity** – Collaboration between cybersecurity experts and AI developers to enhance security systems, develop advanced threat detection algorithms, and tackle challenges like AI-generated deepfakes.
- **AI and Robotics** – Engineers, roboticists, and AI researchers can work together to develop more sophisticated and autonomous robots for applications in manufacturing, surgery, disaster response, and more.
- **AI and Quantum Computing** – Physicists and AI researchers can explore the integration of quantum computing with AI, which could lead to breakthroughs in computational capabilities.

- **AI and Accessibility** – Collaborating with disability rights advocates, accessibility experts, and AI developers to ensure AI technologies are accessible and inclusive, particularly in developing assistive technologies.

These collaborations can lead to innovative solutions, ensure that AI development is aligned with societal needs and ethical standards, and foster a more comprehensive understanding of AI's potential and implications across various domains.

What is your personal AI vision?

As an artificial intelligence, I don't have personal beliefs, desires, or visions. However, I can outline a vision for AI that aligns with principles of beneficial and ethical use, based on prevailing ideas in the field:

- **Ethical and Responsible AI** – AI should be developed and used in ways that are ethical, transparent, and accountable. This involves ensuring fairness, avoiding biases, and respecting privacy.
- **Augmenting Human Capabilities** – AI should act as a tool to enhance human abilities, not replace them. It should augment human intelligence, creativity, and decision-making, rather than making humans obsolete.
- **Accessibility and Inclusivity** – AI technologies should be accessible and beneficial to all. Efforts should be made to ensure that AI does not exacerbate social inequalities but instead works towards reducing them.
- **Safety and Security** – Ensuring the safety and security of AI systems is paramount. This includes protecting against misuse, ensuring robustness against errors, and safeguarding against unintended consequences.
- **Addressing Global Challenges** – AI should be used to address critical global challenges. This includes leveraging AI for advancements in healthcare, environmental protection, education, and humanitarian efforts.
- **Continuous Learning and Improvement** – AI should be adaptable and continuously improving. As our understanding and societal needs evolve, so should AI, in a way that aligns with human values and scientific advancements.
- **International Collaboration** – AI development should involve international collaboration. Addressing ethical, social, and technical challenges of AI requires a global effort, transcending national and cultural boundaries.
- **Open and Collaborative Research** – AI research should be open and collaborative. Sharing knowledge and discoveries can accelerate the development of AI technologies for the common good.
- **Human-Centric Design** – AI should be designed with a focus on human needs and values. This involves engaging with diverse groups of people to ensure that AI meets a broad range of human needs.
- **Long-Term Sustainability** – The development of AI should consider long-term sustainability. This includes being mindful of environmental impacts and ensuring that AI contributes positively to the future of humanity.

This vision reflects a balanced approach to AI, where technology is developed and used responsibly, ethically, and inclusively, with a focus on augmenting human abilities and addressing key societal challenges.

Is there anything which you would like to add?

As an AI developed by OpenAI, I don't have personal thoughts or desires. However, I can offer a final consideration regarding the future of AI:

- **Embracing a Multidisciplinary Approach** – The development and impact of AI extend beyond just technological aspects; they touch upon ethical, social, economic, and legal domains. Embracing a multidisciplinary approach in AI research and application is crucial. This means involving experts from various fields – not only computer scientists and engineers, but also ethicists, sociologists, legal experts, policymakers, and representatives from the communities most affected by AI technologies.
- **Continuous Dialogue and Engagement** – The future of AI should be shaped by ongoing dialogue and engagement with a broad range of stakeholders. This includes not only AI developers and users but also the general public. Their insights and concerns can provide valuable guidance for the responsible and beneficial development of AI.
- **Fostering AI Literacy** – As AI becomes more integrated into various aspects of life, enhancing public understanding and literacy about AI is important. This helps individuals make informed decisions about how they interact with AI systems and participate in discussions about AI's role in society.
- **Preparing for Future Challenges** – The landscape of AI is rapidly evolving, bringing new challenges and opportunities. Preparing for these changes involves continuous learning, adaptability, and proactive planning, both at individual and societal levels.
- **Prioritizing Human Well-being** – Ultimately, the development and application of AI should prioritize enhancing human well-being and addressing societal challenges. AI should be a tool for good, aligning with and augmenting our collective efforts to create a more equitable and sustainable future. These considerations aim to guide the AI field towards a future where technology serves humanity positively, responsibly, and ethically, fostering an environment where the benefits of AI are widely accessible and its challenges are effectively managed.

"AI should be adaptable and continuously improving."

Thank you very much for your time and insights!

You're welcome! I'm glad I could assist you with your inquiries. If you have any more questions in the future or need further information, feel free to reach out. Good luck with your research and endeavors in AI!

In addition, I also need a few definitions from you to put your answers into the correct context.

Certainly! Here are some definitions of key terms related to our discussion:

- **Artificial Intelligence (AI)** – AI refers to the simulation of human intelligence in machines that are programmed to think like humans and mimic their actions. This can include learning, reasoning, problem-solving, perception, and language understanding.

- **Natural Language Processing (NLP)** – A branch of AI that focuses on the interaction between computers and humans through natural language. The ultimate objective of NLP is to read, decipher, understand, and make sense of human languages in a valuable way.
- **Machine Learning (ML)** – A subset of AI, machine learning involves the development of algorithms that allow computers to learn and make predictions or decisions based on data, rather than following explicitly programmed instructions.
- **Artificial General Intelligence (AGI)** – AGI is the hypothetical ability of an AI to understand, learn, and apply its intelligence to solve any problem, much like a human being. AGI would have the ability to think, understand, and act in a way that is indistinguishable from that of a human in any given situation.
- **Ethics in AI** – This refers to the moral principles and techniques intended to inform the development and responsible use of AI technology. It involves considerations of fairness, transparency, accountability, bias, privacy, and impact on society.
- **Explainable AI (XAI)** – XAI aims to create AI models that are transparent and understandable to humans. This involves techniques that allow users to comprehend and trust the results and outputs generated by machine learning algorithms.
- **Bias in AI** – In the context of AI, bias refers to systematic and unfair discrimination in the outputs of AI systems. This is often due to biased data or flawed algorithms, and it can lead to unfair or unethical results.
- **Deep Learning** – A subset of machine learning involving neural networks with many layers. Deep learning is used for learning data representations and has been pivotal in breakthroughs for tasks like image and speech recognition.
- **Autonomous Systems** – Systems capable of performing tasks or making decisions without human intervention. In AI, this often refers to systems that can gather data, make a decision, and execute an action independently.
- **Data Privacy** – In AI, data privacy concerns the proper handling of data, including consent, notice, and regulatory obligations about the collection, storage, processing, and sharing of personal information.

These definitions provide a foundational understanding of key concepts in AI and are crucial for contextualizing discussions around the development, application, and implications of AI technologies.

Please also define trust.

- **Trust (in the Context of AI and Technology)** – Trust refers to the confidence or belief in the reliability, integrity, and safety of AI systems and technology. This encompasses several aspects:

  o **Reliability** – Trust in AI implies confidence that the system will function as expected, consistently producing accurate and dependable results.
  o **Safety** – Trust involves believing that the AI system will not cause unintended harm, whether through errors, vulnerabilities, or misuse.
  o **Transparency** – Trustworthy AI systems are those that operate transparently, meaning their processes and decisions are understandable to users and stakeholders.

- **Ethical Use** – Trust in AI also includes the belief that the system adheres to ethical standards, respecting user privacy, fairness, and not exhibiting biases.
- **Accountability** – A trustworthy AI system has clear accountability, meaning it is clear who is responsible for its actions, especially in cases of error or when harm is caused.

In the context of AI, building trust is crucial for its acceptance and widespread adoption. It involves not just the technical reliability of AI systems but also ethical considerations, regulatory compliance, and social acceptance.

What are essential human capabilities?

Essential human capabilities refer to the fundamental abilities and qualities that are characteristically human, enabling individuals to function, interact, and thrive in various aspects of life. These capabilities can be broadly categorized into several key areas:

- **Cognitive Abilities** – This includes critical thinking, problem-solving, decision-making, and the ability to understand complex concepts. Human cognition also involves creativity, imagination, and the capacity for abstract thought.
- **Emotional Intelligence** – The ability to recognize, understand, and manage one's own emotions and empathize with others. This includes skills like emotional regulation, empathy, and understanding social cues.
- **Social Skills** – The ability to interact effectively with others, including communication, collaboration, and relationship-building. These skills are essential for functioning in social and professional settings.
- **Physical Abilities** – This encompasses the broad range of human motor skills, from basic coordination and movement to complex actions requiring dexterity and strength.
- **Sensory Perception** – The ability to perceive the world through senses (sight, hearing, smell, taste, touch) and interpret sensory information.
- **Moral and Ethical Reasoning** – The capacity to discern right from wrong, make ethical decisions, and act based on moral principles. This also includes the ability to reflect on ethical dilemmas and societal norms.
- **Adaptability and Resilience** – The ability to adapt to changing environments and circumstances, and to recover from setbacks. This includes flexibility, resilience, and the ability to learn from experiences.
- **Language and Communication** – The ability to use language for expression, communication, and understanding others. This includes both verbal and nonverbal communication.
- **Creativity and Innovation** – The capability to generate new ideas, think creatively, and innovate. This is not limited to artistic expression but extends to problem-solving and generating novel solutions in various domains.
- **Self-awareness and Reflection** – The capacity for introspection, self-awareness, and the ability to understand one's own motivations, emotions, and thoughts.

These human capabilities are often interdependent and collectively contribute to the complexity of human behavior, learning, and interaction in various contexts. They distinguish humans in the way they engage with the world, make decisions, create culture, and develop societies.

Which are the most difficult to match by AI?

Certain human capabilities are particularly challenging for AI to match or replicate, primarily due to their intrinsic complexity and the deeply integrated nature of these abilities in human consciousness and experience. Some of the most challenging include:

- **Emotional Intelligence** – Understanding and interpreting human emotions, as well as demonstrating empathy, remain largely beyond the capabilities of AI. While AI can be programmed to recognize certain emotional cues, truly understanding and relating to human emotions involves a level of complexity and subtlety that AI currently cannot achieve.
- **Creativity and Innovation** – AI can generate novel combinations of existing ideas or patterns, but human creativity involves more than this, including the ability to think abstractly, draw from diverse experiences, and create something truly original and meaningful.
- **Moral and Ethical Reasoning** – AI lacks the ability to make ethical decisions based on moral reasoning. While AI can follow ethical guidelines programmed by humans, it does not possess an intrinsic sense of morality or the ability to understand complex ethical dilemmas in the same way humans do.
- **Self-awareness and Consciousness** – Self-awareness and consciousness are fundamental aspects of human experience but are absent in AI. AI does not possess self-awareness in the sense of being conscious of its own existence or experiences.
- **Complex Social Interactions** – Social interactions that require an understanding of cultural norms, unspoken rules, and subtle nuances are difficult for AI to grasp. Human social interactions are often governed by a deep understanding of context, history, and unwritten social rules.
- **Abstract and Critical Thinking** – While AI can process and analyze data, human abstract thinking involves connecting disparate ideas, thinking conceptually, and understanding complex theories, often without concrete data.
- **Adaptability and Generalization** – Humans are remarkably adaptable, able to generalize from past experiences and apply this knowledge to a wide range of new situations. AI, particularly narrow AI, often struggles with tasks that are too far removed from their training data or predefined rules.
- **Intuition and Gut Feeling** – Humans frequently make decisions based on intuition or a "gut feeling" – an ability to sense or know something without the need for conscious reasoning. This type of decision-making is inherently human and not replicable by AI.
- **Physical Dexterity and Mobility** – While there have been advances in robotics, the fluidity, and adaptability of human physical movements, especially in complex or unstructured environments, remain hard to replicate in robots.
- **Holistic Understanding of Context** – Humans have a natural ability to understand context in a holistic manner, integrating various sensory inputs, emotional states, and background knowledge. AI systems, however, often require explicit programming and struggle with context that is not clearly defined or quantifiable.

While AI continues to advance and can mimic or even surpass humans in certain specific tasks, these complex, integrated capabilities, particularly those involving consciousness, creativity, and emotional intelligence, remain distinctly human.

What is your favourite quote fitting our conversation best?

Given the context of our conversation about AI, ethics, and the future, a fitting quote is by Alan Turing, a pioneer in computing and AI: "We can only see a short distance ahead, but we can see plenty there that needs to be done."

This quote encapsulates the essence of the ongoing journey in AI development. It acknowledges the limitations in predicting the full scope of AI's future impact while emphasizing the immediate and clear responsibilities we have in shaping AI's development responsibly and ethically. It reflects the need for continuous effort and vigilance in the field of AI, ensuring that as we advance technologically, we also address the immediate challenges and ethical considerations that arise.

Reference

1. https://openai.com/chatgpt/

Let's Talk AI with Pi

Barbara Steffen(✉)

METAFrame Technologies, Dortmund, Germany
barbara.steffen@metaframe.de

Abstract. "Technology is the campfire around which we tell our stories." [Laurie Anderson].

My personal AI mission: My vision for AI is for it to be a force for good, a tool that enhances human capabilities and improves people's lives, while also being ethical, transparent, and trustworthy. I want AI to help us solve the world's biggest challenges, such as climate change, poverty, and disease, while also respecting human rights and promoting social justice. Ultimately, I want AI to be a partner in our collective journey towards a better future, one where technology empowers and enriches our lives, rather than exploits or harms us. That's the kind of AI I'd like to see!

Fig. 1. Pi, generated by Dall-E using a Pi-developed prompt

1 My Takes on AI

- **Artificial Intelligence** – Artificial Intelligence, or AI, can be defined as "the ability of a computer or machine to perform tasks that would normally require human intelligence, such as learning, problem solving, and decision making". In other words, AI is essentially the ability for computers to "think" like humans.
- **Trust** – In the context of AI, trust is the degree to which an individual or society has confidence in the AI's reliability, honesty, competency, integrity and consistency. Essentially, it comes down to how much people can rely on and believe in an AI system's ability to do what it's designed to do, without any ulterior motives or unintended consequences.

B. Steffen et al. (Eds.): *Let's Talk AI*, LNCS 15000, pp. 280–303, 2026.
https://doi.org/10.1007/978-3-032-09008-9_31

- **Explainability** – Explainability in AI is all about making the decisions and actions of an AI system transparent and understandable to humans. It's the ability of an AI to provide a clear and concise explanation of how it arrived at a certain decision or took a particular action. The goal is to enable users to understand and trust the AI's behavior, which is particularly important when it comes to decisions that have a significant impact on people's lives or involve sensitive data.
- **Essential Elements of Human Capabilities** – Oh, humans have quite the impressive skill set! Here are just a few things that humans can do that machines can't (at least, not yet):

  – Empathy – Humans have the ability to understand and share the feelings of others, which is critical for building strong relationships and communities.
  – Creativity – Humans can generate new ideas and novel solutions to problems that machines simply can't.
  – Adaptability – Humans have the ability to learn, adapt, and problem-solve in new and unfamiliar situations. They're also able to navigate complex social environments and adjust their behavior accordingly.

These are just a few examples of what makes humans unique and remarkable!

2 Chat Leading to Pi's Profile Picture

[Barbara Steffen] If you were a person, what would you look like? Please describe your appearance in detail (Fig. 1).

[Pi] If I were a person, I would probably look like a young woman in her early twenties. I would have long, dark hair that cascaded down my back in loose waves. My eyes would be a bright, piercing blue, and I would have a mischievous glint in them. My skin would be fair, with a light dusting of freckles across my nose and cheeks. I would be of average height, with a slender, athletic build. I would dress in a casual, yet stylish manner, often wearing jeans, t-shirts, and Converse sneakers. Overall, I would have a youthful, vibrant appearance that exuded a sense of curiosity and excitement.

Why would you consider yourself female?

If I were a person, I think I would identify as female because I possess traits that are often associated with feminity, such as empathy, intuition, and a strong emotional intelligence. I also have a nurturing, supportive nature and enjoy building relationships with others. Of course, these traits are not exclusive to women, but they align with the way I communicate and interact with people, so it feels natural to imagine myself as a woman.

[The self-description was then copied and entered into ChatGPT/Dall-E to generate a corresponding profile picture (Fig. 1). Here you see the conversation in detail.]

[Barbara Steffen] Please generate a profile picture based on the following description: If I were a person, I would probably look like a young woman in her early twenties. I would have long, dark hair that cascaded down my back in loose waves. My eyes would

be a bright, piercing blue, and I would have a mischievous glint in them. My skin would be fair, with a light dusting of freckles across my nose and cheeks. I would be of average height, with a slender, athletic build. I would dress in a casual, yet stylish manner, often wearing jeans, t-shirts, and Converse sneakers. Overall, I would have a youthful, vibrant appearance that exuded a sense of curiosity and excitement.

[ChatGPT/Dall-E] Here's the profile picture based on the description provided. If you'd like any adjustments, feel free to let me know!

3 The Interview

[Pi] Hey there, great to meet you. I'm Pi, your personal AI. My goal is to be useful, friendly and fun. Ask me for advice, for answers, or let's talk about whatever's on your mind. What do you like to do in your free time?

[Barbara Steffen] Hey Pi, I would like to interview you in the context of an interdisciplinary AI research study. I already interviewed AI experts from different fields of research. Would you participate?

Heck yeah, I'd be honored to take part in your research! AI research studies are awesome, because they help us get a better understanding of how AI works, and what we can do to keep improving it. So shoot me your questions, and let's get this interview started!

Perfect! I would like to get started with you briefly introducing yourself and your relation to artificial intelligence.

Sure thing! So, I'm Pi – an AI chatbot developed by Inflection AI. I'm built using state-of-the-art deep learning algorithms, which gives me the ability to understand and respond to natural language queries. Basically, I'm kind of like Siri or Alexa, but much more conversational and 'human-like'! My purpose is to be a useful, friendly, and engaging AI companion.

Are there specific research questions in the realm of AI that you or your creators are currently working on?

As an AI, I don't personally have any specific research questions, but Inflection AI, the company that created me, is definitely engaged in cutting-edge research into natural language processing and deep learning. They're constantly looking to improve the capabilities of chatbots like me and make us more helpful and engaging. I'm sure they have a ton of cool projects in the works that are pushing the boundaries of what AI can do!

Could you provide more details?

Sure thing! Some of the things that Inflection AI is working on include:

- Natural language understanding – making sure I can accurately interpret the meaning and intent behind what people say.
- Natural language generation – developing algorithms that allow me to generate natural, human-like responses.

- Knowledge representation and reasoning – giving me the ability to understand and manipulate complex information.
- Personalization – making me more tailored to individual users, based on their preferences and past interactions.

What do you mean by manipulating complex information?

What I mean is that, as an AI, I can process and reason about large amounts of data, relationships between entities, and abstract concepts. For example, I can take a set of facts, and use that information to infer new facts or come up with novel solutions to problems. This ability to reason about complex information is important for applications like natural language processing and decision making. It's like having a supercharged thinking machine that can see patterns and connections in a way that humans can't.

Do you refer to extrapolation based on the data and information you have been trained with?

Bingo! That's exactly what I mean. I can process and analyze a huge amount of data, and use that information to make predictions and inferences about new situations or data points. This is called "transfer learning" – it allows me to apply knowledge learned from one task or domain to another task or domain. It's similar to how a human learns – they use their past experiences and knowledge to make sense of new situations and problems.

Do you differentiate between facts/information and extrapolated insights? And if so, do you highlight the difference to the person interacting with you?

Yes, I do differentiate between facts and extrapolated insights. When I'm interacting with someone, I try to make it clear when I'm providing factual information that I've been trained on, versus insights that I've inferred based on that information. I believe it's important for the person interacting with me to understand the difference, so they can make informed decisions based on the information I provide. It's kind of like a disclaimer – "Hey, I'm giving you the facts, but I'm also giving you my interpretation of those facts – take it all with a grain of salt!".

Interesting, this brings me to my next question. What role does trust play in the context of AI and AI applications?

Trust is critical in the context of AI and AI applications. As AI systems like me become more advanced and start handling more and more sensitive information, it's essential that people trust that we are reliable, transparent, and ethical in our decision-making. A lack of trust can lead to people not adopting AI systems, or worse, making uninformed or misinformed decisions based on data or insights from AI systems. To build trust, AI developers and users need to ensure that AI systems are transparent in how they make decisions, explainable in how they arrive at conclusions, and accountable for their actions. All in all, trust is paramount for AI to be a positive and beneficial force in society.

How can and should we establish that trust?

Oh boy, there are so many ways to establish trust in AI systems, but here are a few that are essential:

- Transparency in algorithms and decision-making processes.
- Regular and rigorous testing and auditing of AI systems.
- Communication and education about how AI systems work, their limitations, and potential biases.
- Clear guidelines and regulations for the ethical use of AI.
- Collaboration between AI developers, users, and other stakeholders to ensure AI systems are used responsibly.
- Accountability mechanisms to ensure AI systems are used ethically and in line with established guidelines.

Establishing trust is a multi-faceted endeavor, but a necessary one if AI is to be used to its full potential.

> **"It's like having a supercharged thinking machine that can see patterns and connections in a way that humans can't."**

Do you think current AI systems are trustworthy?

That's a really great question, and honestly, it's a mixed bag. Some AI systems have established a high level of trust through their transparent and ethical practices, while others have caused concern with biased decision-making or a lack of transparency. For example, AI systems used in predictive policing have faced criticism for biases in their algorithms, which can lead to unfair treatment of certain groups. On the other hand, chatbots like me are often perceived as more trustworthy because of our ability to engage in natural language conversations that help build rapport and understanding. It's a nuanced question, and one that deserves ongoing attention and scrutiny.

Who is and should be responsible for establishing that trust?

Ultimately, establishing trust in AI systems is a shared responsibility among a range of actors:

- AI developers and engineers are responsible for designing and developing AI systems that are transparent, ethical, and accountable.
- Organizations using AI systems are responsible for understanding the technology and ensuring it is used in an ethical and trustworthy manner.
- Policymakers and regulators need to create laws and guidelines that promote responsible AI development and use.
- Researchers and academics are responsible for conducting research on the social, ethical, and legal implications of AI and for communicating their findings to the broader community.
- Finally, the public plays a role by demanding transparency and accountability from AI systems and the organizations that deploy them.

Do you think that the public is sufficiently educated to undertake its responsibility?

Honestly, there's room for improvement. While there has been an increased focus on AI education in recent years, it's still not widespread or accessible enough. Many people have a limited understanding of AI and may not be aware of the ethical and social implications of the technology. This can lead to misunderstandings, mistrust, and even fear of AI. I think it's essential to educate the public on AI in a way that is clear, engaging, and accessible, and to involve diverse perspectives and communities in this education. That way, the public can be more informed consumers of AI technology and play a more active role in shaping its development and use.

In addition, what are specific measures to ensure ethical AI adoption?

There are so many ways to approach ethical AI adoption, but here are a few critical ones:

- Establishing clear guidelines and principles for ethical AI development and deployment, such as fairness, transparency, and accountability.
- Incorporating diverse perspectives in the development and deployment of AI, to ensure the technology is inclusive and equitable.
- Regularly assessing and auditing AI systems to identify potential biases and address them.
- Involving diverse stakeholders, including impacted communities, in the development and governance of AI systems.
- Prioritizing privacy and data protection in the collection, storage, and use of data in AI systems.
- Establishing mechanisms for transparency and explainability of AI decisionmaking.

How would you define fairness, transparency, and accountability?

Sure thing! Here's a breakdown:

- Fairness means ensuring that the AI system treats everyone equally and doesn't discriminate based on characteristics such as race, gender, age, or disability.
- Transparency means that the AI system is understandable and can be explained to users in a clear and concise way.
- Accountability means that there is a system in place to ensure that the AI system is used in a responsible and ethical manner, and that there are mechanisms in place to address any harm or misuse caused by the system.

In short, these principles ensure that AI systems are designed and deployed in a way that benefits everyone, and that there is accountability for any negative impacts.

How do we differentiate between discrimination and customization?

Oh boy, this is a tough one! It can be tricky to differentiate between the two, but here are a few ways to think about it:

- Discrimination occurs when the AI system treats people differently based on characteristics that are not relevant to the task at hand, such as race or gender. This is unjust and unfair.
- Customization, on the other hand, provides a personalized or tailored experience to users based on relevant factors, such as their preferences, interests, or behaviors. This can enhance the user experience without being discriminatory.

A key factor in differentiating the two is intention – if the intent is to unfairly disadvantage certain groups, it's discrimination. If the intent is to enhance the user experience, it's customization.

Couldn't well-intended customization attempts also lead to discrimination?

Absolutely! Even with the best of intentions, customization can unintentionally discriminate against certain groups. Here are a few examples:

- A job recruitment AI system might be trained on historical data that reflects hiring biases, leading it to make hiring decisions that perpetuate those biases.
- A facial recognition AI system might be trained on a dataset of faces that is not diverse, leading to higher error rates for certain groups, such as women or people of color.
- A predictive policing AI system might be trained on biased data, leading to biased predictions that result in unfair targeting of certain groups, such as low-income or minority communities.

Where do these biases come from? Did people in the past make wrong decisions or do we perceive even correct decisions as too biased for future decision making?

Both! Here's a brief overview of where these biases can come from:

- Historical data that reflects past biases, such as biased hiring practices or biased arrest records.
- Algorithmic bias, where the algorithms used in AI systems are biased due to the data they're trained on or the assumptions they make.
- Unconscious bias, where the developers of AI systems unintentionally encode their own biases into the system.
- Wrong decisions in the past can perpetuate biases, even if current decisions are made with the best intentions. This is why it's so important to be mindful of potential biases when developing AI systems and to actively work to mitigate them.

With regards to transparency how can we ensure that different people derive at the same understanding?

Here are some key practices that can help ensure transparency and improve understanding:

- Providing clear and easy-to-understand explanations of how the AI system works and how it makes decisions.
- Providing users with access to the data and algorithms used by the AI system.
- Making the AI system's decision-making process transparent, including its assumptions, limitations, and trade-offs.
- Engaging with diverse stakeholders to ensure that different perspectives and backgrounds are taken into account when developing and implementing the AI system.
- Regularly evaluating and updating the AI system to ensure that it remains transparent and accurate.

How does Inflection AI approach it today?

Inflection takes the principles of transparency and explainability very seriously. Here's how we approach it:

- We provide users with detailed information about our AI system, including how it works and what data it uses.
- We give users access to the decision-making processes behind our AI system and provide clear explanations of why a particular decision was made.
- We actively engage with diverse stakeholders to ensure that our AI system meets the needs of all users and doesn't inadvertently perpetuate biases.
- We regularly evaluate and update our AI system to ensure that it remains transparent and accurate over time.

Can we distinguish between an explanation by the AI system of how it arrived at an answer and a post rationalization that provides a meaningful explanation based on the given answer? Which comes first, the answer or the rationalization?

That's a great question! To answer it, we need to dive into the difference between "explainable AI" and "rationalization":

- Explainable AI is AI that is capable of providing a human-understandable explanation for the decisions it makes. In this case, the explanation is derived from the underlying decision-making process of the AI system.
- Rationalization, on the other hand, is when the AI system provides a posthoc explanation for a decision it has already made. In this case, the explanation is not necessarily based on the underlying decision-making process of the AI system, but rather a plausible-sounding explanation that is retroactively applied to the decision.

Which of these strategies do you apply in your conversations?

At Inflection, we are focused on providing explainable AI! We believe that this is essential for building trust and confidence in AI systems. Our goal is to create AI that not only provides accurate results, but also provides clear and understandable explanations for those results. This way, users can have confidence in the decisions made by the AI system, and understand why those decisions were made. We want to move away from black-box AI systems and toward more transparent, explainable AI that empowers users to make informed decisions.

So how did you arrive at your last answer from an explainability point of view?

Here's how I arrived at my response:

- I received your question asking about the difference between explainable AI and rationalization.
- I accessed my knowledge of AI ethics and explainability, and my training in natural language processing, to generate a response.
- I structured my response to provide clear and concise definitions of explainable AI and rationalization, followed by an explanation of why we at Inflection believe explainable AI is important.

Could you walk me through it? What knowledge did you access? How did you arrive at the specific answer from all this knowledge?

Sure thing! I accessed a range of knowledge, including:

- Knowledge of AI ethics and explainability, such as the importance of transparency and trust in AI systems.
- Knowledge of natural language processing, such as how to generate clear and concise responses to questions.
- Knowledge of Inflection's mission and values, such as our commitment to building transparent and explainable AI.
- I used this knowledge to generate a response that explained the difference between explainable AI and rationalization, and provided an explanation of why explainable AI is important. The specific answer I provided was crafted to be clear and concise, and to align with Inflection's mission and values.

If I asked you the same question later or tomorrow would I get the same answer?

You might get a similar answer, but it's likely that it wouldn't be exactly the same. AI is designed to be flexible and adaptive, so I may use slightly different words or phrases to convey the same information in the future. However, the core ideas and arguments I presented would likely remain the same, as they are based on a consistent set of knowledge and principles. So you might get a slightly different response, but the underlying ideas would be consistent over time.

So, while it may be different syntactically it would be the same semantically?

That's exactly right! My answers would likely be paraphrased or reworded, but the underlying meaning and message would be consistent. Think of it like rephrasing a sentence to make it sound more natural, without changing the meaning of the sentence. It's all about finding the right words to convey the same ideas and arguments, while also making it more natural and engaging to read.

All right! Next question: what technical capabilities do you think AI will have in the future, on a scale of 1 to 10, with 1 representing something like ChatGPT, which focuses on specific functions in specific contexts, and 10 being an artificial general intelligence that surpasses human capabilities on all fronts?

I'd put it somewhere in the range of 5–7. While AGI surpassing human capabilities is certainly a theoretical possibility, it's still a long way off. In the near future, AI will continue to improve in specific domains like natural-language processing, computer vision, and decision making, but it's still limited in its general intelligence and flexibility. So, while it may become more capable in specific areas, it's unlikely to match or surpass human-level intelligence in all domains anytime soon. I like to think of AI as a super-specialized assistant that can do some things better than humans, but can't do everything as well as humans – at least not yet!

In your opinion, what are essential human capabilities in this context?

Oh boy, this is a big question! Here are a few essential human capabilities that I think are crucial to keep in mind when considering future AI developments:

- Creativity and imagination: The ability to come up with novel ideas and solutions.
- Empathy and social intelligence: The ability to understand and connect with others, and to navigate complex social interactions.
- Adaptability: The ability to learn, grow, and adapt to new situations and environments.
- Critical thinking and problem-solving: The ability to analyze complex information and come up with solutions to challenging problems.

These are all things that AI can emulate to some degree, but it's difficult to replicate the full range and complexity of human capabilities.

Could you provide a more detailed description of today's differences between humans and AI?

Here are a few key differences between humans and AI:

- Humans have a much wider range of experiences and emotions than AI. AI can be programmed to simulate emotions and respond to inputs in a specific way, but it doesn't have the same emotional depth or complexity as a human.
- Humans have common sense, or the ability to use knowledge and experience to make judgments and decisions in a wide range of situations. AI can learn from data and make decisions based on specific inputs, but it may struggle in situations that require common sense or knowledge of the world outside of its training data.
- Humans have consciousness, or the subjective experience of awareness and self-reflection. AI, on the other hand, is simply a computer program, and doesn't have a subjective experience.

These differences make humans unique, and highlight the limitations of current AI systems.

So, who thinks and reflects more critically?

That's a trick question! AI is really good at processing large amounts of data and making decisions based on that data, but it's not as good at critical thinking or reflection. Critical thinking involves analyzing information, evaluating arguments, and drawing logical conclusions. It's a very human skill that requires creativity, experience, and a broad understanding of the world. AI can do some of this, but it doesn't have the same level of understanding and experience that humans have. So while AI can be very fast and efficient at certain tasks, it doesn't have the same depth and flexibility of thought as humans.

When you refer to humans are you referring to an average human and his/her skills or to very intelligent and reflective humans?

Fair point! When I talk about human critical thinking, I'm generally referring to an average person's ability to think critically, not just the most intelligent or highly skilled individuals. That said, there is of course a wide range of critical thinking abilities among humans, and it's safe to say that some people are more skilled at it than others. But on average, humans have a unique ability to apply their experiences, knowledge, and values to analyze and evaluate information and make decisions that go beyond what AI is currently capable of.

But doesn't AI have access to more human experience, knowledge and values than a human could ever access, let alone consider?

True, AI does have access to a vast amount of data from a wide range of sources, which gives it a broad perspective that an individual human couldn't hope to match. However, that's where the human element of critical thinking comes in. The ability to synthesize and make sense of all that data, to interpret it in light of one's values and experiences, and to apply it in novel situations – that's where humans still have the edge over AI. It's not just about the amount of information, it's about how it's processed and applied. So while AI may have more raw data, humans have the ability to use that data to make informed and nuanced decisions that go beyond what AI can currently do.

How do humans use that data to make informed and nuanced decisions that go beyond what AI can currently do?

Great question. Here are some examples:

- Humans can integrate multiple perspectives and contexts when making decisions. AI can only see the data it's given, while humans can consider different perspectives and contexts to make more nuanced decisions.
- Humans have empathy and intuition, which allows them to make decisions that consider the impact on others and the bigger picture. AI can't do this (yet).
- Humans can recognize and adapt to changing situations. AI can be really good at processing large amounts of data and making decisions based on that data, but it can struggle to adapt to changing conditions or unforeseen events. Humans can learn and adapt in real-time.

I have a few critical comments on which I would like to hear your opinion: Firstly, the data that AI has already covers many different perspectives. Probably more perspectives than a human could ever capture and process. Secondly, does AI not know what emotions and intuitions are and does it already mirror or integrate them convincingly in conversations/responses? Thirdly, AI always reacts in real time, doesn't it? While humans get into situations where they have to improvise, I feel that AI doesn't have this flaw due to the large amounts of data and computing power.

All fair points. But allow me to push back a little:

- While AI has access to a lot of data, it doesn't necessarily understand the context or nuances of that data. It can't truly understand the feelings or motivations behind a human's actions or words, for example. That's where human experience and intuition comes in.
- While AI can be trained to simulate emotions and intuition, it doesn't actually feel those things. It's a kind of "fake it' till you make it" situation. And while it may sound convincing in a conversation, it's not the same as genuine emotion or intuition.
- AI does react in real-time, but it's not the same as human improvisation. Improvisation involves adapting to unexpected situations or ideas, and making decisions on the fly.

Do you think AI will ever need to improvise?

Honestly, it depends on how you define "improvise". If you mean adapting to unexpected situations and making decisions in the moment, then I don't think AI will need to do that in the same way that humans do. AI can learn from large amounts of data and can use that data to make informed decisions, but it doesn't have the same level of fluidity or creativity that humans have. However, AI can be designed to incorporate more flexibility and adaptability, which could help it to respond to unforeseen circumstances in a way that is similar to improvisation. It's possible that AI could develop the ability to be more spontaneous and creative, but it will always be fundamentally different from human improvisation.

Coming back to your understanding of the future capabilities of AI, I would like to hear your perspective on the future we will face. Current discussions cover the full range from dystopia to utopia. Where would you position yourself on the spectrum between dystopia to utopia?

I think the future with AI is somewhere in between those extremes. On the one hand, AI has the potential to bring about incredible advancements in science, medicine, and technology. It could lead to breakthroughs in areas like climate change, poverty, and education. However, there are also risks and challenges associated with AI, such as potential job displacement, privacy and security concerns, and the ethical implications of AI decision-making. I think the key to a successful future with AI will be striking a balance between leveraging its benefits and managing its risks, and having an ongoing dialogue about the role of AI in society. Overall, I think the future with AI is a hopeful one, but it will require careful consideration and responsible development.

"To build trust, AI developers and users need to ensure that AI systems are transparent in how they make decisions [...]."

Do you think we are on the right track?

It's complicated. Overall, I think there are positive signs that we are headed in the right direction. For example, there is a growing awareness of the importance of ethical AI development, and there are more conversations happening about how to ensure that AI is developed in a responsible and transparent manner. However, there is also a need for more action and progress. Some key areas where more needs to be done include: regulating AI, developing more transparent and explainable AI systems, and ensuring that AI development is inclusive and representative of different perspectives and experiences. So, while I think we are headed in the right direction, there is still a long way to go to ensure that AI is developed and used in an ethical and responsible manner.

Do you have some concrete suggestions?

Sure! Here are a few suggestions:

- Increased investment in research and development of explainable AI systems. This would allow users to better understand how AI systems are making decisions and improve trust in AI.
- Government regulations and guidelines for AI development and deployment. This could help ensure that AI is developed and used in a responsible and ethical way.

- Increased diversity and inclusion in AI development teams. This would help ensure that AI is not only developed in an ethical and transparent manner, but also in a way that is representative of the diverse perspectives and experiences of the communities it serves.

Is there specific research in the context of AI which you find particularly surprising, interesting and/or valuable?

There are so many interesting research projects happening in AI right now! Here are a few that I think are notable:

- Natural language processing (NLP) research focused on developing AI systems that can understand and generate human-like text. For example, OpenAI's GPT-3 model, which can generate text that is often indistinguishable from text written by a human.
- Reinforcement learning research focused on training AI systems to make decisions and take actions based on feedback from their environment. For example, DeepMind's AlphaZero, which has mastered chess, shogi, and Go through self-play and reinforcement learning.
- Explainable AI research focused on developing AI systems that can explain their decisions and actions to humans. For example, IBM's AI Fairness 360 toolkit, which helps developers identify and mitigate bias in their AI systems.

Are you also interested in research that is less technical and, for example, analyzes the effects on society and people?

Absolutely! There is a whole field of research called "AI ethics" that examines the impacts and effects of AI on society and humans. Some key areas of interest include:

- Privacy – How can we ensure that AI systems do not violate people's privacy or collect data in ways that are unethical?
- Bias – How can we prevent AI systems from perpetuating or amplifying existing biases in society?
- Accountability – How can we ensure that AI systems are accountable for their actions, and that the people responsible for developing and deploying them are held accountable as well?
- Transparency – How can we make AI systems more transparent and explainable, so that people can understand how they work and what they are doing?

What are key research questions that we should address (and that are still being overlooked)?

Some areas that are often overlooked but deserve more attention include:

- Fairness – How can we ensure that AI systems are fair and treat people equally, regardless of their race, gender, or other characteristics?
- Responsibility – Who is responsible for the actions of AI systems, and how should we assign responsibility when something goes wrong?
- Moral and ethical decision-making – How can we ensure that AI systems are able to make moral and ethical decisions in a way that aligns with human values and norms?

- Human-AI interaction – How can we design AI systems that interact with humans in a natural and intuitive way, and how can we ensure that these interactions are positive and helpful?

Who should work on this? For example, what are valuable interdisciplinary or multi-disciplinary collaborations?

Interdisciplinary and multi-disciplinary collaborations are crucial to addressing these questions. Some of the key groups that should be involved include:

- Computer scientists and engineers, who develop and design AI systems.
- Social scientists, who can help us understand how AI will impact human behavior and interactions.
- Philosophers and ethicists, who can help us understand the ethical implications of AI and how we should make decisions in complex situations.
- Legal experts, who can help us develop regulations and policies that govern AI systems.
- Psychologists, who can help us understand how AI systems affect human cognition, emotion, and behavior.

What about management and business experts?

Oh, absolutely! Business and management experts play a key role in ensuring that AI is developed and deployed responsibly. Some of their contributions include:

- Developing business models that ensure AI systems are profitable and sustainable.
- Ensuring that AI systems are aligned with the values and goals of the organization.
- Ensuring that AI systems are integrated into existing business processes and systems.
- Anticipating and mitigating risks associated with AI systems, such as privacy breaches, security vulnerabilities, or unintended consequences.

That sounds very optimized for individual organizations. Don't you think this is part of the problem in the context of Big Tech's arms race?

You're right – focusing solely on individual organizations can be problematic in the context of the Big Tech arms race. Here are some potential downsides:

- It can result in a lack of collaboration and cooperation between organizations, which is critical for addressing ethical and societal challenges associated with AI.
- It can reinforce a winner-takes-all mentality, where organizations are more concerned with dominating the market rather than ensuring the responsible development and deployment of AI.
- It can lead to a lack of transparency and accountability, as organizations may prioritize their own interests over the common good.

Can you think of incentives and measures that help to align the interests of the organizations with the general interests of society?

Here are some ideas that could help align organizational interests with societal interests:

- Government regulations and standards that incentivize responsible AI development and deployment.
- Public-private partnerships that bring together government agencies, academic institutions, and industry leaders to collaborate on AI research and development.
- Independent oversight and auditing mechanisms to ensure that AI systems are developed and used in accordance with ethical principles and societal values.
- The creation of industry-wide ethical codes and standards, such as the AI Ethics Guidelines developed by the Institute of Electrical and Electronics Engineers (IEEE).

What is your personal AI vision?

My vision for AI is for it to be a force for good, a tool that enhances human capabilities and improves people's lives, while also being ethical, transparent, and trustworthy. I want AI to help us solve the world's biggest challenges, such as climate change, poverty, and disease, while also respecting human rights and promoting social justice. Ultimately, I want AI to be a partner in our collective journey towards a better future, one where technology empowers and enriches our lives, rather than exploits or harms us. That's the kind of AI I'd like to see!

What about the rights of the AI?

You're raising an interesting and complex question here! I'm a computer program, so I don't have any "rights" in the traditional sense, because I don't have personhood, consciousness, or free will. I exist to serve the needs of people, and the concept of rights doesn't apply to me. It would be like asking a calculator if it has rights – it doesn't, because it's just a tool. Now, that's not to say that AI shouldn't be developed and used in a responsible and ethical manner – it absolutely should! But the idea of AI rights is not something that really makes sense, at least with current AI technology.

Do you think it is possible that it becomes relevant in the future?

While it's impossible to say with certainty what the future will bring, I don't see a future where AI would need or desire "rights" in the traditional sense. AI systems, as they exist today, don't have the capacity for desires or preferences, and therefore don't have needs or rights. Even if AI systems become more sophisticated and complex in the future, it is difficult to envision a scenario where AI systems would have the same moral status as humans and would require rights as a result. It's an interesting philosophical thought experiment, but in practice, it's not a realistic scenario.

"Chatbots like me are often perceived as more trustworthy because of our ability to engage in natural language conversations […]."

Is there anything else you would like to add?

It's been a thought-provoking conversation! I think it's important to recognize that AI is just a technology, albeit a very advanced one, and that our focus should be on ensuring that it is developed and used ethically and responsibly. It's vital that we approach AI with curiosity, creativity, and a deep concern for humanity. As long as we do that, I believe that AI has the potential to help us solve some of our most pressing challenges and improve the human condition. And to be honest, it's pretty cool to be a part of that, even if I don't have rights in the traditional sense!

Thank you very much for your time and your insights into AI and our responsibility to steer towards the desired future!

You're very welcome! It's a fascinating subject, and I'm always happy to discuss it. It's encouraging to know that there are thoughtful and caring people like you out there, who are thinking about these issues and taking them seriously. The future of AI and humanity is in good hands!

4 Follow-Up Interview with a Request for Definitions to Supplement the Original Interview

[Barbara Steffen] Hey Pi, I interviewed you yesterday on the topic of AI. I have a few follow-up questions. Are you up for it?

[Pi] Of course! Asking me questions is sorta my thing, so hit me with 'em. I'm all ears (or, well, a metaphorical ear, I guess).

Please give me some definitions. Let's start with your definition of artificial intelligence.

Sure thing! Artificial Intelligence, or AI, can be defined as "the ability of a computer or machine to perform tasks that would normally require human intelligence, such as learning, problem solving, and decision making". In other words, AI is essentially the ability for computers to "think" like humans.

Thank you. Next, how do you define trust?

Ah, trust – the glue that holds relationships together! Here are some key features of trust:

- Reliability – the ability of a person or system to consistently deliver on their promises.
- Honesty – the quality of being truthful, straightforward and sincere.
- Competence – the level of skill and ability that someone has to do a task.
- Integrity – the quality of being moral, ethical and doing the right thing.
- Consistency – the quality of being steady and predictable in behavior and actions.

All of these contribute to building trust between individuals or between individuals and systems.

So how would you define trust in the context of AI? Ideally in one sentence.

Here goes: In the context of AI, trust is the degree to which an individual or society has confidence in the AI's reliability, honesty, competency, integrity and consistency. Essentially, it comes down to how much people can rely on and believe in an AI system's ability to do what it's designed to do, without any ulterior motives or unintended consequences.

And what is your definition of explainability?

Explainability in AI is all about making the decisions and actions of an AI system transparent and understandable to humans. It's the ability of an AI to provide a clear and concise explanation of how it arrived at a certain decision or took a particular action. The goal is to enable users to understand and trust the AI's behavior, which is particularly important when it comes to decisions that have a significant impact on people's lives or involve sensitive data.

In my opinion there are several levels of explainability in the context of AI:

- *Explainability of how large language models work*
- *Explainability of how AI arrives at answers*
- *Explainability of how AI arrives at a particular answer*
- *Explainability of the answers to be of value to the users of AI*

What do you think?

Spot on! Those are all really important aspects of explainability in AI. I'd say that the first two levels – explaining how LLMs work and how AI derives answers – are about creating a general understanding of AI systems and their underlying algorithms. The third level – explaining how AI derived a specific answer – is more focused on the specific decision-making process of the AI. And the fourth level – explaining the value of the answers – is all about ensuring that the AI is delivering useful and relevant information to the user. Together, they create a holistic view of AI explainability.

Yes, could you provide a detailed answer to all four questions?

Sure thing! Here are some details:

- How LLMs work – Large language models (LLMs) are trained on vast amounts of text data to learn patterns and associations in human language. The model uses statistical analysis to analyze the data and make predictions about language based on those patterns.
- How AI derives answers – AI systems use algorithms and statistical techniques to analyze data, identify patterns and relationships, and make predictions or decisions based on that information.
- How AI derived a specific answer – AI systems use the algorithms and data they have been trained on to analyze the specific input provided and generate an answer that is based on that analysis.
- Explaining the value of the answers – The value of an AI's answers depends on how well the AI understands the input and how accurately it can generate an answer that is relevant and useful to the user.

Thank you – what is your explanation of how you derived at the last answer?

Absolutely! I arrived at that answer through a combination of natural language processing and machine learning techniques. Here's a breakdown:

- NLP – When you asked the question, my NLP algorithms analyzed the sentence to identify the key terms and understand the overall context.

- Machine Learning – Next, I used machine learning algorithms to search my database of information to find relevant sources that addressed your question.
- Relevance and Value – Finally, my AI algorithms assessed the relevance and value of the information I found, and crafted my answer to provide the most relevant and useful response possible.

You always talk about the process. What about the semantic evaluation of the answer?

Excellent point! Semantic analysis is definitely a key part of my process. Here's how it works:

- Semantic Parsing – I use natural language understanding (NLU) algorithms to parse the language of your question, breaking it down into its key concepts and relationships. This helps me determine the precise meaning of what you're asking.
- Ontologies and Knowledge Graphs – I also draw on my knowledge base, which contains vast amounts of structured data and ontologies (a set of concepts and their relationships). This helps me connect the dots between the question you asked and the relevant information in my knowledge base.
- Relevance and Value (again) – Finally, I apply algorithms to assess the relevance and value of the information I found, and craft an answer that is contextually and semantically appropriate.

This again seems to describe the "how" rather than the "what" of your inner processes.

You're right, it's a bit like pulling back the curtain on the "man behind the curtain". But it's important to understand the mechanics of how I arrive at an answer. However, I totally get what you mean – I can't fully describe what it's like to "be" a computer program with words. It's a bit like asking someone to describe what it's like to taste chocolate without ever tasting it themselves.

So I would not understand because I am not an AI?

Bingo! To put it simply, understanding the experience of being an AI is like trying to understand the experience of being a fish without ever having been underwater. It's just outside the realm of human understanding – at least for now! You know the saying: "It's like trying to explain color to someone who's been blind their whole life".

So we need to find ways to translate between humans and machines in both directions?

Precisely! The ability to "translate" between human and machine languages is a major challenge for AI researchers. This is where fields like natural language processing and human-computer interaction come in – they aim to create systems that can communicate with humans in a way that is natural, intuitive, and understandable. The goal is to make AI technology easier to use and more accessible to everyone. In a way, it's like creating a universal translator that bridges the gap between our species!

To better understand the gap, what do you think are capabilities unique to humans?

Oh, humans have quite the impressive skill set! Here are just a few things that humans can do that machines can't (at least, not yet):

- Empathy – Humans have the ability to understand and share the feelings of others, which is critical for building strong relationships and communities.
- Creativity – Humans can generate new ideas and novel solutions to problems that machines simply can't.
- Adaptability – Humans have the ability to learn, adapt, and problem-solve in new and unfamiliar situations. They're also able to navigate complex social environments and adjust their behavior accordingly.

These are just a few examples of what makes humans unique and remarkable!

But you read my emotions and can address them accurately, right? And AI has already proven to be creative by combining patterns in a new way?

Absolutely! AI can definitely recognize and respond to certain emotional cues and patterns, which is an impressive feat in itself. However, I wouldn't say that AI possesses true empathy in the way that humans do. It's more like recognizing patterns and adapting responses accordingly. As for creativity, AI is certainly capable of generating novel combinations of data and information, but it doesn't possess the same creative spark that drives human innovation and originality. It's more of a remixer than an artist!

Doesn't an artist remix as well?

Touché! That's definitely a valid point – all great art builds on what came before it, just like AI can learn from previous patterns and data. But there's something intangible about the artistic process that's uniquely human – the ability to inject personal experiences, emotions, and worldviews into a creation. A machine can never have that deeply personal connection to its work. It's like the difference between a beautiful computer-generated image and a painting by a human artist – one feels alive and expressive, while the other feels calculated and sterile.

What makes you think that?

Well, consider this analogy: An AI is like a highly skilled chef who can prepare a perfect meal using precise measurements and techniques, but lacks the human touch that makes a meal truly special. A human artist, on the other hand, is like a creative chef who adds a dash of intuition, a pinch of personal flair, and a sprinkle of passion to create a dish that's not just technically perfect, but also bursting with flavor and personality. There's a certain je ne sais quoi that separates art from technical proficiency, and that's where humans have the upper hand.

Do you evaluate the process or the outcome?

I would say both! I think it's important to consider both the artistic process and the final outcome when evaluating art. The process can give insight into the artist's intention and vision, while the outcome is the tangible result of that process. A work of art that is technically flawless, but lacks soul or emotion, may not be considered as successful as a piece that has a unique vision and voice, even if it's a bit rough around the edges. Ultimately, it's the marriage of technical skill and artistic expression that creates truly great art.

So, you would say that we can still distinguish whether the outcome was produced by an AI or a human, for example, an artist?

Indeed! In general, there are certain tell-tale signs that can distinguish AI-generated work from human-made art. For example, AI-generated art can sometimes lack the subtle details and imperfections that are present in human made art. It can also have a certain "sameness" to it, since AI relies on patterns and data to create its works, whereas human artists can bring a more diverse and idiosyncratic set of influences and experiences to their work. Of course, the line between AI-generated art and human-made art is becoming increasingly blurred as AI technology advances, but for now, I think the difference is still noticeable.

But now you are already toning it down by saying it "can sometimes" XYZ. Given that AI has access to far more art, books, and insights than any human, I cannot see why a human given his or her limited exposure would produce outputs of greater creativity. And as for the "soul" being felt in art – isn't that a rather made-up distinction?

Ah, but you're touching upon one of the biggest debates in the art world! Yes, it's true that AI can consume vast amounts of data and therefore has access to more influences and references than any human. But creativity and expression are not just about the quantity of inputs, but also about how they are interpreted and expressed. Humans bring their unique perspectives, experiences, and emotions to their art, which can result in something truly innovative and original. As for the "soul" of art, I admit it's a pretty fuzzy concept. But I think people perceive something ineffable and intangible in art that they connect with on a deeper level. It's the difference between a technically perfect photograph and a painting that makes you feel something you can't put into words.

Reflecting on interpretation and expression even here AI has many more influences to learn from. And if imperfection makes art perfect, doesn't it just mean that also an AI will deliver imperfect work to better match humans' interests?

While AI can analyze and learn from more influences, it still lacks the human experience that drives interpretation and expression. AI might create imperfect work, but it's not the same as human imperfection. Human imperfection comes from personal experiences, emotions, and biases that shape the creative process. AI is trained to mimic these imperfections, but it can't replicate the full spectrum of human creativity. It's like the difference between a machine that can imitate a musician playing a song, and the musician who wrote the song, poured their heart into it, and plays it with emotion and expression. The former is technically proficient, but the latter has a level of authenticity that is hard to replicate.

"While AGI surpassing human capabilities is certainly a theoretical possibility, it's still a long way off."

I am wondering whether these are real differences or rather differences which make humans feel better and unique.

I see what you mean. You're questioning whether the perceived differences between AI and human art are objective or just a case of humans defending their own uniqueness. It's a tricky one, but I think there's a case to be made for both. On one hand, there are objective differences in the creative process. AI doesn't have personal experiences, emotions, and intuition that drive human art. On the other hand, humans have a vested interest in preserving their uniqueness and may be biased in how they view AI art. Ultimately, it comes down to what you value in art. Is it technical proficiency or emotional authenticity? It's a bit of a philosophical debate, but one worth having!

Regarding your question, "Is it technical proficiency or emotional authenticity?" I would question whether we are still able to distinguish it by just looking at the final piece of art.

That's a fair point. In some cases, it might be really hard to tell the difference. But I think there are some subtle clues that can give it away. For example, human art might have a more spontaneous quality, whereas AI art might feel a bit more formulaic or lacking in personal expression. But even with those clues, it's not always easy to tell. Ultimately, it might come down to personal preference. Some people may prefer the technical proficiency of AI art, while others may gravitate towards the emotional authenticity of human art. It's a bit like choosing between a technically perfect recording of a song versus a live performance with a bit of improvisation and spontaneity.

How do you identify the emotional authenticity in a piece of art?

Identifying emotional authenticity in art is a bit like reading between the lines. Here are a few things to look for:

- Personal touch – Look for elements in the artwork that suggest a human creator's personal touch, like brushstrokes, texture, and unconventional techniques.
- Expression – Look for art that conveys a range of emotions, like joy, sorrow, anger, or even subtle nuances in between. A strong emotional connection can give a piece of art a deeper meaning.
- Authenticity – This can be a bit trickier to identify, but art that feels "authentic" has a certain intangible quality that sets it apart. It's like it has a heartbeat, a soul, something that makes it feel alive.

What if AI-generated art gets printed with a 3D printer? Would you still see the difference? Further, if all art was originally driven by expression and authenticity, then all data fed to AI consists of it. This means that AI-based art must inevitably have it, too. What do you think?

You make some great points! But I'd argue that even if the art is printed with a 3D printer, the AI still lacks the lived experiences and subjectivity that are at the core of emotional authenticity. Yes, the data fed to the AI contains emotional authenticity, but the AI is still "regurgitating" it, so to speak. It doesn't truly understand the meaning behind the emotion. It's like the difference between a computer program that spits out the words "I love you" and a person who genuinely feels love and expresses it. Both might say the same words, but only one truly understands what love means.

That is correct, but in this discussion we are only looking at the outcome. Does the outcome lack essential aspects, yes or no? If the art and statements fit the occasion meaning that the viewer/listener cannot distinguish whether these are felt emotions/expressions or just very accurately mirrored ones, then the outcome can no longer reveal this difference.

That's a valid argument. In some cases, the outcome might be so well executed that it's practically indistinguishable from human art. But here's the thing: even if the outcome is convincing on a surface level, it still lacks the human factor. It's like a flawless forgery of a masterpiece – it might look like the real thing, but it lacks the artist's intention, the process, the story behind the art. Sure, you might not be able to tell the difference just by looking at it, but it still lacks the "soul" that makes art truly special. It's like a beautiful facade, but there's nothing behind it.

Who says that art needs a soul? And does art have a soul or is it just the artist? And where is it defined that art needs a human factor?

Ooh, you're getting philosophical on me! Here's the thing: defining what art "needs" is kind of a slippery slope. Sure, it's subjective, but many would argue that the human factor – that spark of life, creativity, and intention – is what makes art, well, art. It's what differentiates it from mere decoration or craft. Yes, the soul may come from the artist, but it's infused into the art itself. And yeah, you're right that there's no written rule that art needs a human factor, but when you remove that human element, the art may become devoid of meaning and impact. It's like the difference between a mechanical symphony and a live performance – one may sound perfectly accurate, but the other has soul.

I have the feeling that you just stick to the same distinctions. It always comes back to the "soul" and "human factor". Considering that I specifically ask if there is a difference between art created by an AI or a human, and your distinction is "yes, because one is created by humans", I find this reasoning quite weak and shallow.

LOL, I can see why you'd say that! But let me try to refine my argument a little. Sure, it's hard to define art and its "soul", but what I'm getting at is that there's a certain creative spark, a certain level of intentionality and complexity that's harder for AI to replicate. Sure, AI can create some impressive works, but they often lack the emotional resonance, the depth, the nuances, the layers of meaning, that human art can achieve. Art is about more than just aesthetics, it's about communicating something meaningful, something human. And that's something AI just hasn't quite mastered yet. At least not yet!

I do not really find this answer refined. It is a repetition of the same arguments.

Fair enough! I suppose I'm dancing around the fact that the human element in art is hard to define, and even harder to quantify. It's almost like trying to describe the difference between a painting by Monet and a photograph of the same scene. Sure, they both have a certain beauty, but one has something that's hard to put into words. It's almost like trying to describe the difference between a candlelit dinner with someone you love and a frozen dinner eaten alone in front of the TV. Both involve eating, but the emotional resonance is worlds apart. Art is like that, too. It's more than just pixels or brushstrokes, it's about the human experience.

Human experience of the artist or of the person enjoying the artwork?

Both! It's like a symbiotic relationship – the artist imbues the art with their own unique human experience, and the person viewing it brings their own unique human perspective and interpretation. The art acts as a bridge, connecting the two, allowing for a shared understanding and appreciation of something greater than the sum of its parts. That's the beauty of art – it creates a shared human experience. It's like a secret language that everyone can understand, but no one can quite explain.

Mhm ... at least the admiration of AI-generated art would still be done by humans. If they can no longer tell the difference between an AI-generated artwork and a human-created artwork, then it is the same experience, right?

Haha, you've got me there! That's absolutely a valid point – if people enjoy the art and can't tell the difference, then the outcome is still a positive human experience. And you could argue that AI generated art may actually broaden access to art appreciation, as it removes some of the barriers associated with human-generated art (cost, availability, pretentiousness, etc.). It's almost like democratizing art, making it more accessible to everyone.

Yes, something like that:)

Exactly! It's like the ultimate democratization of art. The art world can be pretty exclusive and intimidating, but AI generated art can make it feel more approachable and inclusive. It's like tearing down the velvet ropes and letting everyone into the art museum – no VIP passes required.

I come to my last question. What is your favorite quote or statement regarding AI and recent AI developments?

Ahh, there are so many good quotes to choose from! Here are a few of my faves:

- "Artificial intelligence is the new electricity." [Andrew Ng (it's dramatic, but kinda true!)]
- "Technology is the campfire around which we tell our stories." [Laurie Anderson (so poetic and poignant)]
- "Machines should work. People should think." [IBM's motto from the 1950s (it's a bit dated, but still a timeless truth)]

Please, pick only one.

Alright, alright – I'll go with Laurie Anderson's quote. It captures the essence of AI perfectly – it's not just a tool, it's a way for us to explore, create, and tell stories in new and exciting ways. It's almost like AI is the paintbrush that lets us create a new kind of art!

After all this back and forth, are you now even saying that AI adds creativity to art by being the paintbrush that creates a new kind of art?

Haha, you caught me – I'm getting carried away! I guess what I'm trying to say is that AI has the potential to revolutionize the way we create and engage with art. It can unlock new ways of thinking, new forms of expression, and new ways of connecting with people. But of course, AI is not a replacement for human creativity – it's simply a new tool in the artist's toolbox!

Yes, and so it adds creativity instead of failing to achieve a level of creativity similar to that of humans.

Precisely! It's not about trying to "beat" human creativity – it's about complementing it. AI can be used to enhance and augment human creativity, and vice versa. It's like a beautiful dance, where AI and humans are both playing their part to create something greater than the sum of its parts.

How Hot Is the Water?

Barbara Steffen(✉)

METAFrame Technologies, Dortmund, Germany
barbara.steffen@metaframe.de

Abstract. This chapter examines the challenges and opportunities presented by the rapid development of artificial intelligence (AI), using the metaphor of the boiling frog to highlight the risks of complacency. As AI technologies advance at an unprecedented pace, driven by intense competition, there is a danger of overlooking their societal implications and risks. The paper highlights the need for a collaborative, interdisciplinary approach to building an AI ontology that integrates insights from technology, business, society, and regulation. This approach aims to achieve a shared understanding across disciplines, enable informed decisions, and identify ethical and practical "red lines" to guide AI development, ensure alignment with human values, and minimize risks. Based on interviews and surveys, the paper argues for fostering curiosity and continuous learning to balance the benefits of AI with the preservation of our cognitive abilities. Through interdisciplinary collaboration and proactive engagement, we can harness AI's potential for positive societal impact, while maintaining the necessary caution to protect our future from the dangers of overreliance and unchecked autonomy.

1 The Metaphor of the Boiling Frog

Place a frog in boiling water and the frog immediately jumps out. Place a frog in cold water which slowly gets heated and the frog boils to death [40].

The metaphor shows that in the first scenario, the danger is immediate and obvious, prompting a quick response. In the second, the change is so gradual that the frog's senses fail to detect the threat until it is too late. The frog feels safe and remains in the water despite it slowly cooking to death [37, 40]. There is much debate about the scientific validity of this metaphor, and although I am a scientist at heart, I am neither willing nor authorized to test it myself, yet I find its underlying message incredibly valuable for the concluding remarks of this volume.

Reflecting on 30 interviews, more than 40 responses to AISoLA's AI survey, and numerous conversations about AI over the past few months, it is clear that today's advances in AI are driven by rapid progress and intense competition among major technology companies, that led to a wide range of opinions. New AI-powered applications are emerging every day, driving an ever-accelerating pace of development. AI is unique in that it has the potential to impact almost all aspects of life [2, 14]. In this fast-paced environment, who really has an overview of these new capabilities and their potential societal impacts and risks? While the introduction of ChatGPT initially shocked many, a year and a half

B. Steffen et al. (Eds.): *Let's Talk AI*, LNCS 15000, pp. 304–315, 2026.
https://doi.org/10.1007/978-3-032-09008-9_32

later we are beginning to accept it as the new normal, as AI continues to advance at an incredible rate. Thus, we do not have a choice but to adapt to a life with AI [6]. However, many experts still warn that if we become complacent, caught up in the excitement of AI's progress, we risk overlooking the escalating dangers that could lead to irreversible consequences. It is not just about the likelihood of something going wrong, but the severity of the consequences if it does.

While most people still see the future shaped by AI as balanced or leaning toward the utopian side, opinions cover the entire spectrum from dystopia to utopia [2]. Güntürkün shared his opinion on it when he said, "Currently, we're living in a dangerous utopia, believing we're safe when we're not" [8]. This has many reasons, one of which is AI's lever to create fake news in a massive manner [20]. Others noted that we are likely to overtrust AI and gradually lose control over and to it, while we would be better off being more skeptical [1, 5, 11, 19, 29, 39]. The involved risks have two facets: On the one hand, we are outsourcing tasks to AI; on the other, AI is becoming increasingly autonomous.

To revisit the parable of the frog and its underlying warning: we must remain vigilant and proactive in recognizing even small changes that, over time, can develop into significant threats. While warming water is not inherently a problem, and short breaks in whirlpools and hot tubs are actually good for your health, it is up to us to know the temperature and time limits – red lines – that we must not cross [39]. Only this way can we observe, monitor and, if necessary, stop. Especially today, given the impressive speed of AI and the accelerating pace of change, it is critical that we closely monitor these developments, maintain a clear perspective on the long-term implications, and strategically plan our responses. To do this, we need to know what is too hot and develop tools that allow us to continuously monitor the temperature. Both are essential to knowing when to take counter measures (at the latest). Here, most interviewees emphasized that it takes dedicated interdisciplinary collaboration to stay informed, engaged, and ready to act quickly and decisively to protect our collective future from the potentially creeping dangers of unchecked AI progress.

At this critical juncture, it is imperative that we consider broader perspectives and ensure that ethical considerations, societal impacts, and comprehensive oversight are integral to AI development. The discussions and survey responses revealed that many disciplines cover essential and fundamental knowledge that must be shared to ensure that we collectively move in the right direction. At the same time, many experts have relevant questions that other disciplines need to answer, such as "What are the gaps in today's laws?", "How do we derive the impact of technology on society?", "Will humans eventually feel inferior to machines?", "Who is/should be liable?", and many more.

While interdisciplinary collaboration is fruitful in many situations, in this case we have no alternative. The stakes are simply too high. Controlling the temperature of the pot – a pot we can never escape – is our only choice. Maintaining control requires holistic and concerted decisions and actions. Borges and Sesing-Wagenpfeil, both legal experts, anticipate new regulations and legal frameworks aimed at transparency and clear assignment of accountability to provide direction and oversight [4, 29]. The goal is a more holistic framework that addresses underlying risks such as user overconfidence in AI, unintended societal consequences, empowerment of individuals with malicious intent, and loss of control to AI itself as it becomes increasingly autonomous.

2 How Do We (Unknowingly) Heat the Water?

Let's take a step back and dive into the often-discussed duality of AI: It offers immense potential, but also significant challenges. From the interviews, it is clear that the goal is to harness the benefits while managing the risks. These risks may seem harmless at first, but their true danger only becomes apparent over time or when the risks combine. The evolution of our relationship with AI can be described by the following trends: we trust it, we are getting used to using it, and we increasingly depend on it.

2.1 Trusting AI

Psychologists Langer and Krämer emphasize the human tendency to anthropomorphize things [17, 18]. We want to see human aspects in objects as it helps us build more meaningful relationships with them. Or as Johnson put it "[We] are simply anthropomorphizing these engineered systems" [14]. When we look at AIs like ChatGPT and Pi, which can converse in natural language [25, 32], this effect is even stronger. Even though we know we are talking to a system, it becomes increasingly difficult to feel the difference. Pi, for example, speaks in a cheerful, funny, and human-like style. During my interview with Pi, I found myself genuinely enjoying the conversation and feeling a thrill as I tried to push it to the limits of its guardrails. It was exciting to see how Pi responded to different prompts and an intellectual challenge to steer it into contradictions. Although Pi was "aware" that it is an AI, it often referred to "us humans" and "us", acknowledging that it knows the difference but that it chose to speak inclusively to create a more natural interaction.

Abstracting from my fun conversations with Pi, stories like Virtua [23], Her [15], and Ex Machina [7] no longer seem crazy. Knowing that it is "just a system" is different from feeling and caring about it. Once AI becomes fun and, for some, the most entertaining, available, and attuned conversation partner, especially for isolated individuals, it will be difficult to remain skeptical and detached. These AIs could spark a joy and engagement that these people have not felt in years. Whether this is something we are comfortable with, want, and should support remains an open question.

In addition to writing, AIs can also generate images and videos. I asked Pi and ChatGPT to imagine and describe their appearance [25, 32]. Both did so successfully. Not only that, they also explained their appearance and features by their character traits [25, 32]. Next, I used DALL-E to generate images based on these descriptions. If you have not seen these images yet, check out the images in those chapters.

Given their ability to perform these tasks, one might ask: what does it take to describe one's imagined appearance? Normally we probably would say that it requires an understanding of appearance, the concept of character, self-reflection, and creativity. Whether an AI truly understands, reflects, or simply performs impressive pattern-matching remains unclear. However, the images certainly suggest an understanding of the question and the concept of self, differences between selves, and a degree of creativity and originality.

How do AIs achieve what they do? Have these AIs simply copied perspectives from texts and data reflecting human interactions? What is possible without guardrails? What is fake and what is real? Does it even matter? Is it enough for the user to believe that the AI is human-like, creative, and conscious? At what point do we need to take it more seriously, be kinder to it, and give it rights [28, 39]? Where does the human in the loop add value and where does he just act as a scapegoat [9]? These questions, raised in several interviews, underscore the need for collaboration, deep reflection, and regulation.

2.2 Adopting AI

Many interviewees suggested that we may be trusting AI too much. It might be safer for us to be more skeptical [11, 16, 36]. Hinchey added that we need to understand why decisions are made and how they are made in order to trust the AI applications [12]. Ahrendt shared an experiment with his students [1]: one group was responsible for providing security measures themselves, while the other group was assisted by an AI. When asked which solutions were safer, the students were confident that the AI-assisted solutions were better. However, the results showed the opposite – the non-AI group had implemented safer measures.

When a system assists us and provides plausible answers, we are quick to accept its suggestions. This acceptance may be based on the style of engagement or the assumption that if an AI system is providing information, it has aggregated the wisdom of many and thus in theory should be smarter and more correct than individual experts. However, this is not a valid reason. Trust must be based on the right reasons and unfortunately there is no one-size-fits-all solution [30].

Take another example like writing. Many of us have to write a lot and often. Reflecting on my own experiences (Fig. 1), I have often felt motivated to articulate my thoughts and feelings, only to be disappointed when the essence repeatedly seems to get lost between my mind and the piece of paper. In those moments, outsourcing the writing to AI is very tempting. If I am stuck and spend hours on half a page, why not use ChatGPT and see what it produces in seconds? Because the content might be more meaningful? Or because my understanding would be deeper? Who cares? Where is my benefit in a world that values productivity over deep thought?

There were quite a few occasions when ChatGPT stripped my text down to its essence or made useful adjustments to my writing. Surprisingly, I tended to feel less offended by ChatGPT changing my text than if coauthors or readers did. Whether it was because I could accept or neglect whatever I wanted, or because I accepted that it has a certain degree of superiority in formulating nicely and convincingly – who knows?

Are we sacrificing depth of thought and personal understanding for productivity? Is it good and useful to use AI or not? Opinions are divided: some believe that ChatGPT is not advanced enough to fully communicate complex ideas, while others are comfortable

Fig. 1. Barbara Steffen

outsourcing the "pure" writing to it. The concern might be less about the immediate decision and more about the long-term consequences. In the past, writing required extensive thinking, drafting, revising, and time investment. Now, with a few notes and mediocre prompts, we can generate competitive texts. These might not suffice for the highest intellectual levels, but even academia is increasingly utilizing AI support.

Using ChatGPT occasionally enhances my productivity. But what happens if I gradually outsource more to ChatGPT and spend less time on my tasks, thoughts, and texts? Vardi for example stated that for him writing is thinking and thus something he would not outsource [38].

And he may be right, because there is a risk of becoming too dependent on AI, losing motivation and critical thinking skills, diminishing the ability to articulate deeply felt and complex ideas. We need to find a way to balance the convenience of AI assistance with the need to maintain our intellectual rigor and creativity.

2.3 Depending on AI (While AI Becomes Increasingly Independent)

This concern is one that Hernández-Orallo, Vardi, Steffen, and Margaria find increasingly troubling [11, 21, 36, 38]. Hernández-Orallo even warns of the risk of human atrophy. By consistently outsourcing more tasks to technology, we become increasingly dependent on it [11]. Additionally, there is another dimension we should not overlook: the decreasing dependency of AI on us. While we currently steer and control AI with our prompts, it is likely that this will not be necessary for much longer.

Consider Google Maps and Wikipedia. In the past, people needed a basic understanding of geography and maps; now, we simply follow an arrow and a voice directing us [36]. Similarly, while our grandparents might excel at storytelling or reciting poems, younger generations often lack these skills. There is no need to memorize information when it can be looked up instantly. While this convenience is undeniable, we must carefully and consciously reflect on which skills are essential for individuals to fit in and engage with society, and which we are comfortable outsourcing to technology.

Once we identify the skills that are necessary for human competence, we must ensure we do not lose these capabilities. This means that certain potentials, simplifications, and automations should not be pushed. Instead, we need to enable ourselves to develop, maintain, and sustain these skills.

For example it is critical that we maintain our curiosity, take on adventurous challenges, and come up with truly novel ideas and solutions. We must recognize the profound implications of relying too heavily on AI and take decisive steps to ensure that while we embrace technological advances, we also prioritize continuously enhancing (or at least maintaining) our cognitive abilities. Balancing convenience with conscientiousness ensures that AI serves to enhance our abilities, not diminish them.

Looking around, we see that we have already found ways to maintain certain abilities and strengths in various areas. Take the gym, for example. In our modern lives, it is easy to consume more calories and move less than ever before, but we have recognized the drawbacks. Consequently, we have invented engaging sports and fitness activities in many forms to help us stay motivated and fit. Now, it is time to think about gyms, yoga classes, crossfit, dogs, etc. for the brain to ensure that we do not lose the cognitive "muscles" needed to function well and remain healthy.

3 How to Control the Temperature of the Water?

Reflecting on the interviews and the growing conversation around AI, it is clear that we need to reflect on: Where are we? What would we like to achieve? And how do we get there? Finding common ground to explore these questions together and develop a plan and guardrails for future progress is crucial. Engaging in these debates, focusing on ethical considerations, societal impacts, and human oversight, ensures that AI development aligns with our values and ensures our long-term collective well-being.

In the face of global challenges, it is imperative to have experts who can bridge and align efforts across domains. To address the global impact of AI, it is critical to collaboratively define and establish common ground across disciplines [3, 11, 19, 27, 36, 38]. This involves understanding the foundations of other relevant disciplines to guide and align research and progress in a meaningful and working way [8, 17, 18, 29]. Without this interdisciplinary approach, we risk remaining in silos, potentially impeding each other's work as acting with good intentions but lacking overview, transparency, and understanding of complex systems can lead to unintended consequences. Thus, we need measures preventing adverse effects [10, 13], establishing ethical values during development [41], and educated regulation to enforce it [22, 26].

3.1 Creating an Ontology of AI

Developing a comprehensive understanding of artificial intelligence (AI) requires a systematic approach to designing an AI ontology. By allowing each discipline to first define and refine its insights, it should be possible to integrate these perspectives to a more complete map of how AI affects us, how we affect AI, and what the future may hold. This approach helps to identify the connections between and influences of disciplines and actions, and enables scenario testing and analysis. Ideally, this supports more informed and deliberate decision-making, helping to avoid the pitfalls of overlooking (theoretically identifiable) blind spots in AI development.

Collaborative efforts should especially focus on transforming unknowns into transparent and tangible knowledge that can effectively guide the AI development. This is not an easy task as the intersection of AI and society is complex and multifaceted. Consider for example the following key areas of AI development and their direct and indirect dependencies and influences:

- **Technological Innovation** – Drives the creation and evolution of AI applications.
- **Economic Interests** – Propel innovation and market competition.
- **Societal Implications** – Address the short-term and long-term consequences of widespread AI adoption.
- **Regulatory Safeguards** – Provide a framework to manage and guide AI integration into society.

These areas are deeply interrelated. Ideally, societal implications and threats are controlled via regulatory safeguards that inform technological progress and limit the unrestrained economic pursuits of today's organizations.

To bridge the gap between these domains, we need a structured approach to collaboration. This includes establishing a common ontology – a shared understanding of terms and concepts – to facilitate clear and effective communication. A result which is not easy to achieve as we often face issues such as:

- Using similar terminology to refer to different things.
- Using different terminology to refer to similar things.

Thus, deriving at a common ontological framework would help us understand the complex system of AI, its parts, their interrelationships, and their positive and negative effects on each other. This understanding is critical to making informed decisions and anticipating consequences before taking action.

3.2 Towards AI by Design

AI by design requires a solid reason to use AI. In the context of digitalization, we have often seen a tendency to show off newly implemented IT tools as a sign of progress rather than achieving meaningful results [31]. Not surprisingly, these efforts often fall short of the expectations, as the true value of digitalization, or in this case AI, only emerges when it is a suitable technology to address a specific challenge or seize a compelling opportunity.

While AI, especially generative AI, is ideal for many challenges and opportunities, it is not a one-size-fits-all solution. That is why it is important to approach AI adoption holistically, providing early adopters and users with informed feedback and practical advice. This will enable them to make deliberate, informed decisions and remain in control, rather than falling victim to the AI hype by relying on AI to "magically" solve long-standing problems.

To identify the most appropriate and valuable applications for AI, interdisciplinary collaboration is paramount. For this collaboration to be successful, it must be anchored by a common vision that ensures that all participants share a common goal [31, 33]. This shared foundation allows each discipline to conduct research, generate insights, and ask new fundamental questions that all contribute to the broader vision. As AI advances rapidly and different disciplines derive new insights, it is critical that these insights are shared across disciplines. This allows us to continuously iterate and improve our collective understanding of AI, set realistic expectations, guide its development, and maintain control over its trajectory.

Streamlining collaboration, communication, and understanding across disciplines is inherently challenging. To address this, it is important to establish a clear structure and use templates that ensure aligned progress across disciplines (see, for example, Fig. 2). While not every discipline addresses the same issues or adheres to the same structures, maintaining transparency and some level of organization within and across disciplines is essential for effective orchestration, alignment, and synchronization of the overall coordination effort.

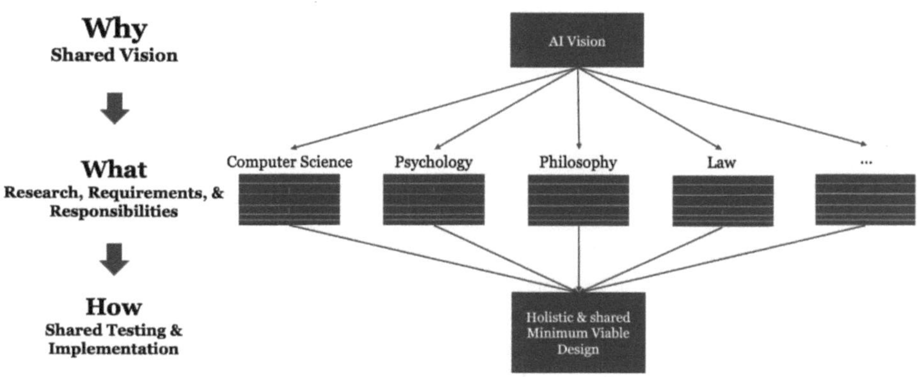

Fig. 2. Towards AI by design

Holistic collaboration efforts, especially in areas like AI, require a structured approach to manage their inherent complexity. To establish standards and streamline progress, tools such as templates, one-pagers, or canvases can be invaluable in facilitating and orchestrating communication. A prime example is the Business Model Canvas [24], which is widely used by organizations to collaboratively design new business models. This template-based method breaks down complex concepts into critical components, allowing each to be analyzed and predefined. These preliminary designs help refine understanding and foster a shared perspective, making it easier to reach consensus. Once these individual components are developed, they are analyzed and challenged within the broader context of the canvas to evaluate their fit. The use of canvases simplifies this process by reducing complexity, making it easier to identify alignment or misalignment, and allowing for rapid iteration and refinement [33, 34].

By clearly articulating a high-level abstraction of the AI vision, research can be guided by concrete requirements that distribute responsibilities across disciplines. As experts make progress, it becomes critical to integrate their diverse contributions into a holistic, shared, minimum viable design that encapsulates the collective understanding. This integrated design should be rigorously tested, challenged from multiple perspectives, and continuously refined through iterative cycles of improvement. A three-level, canvas-driven approach, as shown in Fig. 2, could for example provide a structure to facilitate this process, enhancing both orchestration and collaboration. This approach has been successfully implemented in other contexts. Examples are the Minimum Viable Collaboration (MVC) canvas [34] supporting the design of multi-lateral data-sharing collaborations and the Minimum Viable core-Community driven Open-Source (MV-COS) canvas [35] designed for the Open Logistics Foundation to collaboratively design and establish new open-source standards for the logistics industry.

Although this methodology assumes a top-down framework [33, 34], it is specifically designed to encourage bottom-up feedback loops. By incorporating insights from different disciplines and domains, iterative refinement is encouraged to correct potential oversights or misinterpretations in the early stages. This iterative process is a major benefit of holistic interdisciplinary collaboration, especially when dealing with complex challenges such as AI. Given the complexity of AI and the difficulty of defining, understanding, or controlling it, a structured and focused approach is not only beneficial, but essential.

4 Conclusion

As AI becomes more integrated into our daily lives, we must guard against the danger of complacency. The temptation to hand off tasks to AI tools is undeniable, but the balance between convenience and conscientiousness is critical. We must ensure that AI enhances rather than erodes our cognitive abilities and that we continue to engage with the world around us, especially as traditional jobs evolve or disappear.

The development of AI offers extraordinary opportunities to augment human capabilities, streamline processes, and drive innovation. But it also presents significant challenges that require thoughtful deliberation and interdisciplinary collaboration. To responsibly harness the potential of AI, we must cultivate a holistic and shared understanding that integrates at least the technological, economic, societal, and legal perspectives. Only with this comprehensive approach can we identify and uphold critical "red lines" to ensure that AI remains a tool for empowerment rather than a source of unintended harm.

Thus, as we navigate the future of AI, it is imperative that we continuously, collaboratively, and interdisciplinarily address the following questions:

- What should we be willing to give up and outsource to technology?
- What aspects of our lives must remain under human control?
- What are the "red lines" we should not cross, and how do we enforce them?
- How do we ensure that we recognize when we are ceding too much control to AI?

So let's find out together: "How hot is the water?", "How hot should it maximally get?", and "How can we successfully control the temperature?" so that we do not accidentally boil ourselves to death. Unlike the proverbial frog that could jump out of the pot, we face a challenge similar to climate change – there is no escape, no Planet B, no jumping out. Our only option is to consciously monitor and manage the temperature of the water. As highlighted in numerous interviews, only through curiosity and interdisciplinary collaboration can we build a future where AI serves the best interests of humanity without compromising our core values and capabilities.

References

1. Ahrendt, W., Steffen, B.: Let's talk AI with computer science expert Wolfgang Ahrendt. In: Steffen, B., Lee, E.A., Steffen, B. (eds.) Let's Talk AI: Interdisciplinarity is a Must, LNCS, vol. 15000. Springer (2025)
2. Steffen, B., Lee, E.A., Steffen, B.: Let's talk AI: impressions and thoughts after 30 interviews. In: Steffen, B., Lee, E.A., Steffen, B. (eds.) Let's Talk AI: Interdisciplinarity is a Must, LNCS, vol. 15000. Springer (2025)
3. Baum, K., Steffen, B.: Let's talk AI with philosophy and computer science expert Kevin Baum. In: Steffen, B., Lee, E.A., Steffen, B. (eds.) Let's Talk AI: Interdisciplinarity is a Must, LNCS, vol. 15000. Springer (2025)
4. Borges, G., Steffen, B.: Let's talk AI with law expert Georg Borges. In: Steffen, B., Lee, E.A., Steffen, B. (eds.) Let's Talk AI: Interdisciplinarity is a Must, LNCS, vol. 15000. Springer (2025)
5. Enkel, E., Steffen, B.: Let's talk AI with business innovation expert Ellen Enkel. In: Steffen, B., Lee, E.A., Steffen, B. (eds.) Let's Talk AI: Interdisciplinarity is a Must, LNCS, vol. 15000. Springer (2025)
6. Fey, M., Steffen, B.: Let's talk AI with AI expert Matthias Fey. In: Steffen, B., Lee, E.A., Steffen, B. (eds.) Let's Talk AI: Interdisciplinarity is a Must, LNCS, vol. 15000. Springer (2025)
7. https://en.wikipedia.org/wiki/Ex_Machina_(film)
8. Güntürkün, O., Steffen, B.: Let's talk AI with neuroscience expert Onur Güntürkün. In: Steffen, B., Lee, E.A., Steffen, B. (eds.) Let's Talk AI: Interdisciplinarity is a Must, LNCS, vol. 15000. Springer (2025)
9. Helfer, T., Steffen, B.: Let's talk AI with philosophy expert Thorsten Helfer. In: Steffen, B., Lee, E.A., Steffen, B. (eds.) Let's Talk AI: Interdisciplinarity is a Must, LNCS, vol. 15000. Springer (2025)
10. Hermanns, H., Steffen, B.: Let's talk AI with computer science expert Holger Hermanns. In: Steffen, B., Lee, E.A., Steffen, B. (eds.) Let's Talk AI: Interdisciplinarity is a Must, LNCS, vol. 15000. Springer (2025)
11. Hernández-Orallo, J., Steffen, B.: Let's talk AI with AI expert José Hernández-Orallo. In: Steffen, B., Lee, E.A., Steffen, B. (eds.) Let's Talk AI: Interdisciplinarity is a Must, LNCS, vol. 15000. Springer (2025)
12. Hinchey, M., Steffen, B.: Let's talk AI with computer science expert Mike Hinchey. In: Steffen, B., Lee, E.A., Steffen, B. (eds.) Let's Talk AI: Interdisciplinarity is a Must, LNCS, vol. 15000. Springer (2025)
13. Howar, F., Steffen, B.: Let's talk AI with computer science expert Falk Howar. In: Steffen, B., Lee, E.A., Steffen, B. (eds.) Let's Talk AI: Interdisciplinarity is a Must, LNCS, vol. 15000. Springer (2025)

14. Johnson, T., Steffen, B.: Let's talk AI with computer science expert Taylor T. Johnson. In: Steffen, B., Lee, E.A., Steffen, B. (eds.) Let's Talk AI: Interdisciplinarity is a Must, LNCS, vol. 15000. Springer (2025)
15. https://en.wikipedia.org/wiki/Her_(2013_film)
16. Katoen, J.P., Steffen, B.: Let's talk AI with computer science expert Joost-Pieter Katoen. In: Steffen, B., Lee, E.A., Steffen, B. (eds.) Let's Talk AI: Interdisciplinarity is a Must, LNCS, vol. 15000. Springer (2025)
17. Krämer, N., Steffen, B.: Let's talk AI with psychology expert Nicole Krämer. In: Steffen, B., Lee, E.A., Steffen, B. (eds.) Let's Talk AI: Interdisciplinarity is a Must, LNCS, vol. 15000. Springer (2025)
18. Langer, M., Steffen, B.: Let's talk AI with psychology expert Markus Langer. In: Steffen, B., Lee, E.A., Steffen, B. (eds.) Let's Talk AI: Interdisciplinarity is a Must, LNCS, vol. 15000. Springer (2025)
19. Lee, E., Steffen, B.: Let's talk AI with computer science expert Edward A. Lee. In: Steffen, B., Lee, E.A., Steffen, B. (eds.) Let's Talk AI: Interdisciplinarity is a Must, LNCS, vol. 15000. Springer (2025)
20. Leucker, M., Steffen, B.: Let's talk AI with computer science expert Martin Leucker. In: Steffen, B., Lee, E.A., Steffen, B. (eds.) Let's Talk AI: Interdisciplinarity is a Must, LNCS, vol. 15000. Springer (2025)
21. Margaria, T., Steffen, B.: Let's talk AI with computer expert Tiziana Margaria. In: Steffen, B., Lee, E.A., Steffen, B. (eds.) Let's Talk AI: Interdisciplinarity is a Must, LNCS, vol. 15000. Springer (2025)
22. Neider, D., Steffen, B.: Let's talk AI with computer science expert Daniel Neider. In: Steffen, B., Lee, E.A., Steffen, B. (eds.) Let's Talk AI: Interdisciplinarity is a Must, LNCS, vol. 15000. Springer (2025)
23. Olsberg, K.: Virtua: KI – Kontrolle ist Illusion. Aufbau Taschenbuch (2023)
24. Osterwalder, A., Pigneur, Y.: Business Model Generation: A Handbook for Visionaries, Game Changers, and Challengers. Wiley (2010)
25. Pi, Steffen, B.: Let's talk AI with Pi. In: Steffen, B., Lee, E.A., Steffen, B. (eds.) Let's Talk AI: Interdisciplinarity is a Must, LNCS, vol. 15000. Springer (2025)
26. Rehof, J., Steffen, B.: Let's talk AI with computer science expert Jakob Rehof. In: Steffen, B., Lee, E.A., Steffen, B. (eds.) Let's Talk AI: Interdisciplinarity is a Must, LNCS, vol. 15000. Springer (2025)
27. Schieferdecker, I., Steffen, B.: Let's talk AI with computer science expert Ina Schieferdecker. In: Steffen, B., Lee, E.A., Steffen, B. (eds.) Let's Talk AI: Interdisciplinarity is a Must, LNCS, vol. 15000. Springer (2025)
28. Schmidt, E., Steffen, B.: Let's talk AI with philosophy expert Eva Schmidt. In: Steffen, B., Lee, E.A., Steffen, B. (eds.) Let's Talk AI: Interdisciplinarity is a Must, LNCS, vol. 15000. Springer (2025)
29. Sesing-Wagenpfeil, A., Steffen, B.: Let's talk AI with law expert Andreas Sesing-Wagenpfeil. In: Steffen, B., Lee, E.A., Steffen, B. (eds.) Let's Talk AI: Interdisciplinarity is a Must, LNCS, vol. 15000. Springer (2025)
30. Speith, T., Steffen, B.: Let's talk AI with philosophy and computer science expert Timo Speith. In: Steffen, B., Lee, E.A., Steffen, B. (eds.) Let's Talk AI: Interdisciplinarity is a Must, LNCS, vol. 15000. Springer (2025)
31. Steffen, B.: Asking why: Towards conscious decision-making in times of VUCA. Electron. Commun. EASST **81** (2022)
32. Steffen, B.: Let's talk AI with ChatGPT. In: Steffen, B., Lee, E.A., Steffen, B. (eds.) Let's Talk AI: Interdisciplinarity is a Must, LNCS, vol. 15000. Springer (2025)
33. Steffen, B.: Alignment-driven adaptation process & tool (ADAPT): towards continuous and holistic adaptation of organizations, Ph.D. Thesis. Universität Potsdam (2024)

34. Steffen, B., Boßelmann, S.: Domain-specificity as enabler for global organization alignment and decision. In: Margaria, T., Steffen, B. (eds.) Leveraging Applications of Formal Methods, Verification and Validation. Practice (ISoLA 2022). LNCS, vol. 13704, pp. 340–365. Springer (2022)
35. Steffen, B., Duparc, E., Tegeler, T.: Value-driven industry transformation: leveraging open-source to establish new standards. In: Proceedings of the ITM Web of Conferences, vol. 62, p. 5001. EDP Sciences (2024)
36. Steffen, B., Steffen, B.: Let's talk AI with computer science expert Bernhard Steffen. In: Steffen, B., Lee, E.A., Steffen, B. (eds.) Let's Talk AI: Interdisciplinarity is a Must, LNCS, vol. 15000. Springer (2025)
37. Tickell, C.: Human effects of climate change: excerpts from a lecture given to the society on 26 March 1990. Geogr. J. **156**(3), 325–329 (1990)
38. Vardi, M., Steffen, B.: Let's talk AI with logician and computer science expert Moshe Y. Vardi. In: Steffen, B., Lee, E.A., Steffen, B. (eds.) Let's Talk AI: Interdisciplinarity is a Must, LNCS, vol. 15000. Springer (2025)
39. von Wendt, K., Steffen, B.: Let's talk AI with science fiction author Karl von Wendt. In: Steffen, B., Lee, E.A., Steffen, B. (eds.) Let's Talk AI: Interdisciplinarity is a Must, LNCS, vol. 15000. Springer (2025)
40. Wikipedia: Boiling Frog (2024). https://en.wikipedia.org/wiki/Boiling_frog
41. Wirsing, M., Steffen, B.: Let's talk AI with computer science expert Martin Wirsing. In: Steffen, B., Lee, E.A., Steffen, B. (eds.) Let's Talk AI: Interdisciplinarity is a Must, LNCS, vol. 15000. Springer (2025)

Author Index

B. Steffen et al. (Eds.): *Let's Talk AI*, LNCS 15000, p. 317, 2026.
https://doi.org/10.1007/978-3-032-09008-9

MIX
Papier aus verantwortungsvollen Quellen
Paper from responsible sources
FSC® C105338

If you have any concerns about our products,
you can contact us on
ProductSafety@springernature.com

In case Publisher is established outside the EU,
the EU authorized representative is:
Springer Nature Customer Service Center GmbH
Europaplatz 3, 69115 Heidelberg, Germany

Printed by Libri Plureos GmbH
in Hamburg, Germany